P9-DNU-191

THE
PUSHCART PRIZE, III:
BEST OF THE
SMALL PRESSES

*An annual small press reader assembled with Founding Editors
Anaïs Nin (1903–1977), Buckminster Fuller, Charles Newman,
Daniel Halpern, Gordon Lish, Harry Smith, H.L. Van Brunt,
Hugh Fox, Ishmael Reed, Joyce Carol Oates, Len Fulton,
Leonard Randolph, Leslie Fiedler, Nona Balakian, Paul
Bowles, Paul Engle, Ralph Ellison, Reynolds Price, Rhoda
Schwartz, Richard Morris, Ted Wilentz, Tom Montag, William
Phillips, and others plus Special Contributing Editors for this
edition, and with the cooperation of the hundreds of small
presses whose names follow . . .*

BEST OF THE SMALL PRESSES

THE PUSHCART PRIZE, III:

BEST
OF THE
SMALL
PRESSES

Edited by Bill Henderson
with the Pushcart Prize editors

AVON
PUBLISHERS OF BARD, CAMELOT AND DISCUS BOOKS

AVON BOOKS
A division of
The Hearst Corporation
959 Eighth Avenue
New York, New York 10019

Copyright ⓒ 1978 by The Pushcart Book Press
Published by arrangement with The Pushcart Book Press.
Library of Congress Catalog Card Number: 78-50946
ISBN: 0-380-43059-2

All rights reserved, which includes the right
to reproduce this book or portions thereof in
any form whatsoever. For information address
The Pushcart Press, P.O. Box 845,
Yonkers, New York 10701

First Avon Printing, March, 1979

AVON TRADEMARK REG. U.S. PAT. OFF. AND IN
OTHER COUNTRIES, MARCA REGISTRADA, HECHO EN
U.S.A.

Printed in the U.S.A.

ACKNOWLEDGEMENTS

"Embarkment" by Hugh Seidman ⓒ 1977 *Pequod*, reprinted by permission of Hugh Seidman and *Pequod*.
"The Life That Disappeared" photographs by Roman Vishniac ⓒ 1977 *A Shout In The Street*, reprinted by permission of *A Shout In The Street*.
"Mothers" by Lydia Davis ⓒ 1977 Living Hand Press, reprinted by permission of Living Hand Press.
"Koyokon Riddle Poems" workings by Richard Dauenhauer ⓒ 1977 the editors of *Alcheringa/Ethnopoetics* and The Trustees of Boston University, reprinted by permission of *Alcheringa/Ethnopoetics*. These translations were originally a project of the Alaska Native Education Board, Anchorage, Alaska.
"Vesuvius at Home: The Power of Emily Dickinson" by Adrienne Rich ⓒ 1977 *Parnassus: Poetry In Review* and Adrienne Rich, reprinted by permission of Adrienne Rich.

6

Acknowledgements

"The Crow Is Mischief" by Laura Jensen © 1977 *Open Places*, reprinted by permission of *Open Places* and Laura Jensen.

"Bathroom Walls" by Maura Stanton © 1977 *Ploughshares*, Inc., reprinted by permission of *Ploughshares*, Inc.

"A Puddle" by Larry Eigner © 1977 Larry Eigner, reprinted by permission of Black Sparrow Press.

"Rough Strife" by Lynne Sharon Schwartz © 1977 *Ontario Review*, reprinted by permission of *Ontario Review* and Lynne Sharon Schwartz.

"Key Largo" by Bruce Andrews © 1977 Bruce Andrews, reprinted by permission of *Hills* and Bruce Andrews.

"Charlton Fisk Is My Ideal" by Bernadette Mayer © 1977 North Atlantic Books, reprinted by permission of North Atlantic Books.

"Hey, Is Anyone Listening?" by Stephen Minot © 1977 The University of Northern Iowa, reprinted by permission of *The North American Review*.

"'Armed For War'": Notes on The Antithetical Criticism of Harold Bloom" by Alvin Rosenfeld © 1977 *The Southern Review* and Alvin Rosenfeld, reprinted by permission of *The Southern Review*.

"The Man From Mars" by Margaret Atwood © 1977 *Ontario Review*, reprinted by permission of *Ontario Review*.

"West Virginia Sleep Song" by Ruthellen Quillen © 1977 Sibyl-Child Press, from *Magdalen Women's Literature Series, Volume One*, reprinted by permission of Sibyl-Child Press.

"The Angel and The Mermaid" by Ricardo da Silveira Lobo Sternberg, © 1977 *Small Moon*, reprinted by permission of *Small Moon*.

"Poor God" by Carolyn Cassady © 1977 The Unspeakable Visions of the Individual from *The Beat Diary*, reprinted by permission of The Unspeakable Visions of the Individual.

"Chinatown Sonata" by Yuki Hartman © 1977 Telephone Books and Ailanthus Press, reprinted by permission of Telephone books and Yuki Hartman.

"Even After A Machine Is Dismantled, It Continues to Operate, With or Without Purpose" by Ascher/Straus Collective © 1977 *Chouteau Review*, reprinted by permission of Sheila Ascher and *Chouteau Review*.

"Parting Shot" by Walter Abish © 1977 Walter Abish, reprinted by permission of New Directions Publishing Corporation from *The Future Perfect* and by permission of Fiction Collective, and also by permission of Walter Abish.

"Getting Freedom High" by Wesley Brown © 1977 Persea Books Inc., reprinted by permission of *Persea: An International Review*.

"The Dream of Mourning" by Louise Glück, © 1977 *Salmagundi*, reprinted by permission of *Salmagundi* and Louise Glück.

"Lowell's Graveyard" by Robert Hass © 1977 *Salmagundi*, reprinted by permission of *Salmagundi*, and Robert Hass.

"Wolfbane Fane" by George Payerle © 1977 George Payerle, reprinted by permission of The Kanchenjunga Press from *Wolfbane Fane*.

"What Light There Is" by Mekeel McBride © 1977 *The Agni Review*, reprinted by permission of *The Agni Review*, and Mekeel McBride.

"The Survivors" by Dan Masterson © 1977 *The Georgia Review* reprinted by permission of *The Georgia Review* and Dan Masterson.

"Deer Dance/For Your Return" by Leslie Marmon Silko © 1977 *Columbia*, reprinted by permisson of *Columbia*.

"Meeting Coot" by William Pitt Root © 1977 Confluence Press, reprinted by permission of Confluence Press and William Pitt Root.

"The Wu General Writes From Far Away" by Christopher Howell © 1977 *Northwest Review*, reprinted by permission of *Northwest Review* and Christopher Howell.

"Stepping Back" by Kathleen Collins © 1977 *Story Quarterly*, reprinted by permission of *Story Quarterly*.

"Bons" by Beth Tashery Shannon © 1976 *Chicago Review*, reprinted by permission of *Chicago Review*.

"Letter for A Daughter" by Lorrie Goldensohn © 1977 *Ploughshares*, Inc., reprinted by permission of *Ploughshares*.

"Some Recognition of the Joshua Lizard" by Robert Burlingame © 1977 *New America*, reprinted by permission of *New America*, and Robert Burlingame.

"Turtle" by John Pilcrow © 1977 December Press, reprinted by permission of December Press.

"The Waltz" by Vicente Aleixandre © 1974, 1977 Lewis Hyde, reprinted by permission of The Seventies Press and Robert Bly, translator.

"Everyone Knows Whom The Saved Envy" by James Galvin © 1977 *Antaeus*, reprinted by permission of *Antaeus*.

"The United States" by Robley Wilson, Jr. © 1976 Robley Wilson, Jr., reprinted by permission of the author and the University of Illinois Press.

"To Dance" by Mary Peterson © 1977 Mary Peterson, reprinted by permission of *Fiction International*.

"Utah Died For Your Sins" by Max Zimmer © 1977 *Quarry West*, reprinted by permission of *Quarry West*.

"David" by David McCann © 1977 *Poetry*, reprinted by permission of The Modern Poetry Association and David McCann.

"Snake" by Anne Herbert © 1977 *The CoEvolution Quarterly*, reprinted by permission of *The CoEvolution Quarterly*.

"Moral Fiction" by John Gardner © 1977 *The Hudson Review* and © 1978 John Gardner, reprinted by permission of Georges Borchardt Inc.

"A Sacrifice of Dogs" by William Sprunt © 1977 St. Andrews Press, reprinted by permission of St. Andrews Press.

"Conversation by The Body's Light" by Jane Cooper © 1977 *The Westigan Review*, reprinted by permission of *The Westigan Review*.

"from *A Journey Through The Land of Israel*" by Pinchas Sadeh © 1977 Jewish Publication Society, reprinted by permission of Jewish Publication Society and *TriQuarterly*.

"The Iron Table" by Jane Bowles © 1977 Paul Bowles, reprinted by permission of *Antaeus* and The Ecco Press.

"A Comfort Spell" by Maxine Silverman © 1977 Maxine Silverman, reprinted by permission of Sunbury Press and Maxine Silverman.

"Making A Name for Myself" by Joyce Peseroff © 1977 Alice James Poetry Cooperative Inc., reprinted by permission of Joyce Peseroff.

"How The Hen Sold Her Eggs to the Stingy Priest" by Nancy Willard, © 1977 *Field*, reprinted by permission of *Field*.

"Horst Wessel" by C.W. Gusewelle © 1977 *The Paris Review*, reprinted by permission of *The Paris Review*.

"'Talk To Me Baby'" by Michael Dennis Browne © 1977 *The Iowa Review*, reprinted by permission of Michael Dennis Browne.

"Moral Cake" by Don Hendrie Jr. © 1977 Lynx House Press, reprinted by permission of Lynx House Press and Don Hendrie Jr.

Acknowledgements

"The Tearing of the Skin" by Yvonne © 1977 *Willmore City*, reprinted by permission of *Willmore City*.

Untitled work by Loris Essary © 1977 Loris Essary, reprinted by permission of *Clown War*.

"Two Strange Stories" by Robert Walser © 1977 *Lowlands Review*, reprinted by permission of *Lowlands Review* from Carl Seelig-Stiftung/Robert Walser-Archiv; Zurich.

"There Is A Dream Dreaming Us" by Norman Dubie © 1977 *Porch*, reprinted by permission of *Porch*.

"'All Dressed Up But No Place to Go: The Black Writer And His Audience During The Harlem Renaissance'" by Charles Scruggs, © 1977 *American Literature*, reprinted by permission of Charles Scruggs and *American Literature*.

"Waste of Timelessness" by Anaïs Nin © 1977 Anaïs Nin, reprinted by permission of Magic Circle Press and The Anaïs Nin Trust.

"The Breaker" by Naomi Clark © 1977 Red Earth Press and Naomi Clark, reprinted by permission of Red Earth Press and Naomi Clark.

"Doing Good" by John Balaban © 1976 The Hudson Review, Inc., reprinted by permission from *The Hudson Review*, vol. XXIX, No. 4 (Winter 1976–77).

"The Fat Girl" by Andre Dubus © 1977 David R. Godine, Publisher, reprinted by permission of David R. Godine, Publisher.

"Sweeney Astray" by Seamus Heaney © 1977 *Armadillo*, reprinted by permission of *Armadillo*.

"Whores" by James Crumley © 1977 the *California Quarterly* and The Regents of the University of California, reprinted with their permission.

"The Other Face of Bread" by "The Workers University" © 1977 *Cross Currents*, reprinted by permission of *Cross Currents*.

"The Essential Ellison" © 1977 Ralph Ellison, reprinted by permission of Ralph Ellison from *Y'Bird*.

"My Mother's Novel" by Marge Piercy © 1977 *Painted Bride Quarterly*, reprinted by permission of Marge Piercy and *Painted Bride Quarterly*.

"While The Record Plays" by Gyula Illyés © 1977 *American Poetry Review*, reprinted by permission of Willaim Jay Smith, translator.

"My Mother's List of Names" by Bill Knott, © 1977 Sun Press, reprinted by permission of Bill Knott and Sun Press.

"Monsterfest" by "H. Bustos Domecq" © 1977 *Fiction*, reprinted by permission of *Fiction* and Adolpho Bioy Casares.

This book is for Atticus Lish
and his mom and pop

𝔥 𝔥 𝔥

INTRODUCTION:

About Pushcart Prize III

IN REVIEWING *Pushcart Prize II* last year, Anne Tyler remarked in *The New York Times Book Review* that *"The Pushcart Prize* has become a distinguished annual literary event." The *Times Book Review* also named *II* one of the "noteworthy books of the year." Across the country, the reaction was similar, from *Time* magazine to Lawrence Ferlinghetti at his City Lights Press in San Francisco, "The best small press anthology I've seen."

The editors hope that such recognition will be a tribute to *Pushcart Prize* writers. And since the writers in these editions speak very well for themselves, the briefer Pushcart's annual introductions, the better.

It has never been easy to be a writer of independence and vision, and these days it is especially difficult. Eliot Fremont-Smith, head of The National Book Critics Circle, says it better than we could: ". . . the treatment of writers does, I believe, get more callous every day—in newspapers, magazines, and books as well. More and more, accountants are taking over publishing. Numbers, leading to the holy bottom line, have always counted, but never to such an exclusionary degree. What goes on between the covers, what writers (and yes, good editors) care about becomes more and more peripheral. It used to be that publishing, book publishing especially, was different from the movie and television industries in these respects—that it was somehow more honest and respectful and therefore self-respecting, that it knew and acknowledged that it would be nowhere without good writers." (*Village Voice*, October 10, 1977)

Good writers are what *The Pushcart Prize* series is about. Today such writers are more likely to be found in the publications of small presses than in the packages of conglomerates.

For new authors these presses are often the only place they can receive a reading (slush piles are out of favor with the bottom line folks) and even established authors are depending on small presses. For instance, when the Spanish poet Vicente Aleixandre won the Nobel Prize for Literature in 1977, only The Seventies Press of Madison, Minnesota and The Green Horse Press of Santa Cruz, California had him in print. (A similar situation was documented in the first *Pushcart Prize* edition when Eugenio Montale won the Nobel Prize for Literature in 1975 and was reprinted from New Directions and *Ploughshares*, his only American publishers.) Aleixandre's poem "The Waltz" is included in this edition as it appeared in *Twenty Poems* (The Seventies Press).

Fine poets like Aleixandre have always been nourished by small presses, but recently the same is true of writers of fiction and essays—both traditional and experimental, known and unknown. Our first three volumes have presented work by Saul Bellow, Jorge Luis Borges, Harold Brodkey, John Gardner, William Gass, Henry Miller, and Anaïs Nin—to name but a few recognized writers from a list of over 200 as yet unheralded authors from 142 presses.

The real excitement in literary publishing is the discovery of new talent, and our series has been partial to such talent. Also, we prefer writers who have not been featured in previous *Prize* editions. None of the people in this edition appeared in *Pushcart Prize II*.

We note with pride, however, outstanding work done in 1977 by writers honored in our first or second edition: Jerry Bumpus, Marvin Cohen, Stephen Dixon, H.E. Francis, Patricia Goedicke, Michael Hogan, Richard Hugo, David Kranes, Naomi Lazard, Clarence Major, Joyce Carol Oates, David Ray, Teo Savory and Harvey Shapiro.

As usual most of the presses in *Pushcart Prize III* are new to the series. We welcome here for the first time the following 41 presses: Ailanthus Press, *Alcheringa/Ethnopoetics*, Alice James Books, *American Literature*, *Armadillo*, Black Sparrow, *California Quarterly*, *Chouteau Review*, *Clown War*, CoEvolution Quarterly, *Columbia*, Confluence Press, *Cross Currents*, *December*, *Fiction*, *Fiction International*, The Godine Press, Hills, The Kanchenjunga Press, Living Hand Press, *The Lowlands Review*, Lynx House

Press, Magic Circle Press, *New America*, Oyez Press, *North American Review*, North Atlantic Books, *Northwest Review, Open Places, Pequod*, Persea, Red Earth Press, The Seventies Press, *A Shout In The Street*, Sibyl-Child Press, *Small Moon*, Telephone Books, Unspeakable Visions of the Individual, *Westigan Review, Willmore City, Y'Bird.*

The Pushcart Prize continues to encourage resistance against all types of cultural and political domination. Earlier editions reprinted work from the Russian *samizdat* movement and here we assemble three very different pieces: "While the Record Plays" by Gyula Illýes from Hungary (*American Poetry Review*), "The Other Face of Bread" by "The Workers University" from Belgium (*Cross Currents*), and "Monsterfest" by "H. Bustos Domecq" an underground story from Peron's Argentina of the 1940's (*Fiction*).

Our *Prize* is a democracy of editors (83 on the staff for *III*) with new editors asked to serve for each book. Through such a turnover of opinion, we hope the series will never become stale or representative of any particular style or group. Each Fall we invite over 2,000 small presses to make up to six nominations of their best from the previous calendar year. Our 83 staff editors also make nominations. For *Pushcart Prize III*, almost 4,000 nominations were received. A group of first readers narrowed the selections down to just over 200 and then we asked our staff editors for their advice. The final selection is the result of many voices and visions.

Besides thanking all the Pushcart people and the hundreds of small press editors for their help, Pushcart is grateful to Mrs. Harold Lamport of The Lamport Foundation for providing a ten year program of awards for an outstanding poem, story and essay in each edition. This edition's Lamport Foundation awards of $100 each go to John Gardner for the essay "Moral Fiction" (*Hudson Review*), to Leslie Marmon Silko for the poem "Deer Dance/ For Your Return" (*Columbia*), and to Lynne Sharon Schwartz for the short story "Rough Strife" (*Ontario Review*); as selected by Pushcart.

In a culture as varied as that of today's small presses, no one book can do more than try to present a non-definitive "best". We call the book a "Prize" because it is meant as an honor to those authors who follow in the small press tradition of Whitman, Pound, Sandburg, Joyce, Nin and so many others. The series is also intended as a celebration and a promotion for our non-commercial literary community.

And finally *The Pushcart Prize* editions are meant for the enjoyment of the reader, who perhaps wants to throw away the bestseller lists and discover what is lively, thoughtful and caring in contemporary publishing.

Bill Henderson

THE
PEOPLE WHO HELPED
MAKE THIS BOOK

FOUNDING EDITORS—*Anaïs Nin (1903–1977), Buckminster Fuller, Charles Newman, Daniel Halpern, Gordon Lish, Harry Smith, Hugh Fox, Ishmael Reed, Joyce Carol Oates, Len Fulton, Leonard Randolph, Leslie Fiedler, Nona Balakian, Paul Bowles, Paul Engle, Ralph Ellison, Reynolds Price, Rhoda Schwartz, Richard Morris, Ted Wilentz, Tom Montag, William Phillips. Poetry editor: H.L. Van Brunt.*

EDITORS—*Barbara Damrosch, Carole Gross, Ben Pesta, Bob Seidman, Eugene Redmond, George Plimpton, Harold Brodkey, Harvey Shapiro, John Ashbery, Jerzy Kosinski, Malcolm Cowley, Mary MacArthur, M.D. Elevitch, Michael Hogan, Raymond Federman, Richard Kostelanetz, Teo Savory.*

SPECIAL CONTRIBUTING EDITORS FOR THIS EDITION —*Anne Tyler, Bill Zavatsky, Carol Muske, Carolyn Forché, Colleen McElroy, Cynthia Ozick, David Godine, David Kranes, David Wilk, DeWitt Henry, Grace Schulman, Hallie Burnett, Hayden Carruth, H.E. Francis, Hugh Seidman, Janey Tannenbaum, J.R. Humphreys, John Irving, Jonathan Galassi, Judy Hogan, June Jordan, Karen Kennerly, Lisel Mueller, Louise Simons, Marnie Walsh, Maxine Kumin, Michael Lally, Ntozake Shange, Paula Deitz, Phillip Lopate, Raymond Carver, Robert Boyers, Ron Sukenick, Siv Cedering Fox, Stephen Dixon, Tess Gallagher, Theresa Maylone*

HONORARY EDITORS (These people helped out for previous editions)—*Allan Kornblum, Allen Ginsberg, Bob Miles, Carll Tucker, Clarence Major, Elliott Anderson, Erica Jong, Frederick Morgan, Hilarie Johnston, John Gill, Joel Oppenheimer, Mark Strand, Mark Vinz, Noel Peattie, Noel Young, Robie Macauley, William Saroyan*

DESIGN AND PRODUCTION—*Ray Freiman*

EUROPEAN EDITORS—*Kirby and Liz Williams*

AUSTRALIAN EDITORS—*Tom and Wendy Whitton*

JACKET DESIGN—*Barbara Lish*

POETRY EDITORS FOR THIS EDITION—*Herb Leibowitz, Naomi Lazard*

ASSOCIATE EDITOR—*Lynne Spaulding*

EDITOR AND PUBLISHER—*Bill Henderson*

PRESSES FEATURED IN THE FIRST THREE *PUSHCART PRIZE* EDITIONS

Agni Review
Ahsahta Press
Ailanthus Press
Alcheringa/Ethnopoetics
Alice James Books
American Literature
American Pen
American Poetry Review
Amnesty International (*samizdat*)
Anaesthesia Review
Antaeus
Aphra
Assembling
Aspen Leaves
Barlenmir House
Bilingual Review
Black Rooster
Black Sparrow
Blue Cloud Quarterly
Blue Wind Press
California Quarterly

18 *Presses Featured in the First Three* Pushcart Prize *Editions*
Capra Press
Center
Chariton Review
Chicago Review
Chouteau Review
Cimarron Review
Clown War
CoEvolution Quarterly
Cold Mountain Press
Columbia: A Magazine of Poetry and Prose
Confluence Press
Confrontation
Cosmic Information Agency
Cross Currents
Curbstone Press
Dacotah Territory
Decatur House
December Press
Dryad Press
Duck Down Press
East River Anthology
Fiction
Fiction Collective
Fiction International
Field
Five Trees Press
Gallimaufry
Georgia Review
Ghost Dance
Goddard Journal
The Godine Press
Graham House Press
Greenfield Review
Hard Pressed
Hills
Holmgangers Press
Hudson Review
Icarus
Intermedia
Invisible City
Iowa Review

The Kanchenjunga Press
Kansas Quarterly
Kayak
Latitudes Press
Liberation
The Little Magazine
Living Hand Press
Living Poets Press
Lowlands Review
Lucille
Lynx House Press
Manroot
Magic Circle Press
Massachusetts Review
Montana Gothic
Mulch Press
Nada Press
New America
New Letters
North American Review
North Atlantic Books
Northwest Review
Ohio Review
Ontario Review
Open Places
Oyez Press
Painted Bride Quarterly
Paris Review
Parnassus: Poetry In Review
Partisan Review
Penumbra Press
Pentagram
Persea: An International Review
Pequod
Pitcairn Press
Ploughshares
Poetry
Poetry Now
Prairie Schooner
Promise of Learnings

Quarry West
Raincrow Press
Red Earth Press
Release Press
Salmagundi
San Marcos Press
Seamark Press
Second Coming Press
The Seventies Press
Shenandoah
A Shout In The Street
Sibyl-Child Press
Small Moon
The Smith
Southern Review
Spectrum
St. Andrews Press
Story Quarterly
Sun Press
Sunstone
Telephone Books
Texas Slough
Transatlantic Review
Three Rivers Press
Thorp Springs Press
Toothpaste Press
TriQuarterly
Truck Press
Undine
Unicorn Press
Unspeakable Visions of the Individual
Vagabond
Virginia Quarterly
Westigan Review
Willmore City
Word-Smith
Xanadu
Yardbird Reader
Y'Bird

CONTENTS

Contents

THE
PUSHCART PRIZE, III:
BEST OF THE
SMALL PRESSES

🔥 🔥 🔥

ROUGH STRIFE

fiction by LYNNE SHARON SCHWARTZ

from ONTARIO REVIEW

nominated by ONTARIO REVIEW, *Dewitt Henry, Harry Smith, Joyce Carol Oates, Lynne Spaulding and Ted Wilentz*

> Now let us sport us while we may;
> And now, like am'rous birds of prey
> . . . tear our pleasure with rough strife
> Through the iron gates of life.
> —*Andrew Marvell*

CAROLINE AND IVAN finally had a child. Conception stunned them; they didn't think, by now, that it could happen. For years they had tried and failed, till it seemed that a special barren destiny was preordained. Meanwhile, in the wide spaces of childlessness, they had created activity: their work flourished. Ivan, happy and moderately powerful in a large foundation, helped decide how to distribute money for artistic and social projects. Caroline taught mathematics at a small suburban university. Being a mathematician, she found, conferred a painful private wisdom on her efforts to conceive. In her brain, as Ivan exploded within her, she would involuntarily calculate probabilities; millions of blind sperm and one reluctant egg clus-

tered before her eyes in swiftly transmuting geometric patterns. She
lost her grasp of pleasure, forgot what it could feel like without a
goal. She had no idea what Ivan might be thinking about, scattered
seed money, maybe. Their passion became courteous and automatic
until, by attrition, for months they didn't make love—it was too
awkward.

One September Sunday morning she was in the shower, watching, through a crack in the curtain, Ivan naked at the washstand. He
was shaving, his jaw tilted at an innocently self-satisfied angle. He
wasn't aware of being watched, so that a secret quality, an essence of
Ivan, exuded in great waves. Caroline could almost see it, a cloudy
aura. He stroked his jaw vainly with intense concentration, a self-
absorption so contagious that she needed, suddenly, to possess it
with him. She stepped out of the shower.

"Ivan."

He turned abruptly, surprised, perhaps even annoyed at the
interruption.

"Let's not have a baby any more. Let's just . . . come on." When
she placed her wet hand on his back he lifted her easily off her feet
with his right arm, the razor still poised in his other, outstretched
hand.

"Come on," she insisted. She opened the door and a draft blew
into the small steamy room. She pulled him by the hand toward the
bedroom.

Ivan grinned. "You're soaking wet."

"Wet, dry, what's the difference?" It was hard to speak. She began
to run, to tease him; he caught her and tossed her onto their
disheveled bed and dug his teeth so deep into her shoulder that she
thought she would bleed.

Then with disinterest, taken up only in this fresh rushing need for
him, weeks later Caroline conceived. Afterwards she liked to say
that she had known the moment it happened. It felt different, she
told him, like a pin pricking a balloon, but without the shattering
noise, without the quick collapse. "Oh, come on," said Ivan. "That's
impossible."

But she was a mathematician, after all, and dealt with infinitesimal
precise abstractions, and she did know how it had happened. The
baby was conceived in strife, one early October night, Indian summer. All day the sun glowed hot and low in the sky, settling an amber
torpor on people and things, and the night was the same, only now a

dark hot heaviness sunk slowly down. The scent of the still-blooming honeysuckle rose to their bedroom window. Just as she was bending over to kiss him, heavy and quivering with heat like the night, he teased her about something, about a mole on her leg, and in reply she punched him lightly on the shoulder. He grabbed her wrists, and when she began kicking, pinned her feet down with his own. In an instant Ivan lay stretched out on her back like a blanket, smothering her, while she struggled beneath, writhing to escape. It was a silent, sweaty struggle, interrupted with outbursts of wild laughter, shrieks and gasping breaths. She tried biting but, laughing loudly, he evaded her, and she tried scratching the fists that held her down, but she couldn't reach. All her desire was transformed into physical effort, but he was too strong for her. He wanted her to say she gave up, but she refused, and since he wouldn't loosen his grip they lay locked and panting in their static embrace for some time.

"You win," she said at last, but as he rolled off she sneakily jabbed him in the ribs with her elbow.

"Aha!" Ivan shouted, and was ready to begin again, but she quickly distracted him. Once the wrestling was at an end, though, Caroline found her passion dissipated, and her pleasure tinged with resentment. After they made love forcefully, when they were covered with sweat, dripping on each other, she said, "Still, you don't play fair."

"I don't play fair! Look who's talking. Do you want me to give you a handicap?"

"No."

"So?"

"It's not fair, that's all."

Ivan laughed gloatingly and curled up in her arms. She smiled in the dark.

That was the night the baby was conceived, not in high passion but rough strife.

She lay on the table in the doctor's office weeks later. The doctor, whom she had known for a long time, habitually kept up a running conversation while he probed. Today, fretting over his weight problem, he outlined his plans for a new diet. Tensely she watched him, framed and centered by her raised knees, which were still bronzed from summer sun. His other hand was pressing on her stomach. Caroline was nauseated with fear and trembling, afraid of the verdict. It was taking so long, perhaps it was a tumor.

"I'm cutting out all starches," he said. "I've really let myself go lately."

"Good idea." Then she gasped in pain. A final, sickening thrust, and he was out. Relief, and a sore gap where he had been. In a moment, she knew, she would be retching violently.

"Well?"

"Well, Caroline, you hit the jackpot this time."

She felt a smile, a stupid, puppet smile, spread over her face. In the tiny bathroom where she threw up, she saw in the mirror the silly smile looming over her ashen face like a dancer's glowing grimace of labored joy. She smiled through the rest of the visit, through his advice about milk, weight, travel and rest, smiled at herself in the window of the bus, and at her moving image in the fenders of parked cars as she walked home.

Ivan, incredulous over the telephone, came home beaming stupidly just like Caroline, and brought a bottle of champagne. After dinner they drank it and made love.

"Do you think it's all right to do this?" he asked.

"Oh, Ivan, honestly. It's microscopic."

He was in one of his whimsical moods and made terrible jokes that she laughed at with easy indulgence. He said he was going to pay the baby a visit and asked if she had any messages she wanted delivered. He unlocked from her embrace, moved down her body and said he was going to have a look for himself. Clowning, he put his ear between her legs to listen. Whatever amusement she felt soon ebbed away into irritation. She had never thought Ivan would be a doting parent—he was so preoccupied with himself. Finally he stopped his antics as she clasped her arms around him and whispered, "Ivan, you are really too much." He became unusually gentle. Tamed, and she didn't like it, hoped he wouldn't continue that way for months. Pleasure lapped over her with a mild, lackadaisical bitterness, and then when she could be articulate once more she explained patiently, "Ivan, you know, it really is all right. I mean, it's a natural process."

"Well I didn't want to hurt you."

"I'm not sick."

Then, as though her body were admonishing that cool confidence, she did get sick. There were mornings when she awoke with such paralyzing nausea that she had to ask Ivan to bring her a hard roll from the kitchen before she could stir from bed. To move from her awakening position seemed a tremendous risk, as if she might spill out. She rarely threw up—the nausea resembled violent hunger. Something wanted to be filled, not expelled, a perilous vacuum occupying her insides. The crucial act was getting the first few mouthfuls down. Then the solidity and denseness of the hard unbuttered roll stabilized her, like a heavy weight thrown down to anchor a tottering ship. Her head ached. On the mornings when she had no classes she would wander around the house till almost noon clutching the partly-eaten roll in her hand like a talisman. Finishing one roll, she quickly went to the breadbox for another; she bought them regularly at the bakery a half-dozen at a time. With enough roll inside her she could sometimes manage a half-cup of tea, but liquids were risky. They sloshed around inside and made her envision the baby sloshing around too, in its cloudy fluid. By early afternoon she would feel fine. The baby, she imagined, claimed her for the night and was reluctant to give up its hold in the morning: they vied till she conquered. She was willing to yield her sleeping hours to the baby, her dreams even, if necessary, but she wanted the daylight for herself.

The mornings that she taught were agony. Ivan would wake her up early, bring her a roll, and gently prod her out of bed.

"I simply cannot do it," she would say, placing her legs cautiously over the side of the bed.

"Sure you can. Now get up."

"I'll die if I get up."

"You have no choice. You have a job." He was freshly showered and dressed, and his neatness irritated her. He had nothing more to do—the discomfort was all hers. She rose to her feet and swayed.

Ivan looked alarmed. "Do you want me to call and tell them you can't make it?"

"No, no." That frightened her. She needed to hold on to the job, to defend herself against the growing baby. Once she walked into the classroom she would be fine. A Mondrian print hung on the back wall—she could look at that, and it would steady her. With waves of nausea roiling in her chest, she stumbled into the bathroom.

She liked him to wait until she was out of the shower before he left for work, because she anticipated fainting under the impact of the water. Often at the end she forced herself to stand under an ice cold flow, leaning her head way back and letting her short fair hair drip down behind her. Though it was torture, when she emerged she felt more alive.

After the shower had been off a while Ivan would come and open the bathroom door. "Are you O.K. now, Caroline? I've got to go." It made her feel like a child. She would be wrapped in a towel with her hair dripping on the mat, brushing her teeth or rubbing cream into her face. "Yes, thanks for waiting, I guess this'll end soon. They say it's only the first few months."

He kissed her lips, her bare damp shoulder, gave a parting squeeze to her toweled behind, and was gone. She watched him walk down the hall. Ivan was very large. She had always been drawn and aroused by his largeness, by the huge bones and the taut legs that felt as though he had steel rods inside. But now she watched with some trepidation, hoping Ivan wouldn't have a large, inflexible baby.

Very slowly she would put on clothes. Selecting each article seemed a much more demanding task than ever before. Seeing how slow she had become, she allowed herself over an hour, keeping her hard roll nearby as she dressed and prepared her face. All the while, through the stages of dressing, she evaluated her body closely in the full-length mirror, first naked, then in bra and underpants, then with shoes added, and finally with a dress. She was looking for signs, but the baby was invisible. Nothing had changed yet. She was still as she had always been, not quite slim yet somehow appearing small, almost delicate. She used to pride herself on strength. When they moved in she had worked as hard as Ivan, lugging furniture and lifting heavy cartons. He was impressed. Now, of course, she could no longer do that—it took all her strength to move her own weight.

With the profound sensuous narcissism of women past first youth, she admired her still-narrow waist and full breasts. She was especially fond of her shoulders and prominent collarbone, which had a fragile, inviting look. That would all be gone soon, of course, gone soft. Curious about how she would alter, she scanned her face for the pregnant look she knew well from the faces of friends. It was far less a tangible change than a look of transparent vulnerability that took over the face: nearly a pleading look, a beg for help like a message from a powerless invaded country to the rest of the world. Caroline did not see it on her face yet.

From the tenth to the fourteenth week of her pregnancy she slept, with brief intervals of lucidity when she taught her classes. It was a strange dreamy time. The passionate nausea faded, but the lure of the bed was irresistible. In the middle of the day, even, she could pass by the bedroom, glimpse the waiting bed and be overcome by the soft heavy desire to lie down. She fell into a stupor immediately and did not dream. She forgot what it was like to awaken with energy and move through an entire day without lying down once. She forgot the feeling of eyes opened wide without effort. She would have liked to hide this strange, shameful perversity from Ivan, but that was impossible. Ivan kept wanting to go to the movies. Clearly, he was bored with her. Maybe, she imagined, staring up at the bedroom ceiling through slitted eyes, he would become so bored he would abandon her and the baby and she would not be able to support the house alone and she and the baby would end up on the streets in rags, begging. She smiled. That was highly unlikely. Ivan would not be the same Ivan without her.

"You go on, Ivan. I just can't."

Once he said, "I thought I might ask Ruth Forbes to go with me to see the Charlie Chaplin in town. I know she likes him. Would that bother you?"

She was half-asleep, slowly eating a large apple in bed and watching *Medical Center* on television, but she roused herself to answer. "No, of course not." Ruth Forbes was a divorced woman who lived down the block, a casual friend and not Ivan's type at all, too large, loud and depressed. Caroline didn't care if he wanted her company. She didn't care if he held her hand on his knee in the movies as he liked to do, or even if, improbably, he made love to her afterwards in her sloppy house crawling with children. She didn't care about anything except staying nestled in bed.

She made love with him sometimes, in a slow way. She felt no specific desire but didn't want to deny him, she loved him so. Or had, she thought vaguely, when she was alive and strong. Besides, she knew she could sleep right after. Usually there would be a moment when she came alive despite herself, when the reality of his body would strike her all at once with a wistful throb of lust, but mostly she was too tired to see it through, to leap towards it, so she let it subside, merely nodding at it gratefully as a sign of dormant life. She felt sorry for Ivan, but helpless.

Once to her great shame, she fell asleep while he was inside her. He woke her with a pat on her cheek, actually, she realized from the faint sting, a gesture more like a slap than a pat. "Caroline, for Christ's sake, you're sleeping."

"No, no, I'm sorry. I wasn't really sleeping. Oh, Ivan, it's nothing. This will end." She wondered, though.

Moments later she felt his hands on her thighs. His lips were brooding on her stomach, edging, with expertise, lower and lower down. He was murmuring something she couldn't catch. She felt an ache, an irritation. Of course he meant well, Ivan always did. Wryly, she appreciated his intentions. But she couldn't bear that excitement now.

"Please," she said. "Please don't do that."

He was terribly hurt. He said nothing, but leaped away violently and pulled all the blankets around him. She was contrite, shed a few private tears and fell instantly into a dreamless dark.

He wanted to go to a New Year's Eve party some close friends were giving, and naturally he wanted her to come with him. Caroline vowed to herself she would do this for him because she had been giving so little for so long. She planned to get dressed and look very beautiful, as she could still look when she took plenty of time and tried hard enough; she would not drink very much—it was sleep-inducing—and she would not be the one to suggest going home. After sleeping through the day in preparation, she washed her hair, using something she found in the drugstore to heighten the blonde flecks. Then she put on a long green velvet dress with gold embroidery, and inserted the gold hoop earrings Ivan bought her some years ago for her twenty-fifth birthday. Before they set out she drank a cup of black coffee. She would have taken No-Doze but she was afraid of drugs, afraid of giving birth to an armless or legless baby who would be a burden and a heartache to them for the rest of their days.

At the party of mostly university people, she chatted with everyone equally, those she knew well and those she had never met. Sociably, she held a filled glass in her hand, taking tiny sips. She and Ivan were not together very much—it was crowded, smoky and loud; people kept moving and encounters were brief—but she knew he was aware of her, could feel his awareness through the milling bodies. He was aware and he was pleased. He deserved more than the somnambulist she had become, and she was pleased to please him. But after a while her legs would not support her for another instant. The skin tingled: soft warning bells rang from every pore.

She allowed herself a moment to sit down alone in a small alcove off the living room, where she smoked a cigarette and stared down at her lap, holding her eyes open very wide. Examining the gold and rose-colored embroidery on her dress, Caroline traced the coiled pattern, mathematical and hypnotic, with her index finger. Just as she was happily merging into its intricacies, a man, a stranger, came in, breaking her trance. He was a very young man, twenty-three, maybe, of no apparent interest.

"Hi. I hear you're expecting a baby," he began, and sat down with a distinct air of settling in.

"Yes. That's quite an opening line. How did you know?"

"I know because Linda told me. You know Linda, don't you? I'm her brother."

He began asking about her symptoms. Sleepiness? Apathy? He knew, he had worked in a clinic. Unresponsive, she retorted by inquiring about his taste in music. He sat on a leather hassock opposite Caroline on the couch, and with every inquisitive sentence drew his seat closer till their knees were almost touching. She shifted her weight to avoid him, tucked her feet under her and lit another cigarette, feeling she could lie down and fall into a stupor quite easily. Still, words were coming out of her mouth, she heard them; she hoped they were not encouraging words but she seemed to have very little control over what they were.

"I—" he said. "You see—" He reached out and put his hand over hers. "Pregnant women, like, they really turn me on. I mean, there's a special aura. You're sensational."

She pulled her hand away. "God almighty."

"What's the matter? Honestly, I didn't mean to offend you."

"I really must go." She stood up and stepped around him.

"Could I see you some time?"

"You're seeing me now. Enjoy it."

He ran his eyes over her from head to toe, appraising. "It doesn't show yet."

Gazing down at her body, Caroline stretched the loose velvet dress taut over her stomach. "No, you're right, it doesn't." Then, over her shoulder, as she left their little corner, she tossed, "Fuck you, you pig."

With a surge of energy she downed a quick Scotch, found Ivan and tugged at his arm. "Let's dance."

Ivan's blue eyes lightened with shock. At home she could barely walk.

"Yes, let's." He took her in his arms and she buried her face against his shoulder. But she held her tears back, she would not let him know.

Later she told him about it. It was three-thirty in the morning, they had just made love drunkenly, and Ivan was in high spirits. She knew why—he felt he had her back again. She had held him close and uttered her old sounds, familiar moans and cries like a poignant, nearly-forgotten tune, and Ivan was miraculously restored, his impact once again sensible to eye and ear. He was making her laugh hysterically now, imitating the eccentric professor of art history at the party, an owlish émigré from Bavaria who expounded on the dilemmas of today's youth, all the while pronouncing "youth" as if it rhymed with "mouth." Ivan had also discovered that he pronounced "unique" as if it were "eunuch." Then, sitting up in bed cross-legged, they competed in making up pretentious scholarly sentences that included both "unique" and "youth" mispronounced.

"Speaking of 'yowth,'" Caroline said, "I met a weird one tonight, Linda's brother. A very eunuch yowth, I must say." And giggling, she recounted their conversation. Suddenly at the end she unexpectedly found herself in tears. Shuddering, she flopped over and sobbed into her pillow.

"Caroline," he said tenderly, "please. For heaven's sake, it was just some nut. It was nothing. Don't get all upset over it." He stroked her bare back.

"I can't help it." she wailed. "It made me feel so disgusting."

"You're much too sensitive. Come on." He ran his hand slowly through her hair, over and over.

She pulled the blanket around her. "Enough. I'm going to sleep."

A few days later, when classes were beginning again for the new semester, she woke early and went immediately to the shower, going through the ritual motions briskly and automatically. She was finished and brushing her teeth when she realized what had happened. There she was on her feet, sturdy, before eight in the morning, planning how she would introduce the topic of the differential calculus to her new students. She stared at her face in the mirror with unaccustomed recognition, her mouth dripping white foam, her dark eyes startled. She was alive. She didn't know how the miracle had happened, nor did she care to explore it. Back in the bedroom she dressed quickly, zipping up a pair of slim rust-colored woolen slacks with satisfaction. It didn't show yet, but soon.

"Ivan, time to get up."

He grunted and opened his eyes. When at last they focused on Caroline leaning over him they burned blue and wide with astonishment. He rubbed a fist across his forehead. "Are you dressed already?"

"Yes. I'm cured."

"What do you mean?"

"I'm not tired any more. I'm slept out. I've come back to life."

"Oh." He moaned and rolled over in one piece like a seal.

"Aren't you getting up?"

"In a little while. I'm so tired. I must sleep for a while." The words were thick and slurred.

"Well!" She was strangely annoyed. Ivan always got up with vigor. "Are you sick?"

"Uh-uh."

After a quick cup of coffee she called out, "Ivan, I'm leaving now. Don't forget to get up." The January air was crisp and exhilarating, and she walked the half-mile to the university at a nimble clip, going over her introductory remarks in her head.

Ivan was tired for a week. Caroline wanted to go out to dinner every evening—she had her appetite back. She had broken through dense earth to fresh air. It was a new year and soon they would have a new baby. But all Ivan wanted to do was stay home and lie on the bed and watch television. It was repellent. Sloth, she pointed out to him more than once, was one of the seven deadly sins. The fifth night she said in exasperation, "What the hell is the matter with you? If you're sick go to a doctor."

"I'm not sick. I'm tired. Can't I be tired too? Leave me alone. I left you alone, didn't I?"

"That was different."

"How?"

"I'm pregnant and you're not, in case you've forgotten."

"How could I forget?"

She said nothing, only cast him an evil look.

One evening soon after Ivan's symptoms disappeared, they sat together on the living-room sofa sharing sections of the newspaper.

Ivan had his feet up on the coffee table and Caroline sat diagonally, resting her legs on his. She paused in her reading and touched her stomach.

"Ivan."

"What?"

"It's no use. I'm going to have to buy some maternity clothes."

He put down the paper and stared. "Really?" He seemed distressed.

"Yes."

"Well, don't buy any of those ugly things they wear. Can't you get some of those, you know, sort of Indian things?"

"Yes. That's a good idea. I will."

He picked up the paper again.

"It moves."

"What?"

"I said it moves. The baby."

"It moves?"

She laughed. "Remember Galileo? *Eppure, si muove.*" They had spent years together in Italy in their first youth, in mad love, and visited the birthplace of Galileo. He was a hero to both of them, because his mind remained free and strong though his body succumbed to tyranny.

Ivan laughed too. "*Eppure, si muove.* Let me see." He bent his head down to feel it, then looked up at her, his face full of longing, marvel and envy. In a moment he was scrambling at her clothes in a young eager rush. He wanted to be there, he said. Caroline, taken by surprise, was suspended between laughter and tears. He had her on the floor in silence, and for each it was swift and consuming.

Ivan lay spent in her arms. Caroline, still gasping and clutching him, said, "I could never love it as much as I love you." She wondered, then, hearing her words fall in the still air, whether this would always be true.

Shortly after she began wearing the Indian shirts and dresses, she noticed that Ivan was acting oddly. He stayed late at the office more than ever before, and often brought work home with him. He appeared to have lost interest in the baby, rarely asking how she felt, and when she moaned in bed sometimes, "Oh, I can't get to sleep, it keeps moving around," he responded with a grunt or not at all. He asked her, one warm Sunday in March, if she wanted to go bicycle riding.

"Ivan, I can't go bicycle riding. I mean, look at me."

"Oh, right. Of course."

He seemed to avoid looking at her, and she did look terrible, she had to admit. Even she looked at herself in the mirror as infrequently as possible. She dreaded what she had heard about hair falling out and teeth rotting, but she drank her milk diligently and so far neither of those things had happened. But besides the grotesque belly, her ankles swelled up so that the shape of her own legs was alien. She took diuretics and woke every hour at night to go to the bathroom. Sometimes it was impossible to get back to sleep so she sat up in bed reading. Ivan said, "Can't you turn the light out? You know I can't sleep with the light on."

"But what should I do? I can't sleep at all."

"Read in the living room."

"It's so cold in there at night."

He would turn away irritably. Once he took the blanket and went to sleep in the living room himself.

They liked to go for drives in the country on warm weekends. It seemed to Caroline that he chose the bumpiest, most untended roads and drove them as rashly as possible. Then when they stopped to picnic and he lay back to bask in the sharp April sunlight, she would always need to go and look for a bathroom, or even a clump of trees. At first this amused him, but soon his amusement became sardonic. He pulled in wearily at gas stations where he didn't need gas and waited in the car with folded arms and a sullen expression that made her apologetic about her ludicrous needs. They were growing apart. She could feel the distance between them like a patch of fog, dimming and distorting the relations of objects in space. The baby that lay between them in the dark was pushing them apart.

Sometimes as she lay awake in bed at night, not wanting to read in the cold living room but reluctant to turn on the light (and it was only a small light, she thought bitterly, a small bedside light), Caroline brooded over the horrible deformities the baby might be born with. She was thirty-one years old, not the best age to bear a first child. It could have cerebral palsy, cleft palate, two heads, club foot. She wondered if she could love a baby with a gross defect. She wondered if Ivan would want to put it in an institution, and if there were any decent institutions in their area, and if they would be spending every Sunday afternoon for the rest of their lives visiting the baby and driving home heartbroken in silence. She lived through these visits to the institution in vivid detail till she knew the doctors' and nurses' faces well. And there would come a point when Ivan would refuse to go any more—she knew what he was like, selfish with his time and impatient with futility—and she would have to go alone. She wondered if Ivan ever thought about these things, but with that cold mood of his she was afraid to ask.

One night she was desolate. She couldn't bear the loneliness and the heaviness any more, so she woke him.

"Ivan, please. Talk to me. I'm so lonely."

He sat up abruptly. "What?" He was still asleep. With the dark straight hair hanging down over his lean face he looked boyish and vulnerable. Without knowing why, she felt sorry for him.

"I'm sorry. I know you were sleeping but I—" Here she began to weep. "I just lie here forever in the dark and think awful things and you're so far away, and I just—"

"Oh, Caroline. Oh, God." Now he was wide awake, and took her in his arms.

"You're so far away," she wept. "I don't know what's the matter with you."

"I'm sorry. I know it's hard for you. You're so—everything's so different, that's all."

"But it's still me."

"I know. I know it's stupid of me. I can't—"

She knew what it was. It would never be the same. They sat up all night holding each other, and they talked. Ivan talked more than he had in weeks. He said of course the baby would be perfectly all right, and it would be born at just the right time, too, late June, so she could finish up the term, and they would start their natural childbirth group in two weeks so he could be with her and help her, though of course she would do it easily because she was so competent at everything, and then they would have the summer for the early difficult months, and she would be feeling fine and be ready to go back to work in the fall, and they would find a good person, someone like a grandmother, to come in, and he would try to stagger his schedule so she would not feel overburdened and trapped, and in short everything would be just fine, and they would make love again like they used to and be close again. He said exactly what she needed to hear, while she huddled against him, wrenched with pain to realize that he had known all along the right words to say but hadn't thought to say them till she woke him in desperation. Still, in the dawn she slept contented. She loved him. Every now and then she perceived this like a fact of life, an ancient tropism.

Two weeks later they had one of their horrible quarrels. It happened at a gallery, at the opening of a show by a group of young local artists Ivan had discovered. He had encouraged them to apply to his foundation for money and smoothed the way to their success. Now at their triumphant hour he was to be publicly thanked at a formal dinner. There were too many paintings to look at, too many people to greet, and too many glasses of champagne thrust at Caroline, who was near the end of her eighth month now. She walked around for an hour, then whispered to Ivan, "Listen, I'm sorry but I've got to go. Give me the car keys, will you? I don't feel well."

"What's the matter?"

"I can't stop having to go to the bathroom and my feet are killing me and my head aches, and the kid is rolling around like a basketball. You stay and enjoy it. You can get a ride with someone. I'll see you later."

"I'll drive you home," he said grimly. "We'll leave."

An awful knot gripped her stomach. The knot was the image of his perverse resistance, the immense trouble coming, all the trouble congealed and solidified and tied up in one moment. Meanwhile they smiled at the passers-by as they whispered ferociously to each other.

"Ivan, I do not want you to take me home. This is your event. Stay. I am leaving. We are separate people."

"If you're as sick as you say you can't drive home alone. You're my wife and I'll take you home."

"Suit yourself," she said sweetly, because the director of the gallery was approaching. "We all know you're much bigger and stronger than I am." And she smiled maliciously.

Ivan waved vaguely at the director, turned and ushered her to the door. Outside he exploded.

"Shit, Caroline! We can't do a fucking thing anymore, can we?"

"You can do anything you like. Just give me the keys. I left mine home."

"I will not give you the keys. Get in the car. You're supposed to be sick."

"You big resentful selfish idiot. Jealous of an embryo." She was screaming now. He started the car with a rush that jolted her forward against the dashboard. "I'd be better off driving myself. You'll kill me this way."

"Shut up," he shouted. "I don't want to hear any more."

"I don't care what you want to hear or not hear."

"Shut the hell up or I swear I'll go into a tree. I don't give a shit anymore."

It was starting to rain, a soft silent rain that glittered in the drab dusk outside. At exactly the same moment they rolled up their windows. They were sealed in together. Caroline thought, like restless beasts in a cage. The air in the car was dank and stuffy.

When they got home he slammed the door so hard the house shook. Caroline had calmed herself. She sank down in a chair, kicked off her shoes and rubbed her ankles. "Ivan, why don't you go back? It's not too late. These dinners are always late anyway. I'll be O.K."

"I don't want to go anymore," he yelled. "The whole thing is spoiled. Our whole lives are spoiled from now on. We were better off before. I thought you had gotten over wanting it. I thought it was a dead issue." He stared at her bulging stomach with such loathing that she was shocked into horrid, lucid perception.

"You disgust me," she said quietly. "Frankly, you always have and probably always will." She didn't know why she said that. It was quite untrue. It was only true that he disgusted her at this moment, yet the rest had rolled out like string from a hidden ball of twine.

"So why did we ever start this in the first place?" he screamed.

She didn't know whether he meant the marriage or the baby, and for an instant she was afraid he might hit her, there was such compressed force in his huge shoulders.

"Get the hell out of here. I don't want to have to look at you."

"I will. I'll go back. I'll take your advice. Call your fucking obstetrician if you need anything. I'm sure he's always glad of an extra feel."

"You ignorant pig. Go on. And don't hurry back. Find yourself a skinny little art student and give her a big treat."

"I just might." He slammed the door and the house shook again.

He would be back. This was not the first time. Only now she felt no secret excitement, no tremor, no passion that could reshape into lust; she was too heavy and burdened. It would not be easy to make it up—she was in no condition. It would lie between them silently like a dead weight till weeks after the baby was born, till Ivan felt he could reclaim his rightful territory. She knew him too well. Caroline took two aspirins. When she woke at three he was in bed beside her, gripping the blanket in his sleep and breathing heavily. For days afterward they spoke with strained, subdued courtesy.

They worked diligently in the natural childbirth classes once a week, while at home they giggled over how silly the exercises were, yet Ivan insisted she pant her five minutes each day as instructed. As relaxation training, Ivan was supposed to lift each of her legs and arms three times and drop them, while she remained perfectly limp and passive. From the very start Caroline was excellent at this routine, which they did in bed before going to sleep. A substitute, she thought, yawning. She could make her body so limp and passive her arms and legs bounced on the mattress when they fell. One night for diversion she tried doing it to Ivan, but he couldn't master the technique of passivity.

"Don't do anything, Ivan. I lift the leg and I drop the leg. You do nothing. Do you see? Nothing at all," she smiled.

But that was not possible for him. He tried to be limp but kept working along with her; she could see his muscles, precisely those leg muscles she found so desirable, exerting to lift and drop, lift and drop.

"You can't give yourself up. Don't you feel what you're doing? You have to let me do it to you. Let me try just your hand, from the wrist. That might be easier."

"No, forget it. Give me back my hand." He smiled and stroked her stomach gently. "What's the difference? I don't have to do it well. You do it very well."

She did it very well indeed when the time came. It was a short labor, less than an hour, very unusual for a first baby, the nurses kept muttering. She breathed intently, beginning with the long slow breaths she had been taught, feeling quite remote from the bustle around her. Then, in a flurry, they raced down the hall on a wheeled table with a train of white-coated people trotting after, and she thought, panting, No matter what I suffer, soon I will be thin again, I will be more beautiful than ever.

The room was crowded with people, far more people than she would have thought necessary, but the only faces she singled out were Ivan's and the doctor's. The doctor, with a new russet beard and his face a good deal thinner now, was once again framed by her knees, paler than before. Wildly enthusiastic about the proceedings,

he yelled, "Terrific, Caroline, terrific," as though they were in a
noisy public place. "O.K., start pushing."

They placed her hands on chrome rails along the table. On the
left, groping, she found Ivan's hand and held it instead of the rail.
She pushed. In surprise she became aware of a great cleavage, like a
mountain of granite splitting apart, only it was in her, she realized,
and if it kept on going it would go right up to her neck. She gripped
Ivan's warm hand, and just as she opened her mouth to roar someone
clapped an oxygen mask on her face so the roar reverberated inward
on her own ears. She wasn't supposed to roar, the natural childbirth
teacher hadn't mentioned anything about that, she was supposed to
breathe and push. But as long as no one seemed to take any notice
she might as well keep on roaring, it felt so satisfying and necessary.
The teacher would never know. She trusted that if she split all the
way up to her neck they would sew her up somehow—she was too
far gone to worry about that now. Maybe that was why there were so
many of them, yes, of course, to put her back together, and maybe
they had simply forgotten to tell her about being bisected; or maybe
it was a closely guarded secret, like an initiation rite. She gripped
Ivan's hand tighter. She was not having too bad a time, she would
surely survive, she told herself, captivated by the hellish bestial
sounds going from her mouth to her ear; it certainly was what her
students would call a peak experience, and how gratifying to hear
the doctor exclaim, "Oh, this is one terrific girl! One more, Caroline,
give me one more push and send it out. Sock it to me."

She always tried to be obliging, if possible. Now she raised herself
on her elbows and, staring straight at him—he too, after all, had
been most obliging these long months—gave him with tremendous
force the final push he asked for. She had Ivan's hand tightly around
the rail, could feel his knuckles bursting, and then all of a sudden the
room and the faces were obliterated. A dark thick curtain swiftly
wrapped around her and she was left all alone gasping, sucked
violently into a windy black hold of pain so explosive she knew it
must be death, she was dying fast, like a bomb detonating. It was all
right, it was almost over, only she would have liked to see his blue
eyes one last time.

From somewhere in the void Ivan's voice shouted in exultation,
"It's coming out," and the roaring stopped and at last there was peace
and quiet in her ears. The curtain fell away, the world returned. But

her eyes kept on burning, as if they had seen something not meant for living eyes to see and return from alive.

"Give it to me," Caroline said, and held it. She saw that every part was in the proper place, then shut her eyes.

They wheeled her to a room and eased her onto the bed. It was past ten in the morning. She could dimly remember they had been up all night watching a James Cagney movie about prize-fighting while they timed her irregular mild contractions. James Cagney went blind from blows given by poisoned gloves in a rigged match, and she wept for him as she held her hands on her stomach and breathed. Neither she nor Ivan had slept or eaten for hours.

"Ivan, there is something I am really dying to have right now."

"Your wish is my command."

She asked for a roast beef on rye with ketchup, and iced tea. "Would you mind? It'll be hours before they serve lunch."

He brought it and stood at the window while she ate ravenously.

"Didn't you get anything for yourself?"

"No, I'm too exhausted to eat." He did, in fact, look terrible. He was sallow; his eyes, usually so radiant, were nearly drained of color, and small downward-curving lines around his mouth recalled his laborious vigil.

"You had a rough night, Ivan. You ought to get some sleep. What's it like outside?"

"What?" Ivan's movements seemed to her extremely purposeless. He was pacing the room with his hands deep in his pockets, going slowly from the foot of the bed to the window and back. Her eyes followed him from the pillow. Every now and then he would stop to peer at Caroline in an unfamiliar way, as if she were a puzzling stranger.

"Ivan, are you O.K.? I meant the weather. What's it doing outside?" It struck her, as she asked, that it was weeks since she had cared to know anything about the outside. That there was an outside, now that she was emptied out, came rushing at her with the most urgent importance, wafting her on a tide of grateful joy.

"Oh," he said vaguely, and came to sit on the edge of her bed. "Well, it's doing something very peculiar outside, as a matter of fact. It's raining but the sun is shining."

She laughed at him. "But haven't you ever seen it do that before?"

"I don't know. I guess so." He opened his mouth and closed it several times. She ate, waiting patiently. Finally he spoke. "You know, Caroline, you really have quite a grip. When you were holding my hand in there, you squeezed it so tight I thought you would break it."

"Oh, come on, that can't be."

"I'm not joking." He massaged his hand absently. Ivan never complained of pain; if anything he understated. But now he held out his right hand and showed her the raw red knuckles and palm, with raised flaming welts forming.

She took his hand. "You're serious. Did I do that? Well, how do you like that?"

"I really thought you'd break my hand. It was killing me." He kept repeating it, not resentfully but dully, as though there were something secreted in the words that he couldn't fathom.

"But why didn't you take it away if it hurt that badly?" She put down her half-eaten sandwich as she saw the pale amazement ripple over his face.

"Oh, no, I couldn't do that. I mean—if that was what you needed just then—" He looked away, embarrassed. "Listen," he shrugged, not facing her, "we're in a hospital, after all. What better place? They'd fix it for me."

Overwhelmed, Caroline lay back on the pillows. "Oh, Ivan. You would do that?"

"What are you crying for?" he asked gently. "You didn't break it, did you? Almost doesn't count. So what are you crying about. You just had a baby. Don't cry."

And she smiled and thought her heart would burst.

DEER DANCE/FOR YOUR RETURN

(FEBRUARY, 1977)

by LESLIE MARMON SILKO

from COLUMBIA: A MAGAZINE OF POETRY AND PROSE

nominated by Nona Balakian and Daniel Halpern

Note on the Deer Dance:

In the fall, the Laguna hunters go to the hills and mountains around Laguna Pueblo to bring back the deer. The people think of the deer as coming to give themselves to the hunters so that the people will have meat through the winter. Late in the winter the Deer Dance is performed to honor and pay thanks to the deer spirits who've come home with the hunters that year. Only when this has been properly done will the spirits be able to return to the mountain and be reborn into more deer who will, remembering the reverence and appreciation of the people, once more come home with the hunters.

If this
will hasten your return
then I will hold myself above you all night
blowing softly
down-feathered clouds
that drift above the spruce
and hide your eyes
as you are born back
to the mountain.

Years ago
through the yellow oak leaves
antlers polished like stones
in the canyon stream-crossing
   Morning turned in the sky
   when I saw you
   and I wanted the gift
   you carry on moon-color shoulders
   so big
   the size of you
   holds the long winter.

You have come home with me before
a long way down the mountain
The people welcome you.
I took
the best red blanket for you
the turquoise the silver rings
were very old
   something familiar for you
   blue corn meal saved special.

While others are sleeping
I tie feathers on antlers
whisper close to you
   we have missed you
   I have longed for you.

Losses are certain
in the pattern of this dance
Over the terrain a hunter travels
blind curves in the trail
seize the breath
until it leaps away
loose again
to run the hills.
   Go quickly.

How beautiful
this last time
I touch you
            to believe
            and hasten the return
            of lava-slope hills and
            your next-year heart
Mine still beats
in the tall grass
where you stopped.
                    Go quickly.

Year by year
after the first snow-fall
I will walk these hills and
        pray you will come again
I will go with a heart full for you
        to wait your return.

The neck pulse slacks,
then smooths.
It has been a long time
Sundown forms change
Faces are unfamiliar
            As the last warmth goes
            from under my hand
            Hooves scatter rocks
            down the hillside
            and I turn to you
The run
for the length of the mountain
is only beginning.

MORAL FICTION

by JOHN GARDNER

from THE HUDSON REVIEW

nominated by DeWitt Henry

SOCIETIES ARE CREATED and destroyed by myth. The question a dying society must ask is (and let us assume for the moment that the fashionable wail is right and ours is dying), Where, Lord, did our fictions go wrong? How can we be saved? The answer is a little old-fashioned, but it's true.

True fiction—life-sustaining myth—is moral. One need not call up theory; one only need think of the fictions that have lasted, the *Iliad* and *Odyssey*, the tragedies of Aeschylus, Sophocles, and Euripides, Virgil's *Aeneid*, Dante's *Commedia*, the plays of Shakespeare and Racine, the novels of Tolstoy, Melville, Thomas Mann . . . Yet it is not true, as optimists imagine, that the morality of fiction

© 1978 John Gardner

takes care of itself. Good fiction is always in competition with bad, and the writer of good fiction can easily fall into a disadvantage, since he can see the virtues in the kind of fiction he prefers not to write, can make up excuses and justifications for even the cheapest pornography—to say nothing of more pretentious, more "serious" false art—while the writer of trash is not always so careful to be just. It is a fact of life, as Melville pointed out in *Israel Potter,* that noble ideas, noble examples of human behavior, can drop out of fashion though they remain as real and applicable as ever—can simply come to be forgotten, plowed under by "progress."

I would not claim that even the worst bad fiction should be outlawed or burned; morality by compulsion is a fool's morality. But I do think the arguments for the best kind of fiction, one of the bases of true morality, need to be mentioned from time to time, because it seems to me true that art has an effect on society. No one who has studied the evidence can doubt that violence on TV has at least a strong tendency to breed violence in the streets, or that when poet after poet claims, wringing his hands, "America is dead," readers may begin to believe it. The effect of the best fiction is to humanize, to clear the air, increase our understanding and offer models of just behavior. To put it another way, mankind has always lived by myth, religious or poetic. By myth we shape our understanding of ourselves and lay the foundations of our future. By bad myths—by myths of man as innately evil and inescapably doomed, or of man as inherently irrational, violent, depraved, loveless, or of all man's values as seminally corrupt, so that loyalty, restraint, justice, compassion are all, as Nietzsche thought, mere cyphers of cowardice and weakness—we plant the future in land mines.

Since "morality" has become a suspect term—a favorite cry of tyrannical oppressors from Russia and China to South Africa and Argentina—it is natural that you should ask, squinting suspiciously, exactly what I mean by "moral fiction." I mean two things, neither of which can stand without the other. First, moral fiction holds up models of decent behavior: characters whose basic goodness and struggle against confusion, error, and evil—in themselves and in others—give firm intellectual and emotional support to our own struggle. One thinks of such characters as Tolstoy's Pierre, in *War and Peace,* or Dostoevsky's brothers Karamazov. Sometimes—as in certain works of Chaucer and Shakespeare—the model is indirect, as when the moral confusion of the Pardoner or Macbeth leaves true morality at least partly to implication or at best in the hands of some minor character. Without denying for a moment that *The Pardoner's Tale* and *Macbeth* are masterworks that no writer living can come anywhere near, and realizing that my judgment is likely to annoy, I would call these morally secondary, though moral nonetheless. My reason is merely that it is easier and more natural to be moved to right action by the model of an admirable character than it is to be moved by recognition of an evil man's mistakes.

Life's imitation of art, after all, is direct and not necessarily intelligent. After Marlon Brando appeared in *On the Waterfront*, an entire generation took to slumping, mumbling, turning up its collar, and hanging its cigarette casually off the lip. After the appearance of Roy Rogers, a generation took to squinting. It is because of life's tendency to follow art that Tolstoy argued, in "What Is Art?," for establishing noble models. "By evoking under imaginary conditions the feeling of brotherhood and love, religious (i.e., moral) art will train men to experience those same feelings under similar circumstances in actual life. . . ." Today, though perhaps not in Shakespeare's day, the resolution never to behave like Macbeth does not inevitably carry any clear implication of what to do instead.

The first quality of moral fiction, then, is that it holds up useful models. These should not be stereotypic and sentimental models, needless to say, that is, models which merely confirm our unconsidered moral prejudices and cheap self-righteousness; and they will not be such models if the writer understands and submits himself to the second essential quality of moral art: to be moral a work of fiction must be the result of a creative process which is in total—and in specific ways—an intensely honest and rigorous mode of thought, an investigation in concrete (as opposed to abstract, or merely logical) philosophy.

For the person who looks at fiction mainly from the point of view of the reader or critic, it is easy to get the idea that fiction is serious, thoughtful, or "philosophical" merely because—and merely in the sense that—some writers of fiction are intelligent thinkers who express their profound ideas through stories. Thus Henry James "tells us" about American innocence, Melville "shows us" how the quality of life is affected by the proposition of an indifferent universe, and so on. What literary critics claim is true: writers do communicate ideas. What the writer understands, though the student or critic of literature need not, is that the writer discovers, works out, and tests his ideas in the process of writing. Thus at its best fiction is, as I've said, a way of thinking, a philosophical method.

It must be granted at once that some good and "serious" fiction is merely first-class propaganda—fiction in which the writer knows before he starts what it is that he means to say and does not allow his mind to be changed by the process of telling the story. A good deal of medieval literature works this way: the doctrine is stock, and the actions of ladies, gentlemen, and beasts are merely devices for communicating doctrine in a pleasing way. This is the method Boccaccio describes in his *Genealogy of the Gods* as the essential technique of allegory; it produces the kind of poetry Sidney defends in his *Defense:* instruction clothed in delight. *Pilgrim's Progress* and *Gulliver's Travels* (to some extent) are fictions of this kind, as are (to a large extent) such modern works as *Gravity's Rainbow* and John Barth's superb tract on justice between the sexes, *Chimera*. Fiction of this sort, dogmatic or ironic-dogmatic fiction, may be highly entertaining, may be fully persuasive, may have the clear ring of art, but such fiction is closer to the sermon than to the true short story or novel, closer to the verse essay as practiced by Pope than to the Elizabethan play. Such fiction may be—and usually is—*moralistic*, and the writer, in creating it, may be morally careful, that is, may work hard at telling nothing but the truth; but in what I am describing as true moral fiction the "art" is not merely ornamental: it controls the argument and gives it its rigor, forces the writer to intense yet dispassionate and unprejudiced watchfulness, drives him—in ways abstract logic cannot match—to unexpected discoveries and, frequently, a change of mind.

Moral fiction communicates meanings discovered by the process of the fiction's creation. We can see the process working when we look through the drafts of a certain kind of writer's work. Thus we see Tolstoy beginning with one set of ideas and attitudes in *Two Marriages,* an early draft of *Anna Karenina*—in which Anna, incredible as it seems, marries Vronsky—and gradually discovering, draft by draft, deeper and deeper implications in his story, revising his judgments, stumbling upon connections reaching new insights, until finally he nails down the attitudes and ideas we find dramatized, with such finality and conviction that it seems to us unthinkable that they should not have burst full-grown from Tolstoy's head, in the published novel. So Dostoevsky agonized over the better and worse implications of Myshkin's innocence and impotence. We see the same when we look at successive drafts of work by Kafka, or even the two drafts of Chaucer's *Troilus and Criseyde*.

The writing of a fiction is *not* a mode of thought when a good character and a bad one are pitted against each other. There is nothing inherently wrong with such fiction. It may be funny, or biting, or thrillingly melodramatic; it may be unspeakably witty, or grave, or mysterious, or something else; but it can contain only cleverness and preachments, not the struggle of thought. When fiction becomes thought—a kind of thought less restricted than logic or mere common sense (but also impossible to verify)—the writer makes discoveries which, in the act of discovering them in his fiction he communicates to the reader.

He makes these discoveries in several ways. Much of what a writer learns he learns simply by imitation. Making up a scene, he asks himself at every step, "Would she really say that?" or "Would he really throw the shoe?" He plays the scene through in his imagination, taking all the parts, being absolutely fair to everyone involved (mimicking each in turn, as Aristotle pointed out, and never sinking to stereotype for even the most minor characters), and when he finishes the scene he understands by sympathetic imitation what each character has done throughout and why the fight or accident, or whatever, developed as it did. The writer does the same with the total action, Aristotle's *energeia*, the actualization of the potential which exists in character and situation. Throughout the entire chain of casually related events, the writer asks himself, would *a* really cause *b* and not *c*, etc., and he creates what seems, at least by the test of his own normal imagination and experience of the world, an inevitable development of story. Inevitability does not depend, of course, on realism. Some or all of the characters may be fabulous— dragons, griffins, Achilles' talking horses—but once a character is established for a creature, the creature must act in accord with it.

To learn about reality by mimicking it, needless to say, the writer must never cheat, never play tricks. He may establish any sort of *givens* he may please, but once they are established he must follow where, in his experience, nature would lead if there really were, say, griffins. He cannot, for instance, make the reader accept some event on the basis of the writer's stylistic eloquence. By rhetoric any writer worth his salt can convince the reader that an eighty pound griffin falls twice as fast as a forty pound griffin, but if natural law in a world containing griffins is one of the premises the writer has accepted, the rhetoric is a betrayal of honest thought. Neither can the honest writer make the reader accept what he says took place if the writer moves from *a* to *b* by verbal sleight-of-hand, that is, by distracting the reader. It is easy for any clever writer to evoke and fully authenticate a situation (*a*), then digress to something else, then evoke and fully authenticate a situation which pretends to be the direct effect of *a*, a situation *b* which is in fact implausible as a result of *a* but does not seem implausible because the digression has blurred the real and inevitable effect of *a* in the reader's mind. No decent writer, admittedly, would play such games—except, by accident, on himself. Thus one of the ways in which fiction serves thought is this: its laws demand that the writer study out what *a* would lead to, and tell the truth. By style, energy, the power of his voice and the pressure of his feeling, an honest writer may heighten, sharpen, or clarify the importance of causal relationships; but style or no style, *a* must lead to *b* if the writer is claiming causality as the principle of his fiction's profluence. The writer who boasts, "I can make a lady pick up a coffee cup anytime I please" may be amusing, even spell-binding, but he is not, in one important way, serious. Worse, his work will be, in one important way, boring.

Aristotle of course understood this. It is his reason for objecting to a plot-solution by divine machinery. If Aristotle's position were still generally understood, we would need to say no more on this subject; but unfortunately in recent years Aristotle's ideas have fallen out of fashion among some modern writers, a group in some measure led by William Gass, whose theory of fiction as mere language has been widely influential—not, I think, because of any merit in Gass's argument but only because of the appealing verbal richness—the entertainment value—in Gass's way of presenting his outlandish notions.

Gass claims—and perhaps for some readers it is true—that when a writer describes a scene, the reader's imagination seizes only those details the writer has explicitly given, so that, for example, if the writer mentions that a character wears spectacles but says nothing else about that character, the reader forms no impression of the character's nose, eyes, forehead, stature, or clothes. If it is true that words are the writer's only material, then the only kind of richness or interest available to the writer is linguistic, and—given equal linguistic dazzle—there should be no difference between the emotional effect of a story about a lifelike character with some urgent

problem (Gass would disapprove of the word "lifelike") and a character who admits or, indeed, insists that she has no existence except as
words on a page—as does the central figure in Gass's experiment,
Willie Masters' Lonesome Wife. To think of a fictional character as a
person—to weep for little Nell or shudder at the affrontery of
Captain Ahab—is childishly naive, Gass claims.

The trouble with the theory is essentially this: that words have
associations, and groups of words form chains of association. To say
the word *crate* to a native English speaker is to summon up an image
of a crate and, with it, the natural background of that image, which is
a different background from that summoned up by *casque* or *trunk*
or *cube*. etc. To say that a character is built like a crate is to suggest
more than just the character's shape: it is to hint at his personality,
his station in life, even his behavior. This becomes obvious when we
place the character in some setting not at all natural for a crate and
then linguistically reinforce the unnaturalness: *He sat at the tea
table, trying to look small for all his bulk, as stiff and unnatural as a
crate*. It is true only in a trivial sense that the writer's only material is
words. Words conjure images in the reader's mind, and when the
words are put together in the proper way, with the proper
rhythms—long and short sounds, smooth or ragged, tranquil or
rambunctious—we have the queer experience of falling through the
print on the page into something like a dream, an imaginary world so
real and convincing that when we happen to be jerked out of it by a
call from the kitchen or a knock at the door, we stare for an instant in
befuddlement at the familiar room where we sat down, half an hour
ago, with our book. To say that we shouldn't react to fictional
characters as "real people" is exactly equivalent to saying that we
shouldn't be frightened by the things that leap out at us in nightmares.

We will need to return later, in another connection, to this matter
of language as the trigger of a dream, but for the moment the
important point is this: if it is true that metaphor becomes reality
when we read—if it is true, that is, that on encountering the words,
*whenever it is a damp, drizzly November in my soul, whenever I find
myself involuntarily pausing before coffin warehouses, and bringing
up the rear of every funeral I meet*, we involuntarily form images of
the things represented—then there is nothing inherently wrong
with Aristotle's opinion that what chiefly interests us in fiction is

characters in action or, more philosophically, "the actualization of the potential which exists in character and situation." If it is true that we *do* look at characters in fiction as if they were real, and feel curious about what they will do when their safety is threatened or their wishes are opposed, then the only possible objection to fiction which looks carefully at how things come about—how, given the drives and obsessions of Oedipus, situation *a* in his life leads with murderous inevitability to situation *b*—must be that such study is frivolous. (I would not say, myself, that frivolity is ever an argument against anything; but our object here is to discover whether, on any grounds, causality should be considered an undignified or wrong concern.)

What we learn when we look closely at the successive drafts of a writer like Tolstoy—and what one learns if one is oneself a writer who has tested each of his fictional scenes against his experience of how things seem to happen in the world—is that scrutiny of how people act and speak, why people feel precisely the things they do, how weather affects us at particular times, how we respond to some people in ways we would never respond to others, leads to knowledge, sensitivity, and compassion. In fiction we stand back, weigh things as we do not have time to do in life, and the effect of great fiction is to temper real experience, modify prejudice, humanize. One begins a work of fiction with certain clear opinions—for instance the opinion I myself began with in a recent novel, *October Light*, that traditional New England values are the values we should live by: good workmanship, independence, unswerving honesty, and so on—and one tests those values in lifelike situations, puts them under every kind of pressure one can think of, always being fair to the other side, and what one slowly discovers, resisting all the way, is that one's original opinion was oversimple. This is not to say, by any means, that there are no values; only to say that a simulation of real experience is morally educational. To the writer at least, such an experience proves that Aristotle was correct: fiction is a mode of thought—the artist's equivalent to the scientific method—and therefore anything but frivolous.

In this process I describe, the reader is at a disadvantage in that what he has before him is not all the possibilities entertained by the writer and recognized as wrong but only the story the writer eventually came to see as inevitable and right. But the good writer provides his reader, consciously and to some extent mechanically, with a dramatic equivalent of the intellectual process he himself went through. That equivalent is suspense.

Alas, it is even more embarrassing for a serious writer to speak of suspense, these days, than it is to speak of morality or plot. Thirty years ago, when I was an earnest young writer reading books on how to write, I was outraged, I remember, by talk of keeping the reader in suspense. Suspense, it seemed to me—and so those foolish writers on how to write made it seem—was a carrot held out to an idiot donkey, and I had no intention of treating my reader as anything but an equal. But suspense, rightly understood, is a serious business: one presents the moral problem—the character's admirable or unadmirable intent and the pressures of situation working for and against him (what other characters in the fiction feel and need, what imperatives nature and custom urge)—and rather than moving at once to the effect, one tortures the reader with alternative possibilities, translating to metaphor the alternatives the writer has himself considered. Superficially, the delay makes the decision—the climatic action—more thrilling; but essentially the delay makes the decision philosophically significant. Whether the character acts rightly or wrongly, his action reflects not simply his nature but his nature as the embodiment of some particular theory of reality and the rejection, right or wrong, of other theories. When the fiction is "tight," as the New Critics used to say, the alternatives are severally represented by the fiction's minor characters, and no character is without philosophical function. True suspense is identical with the Sartrean anguish of choice.

It goes without saying, though I will say it anyway, that even the most lofty and respectable theories of human motivation—from psychiatrists, biologists, theologians, and philosophers—must always be treated by the serious writer as suspect. The writer's sole authority is his imagination. He works out in his imagination what would happen and why, acting out every part himself, making his characters say what he would say himself if he were a young second-generation Italian, then an old Irish policeman, and so on. When the writer accepts unquestioningly someone else's formulation of how and why people behave, he is not thinking but dramatizing some other man's theory, that of Freud, Adler, Laing, or whoever. Needless to say, one may make some theory of motivation one's premise—an idea to be tested. But the final judgment must come from the writer's imagination. True moral fiction is a laboratory experiment too difficult and dangerous to try in the world but safe and important in the mirror-image of reality in the writer's mind. Only a madman would murder a sharp old pawn-brokeress to test the theory of the Superman; but Dostoevsky can without harm send his imaginary Raskolnikov into just that experiment in a thoroughly accurate but imaginary St. Petersburg.

The writing of fiction is a mode of thought because by imitating we come to understand the thing we imitate. Fiction is thus a convincing and honest but unverifiable science (in the old sense— knowledge): unverifiable because it depends on the reader's sensitivity and clear sense of how things are, a sense for which we have no tests. Some people claim our basic human nature is vicious, some claim otherwise. The cynic can be shown, by definition, to be a cynic, but he cannot be proved wrong. (So far, unhappily, it cannot even be proved conclusively that he grows ulcers more quickly than do nice people.) The kind of knowledge which comes from imitation thus depends for its quality on the sanity and stability of the imitator—according to some standard (Nietzsche would say) of sanity and stability. Clearly no absolute standard exists; but rough estimates are possible. If a writer regularly treats all life bitterly, scorning love, scorning loyalty, scorning decency (according to some standard)—or to put it another way; if some writer's every remark strikes most or many readers as unfair, cruel, stupid, self-regarding, ignorant, or mad—if he has no good to say to anything or anyone except the character who seems to represent himself—if he can find no pleasure in what happy human beings have found good for centuries (children and dogs, God, peace, wealth, comfort, love, hope, and faith)—then it is fair to hazard that he has not made a serious effort to sympathize and understand, that he has not tried to guess what special circumstances would make him behave, himself, as his enemies behave. Whatever some possible divinity might say of such a writer's fictions, the nonomniscient can say this much: he is not using fiction as a mode of thought but merely as a means of preaching his peculiar doctrine.

For Aristotle, imitation was the primary way in which the writer of a fiction makes discoveries. There are other ways. When the writer asks himself, "would she really say that?" or "Would he really throw the shoe?" his imagination is working close to the conscious surface. Given a clearly defined character and circumstance, it takes no genius to determine whether or not she would say that or he would throw the shoe. We all have a sense of the probable. If a fierce, violently angry man whose society and family demands eye-for-eye revenge meets his brother's murderer and is invited to tea, any fool can guess that in all likelihood he will not at once accept the invitation and let bygones be bygones. And the same is true in far more subtle situations. When characters behave out of character, readers notice. They may blink the mistake and accept what the writer claims to have happened, but readers do know. If they read on, they do so for lack of something better to read. A strong imagination makes characters do what they would do in real life. A subtler work of the imagination—a subtler way in which the writing of fiction is a morally serious mode of thought—is symbolic association.

There is a game, often played in the nineteen-fifties by members of the Iowa Writers' Workshop, called "What Kind of Smoke Are You?" It works as follows. The player who is "it" chooses some famous person with whom everyone playing must surely be acquainted (Harry Truman, Madame Mao, Charles de Gaulle, for instance) and tells the other players "I am a dead American," "I am a living Asian," "I am a dead European," and then each of the other players in turn asks one question of the person who is "it," such as, "What kind of smoke are you?" (cigarette, pipe, cigar—or, more specifically, L & M, Dunhill, White Owl) or "What kind of weather are you?" "What kind of insect are you?" or "What kind of transportation?" The person who is "it" answers not in terms of what kind of smoke his character would *like*, if any, but what kind of smoke he would *be* if, instead of being human, he were a smoke, or what kind of weather, insect, transportation, and so forth, he would be if reincarnated as one of those. Thus, for example, Kate Smith if an insect would be a turquoise beetle; Marlon Brando, if weather, would be sultry and uncertain, with storm warnings out; and Harry Truman would be (whatever he may in fact have driven) a Model T Ford. What always happens when this game is played by sensitive people is that the whole crowd of questioners builds a stronger and stronger feeling of the character, by unconscious association, until finally someone says the right name—"Kate Smith!" or "Madame Mao!"—and everyone in the room feels instantly that that's right. There is obviously no way to play this game with the reasoning faculty, since it depends on largely unconscious associations or intuition; and what the game proves conclusively for everyone playing is that our associations are remarkably similar. When one of the players falls into some mistake, for instance saying that Mr. Brezhnev of the U.S.S.R. is a beaver instead of, more properly, a crafty old wood-chuck, all the players at the end of the game are sure to protest, "You misled us when you said 'beaver,'" The game proves more dramatically than any argument can suggest the mysterious rightness of a good metaphor—the one requisite for the poet, Aristotle says, that cannot be taught.

The mainly unconscious or intuitive associations which show up in the game "What Kind of Smoke Are You?" hint at one of the ways in which the writing of fiction is a mode of thought. No one can achieve profound characterization of a person (or place) without appealing to semi-unconscious associations. To sharpen or intensify a characterization, a writer makes use of metaphor and reinforcing background —weather, physical objects, animals—details which either mirror character or give character something to react to. To understand that Marlon Brando *is* a certain kind of weather is to discover something (though something neither useful nor demonstrable) and in the same instant to communicate something. Thus one of the ways in which fiction thinks is by discovering deep (metaphoric) identities. Any given character may happen to be found, of course, in any setting; but a good writer chooses the setting which makes character and situation clear. (I do not mean that a character ought to be discovered in the setting that best reveals him. A man of the mountains may be found in an automat; but if the man's nature is to be clear to the reader, the mountains must be somehow implied.) When fiction is truly a mode of understanding, Raskolnikov can only be a creature of Russia and St. Petersburg; he would not be the same young man at all if raised in Copenhagen. Given a character who's shy and silent, interested in chemistry, socially retiring but happy with his family, it makes all the difference in the world whether he wears brown or gray. When a writer meets a stranger, the writer should be able to tell quite soon—within reasonable limits—how the stranger's living room is furnished.

What possible moral value can there be, it may be asked, in knowing how a stranger's living room is furnished? The answer is of course that it depends on how the knowledge is put to use. We study people carefully for two main reasons: in order to understand them and fully experience our exchange with them, or in order to feel ourselves superior. The first purpose can contribute to art and is natural to art, since the soul of art is celebration and discovery through imitation. The second, perhaps more common, is a mark of petty-mindedness, insecurity, or vice and is the foundation of art that has no value. Both artistic acts, the real and the fraudulent, are obviously egoistic: the true artist is after "glory," as Faulkner said, that is, the pleasure of noble achievement and good people's praise; the false artist is after power and the yawping flattery of his carnivore pack.

The understanding which comes through the discovery of right metaphors can lead the writer to much deeper discoveries, discoveries of the kind made by interpreters of dreams—discoveries, that is, of how one dark metaphor relates to another, giving clues to the landscape of the writer's unconscious and, through these clues, hypotheses on the structure of reality. Pursuit of these clues and hypotheses is the third element—and perhaps the most eerie—in the total creative process which makes fiction a mode of thought.

This is how it works. The writer, let us say, plans his story (some writers do, other writers don't, preferring to make up the story as they go), then writes it in rough draft, employing all his powers of imagination to give clarity and richness, or, to put it another way, make the characters, settings, and events seem real. He knows, for instance, that it is not enough to say *Her father was a drunkard*, since the mere abstract statement does not conjure the image of a drunkard in the reader's mind; instead, the writer must add some concrete image, perhaps some metaphoric expression as well—*she remembered him sitting at the kitchen table, gray as a stone, with his hat on.* Or, again, the writer knows it is not enough to say that some character smoked a pipe; he must, for instance, show the pipe smoke clouding around the face. So the writer continues, character by character, scene by scene, event by event, constantly insisting on concrete images, perhaps backing them with poetic suggestion, until the draft is complete. Many writers stop here, perhaps including some great ones, but it's a mistake. If the writer looks over his story carefully, again and again, reading aloud, his whole soul as tense as any stalking beast, he will begin, inevitably, to discover odd connections, strange and seemingly inexplicable repetitions. On page four he finds the drunkard, gray as a stone, with his hat on; and on page 19 he finds, say, an image of a hushed gray mountain with a hat of low clouds.

In art repetition is always a signal, intentional or not, and when the moral artist finds in his work some such accident of language as the one I've just fabricated, he refuses to rest until he has somehow understood—or can emotionally confirm—the accident. He asks himself consciously—perhaps writes it down on a slip of yellow paper—"Why is this particular drunken father like this particular mountain?" Occasionally the question remains stubbornly unanswerable, and the writer, convinced by the prickling of his thumbs that the mysterious equation is significant, God knows how, will simply let it stand, or will perhaps reinforce it with some further related image which feels equally right, God knows why. There's nothing wrong in this. At a certain point in human thought, rationality breaks down and can speak to us only of the mundane. But whether or not the writer can finally answer the questions his writing fishes up from the bog of the unconscious, he asks them carefully, again and again. He reevaluates, in the light of the messages he has received from the swamp, all that his fiction has labored to maintain. If he has claimed, for instance, that a particular character is sterile and empty, yet accidents of language or of image-echo have secretly identified that character with forces of fecundity and fullness, the writer tries the hypothesis that his first opinion was wrong. He plays part against part, hunting out each part's secrets, until something clicks.

In short, the discoveries or "epiphanies" in great fiction are not planned in advance: they evolve. So Anna, to Tolstoy's surprise, commits suicide, though he'd been brooding on that mangled young body on the tracks for years. So Mrs. Eustace, to Trollope's astonishment, stole her own diamonds.

This is not, for the moral writer, a mere device, a way of coming up with interesting surprises for the audience. It reflects a fundamental conviction of the artist that the mind does not impose structures on reality (as existentialists claim), arbitrarily maintaining now this, now that, but rather, as an element of total reality, a capsulated universe, discovers, in discovering itself, the world. The artist's theory, as revealed by his method (however artists may deny it), is that the things he thinks when he thinks most dispassionately—not "objectively," quite, but with passionate commitment to discovering whatever may happen to be true (not merely proving that some particular thing is true)—that the ideas the artist gets, to put it another way, when he thinks with the help of the full artistic method, are absolutely valid, true not only for himself but for everyone, or at least for all human beings—and some artists would go further. (Tolstoy never doubted his understanding of dogs and horses.)

To someone who has never written real poetry or fiction, all this may seem doubtful; but it is a method that can be studied wherever great writers have left sketches and consecutive drafts. That the method is still common is easily verified: simply ask writers how they work, if you can get them not to lie. The method is not always as conscious as I've made it seem, of course. Some writers may claim that they simply keep tinkering until everything works. But however the given writer expresses it, this feeling-out of the fiction's implications, this refusal to let the fiction go until it has proved itself a closed and self-sustaining system, an alternative reality, an organism, this is the true writer's check on himself, and his road to understanding. It is here that fake art hopelessly breaks down. One does not achieve the dense symbolic structure of *Death in Venice*, *The Sound and the Fury*, or *Under the Volcano* by planning it all out on butcher paper—though one does make careful plans. True writing, as William Gaddis says, is:

> like living with a God damned invalid . . . eyes follow you around the room wave his God damned stick figure out what the hell he wants, plump the God damned pillow change bandage read aloud move a clause around wipe his chin new paragraph. . . .

I will mention one last check on fiction's honesty: tradition. No writer imagines he exists in a literary void. Though writers rarely read as widely as do critics, partly because writers can afford to be critical, throwing out books because of annoying little flaws of conception or execution, it is nevertheless true that writers would not be what they are if they didn't have a liking for books. A particular writer may read no one but George Gissing or, perhaps, Aristophanes; but he knows full well that one of the things he's doing when he writes is laboring to achieve an effect at least somewhat similar to effects he has gotten out of other people's books. When a writer begins a story *It was winter of the year 1833. A large man stepped out of a doorway,* that writer has a literary tradition in mind, and part of his purpose is to be—besides interesting and original— true to the tradition (or anyway steadily aware of it). When he begins a story, *She was no longer afraid of the long drive home,* he has another distinct tradition in mind, and still another when he begins,

"Henry, come clean off them boots," Mrs. *Cobb called out the woodshed door.* The medium of literary art is not language but language plus the writer's experience and imagination and, above all, the whole of the literary tradition he knows. Just as the writer comes to discoveries by studying the accidental implications of what he's said, he comes to discoveries by trying to say what he wants to say without violating the form to which he's committed. It isn't true that, as New Critics used to say with great confidence, "Form is content." The relationship between the two is complex almost beyond description. It *is* true, as Wallace Stevens said, that "A change of style is a change of subject."

The process of discovery through a struggle with tradition is most obvious in the retelling of some traditional myth. In my own retelling of the story of *Jason and Medeia* I shackled myself with one basic rule: I would treat the same events treated in the past (by Apollonios and Euripides), making sure that the characters said approximately the same things, performed the same actions, and made the same friends and enemies among men and gods; but all that happened I would try to understand with a modern sensibility (granting the existence of gods as forces), asking myself how *I*, in these situations, could say and do what these antique figures did. In what sense could I understand the Sirens, or Circe, or the Golden Fleece? What would make me, as a modern woman (as a writer one claims androgyny), kill my children? The result of this process is that one gets the impression, rightly or wrongly, that one has to some extent penetrated what is common in human experience throughout time; and since again and again the ancient poets seem right, and "modern sensibility" seems a fool's illusion, one gets the impression that one has come to grasp, more firmly than before, fragments of the ancient poets' wisdom.

The same process is at work, less obviously, when one decides to write a "gothic," a murder mystery, a family saga, or a country yarn, and at work much more subtly when one commits oneself to a conventional realistic novel—or for that matter to a serious poem in tetrameter quatrains without rhyme. What has gone before exerts its light pressure, teasing the mind just as Tarot cards do toward queer new visions of the familiar.

Such are my arguments for what I have described as "the best kind of fiction." I don't mean in all this to be unduly sober-minded. I have nothing against limericks, tales of boys and dogs, or *Star Trek*. I do object strongly to the cult of sex and violence, and more strongly yet to the cult of cynicism and despair. But I do not really think censorship is the answer. I am convinced that good art easily beats out bad, and that the present scarcity of first-rate literature does not follow from a sickness of society but the other way around. In the past few decades we have shaken off, here in America, the childish naivety and prudishness we see in, for instance, movies of the thirties and forties, where the killers say "Jeez" and the reporters say "Gosh," but in our pursuit of greater truth we have fallen to the persuasion that the cruellest, ugliest thing we can say is likely to be the truest. Real art has never been fooled by such nonsense: real art has internal checks against it.

Real art creates myths a society can live instead of die by, and clearly our society is in need of such myths. What I have tried to show here is that such myths are not mere hopeful fairy tales but products of careful and disciplined thought, that a properly built myth, in other words, is worthy of belief, at least tentatively, that working at art is a moral act, that a work of art is a moral example, and that false art can be known for what it is if one remembers the standards. The black abyss stirs a certain fascination, admittedly, or we would not pay so many writers so much money to keep staring at it. But the black abyss is merely life as it is or as it soon may become, and staring at it does nothing, merely confirms that it is there. It seems to me time that artists start taking that fact as pretty firmly established, and stop fooling around.

THE SURVIVORS

by DAN MASTERSON

from THE GEORGIA REVIEW

nominated by THE GEORGIA REVIEW

I. Catherine Anne Hanley

They knew scarlet fever when they saw it,
and they saw it on her neck and arms,
could feel it in the pulse she gave off
as she lay in fever on her bunk twisting
the blanket to her face, a headache
wishing her back to Dublin, to her own
bed, her own window where the breeze
brought the garden inside.

In three days it would be her ears;
in a week she would let go
of her fourth winter, her parents' faces
blurring away, her sisters' eyes turning
into stars as she eased out of pain,
wrapped in their blankets, surrounded
by everything she'd touched, swirling
with her in a weighted sack, to the floor
of the Atlantic.

II. James Edward Hanley

They were told to return to steerage
where they belonged, but stayed,
the father's eyes ending any argument
on deck; a tanner by trade, his hands

were mostly leather; the arms, massive
as country fence posts, curved
around his family bent at the railing
in prayer.

In time, they asked for more blankets
and took the children below,
where they lay broken in the first grief
they had ever known, their mother close
to the father, speaking in whisper,
learning again that his strength was only
partly his own.

III. Laura Marie Hanley

The child's third night was fitful; at dawn
she awoke in chill; by noon the headaches
began, the spots scattered themselves,
and the countrymen nearest her bunk
turned their faces to the wall.

They were five days from shore; the hospital
could save her; fresh vegetables and milk
would be waiting, clean linen and gargles,
warm baths and oils when the peeling began;
she was less frail than Catherine, older,
and had never been sick before.

IV. Elizabeth Carroll Hanley

She would bring her daughter through;
after eight weeks of living in stench,
eating like beggars, sleeping in straw,
they would be in America where Uncle Patrick
held a parcel of land in their name.

She would see to it that Laura Marie would be
with them; she would wager her life on it;

through day and night she stayed
with the child, keeping the others away,
restricting her diet to soft foods, listening
to advice from the curious and bereaved

Until her own eyes burned, even when shut; her throat
closed beyond words, and she lay back
on her bunk, rubbing away the strawberry rash
that was forming on her arms.

V. Liza, Mary and Kate Hanley

They stayed below with their father when the men
took the others, the men in thick masks and gloves
who said kind things to the stretchers they carried,
and told James to come back in six weeks, that all
would be fine by then.

In three hours, they were on land, walking ahead
of him, trying not to fall down in the crowd,
feeling his hands urging them on, steering them
wherever the signs told him to go, his voice
telling them all the things they wanted to hear.

A man with a badge gave them white cards to hang
on their coats; their common code, Han-14,
would get them together if lost; on to the end
of the ramp where doctors worked in rooms
with ceilings as far back as you could lean; a man
just ahead had his card torn in half and chalk
scrawled on his sleeve; they took him
out a different door.

They held hands outside and followed their father
to the trains; once aboard, they felt sure of things
and fell asleep, leaving him to watch the buildings
give way to trees; by morning, they were there.

VI. Mrs. James Edward Hanley and Daughter

A prayerful six weeks passed slowly in the house
in upstate New York, but the time came to bring
the rest of his women home; he would travel alone,
leaving Liza in charge, and Mary and Kate
would obey her as they would their mother,
or he would know the why of it.

The trip to Ward's Island was long, but he ran
the gravel road to the hospital, stopping
out of breath at the desk to be told
the third floor office would have that sort
of information; it did:

Two entries. December, 1850, six days apart:

      Cremated due to contagion
      Elizabeth Hanley, age thirty-four
      Laura Marie Hanley, age six

The road to the depot was spotted with snow,
his hands raw where he wrung them, each knuckle
white at the bone.

The last car was empty, its windows heavy with soot;
he saw trees hardened with ice, and a sky going grey
without clouds. He pulled the shade to the sill.

BONS

fiction by BETH TASHERY SHANNON

from CHICAGO REVIEW

nominated by Gordon Lish

Poodys! boo! theres things when you dye, but all the time really. Just they are on dead peopso you can see em. Undie you meat, your bons. All the bons makeup a Poody.

Poodys are use by Drs. so they can know what won look like. If thare Drs. and wad to no they git em some. Then they do. Kno. Werd for Poodys comes frum a laddin werd means gnaw-bon.[Z] Lots laddin wrd. use by drs. Ther main name is of the first Dr., Hippocrites and his oats.

But som Poodos Drs. themsefs. They gnaw why Drs. wants to poke at em. Then the DRs. has to run awa. So most Ds. make there Poodys their selves. If they can get the blypes off.

The history of Poodys is that some Poodys diffaurant size; Some come from caves. If you sea cav, you know a Poody migt live in. Some Poodys not even Poodys At All! The called: Mumblies. If all dryd up and wear a mask you kno its a: mumbly.

Theirs Poodys ever day of the weak.

Black peops have white Poodys and Whit peo blak Poodys. Poody never get cold; but can, however, loose thei'r bons. That is, everhow, the storey of Bloody Bon. You, evhower, know abot it under the stairs. But thee Red Hand is no a Poody. He put peopoles in jars indies attic.

Nothin can doo ab out Poodys. Everwher! Even there's one inn you! Just try not be skared.

There advantageous to Poodsy. For instant; slugs donut hava P. If withouten Puti you might be a ear. ᶻᶻ

Inside Pood y ou make your bloot.

Som bonns bent. Wishbons. Nother person you can pull em & get you're wished.

There's al so Crossbons. Skull an. The are poison. Standin at thee Crossbons Im tryn to flad aride.

A few reminder abo Podos: No don't forget!

3. Poodo, Poodo, stay inside.

3. Fun too have your ver owned Poodi!

3. No Poodys at the tabl. ᶻᶻᶻ

Even nakes have Pooys.

The time you can seye yrs own is an exeroys. Exeroys when the shot you with Alpha Rays mik a pickture.

Som bons r carpals. Once upon a tim were those Poodys Orville Ogle, Factory Ferd and thee flyin carpal. Who were P.s. and Drs. all metupona comment where had stopped for he loved to stop on streed comments and have as moke. Up a bon Orville Ogle.

"Boo. Is that you'res mokin," ask Orville Orgle with gret interest.

"Oooooh. Since when you don't know," popped Dr. Ferd, handing his money back.

"Wooo. But it smell like it were cut with camelear wax." said the Poody. "and I haven't anywhat to eat."

But Orville Oble was nothing haunted.

Whereupon Factory Fur.

A pausing stranger pulled a carpal and sit on it spiderwise. Orville Tuba did not know, haveing a lot upon his mind.

"It looks vacant, is it forsale;" the stranger spyderwise.

Nunsuch embareassed Orgle Oval yeld, "Boo! You bag of bons, is it so much to your get off that carpal all spiderwise and what make you think they are anyhow?"

"So many,: were the answers, smiling.

Whereon off a suddien Orgle Odr. an Factory Ferd dr. jump into a maze! for the carpal were actual beginn to fly! As the took of, bit by bite, gnaw by bon, with Factoryoutlet Ferdinand atop, who were even seen again.

---

[z]Gnaw-bon, Idniana. Salt Creak Valley Horrey!

[zz]ears have no Poddys.

[zzz]your teeth all poodys.

[zzzz]but you don't have to brush te rest of it.

MORAL CAKE

fiction by DON HENDRIE JR.

from SCRIBBLE, SCRIBBLE, SCRIBBLE (Lynx House Press)

nominated by John Irving

HE DRANK IN QUICK succession four Canadian beers. He was a childless American of modest means, supported by his wife, and now and then bartending tips. The man—Lock Jennish—sat on a padded stool at the darker end of the Freneau Taproom's bar, Hancock, New Hampshire. It was four o'clock on the October afternoon of his thirty-eighth birthday, and he was alone but for the odd look-in of the night man Roger, busy hustling stock in the room behind the bar's aged mirror. Lock held a long filterless cigarette between the third and fourth fingers of his left hand; the right hand caressed the most recent glass of beer. Smoke drifted from his mouth and through the filter of his generous salt-and-pepper mustache. He rubbed at his temple with his left hand, quite aware of the vein that pulsed dumbly just under the taut skin. And he would remember this evidence of his sober existence, because just then—his brow felt the tad of heat from the cigarette—someone entered the bar from the street and said in a throttled, awful voice, "Lock! . . . Your wife's killed on the Dublin road!"

"What do you mean?"

That morning Lock Jennish had worked out his own suicide. He would take a shovel and a rectangle of heavy plywood from the shed behind his house and walk with them across the saucer meadow until he reached the tree line. Several yards into the trees, well hidden from their kitchen window's view, he would commence to dig his grave to a depth of some five feet. At one end of the pit would be a slot just wide enough and sloped for him to make his ground hog's entrance. This after he had replaced the earth on top of the plywood set into the walls of the grave eighteen inches above its bottom. Beneath the plywood would lie his twelve gauge shotgun. Once the grave was filled and the entrance securely capped with a slab of granite, he would wait however long it took for his labors to be obscured by nature—a week? a month? Then, when the time was perfect, he would lift the rock, descend feet-first, and after replacing the rock would wiggle his black way under the plywood, embrace the shotgun, and cause to happen a dirt-muffled explosion that Lyn might well hear as she sat in her clothespin factory a half mile up the Dublin road: *Oh . . . Lock's got another pheasant.*

Lock Jennish, Missing Person.

He would do this secretive, foolproof thing because he had decided he was a prick of misery.

Officer Lonnie Swett, constable of Hancock, stood in front of Lock, a sheen of tears covering his cheekbones. "I hate a hit and run more'n anything, Lock," he moaned. Lock stared at himself in Swett's reflecting sunglasses, so as to avoid the peripheral sight of Lyn's insanely meagre heap . . . a rubber-sheeted brokenness on the shoulder of the road. "The impact knocked her right up against that maple," Swett went on, unnecessarily; Lock had been told whatever was worth knowing by his friend Tip Insinger, the man who had brought the rotten news to the Freneau. But Swett babbled, "They'll take her to Peterborough, Lock. A doctor's got to . . . The little Brown girl saw a VW bus going down towards your house just before. The bastard!"

Lock watched himself nod.

"Thanks, Lonnie," he heard himself say as he touched the man's tricep for a moment before turning away and puking the Canadian beers onto the roadside, a car length away from what was probably Lyn's concussant head.

After the funeral Tip took Lock to a bar in Hillsboro. Burly Tip tore at the label of his beer until Lock saw fit to say something. The something was to the effect that John McElwain, the eighteen year old driver of the VW bus, who had been apprehended in Goffstown the morning after the killing, should be treated with mercy.

"But why?" Tip cried. "You know he's lying!"

"What if he's not? What if she did jump smack in front of his car?"

Tip's grimace was not covered by an angry pull at his beer. "She's the calmest person I ever knew in my life."

Then Lock told his friend a story that Tip had not heard in the four years that they had known one another.

"When we came to New Hampshire we rented a farmhouse about fifteen miles north of here. There was one other house we could see, a cheap-shingled shack across the road, within hearing distance. Inside was a man named Winston Crockett, his wife Doris, and three kids, the smallest being a boy of three called—I don't know why— Loop. Crockett worked at the paper mill and drank like a fish. We didn't see much of Doris, but in summer the kids played in their miserable yard, and sometimes the older one, Bobby, would come over and watch me work in the shop."

"What kind of shop?" Tip asked.

"I thought of myself as a cabinet maker then . . . Neither Lyn nor I liked the Crocketts much. They were slovenly and unfriendly. But Lyn thought well enough of Loop, or the *idea* of a three year old, to buy him a birthday present. A wooden rocking horse. When she took it over on a Sunday afternoon, Mr. Winston Crockett intercepted the gift and in a drunk rage broke the head right off. 'Don't come round here with your cock horses, lady,' is what he said.

"That was in the beginning of the summer. More and more we heard all kinds of stuff coming from over there, especially at night. Shouts and curses, even screaming from Doris. Kids bawling. Lyn would sit in our living room, all the windows open, and bite her nails while she tried to read some book."

"Lock, have another beer."

"Sometimes we talked about having a chat with Crockett at a sober moment, but I could never quite see such interference from strangers. So it went on; got worse in July after he lost his job, Bobby told us. On the seventeenth, in the late afternoon when I was trying to put a finish on the first piece I'd managed to *sell*, Lyn came into the shop and said hell had broken loose across the road and she was damn well going to go over there. God help me, in my abstraction I said okay, okay, Lyn, yell if you need any help. In maybe fifteen minutes I heard her—the shop was on the other side of our house from theirs—shouting my name. **LOCK!**"

Tip started, again drank to cover it.

"My asshole name. I ran and found every one of them in their yard, Crockett flat-out on his back and plainly dead drunk passed out. Bobby was crying and Loop was huddled against a tree sucking his thumb and the other one was sniveling, but Doris looked as serene as a meringue pie. Lyn was standing over Crockett and she had loose in one hand a kid's baseball bat. She looked at me quizzically . . . and said, she said this exactly, Tip, 'He was kicking Loop and when he wouldn't stop I hit him across the chest with this and he turned purple and fell and I think he's dead.' 'That's right,' Doris said, 'the pot face is deader'n a mackerel.'"

"Jesus," Tip breathed.

"Death by misadventure, the coroner's inquest decided. Doris Crockett maintained her husband had got apoplexy in the process of beating the shit out of their youngest child."

"But . . ."

"See, Doris insisted . . . and Lyn and I didn't argue. What would you have done?"

Lock sat across the scarred table from John McElwain, whose long hair fell in dirty coils to the level of his collar bone. He seemed so frightened his lips had split from licking. "My mother," he was saying in a voice devoid of accent, "won't come and see me. She says the devil has come a rampage in my heart, she says these things in letters they lay on me every day, and the jailer in my wing thinks she's right, Mr. Jennish!"

"Well," Lock said quietly, "can you tell me why I should believe you."

McElwain raised his eyes to the ceiling and clasped his hands before his narrow chest. "May Yahweh make a eunuch of this person if he is lying." His eyes returned to Lock's; they were bright blue. "Your wife *leaped*, sir . . . She was in the *air* when my bus struck her. If there was sin . . . it was that her face at that moment was full of *rapture*. Can you dig it, your wife?"

"It's hard," Lock murmured, twisting at one end of his mustache. "Christ, man, then why didn't you at least stop for her? Help her or something. Maybe she wasn't even dead yet."

For a second McElwain's tongue explored his famished lower lip. He moved his hands from his chest to the table and appeared to be exerting considerable pressure down upon it. "I don't know sir. Maybe you know. Do you suppose I resented being *used*? You know, an innocent passer-by. Another point of view would be that I was enthralled, chicken, panicked, *sir*."

After a long breath, Lock asked, "What do you want me to do, assuming I believe you? Should I call your mother? Do you have a lawyer?"

McElwain snorted. "They say one will be assigned. It's my right. My mother would have me stoned." Now he giggled and leaned forward until Lock could see every white chap line on his lips. "You could *testify* that your wife had maybe a secret *aching* for death, that she got off on it." Having said his piece McElwain went to the door and rapped for his jailer.

Lock remembered a time when any manner of lie detecting tests performed upon himself would have offered only negative results. Respiration? Pulse? Sweat? Blood pressure? Voice? Each would have signified a man in harmony with himself. What leap had been made?

Long after the death of Winston Crockett and not so long after Lock and Lyn had moved from the farmhouse to their place in Hancock, Tip Insinger came into the Freneau with a woman, a Southern woman of about forty whose name—Fay Thames—Lock did not learn until after he had prepared her second vodka martini on the rocks. Handsome, regal, dark blonde, a blouse of white raw silk. . . . Only the dark glasses kept on despite the afternoon dimness of the bar suggested any sort of secret abuse of her limber body.

"Now Lock here," Tip said to Fay Thames, "he's married to a woman from New York City who now manufactures excellent wooden clothespins."

"Really," the neutral response from Fay. "My husband was the maize baron of Dalhart, Texas."

"What brings you up here?" Lock asked politely.

"Before poor Jack passed away he bought me a little place near Marlborough so I could come during autumn and enjoy the foliage, if I wanted."

"The old Jarndyce farm," Tip told Lock. "All four hundred acres of it."

Fay finished her drink and tinkled the ice. "But now I reckon I'll stay on through the winter. Jack Jr.'s in prep school nearby."

Lock built her another drink and wondered idly what she did to her skin to keep it so like the edible flesh of a brook trout.

This conversation meant little to Lock at the time. Dozens like it transpired before his face. In such a small town every stranger is at first exotic, then—to the amiable afternoon bartender—either becomes a regular vodka martini on the rocks, or goes on down the road. Fay Thames would do neither. Before she left with Tip she placed a ten dollar bill in Lock's outstretched palm and with her other hand lowered her glasses. The eyes were so brown as to be opaque, messageless. "Y'all come see me. Mr. Lock Clothespin," she might have whispered, and more loudly, "That change is yours."

Lock did not hesitate over the money. He smiled his thanks.

Time passed. The foliage arrived on schedule, and with it drinkers, assholes, even the Mayor of Boston. Lyn slowed the factory down, her product being a summer item, and by the time Lock had returned to his work-when-needed routine, he had forgotten about Mrs. Jack Thames.

Yet, on October nineteenth, he found himself mindlessly splitting wood for the seven fireplaces of the old Jarndyce house, a cream and brown manse built in 1852. He would remember as one conversation, commencing in mid-afternoon of the day when by accident he encountered Fay in the Marlborough General Store, these snippets of his seduction:

"There is no central heating, can you imagine?"

"Eight cords of hardwood, but they aren't broken . . . Oh, I mean split."

"My boy finds no dignity in work."

"Would you really? That's lovely. Follow me."

"A axe, wedges, sledge hammer, and you can holler for refreshment."

"A sort of catch-as-catch-can dinner. . . . If you want to call your wife there's the phone."

"Applejack. Vodka, if you please. All this beer, and a half gallon of zinfandel."

". . . so Jack ordered a special kind of quirt from Abercrombie's [she whooped, like a cowgirl], a chamois quirt for the beleaguering of my poor skin."

"I like a grey eye and a thick mustache, I like a close-mouthed fellow with dried sweat on his coccyx, I like. . . ."

"My grandmother made this quilt while she was still at the asylum in Lubbock."

"That's some soft mustache, Senor Jennish."

"Are you going to fuck me or not?"

Thus he leaped.

On the morning following his visit to John McElwain, Lock rose to a solitary breakfast of tea and a cigarette. In the bathroom, shitting, he told his sins. They were: Unearned Pride, Concealed Sloth, Moral Deafness, and a Soft Venery that had moved him like sludge toward Deception, Guilt, and Death. At the mirror he scowled, grinned horribly, relaxed every muscle in his body and became old, sexless . . . a tan mummy.

"Dipshit," he muttered. A percolation from his boyhood. Then he was abruptly at the door of the living room closet, and the shotgun seized. Shells. Canvas game bag. Rubber boots. And walking across the damp meadow and into the trees where he passed his own imaginary grave site, an event which gave the fleeing widower little pause as he made his way in the direction of the weird Lorelei cry of a ring-necked pheasant.

After he shot the second—the shot blew the bird smack against the standing trunk of a rotting birch—Lock returned to his home and called Tip on the telephone. He told his friend that he had decided to testify on the behalf of young John McElwain.

Tip allowed as how, in his opinion, Lock was crazy.

Lock said that redemption came in strange ways, and that Death could not have the last crumbs of his moral cake.

Tip did not seem to understand. He asked if Lock had any frozen pheasant on hand, manna for Tip's coming marriage to Fay.

A SACRIFICE OF DOGS

by WILLIAM SPRUNT

from A SACRIFICE OF DOGS (St. Andrews College Press)

nominated by St. Andrews College Press

The room is alive with dogs
Playing dead on wooden tables.
Nostrils flare like empty vases.
Tongues dry at half mast.
The hornless scapegoat snores unrecognized.

The skin is anointed with iodine,
And a signature appears in red.
Lungs collapse like balloons
Crepitant with micro barks.
A fist of heart gives in to a knife.

We extirpate the wonder in a search
For new technics, replace the faultless
Valves with plastic, leave
Polyester tubes for arteries.
The remainder will serve another day.

Aesculapius is pleased
And sends a shower of paper
Interpreted by the priest
As permission to extend
Our experiments to man.

THE WU GENERAL WRITES FROM FAR AWAY

by CHRISTOPHER HOWELL

from NORTHWEST REVIEW

nominated by NORTHWEST REVIEW

My dear friend
        It is snowing
in the house of my body, and beyond
    tarnishing childhood
song, below the red
black earth our grandfathers loved.
        What shall I say of this Summer
in which it is snowing
so often? I have no voice to describe
the delicacy of grasses, the scarlet horns
of new birds crying *feed feed*.
Every swayed branch stops the world
freshly. Every doe
browsing in sunlight beyond the meadow of tents
is a woman
releasing her braid on plain white silks.
    But it is going, it is all
going again through glass lips
of the hour. Soon cold will step from hiding;
the bears stagger comically to sleep; poor
beggars die out the crime of luck. Even now
courtesans lean to practiced grace
alone, shamed
as brushes draw youth on.
        Where shall we find hope

that cruelty is a passing accident, balance
the true gauge?
  I long to speak again kindly
with the thin dead
blossoms
who followed me here. I want to caress
the rose of peace before it empties; to abandon
storms over the ancestors of bodiless order.
  Tell me you have found it, the drowned
key, the footprint waking peacocks
at the last minute which
stops. You who followed the absent fortune
of pilgrims, come back to your friend
rooted here, sealed
in harm's garden of jars. Tell all
before snow retakes the road
to feeling,
this foreign ground.

GETTING FREEDOM HIGH

fiction by WESLEY BROWN

from PERSEA: AN INTERNATIONAL REVIEW

nominated by PERSEA: AN INTERNATIONAL REVIEW

PAULINE HAD REALLY gotten next to me. I didn't want to believe
that my only reason for not going into the army was to get attention. I
had thought a lot about my motives while I was in prison. Otis had
schooled me early in the importance of the sound and not the sense
of words. And I had to admit that my beliefs were often shaped by
the attention I thought I would get. But something happened that
showed me how believing in something could bring a kind of attention I hadn't bargained for.

I was walking along One Hundred Twenty-fifth Street. At the
corner of Seventh Avenue a crowd had gathered and was listening to
a man speak. He was standing on a milk crate. There wasn't much of

him, just a hanger-thin frame on which his clothes were hung. He moved like a torch singer, using his body to make the lyrics of a song do something there were no words for. And his mouth was a reckless gash with lethal doses of anger jerking at the edge of his voice. What he was saying must have slipped up on something familiar inside those present because necks were craned forward and attention claimed every face.

There had been some disturbance in the street earlier. The police had moved in to disperse the crowd and arrested a boy who didn't move quickly enough.

"I may be young, but I'm old enough to know that youth ain't never been a reason for gettin away clean . . . "

Heads nodded in rocking-chair fashion.

"That boy couldn't a been more than thirteen. But they busted him for not movin fast enough. But where was he movin to? And who wasn't it fast enough for?"

"Talk about it!" someone shouted.

"I'm not running for nuthin," he said, "and I don't wanna be in charge. I just wanna run this," he said, jabbing his two index fingers into his chest. "But I can't do that if I don't go over to the precinct and see about that kid who didn't move fast enough . . . Some of you may think messin with the po-leece is like going barehanded in a brass knuckle affair. Well, strength ain't always a fat mouth parade. It can also come on like a hush that even dogs can't pick up on sometimes."

He jumped down off the milk crate and began walking down Seventh Avenue. Almost immediately people began filling in behind him. I joined the procession and soon it extended the length of the block. I don't really know why I followed him, but I think it had something to do with the way his outrage recomposed itself in a word design that x-rayed his hold cards. It scared the shit out of me that anyone would open up like that in front of strangers. My senses were aroused in a way I'd never experienced before. And I wanted more. So like everyone else I latched onto the whirlwind he'd created and rode his guts.

At each corner our ranks swelled, thickening the primer with another coat. And the hitting of all those feet on the pavement became a drum roll. When we got to the precinct some police were waiting on the steps. A beefy one with a chest studded with trinkets that might have been left over from the sale of Manhattan stepped forward.

"What seems to be the trouble?" he asked.

"We want to know what happened to the boy you arrested," asked the man we'd followed.

"Are you speaking for all these people?"

"No, I'm speakin for myself. But we're all here for the same reason."

"He's all right. We're just asking him a few questions."

"We wanna see him."

"Everybody can't come in but since you seem to be the spokesman, you can come in."

"I'm goin in," he hollered back to us.

"Don't you go in there alone blood!" someone shouted.

"It's either you or nobody," the policeman said.

"I'll be all right," he assured us and went in.

After about fifteen minutes the boy came out. A brassy cheer went up as the boy disappeared into the crowd. Everyone began to leave and I was about to go when I saw the beefy policeman put his hand on our spokesman's shoulder. He nodded to what was said to him and then followed the cop back inside the precinct house. In the jubilation over the boy's release this went unnoticed.

I waited around after everyone had left to see when he would come out. When he did it was almost dark. His head was down and his arms were wrapped around him as if he were trying to hold himself together.

"What happened?" I asked, as he passed me. He raised his head and looked at me with eyes floating in pools of red.

"I didn't move fast enough," he said.

"Ain't you gonna tell anybody what they did to you?"

"What for?"

"So something can be done about it."

"There's no way to prove it. They beat up on me in a way that don't show."

"But if everybody knew what happened —"

"They knew."

"But how? I'm the only one that saw them take you back inside."

"There were others besides you that saw what happened You just the only one that didn't know what was goin on."

"You knew what they would do?"

"Yea! I made them look bad. And they didn't dig it. So in exchange for them cuttin the kid loose I had to take the ass whippin he was gonna get."

"But if you knew what was gonna happen why did you speak up?"

"I didn't intend to. It just happened. Most a the time I don't trouble trouble till trouble troubles me. But this time I just couldn't play it safe."

"But how do you know when not to play it safe?"

"When it happens you'll know. Just don't let nobody else tell you when . . . What you lookin at?"

"Your eyes."

"What about em?"

"They're red."

"Well, if you think that's from cryin, you wrong. They red from overflowin! Thanks for lookin out for me youngblood. Later on."

"The cat shoulda know better," Otis said, when I told him. "He definitely didn't have no smarts."

"But what he was sayin was true."

"That ain't got nuthin to do with it. Whether it's broads or not, you never let anyone know what's really on your mind. If he had really been slick he woulda got somebody else to go inside with the police."

"But if you coulda heard him. He was serious. He didn't care about the police."

"Then he got what he deserved. Talkin that political talk is all right when you in school. But you don't be runnin that shit in the street."

"All he did was say what was on his mind."

"And all the police did was put somethin on his ass! Would you a done what he did?"

"I don't know."

"Shit, you know what you woulda done and so did everybody else who was there. That's why he's the only one that got the ass whippin!"

A distance had begun to crack between us. Otis still believed he had all the answers. But questions were insinuating themselves into me. I was no longer a ready echo for whatever Otis said. And he was surprised to find that more and more after one of his assertions I would not follow up with a refrain but with a theme of my own. This development in our friendship crescendoed when Otis decided to go into the army and I opted for college.

One afternoon during my first semester at City College I was sitting in the snack bar leafing through a textbook.

"Hey my man, didn't you hear about the meeting?" A billy goat-faced dude stood over me, going through a grab-bag of nervous mannerisms that resembled a third base coach flashing signs.

"What meeting?"' I asked.

"The meeting to discuss what's happenin in the South and the ways we can support The Movement. You comin?"

"Yea, I guess I'll check it out."

"My name's Theodore Sutherland. What's yours?"

"Melvin Ellington."

There were about twenty people in the student lounge either sprawling in chairs or sitting on the floor. Just about everyone sprouted the roguey attire of faded dungarees, work shirts, and desert boots. The racial composition was an unequally distributed keyboard favoring the treble white over the bass black. Theodore, who was one of the organizers of the meeting, was the first to speak.

"As you know, the purpose of this meeting is to form a group that will be a second front for The Movement in the South. Since the press has been reluctant to publicize the recent bombings in Alabama, we see it as our function to pressure our elected officials in Congress to call for an investigation of these criminal acts by the Justice Department.

"Secondly, we want to begin, through weekly workshops, to politicize the students of this college to parts of the American profile that they don't see. And finally, in order to raise bail money and other operating expenses for the Movement, we will have parties or what we call, 'freedom highs,' every Friday night. For those of you who decide to join with us in struggle, you should realize that you are not only doctors but are also part of the disease. To explain what I mean, Keith McDermott will rap to you."

A white dude joined Theodore at the front of the room. Long drawn-out hay dogged his face except for his eyes, which glared out of his head like dime-sized pieces of sky blue. He stuck his hands in his front pockets up to the knuckles as he spoke, shifting his weight from one leg to the other.

"What Theo means is that serious commitment demands experiencing someone else's pain. I know it's impossible for me to really know what a black man feels. So what I must do is get into touch with the pain that whites historically have been estranged from. Once his pain is my own, there should be such outrage in me that it would require that I do something to alleviate that condition.

"As a preliminary step toward feeling the black man's pain, all whites who wish to work with our group are required to read in one sitting Ralph Ginsburg's *One Hundred Years of Lynching* in the presence of Theo or one of the blacks in our group. This should begin to put you into touch with the pain of black people. Reading the details of each atrocity without stopping will be a test of your commitment to The Movement."

"I'd like to add," Theo broke in, "that blacks who are joining us are required to read the book too. But without a witness. If you can put this book down after beginning it, you'll have to answer to your own conscience . . . We'll meet again next week at the same time and discuss your experiences with pain while reading *One Hundred Years of Lynching.*"

I tried to get through the book but couldn't. Reading about one atrocity was enough for me. Far from becoming a redcap for every documented lynching in America over a hundred-year period, the cumulative effect of thousands of lynchings left me with no desire to carry the legacy any further than my knowledge of what had happened. And I felt guilt about being unable to keep my outrage up to the level of the horrors recounted in the book.

At the next meeting Theo started off by questioning a white chick whose face played peek-a-boo behind marble cake hair.

"Were you able to experience pain while reading the book?"

"Yes, I did," she said.

"How did it express itself?"

"I threw up."

"And did you continue reading?"

"Yes."

"Why?"

"I felt if black people could survive those horrible experiences, I could tolerate a bad taste in my mouth long enough to finish the book."

"Are you prepared to do anything else besides throwing up?"

"I know I can't undo what's already been done, but now that I've begun to experience black pain I am ready to be the instrument for whatever is required by The Movement."

"What about being white? How do you intend to deal with the resentment you'll face because you're white?"

"I'm willing to do whatever is necessary to change that. And if I can't I'll just have to accept it."

"I see," Theo said, testing the strength of his patchy beard with a few strong tugs. "Keith, why don't you question one of the brothers?"

Keith scanned the room and dropped his two blue dimes on me.

"Your name's Melvin, isn't it?"

"Yeah."

"Well, what did you experience when you read *One Hundred Years of Lynching?*"

"How come you don't question somebody white?" I asked.

"Because the only way to work out antagonisms between blacks and whites is to confront them. That won't happen if I talk to whites. By challenging one another we get the disease out in the open. When that happens, we can sort it out and then go about finding a cure."

"And what's the cure?"

"The cure is to use these sessions as outlets for fucked up attitudes so our political action won't be tainted by contradictions. . . . Now what did you think about the book?"

"I couldn't finish it."

"Why not?"

"It was too much to take all at one time."

"Did you feel any outrage?"

"At first, but then I didn't feel anything."

"Do you think the reason might be that you don't want to deal with history?"

"What's there to deal with? It's already happened!"

"But you've got to put it in its proper perspective."

"And what is that?"

"Do you know why most people in The Movement don't wear ties?"

"No, I don't."

"Wearing ties is a form of contemporary lynch law. In other words, it's the rope revisited. They are part of the official uniform of oppression, lynching people to stiffling jobs and choking their identity. Having this perspective forces us to commit a kind of suicide by murdering our capacity to cop out."

"It also," Theo interjected, "keeps a vigil over our consciousness by not allowing us to become what we despise."

I was impressed. Theo and Keith seemed to have thought it all out, complete with contingency theses to tighten up any snags in their arguments. That night there was a party in the student lounge. I ran into Theo when I got off the subway and we walked over to the school together.

"How are these parties?" I asked.

"They're probably a little different from the sets you're used to."

"In what way?"

"Well, we call them 'freedom highs' because everybody is supposed to slide their fantasies up under somebody else. If the other person digs it, then they both experience it until they've had enough. And that's a freedom high. It's just a way to get all the bullshit out of our system. If you analyze it, you'll see it's not as fucked up as it sounds. It's all political."

The student lounge was lit with the red tone of a traffic light on simmer. Everyone seemed to be heeding the light as a signal to slow down because there was very little movement. "Don't Make Me Over" by Dionne Warwicke was playing, as people went through what I assumed were forms of freedom high. A black dude and a white broad took turns tracing with their fingers the contours of their bodies. Two women, one black and the other white, moved their hands in a massaging motion through each other's hair. A black cat and a white dude faced each other and traded salvos decrying the other's presence in the human race.

"Hello."

It was the peek-a-boo girl behind all the marble cake. For the first time I got a good look at her. Her vanilla skin adhered so closely to bones in her face that skin and cheek bones seemed about ready to change places.

"Hi," I said.

"You wanna get freedom high?"

"I don't know, I'm not really sure how to go about it."

"Get angry at me."

"You haven't done anything."

"All right, I'll help you. . . . Did you know that when you move you look like you're a walking chicken with your ass picked clean?"

I cracked up.

"You're not supposed to laugh."

"I'm sorry, I couldn't help it," I said.

"Okay, let's try again. Say, 'What's the word?'"

"What's the word?"

"Thunderbird! Now say, 'Who drinks the most?'"

"Who drinks the most?"

"Colored folks."

"Where'd you hear that?" I asked.

"You mean you never heard that before?"

"No."

"Doesn't it bother you having a white person talk to you like that?"

"Not really. It's only a freedom high, right?"

"Not if you don't act right it isn't!"

"Now you're getting angry. I thought that's what I was supposed to do?"

"The way you act no one would ever believe you were oppressed," she said, walking away.

I looked around and noticed Keith talking to a black woman. She wasn't paying much attention to him but was looking in my direction. A mane of thick black wool rose above her forehead like a second story. I acknowledged her look with a nod. She excused herself from Keith and walked over to me.

"You're Melvin, aren't you?"

"Yeah."

"I'm Geneva. Theo has told me a lot about you. He says you're a very quiet dude."

"Yeah, I guess so."

"What made you get involved in The Movement?"

"I don't know. . . . I guess it had something to do with seeing this dude stick up for a kid in front of the police. They let the kid go but beat the dude up. At the time I wondered whether it was such a good idea for the cat to have gotten involved. But then when those little girls got blown up in that church in Alabama I realized getting involved didn't have anything to do with whether it was a good idea or not."

I couldn't believe what I'd said. Something I never really understood before was clarified for me at the same moment I tried to explain it to someone else. Geneva's face squinted with curiosity.

"What do you think of this freedom high?" she asked.

"I don't know, but Theo has a way of making just about anything make sense."

"You're right about that. Sometimes I wish he wasn't so good at it."

"Have you know him long?" I asked.

"Long enough to be strung out on him."

"You go to City? I've never seen you around."

"I go to Hunter. I met Theo at a demonstration. We talked. And he made a lot of sense. But lately he hasn't been making any sense. He wants me to make it with Keith as part of this freedom high business. He thinks if I do I'll get the fantasy about getting a white man out of the system. The IDEA of sleeping with a white man as an experiment is something I've never thought about. But white women are definitely on Theo's mind. That's why he concocted these freedom highs, so he could rationalize chasing white women by making it a form of political work."

"But you don't think he's right about it being better to live out your fantasies than repressing them?"

"But it's his fantasy, not mine . . . Look at him over there with that white woman who was talking to you." The woman was transfixed as Theo pointed a menacing finger at her as if it were a gun barrel. "Do you know anything about Gandhi?" she asked.

"Not very much."

"Somebody once asked Gandhi what he thought of Western Civilization, and he said he thought it would be a good idea. He didn't say it should be made into anything. Just that it would be a good idea. But Theo seems to think every idea he gets is worth pursuing."

"You sure you're not jealous?"

"You damn straight I am! And you won't hear me saying it's political."

"What you two running off at the mouth about?" Theo said angrily.

"We're getting freedom high," Geneva said.

"Don't get smart with me, Geneva. I told you what I wanted you to do."

"If asking me didn't get it, telling me definitely won't."

"You just don't have any understanding. All I'm trying to do is get us to go through some things so we won't fuck over each other later."

"Theo, if you want to fuck white girls, go ahead. But don't tell me who to fuck."

"You just have no sense of history."

"And you've lost all sense of anything else."

Theo leaned forward and seemed to be on the verge of jumping all over Geneva's case. Then he eased up, smiled, and walked back over to where the peek-a-boo girl was sitting. Wetness flickered in Geneva's eyes.

"Do you wanna dance?" I asked. She didn't say anything, but turned to me and let me do the rest.

> People get ready
> There's a train a comin
> You don't need no ticket
> You just get on board

She was numb to the insinuation that dancing close to someone usually produces. So we moved, but it wasn't dancing.

"Do you believe that history is everything?" she asked.

"What do you mean?"

"There's a group called the Five Per Centers, and they believe only five per cent of black people know what's going on. They don't believe in history because its HIS-story meaning white folks. Five Per Centers believe in MY-story which is a mystery to most of us. According to them, black folks spend too much time listening to the wrong story."

I didn't know if I'd gotten her full meaning, but if what was going on around us had anything to do with it, mystery didn't stand a chance. People had turned into lazy susans, revolving to the touch of curious hands, picking for a taste of something choice. Geneva took two fistfuls of my back as if her mystery depended on it.

The Friday night parties continued, but as the profile of events in the country became more vile, it was difficult to keep up the masquerade that freedom highs served a remedial purpose. Demonstrations, beatings, jailings, bombings, and murders glazed our eyes. Eventually we used freedom highs as a way to bring our gargoyle side out of hiding and avenge ourselves on any bodies of history that were available.

When Malcolm was killed a memorial service was held in Lewisohn Stadium. I was one of the few hundred shivering people needing to hear someone say something to loosen the full-nelson that Malcom's death had on us. After the first few speakers I was still hungry for words that would be around when I needed them. Like those spoken by that dude standing on the milk crate on One Hundred Twenty-fifth Street. Words that would linger like jade.

And then Theo spoke. As he worked his face, his scattered beard shifted like an earthquake.

" . . . Many have asked why Malcom was killed. The answer to that becomes clear once we understand the things that concerned him in life. He knew that freedom is nothing unless it is dangerous. And it is a source of embarrassment for America that his prescription for a people who have moved from deprivation to realized injustice, resides in the Declaration of Independence . . ."

He was into it, his body doing rope tricks and his hands checking out the air like a lead singer.

"Malcom was the man we thought we were. He showed us how we are victims of very little law and an excess of order, how law has become congealed injustice, how the existing order only hides the everyday violence against body and spirit, how the machinery of society is greased on the misery of the poor, how powerless conscience appeals to conscienceless power, how moral suasion is bastardized before our eyes, and how everywhere the political structure is fossilized . . ."

"Wake em up, brother! Wake em up!"

"So having been a witness to this, we should no longer be legally or morally bound to obey laws which we have had no say in shaping and which seek to arrest our struggle . . . There are those who would counsel us in restraint and in the danger of becoming what we despise. But this is a luxury indulged in by those who do not live the reality of our grievances. I believe Malcolm would agree that you don't talk to a starving man about indigestion. It's only after he's eaten that he concerns himself with the dangers to his health from what or how much he eats!"

"Talk the talk slaves afraid to live!" Theo had us. And when he pushed, we chimed.

"Those who raised the question of the use of violence seem to forget that the development of American democracy has shown that when its political initiatives fail, the use of violence becomes a logical extension of political policy . . . But unlike the government, we understand that although violence can be explained, it can never be explained away . . . And it is the recognition of this distinction that is the difference between a revolutionary who can never be radical, and a radical who can never be revolutionary. . . .

"But Malcolm is dead. And it's important that we ask ourselves what must command the living. Too often we use coming together like this as a kind of moral lightning rod instead of a looking glass. None of us can afford to take refuge in the role of speaker or spectator. We must cease being mere fans of the activity of life and make engagement the substance out of which our lives are made. If we don't do this, we are already at the lip of the grave. That's why this whole proceeding is so inadequate. The words seem to wither away almost as soon as they've been said. Because they're just words. . . ."

We all left the stadium without a word, heeding Theo's admonition not to give up any rap unless it was followed by some political punch. For the next few days I said very little to anyone. And I wasn't alone. Theo was also taking an undeclared fast on talking. Especially to whites. He began putting signs on bulletin boards saying: WHAT'S THERE TO TALK ABOUT? and DON'T SAY IT, DO IT.

Once Theo and I were sitting in the snack bar and Keith came in.

"What's happening Theo?" he asked, sitting down.

"Not you."

"Don't freeze me out like this, Theo."

"There ain't nuthin to freeze cause you ain't even there."

"You talk like I don't even exist."

"As far as I'm concerned, you don't."

"Look Theo, I understand things have changed and we can't hang together like we used to. But you can't shut me out of history. I'm still part of the struggle."

"You're not part of mine."

"You know what Theo, you're still freedom high. But it's all black now. And that's cool with me. What you don't understand is, I'm struggling for my own freedom, not just yours."

"Do you know what a penny buys, whitey?"

"What do you mean?"

"A penny buys a book of matches, muthafucka. So if you really wanna fight for your freedom, make an investment in a book of matches, set yourself on fire, and jump on President Johnson!"

"You know what your problem is, Theo? You've never been able to get over the fact that you pushed Geneva and I together before you changed the rules of freedom high. And now that you've made the game all black, it fucks you up that she didn't come back to you but decided to stay with me."

Theo was on Keith like an ink spot on manila bond paper. Before some others and I could pull him off, he had sledged Keith's face into meatsauce. I'd always wondered what had happened to Geneva. I never saw her again after my first freedom high. And Theo never said anything whenever I asked about her.

After the fight with Keith, Theo cultivated an even more sinister don't-fuck-with-me-honkie-cause-I'm-liable-to-have-a-trick-up-my-sleeve-and-take-your-head look. And I followed suit.

"The Five Per Centers are right about honkie history," Theo said. "You got to admit though, the whiteys got a good starting team, good bench strength, and solid team defense. Their problem is, they only play for ideas and not for fun. Ideas are cool, but when you take the fun out of ideas like freedom, justice, and the American way, something thrilling becomes killing. And if the whiteys have their way, life will eventually be like watching a newsreel . . . That's why we need more mystery, so we can fuck with the standard operational procedure. Make them go for the okey-doke and jump Proteus on them, on general principle. Our rallying cry should be: Wherever We Are Is Already a Minute Ago."

Theo and I walked around City in hooded black sweat suits, calling ourselves the Blue Monks. Whenever someone white said anything to us, we would either ignore them or create mental brick walls by answering with the names of Thelonius Monk tunes like "Little Rootie Tootie"; "Straight, No Chaser"; "Well, You Needn't"; "Epistrophy"; "Off Minor"; "Ruby, My Dear"; "Crepuscule with Nellie" and "Round Midnight."

In our senior year at City it was clear that the draft board would not view our Blue Monk status as meeting the criteria for conscientious objection to the Vietnam War on religious grounds. Theo came up with the idea that we form a group that was less bizarre and more broadly based. We called it the "No Vietnamese Ever Called Me A Nigger" Caucus. There was another group called the "Hell No, We Won't Go" Brigade, which was made up of whites who counseled students and non-students on ways to resist the draft. Theo said what they were doing was irrelevant since they held on to their student deferments. We agreed to give up our deferments as an act of solidarity with the brothers who didn't have the opportunity to go to college.

At our first organizational meeting I was surprised to see Geneva standing just inside the door of the lounge. She looked tired but not from lack of sleep. Lines beneath her eyes like skid marks on asphalt revealed a loss of enthusiasm for playing games of chicken with herself.

"Geneva! How you doing?"

"I'll live. What about you Melvin?"

"I'm hanging in."

"Yeah, I see. When I heard the name of this group, I just knew you and Theo had something to do with it."

"Have you seen Theo?"

"I saw him, but I'm not freedom high over him anymore."

"Are you still mad at him for what he did to Keith?"

"I'm over that too."

"How are you and Keith doing?"

"We broke up. Theo thinks it was because of him, which isn't surprising since he thought he was responsible for bringing Keith and me together in the first place. It never occurred to him that my break-up with Keith might have nothing to do with him."

"What made you come back?" I asked.

"I wanted to see both of you. You're an important part of my life. I have to acknowledge it even though I don't want to repeat it. Especially with Theo. He still doesn't see me as a person. He's hung up on some idea he has about me. This time it's his notion of what a black woman should be . . . It's like that with him in everything. Even when his ideas are sound Theo never tests them against any opposition. He's only interested in what's going on in his own head . . . You don't see him that way, do you?"

"I see what you're saying, Geneva. But Theo has a way of making me understand things even if I can't change them. And this gives me a kind of power that takes away the feeling of being helpless."

"You're not helpless, Melvin. Do you remember at that freedom high when you asked me to dance? You were the freest person there. Everyone else was into terrorism!"

"All I did was ask you to dance."

"But that's what parties are for!"

"All right, can I have your attention?" It was Theo. The lounge had filled to capacity and as I looked at the scowls of those in attendance, most were up to the level of meanness required to give the meeting credibility as serious business.

"The purpose of this meeting," Theo began, "is for black and other Third World students here at City to begin to develop a strategy to move from rhetoric to action. You see, it's not enough to badmouth the system. We must be ready to show by our example that we are prepared to discontinue our participation in its vital functions."

"Criticism is an autobiography," Geneva whispered to me.

"So we of the 'No Vietnamese Ever Called Me A Niggar' Caucus are asking those of you who want to become members to go to the Registrar's Office and demand that your student classifications not be sent to the draft board. We see this as a first step in a national move by Third World students to force the Selective Service System to draft us. If we are united and armed with the correct political ideology, there is no way that the demagogic politicians and their cut buddies, the avaricious businessmen, can mess with us. And it's in that spirit that we can tell President Johnson regarding Vietnam, to pull out, like his father should have!"

"Whoooocap!"

"All right!"

"Teach!"

"Wait a minute," someone way in the back said, "I don't see what good giving up my student deferment will do. The only thing I see happening is me ending up in the service or in jail."

"Melvin," Theo said, "would you update the brother's consciousness?"

"What we are trying to do," I said, stepping forward, "is to heighten the contradictions in the society by forcing the government to use repressive measures against us. By ventilating this aspect of government, people will see how the government really operates."

He had now come out into full view. His skinny haircut, button-down shirt, V-neck sweater, and cuffed trousers made him immediately suspect. Before speaking, he adjusted his thick-lensed glasses.

"I don't know about anyone else but I came to college to get some skills. And I'm not hardly going to blow my education on some bullshit!"

"But brother," I said, "with a united front we can raise enough hell to end the draft."

"You can go ahead and raise all the hell you want. I'm going to raise my grade point average!"

"That's too bad," I said.

"No it isn't," Theo broke in. "In fact, it's very instructive for the brother to be talking this way because he represents a failure of analysis, and as a result doesn't understand the politics of escalation."

"And what you don't understand," the dude said, "is if you sneeze, you'll draw a crowd."

"That's the only way to raise the level of consciousness of the people." Theo fired back.

"And lower your damn self into a grave."

"That's the price you pay when you choose to be part of the solution rather than part of the problem."

"I'm the solution to any problems I got."

"Brothers and sisters, what you see before you is an example of a renegade. He's worse than an Uncle Tom cause he ain't acting. He's a Gunga Din, which means he's exactly what he appears to be. A Tom can be brought home, but a Gunga Din cannot be reformed. And I hope the sisters are listening because you have an important role in making sure the brothers stay righteous."

I turned to look at Geneva but she was gone.

"If brothers knew that if they shucked and jived, the sisters would not get off of any cat food, they would get their shit together in a hurry and be putting messages on community bulletin boards documenting their righteous behavior . . . So I'm glad the brother has exposed himself as a Gunga Din for everyone to see . . . Now I'd like to move on to the business of drawing up a petition to present to the Registrar's Office."

"Wait a minute, I haven't finished yet," the dude said.

"Yes, you have, my man," Theo said, shooting glances at me and some other cats in the room. We converged on him.

"I'm not goin anywhere. Take your fuckin hands off me . . . You said the Vietnamese never called you a nigger. Well, I ain't no Vietnamese, NIGGER!"

Theo streaked in a direct route to where we were struggling with the dude. What followed was the spirited rhubarb atmosphere of a baseball game where enough punches are thrown for everyone to work out his frustrations before calmer heads are allowed to prevail.

As a result of the fighting, the "No Vietnamese Ever Called Me A Nigger" Caucus was banned from campus. We never saw the dude who disrupted the meeting again, which confirmed our belief that he was an agent. I never saw Geneva after that either. Maybe she was an agent too?

With no organization to galvanize the black students, Theo and I continued to play the dozens with America, hoping it would live up to our unflattering portrait. Upon graduation we escalated our strategy to force the Selective Service System into drafting us by writing a letter to the draft board saying if we weren't drafted immediately bumble bees in Mississippi would light out from a donkey's ass and go straight to the brains of the members of the local board, buzz their way in and bloom. We received our draft notices and tokens in the mail within a matter of weeks, which went a long way toward restoring confidence in our analysis of the system and in our belief that we were a threat to its continued existence.

It was then that the wishbone holding Theo and I together broke under the pressure of what we wanted to come true.

"How long do you think it will take people to understand the significance of our act?" I asked Theo, soon after we'd refused induction.

"I been thinking about that and I don't think I'm going to wait around to find out."

"Why not?"

"The shit is getting serious out here. Didn't you see in the papers today about Keith?"

"No, what happened?"

"The fool doused himself with gasoline and set himself on fire while trying to shake hands with Johnson. A secret serviceman shot him through the head before he could even touch Johnson. The picture in the paper shows everybody standing around watching him burn up."

"God damn! You don't think he did that behind what you told him that time?"

"I don't know. But I can't see anybody doing no shit like that to themselves."

"Theo, were you serious when you told him to do that?"

"I don't know. But Keith must a thought so. Ain't that a bitch? He did what I said. And I don't even know if I'll do what I say."

"You didn't go into the service."

"Yeah, but . . . I can't seem to keep up with events anymore. The appropriate response changes every day. There ain't no way I can follow Keith's act."

"Why try?"

"Why not?"

"Because maybe Geneva was right."

"About what?"

"About history not being everything."

"It'll do until something better comes along. In the meantime I'm going underground until I can get some things into focus. I've had my greatest moments of clarity after someone I was close to died. First Malcolm, now Keith. It'll take a little while before I'm ready to inflict a political consequence on America, but when I do it'll be outrageous. And I'll live to tell about it."

Theo wanted me to go with him. When I told him I couldn't he split and left a note saying: HAVING BEEN TREATED EX-TREMELY DICTATES THAT WE TAKE EXTREME ACTION. While in prison I read a newspaper account of an airplane hijacking to Cuba perpetrated by a Theodore Sutherland.

Unlike Theo I didn't recover from my scare with uncertainty so quickly. I had believed with Theo that doubt was a punk half-stepping around self-evident truths. And I was quicker than soon and surer than shit about the shape and point of everything I did. But by the time Keith committed revolutionary suicide, my rap was no longer the foil for disorder I once believed it was. In fact, my command of imagery was dribbling way past composure toward a directionless spree. So being unable to play the political licks put down by Keith and Theo, I laid with what I could play and kept my date in court.

I still couldn't go for Pauline reducing my not going into the army to trying to get attention. Chilly had run the same shit on me in the joint. Geneva was more on the money. I had drained the mystery from my history and as a result stripped my life of enchantment which is a more sincere form of instruction.

THE WALTZ

by VICENTE ALEIXANDRE

from TWENTY POEMS (The Seventies Press)

nominated by The Seventies Press

You are beautiful as a stone,
oh my dead woman!
Oh my living, living woman, you are happy as a ship!
This orchestra which stirs up
my worries like a thoughtlessness,
like an elegant witticism in a fashionable drawl,
knows nothing of the down on the secret mound,
knows nothing of the laugh which rises from the breastbone like an
      immense baton.

A few waves made of bran,
a bit of sawdust in the eyes,
or perhaps even on the temples
or perhaps decorating the women's hair.
Trailing skirts made of alligator tails,
some tongues or smiles made of the shells of crabs.
All those things that have been seen so often
can take no one by surprise.

The ladies wait for their moment seated upon a tear,
keeping their dampness hidden with a stubborn fan,
and the gentlemen, abandoned by their buttocks,
try to draw all looks toward their moustaches.

But the waltz is here.
It is a beach with no waves,
it is a clashing together of seashells, heels, foam and false teeth.
It is the churned up things arriving.

Exultant breasts on the serving tray of arms,
sweet cakes fallen on the weeping shoulders,
a languorousness that comes over you again,
a kiss taken by surprise just as it turns into cotton candy,
as sweet "yes" of glass painted green.

Powdered sugar on the foreheads
gives a simple whiteness to the polished words
and the hands grow short, and rounder than ever
and wrinkle up the dresses as though they were sweet esparto grass.

The heads are clouds, the music is a long piece of rubber,
the tails made of lead almost fly, and the noise
has turned into waves of blood inside the heart,
and into a white liqueur that tastes of memories or a rendezvous.

Goodbye, goodbye, emerald, amethyst, secret,
goodbye, the instant has arrived like an enormous ball,
the precise moment of nakedness head down
when the downy hair begins to penetrate the obscene lips that know.

It is the instant, the moment of pronouncing the word that explodes,
the moment in which the dresses will turn into birds,
the windows into cries,
the lights into "help!",
and the kiss that was over there (in the corner) between two mouths
will be changed into a fishbone
that will distribute death saying:
I love you.

Translated by Robert Bly

WEST VIRGINIA SLEEP SONG

by RUTHELLEN QUILLEN

from MAGDALEN (Sibyl-Child Press)

nominated by Sibyl-Child Press

(for Jim Redmond and Doris Mozer)

You must teach him that when the deer comes into
the corn you shoot without question, and the runts
must be drowned in the kitchen well. Those who pray
they'll die asleep, hands on heart, are choked backwards
into pillow slips and tatted counterpanes.
When the heart is stillborn there is no answer.
An ectoplasm masks the face that will not cry.
This child, you teach him good and more. The nighttime's

made of horses who run on shattered legs.
The blinded pheasant is in its trap to judas
sing. Geraniums in coffee cans and tires
of marigolds spindle when there is no sun.
Those who come from churches never dream there're some
whose fathers lock closet doors on fists that pray
they haven't sinned. A great moon rises on all
the tar-papered shacks and cinderblocks; some

fire blindly at Orion unable to touch
a moment of their lives. I will or can't or
must: there's no necessity. You rhyme or scan
this song which settles where the roofs are tin and
the houses bluer than violets or pink as glazes

on supper rolls, where children take worms
into their feet and mouths, and dulcimers hang from
gouty hands. I give you penny whistles,

washboards, cups, and pans to bang the spooks away.
Jefferson County, home of pole beans, black lung,
twists in the road, and chevvies of sudden death,
some lullaby on bone pipes ought to be played
cross the fields of sorghum and civil war; it
staggers. I am afraid of music. I
buck and clog over this sag of porch and think:
my babies, this dirt will catch you when you fall from me.

Your cowls are going to be buried where the roads
cross, soon the rags of curtains will flap like crows
above your cradles. God help you. Here's grief pushed
into a corner of broken looking-glass
and comb, with patched-up screens and the husks of moths.
Those who think of other things, they can bind
the cut cord or let you bleed. I bleed. I ache
because I'm out of joint. The sons and daughters

damned to hell, the country stores, the glider swings,
the breasts tucked-in at underskirts, the river gnats,
the cataracts that half-cloud these eyes, the knives
too dull to cut even this simple pain, this fear
away. You keep this wrapped in eiderdown
for him who comes, half-dreamed of now on attic
stairs, in hunting roots, when cooling cider down.
You keep these patches and fits of love; they're all

I have to wrap him with against that night of
no sleep when I am plastered to this bed
of tied-up springs and corn and feather matresses
and bite down to crown his head or thrust his feet
into a world where lullabies slide out through broken teeth.

From A JOURNEY THROUGH THE LAND OF ISRAEL

by PINCHAS SADEH

from TRIQUARTERLY

nominated by TRIQUARTERLY

Moses, or God's disappointment in love

And I entreated the Lord at that time saying, "My Lord God, thou hast only begun to show thy servant thy greatness.. . . . Pray let me go over and see the good land that is beyond the Jordan, those fair mountains and the Lebanon." But the Lord was angry with me on your account and would not listen. And the Lord said to me, "Enough, say not to me another word about this matter."

I rarely have occasion to glance at the Book of Deuteronomy. Its rules and codes of law do not appeal to me. Given man's condition in the universe, it's my feeling that no saving grace can come from the pips he throws away after eating of the tree of the knowledge of good and evil. Yet as I leafed through the Bible one day, my eyes fell on the words, "And I entreated." I caught my breath and read them again: *And I entreated . . .* How curiously misplaced they seemed here!

I read on: *My Lord God . . . pray let me go over and see . . . but the Lord was angry with me . . . and would not listen.* Something tugged at my heart. I felt that my eyes were moist. What on earth was the matter with me? The event had taken place many thousands of years ago. I looked up from the book. The shadowy room was lighted only by the reading lamp on my desk. No voices reached me from the city outside my window. The night sweltered with a dry desert heat. When I looked back at the printed page, it was as though the event were happening in front of me.

Once more I read the story—only four verses long and told by Moses himself—of how this titanic man had pleaded like a little child for one more thing before his death: to be allowed to see the goodly, longed-for, legendary land. *Pray let me go over and see . . . those fair mountains. . . .* But God cruelly refused him.

Yet was God really so cruel to you, Moses? True, He rejected your plea, and unkindly at that. Soon, however, you of all mortals were destined to die by a kiss from His own mouth, and He would bury you Himself in a canyon in the land of Moab, across from the plains of Jericho. What other man in history was ever privy to such great, such terrible, such lonely love as you?

2

So I mused while the words came to life in the shadowy stillness of my room. And yet it was obvious that God *had* been cruel to Moses. But why? Why be angry with him? It wasn't his fault. He had said so clearly himself: *on your account.*

It could only be, it suddenly occurred to me, that God had known some great disappointment, which He needed to pass on to Moses. It could only be—as absurd as it seemed—that God had been in some sort of trouble.

But what disappointment and what trouble, if it was possible to conceive of God's being in trouble at all? And even if it were, why treat Moses as He did? The more I thought about it, the stranger and more nebulous my thoughts became. Only with the greatest effort was I able finally to put them into words. First, though, I needed to reread the whole story of Moses from the beginning.

I leafed again through the pages of the book. "Now there went forth a man from the house of Levi and married the daughter of a Levite. And the woman conceived and bore a son; and she saw that he was in good health, and she hid him for three months." Yet death's shadow hung over the infant. Then comes the story of the cradle of reeds and Pharaoh's daughter, who comes to bathe in the Nile and finds the child crying. And the boy grew up, and he became her son, and she called him Moses.

Just as his origin is not without mystery, so nothing is told us of his youth. The years go by. "And Moses matured, and went out to his brethren, and saw their sufferings." He sees an Egyptian flogging a Hebrew and hurls himself on that Egyptian. Yet even in his anger he is prudent, for before slaying the oppressor he looks "this way and that, and sees that no man is watching." Nevertheless, he is compelled to flee. He escapes to the land of Midian, where he meets, as did Jacob in his flight from Esau, a girl by a well. Like Jacob, he goes to live in her father's house and takes her for his wife.

3

While tending his father-in-law's sheep, Moses comes to Mount Horeb. Nothing is known today of this mountain's location. It has been identified with Jebel Musa in the Sinai Peninsula, with the nearby Jebel Serbil, and with places much farther away. In any case, at the foot of Mount Horeb Moses sees a bush that burns on and on. He stares at the tongues of fire, which are nearly transparent in the shimmering desert air (at least so I imagine it, though nowhere does it say that the vision took place in daylight, and perhaps it happened at night), and resolves, "I will turn aside and see this great sight, why the bush is not consumed." How innocent is this curiosity of his, which alone, it would seem, entices him to approach closer.

"And when God saw that he had turned aside to look at it, He called to him out of the bush: 'Moses, Moses!' And he said: 'Here I am.'" At which point God informs him: "I am the God of Abraham, the God of Isaac, and the God of Jacob. . . . Go, for I am sending you unto Pharaoh." Moses now asks two questions. The first is about himself: "Who am I that I should go unto Pharaoh?" The second is, "But what if I should go to the Children of Israel and say to them, 'The God of your fathers has sent me to you,' and they say to me,

'What is His name?', what shall I tell them?" The second question is about God, yet the two are connected because man has no being apart from God.

God's answer to the first question is as much as a man might hope for: "For I will be with you!" In other words, my being will be yours. To the second question, however, His answer is elusive: "I am who I am." Perhaps such conundrums are characteristic of the language of the gods, for on the statue of the Egyptian goddess Isis it is said to have been written, "I am all that there is"; while engraved on the pyramid of Sais were the words, "I am all that is, was, and will be." Jacob, too, when asking for the name of the angel he wrestled with through the night, received no clear answer. The answer is in the struggle, the darkness, the blessing, the experience itself. It cannot be given in names or words, or in any manner that the mind can grasp. It is beyond mind.

4

I continued to read about how Moses returned to Egypt. "And at a camping place in the course of his journey the Lord encountered him and tried to kill him." Nothing can adequately explain this macabre tale. Just a while ago God has lavished His grace upon Moses from the burning bush; now, in a reversal that might be fathomed in a moment of nightmarish madness but never in one of lucidity, He seeks to ambush and murder him on his way. Can it be, strange as it may sound, that God now regrets having revealed Himself to Moses and having sent him on his mission to Pharaoh? Or is God now revealing another side of Himself, not only different from, but actively opposed to, its predecessor? Perhaps the Bible is concerned with that side or face of God when it calls Him "a consuming fire," "vengeful and jealous," and when Paul writes that "it is terrible to fall into the hands of the living God." That is the face of God which makes "the hairs stand up on the flesh" of Job's friend Eliphaz when it appears to him in a dream; which reveals itself to Abraham, even while blessing Him, as "a great and awful gloom"; and of which Jacob exclaims upon awakening from his dream, "How terrible is this place!" Such infinite, indefinable dread is perhaps the original sense of the phrase "the fear of God." Man gazes for an instant into the abyss, then shuts his eyes again.

I myself knew such a moment of dread only once, a moment in which everything else seemed to drop right out of the world—and I

knew then that I could never live through it again. But I also knew
that whether or not I would have to did not depend on me. As the
Psalmist, who generally seeks God's company, unexpectedly puts it,
"Whither shall I flee from thee?" Sometime later I was moved to
write a poem that began with the words, "I sue for mercy at the onset
of the night." Lest that which comes suddenly will come. For then
all defenses are down. And a man grows icy with fear. With the
coming of the time of the abyss. Yea, You have created that too. And
You know and You understand. I pray, then, if only it please You. For
there is no other defense. I sue for mercy from God.

5

It is perhaps more than coincidence (though what it may signify I
don't know) that both Moses and Jacob encounter this terrifying
divinity on their way home; that is, on their way back to the homeland from which they have fled. Moreover, each has run away by
himself and is now returning with a family. Can God's assault on
Moses be connected with these facts? No one can say. At any rate,
Jacob is physically injured in the struggle, while Moses' ordeal also
ends with a bloody injury to his son. Nor is this all that the two have
in common.

He who is destined to make contact with God must first break the
laws of men and be compelled to flee. Jacob robs Esau of his
birthright; Moses kills the Egyptian. Each seeks refuge—one in
Haran, the other in Midian. Each encounters on arrival a maiden by
a well, and for each this confirms that he is on the right path. True
femininity, that which stands astride living water, is a source of
confirmation in this world, of love and of life. Until her man comes,
the maiden must stand and wait. She cannot drink from the well,
whose waters flow under the bare soles of her feet, until Jacob rolls
the stone from its mouth, or Moses drives away the bad shepherds.

6

The night was hot. Silence. I looked up from my papers and books.
The clock said two A.M. A gecko darted from behind the bookcase. It
moved slowly along the wall toward the circle of light thrown by the
lamp on my desk. I knew this lizard who lived back of my books. I,
too, am a creature of the night. There are spiders in my room also.
They live their lives and I live mine. The gecko lay in ambush on the
fringe of the circle of light, glued to the wall. It was petite, nearly

transparent. A moth moved innocently toward it. The gecko regarded it frozenly. The moth came closer and was suddenly between its jaws. It beat its astounded wings but no succor came. I made a slight movement and the gecko glanced suspiciously around. It scrambled away with its prey between its teeth and disappeared behind the bookcase. I could still hear the flap of the moth's wings. In the darkness, death was taking place. There was unspeakable horror there. A small lizard and a blameless moth, yet what utter blackness. The underworld had opened its mouth to yawn.

Silence. I sat quietly smoking. Through the windows I could see the pale sickle of a halo-limned moon. Shadows of trees. Of houses. For an instant I was almost sure that I saw, not far from me in the darkness, a short, burly, full-bearded man who reminded me of Tolstoy. There was just enough time for him to say, roguish gleam in his eyes, "But suppose there isn't any God at all, eh?" And I knew that he had thought about it a great deal, a great deal. Quickly, for I had to answer before he could vanish, I said, "Well, what if you're right and there isn't? Tell me, then—what is there?" He had gone when I added, "In that case, we're simply right back where we started from."

7

I returned to my book and to the story of what happened to Moses at his camping place. It occurred to me that I must try to understand it, not from the divine point of view from which it is told—that is, in terms of God's nature—but from the human point of view, in terms of the man it happened to.

According to Moses—who can be presumed to have related it at a later date (from whom else could it have been known if not from him?)—God attacked and sought to murder him. Nothing in this story enables us to imagine what shape the attacker assumed, but no room is left for doubt that it was God Himself. Humanly speaking, it would seem, one cannot preclude the possibility of a moment of madness.

This moment happened to Moses on his way back, after the exhilarating experience by the bush, where he was cast in the role of prophet and redeemer. Not a word is said about his having been inwardly shaken by this experience, from which we may conclude that he underwent it undauntedly. Abraham, when God revealed Himself to him, fell into a dark and frightful slumber. Ezekiel, after hearing God's call, "went bitterly in aggravation of spirit, and the Lord's hand was hard upon him." Nothing of this sort happened to Moses, yet perhaps the seed of the crisis to come was sown at that time. Now, on the way back, it bursts forth. The terrible dread of returning, of his mission, of his contact with God, awakens in him. In its light, God's face changes from one of lovingkindness to one of nightmarish aggression.

One may say that the human point of view is unimportant, and that the only perspective which matters here is God's. Yet because of our own inadequacy the divine perspective reveals itself only through the human one, which it wears like a mask upon its face.

8

I read on how Moses, accompanied by Aaron, comes to Pharaoh. "And they said to Pharaoh: 'Thus says the Lord, Let my people go.' And Pharaoh said: 'Who is the Lord that I should hearken unto him?'" And Moses was eighty years old.

Now all manner of miracles begin to happen. Moses turns the waters of Egypt to blood and strikes the country with frogs. He turns the earth into lice and sends vermin into the houses. He afflicts the people with pestilence, and with boils, and with hail, and with locusts. "And God said to Moses: 'Stretch out your hand to the sky, that darkness may fall.' . . . So Moses stretched out his hand to the sky, and there was thick darkness throughout the whole land of Egypt. . . . And God said to Moses: 'One more plague will I bring on Pharaoh, and then he will let you go.' . . . And at midnight God struck down all the first-born in the land of Egypt . . . and there arose a great cry." At which point Pharaoh summons Moses in the middle of the night and says, "Rise and go."

Once, when I was in the Louvre in Paris, my glance fell on a statue of Ramses II, who was, there is reason to believe, the Pharaoh of the biblical story. From what is known of him, he was one of the great kings of Egypt, a hard man whose wars and monuments cost the labors and lives of tens of thousands. Somewhere I read that he fathered one hundred sons and sixty daughters. I stood at length before the massive granite sculpture, whose height I judged to be twice that of an average man. Ramses sat upright, his hands on his knees, his eyes staring straight ahead. The shadow of a smile had frozen on his lips. A heavy, sphinxlike composure informed his whole being.

I thought then that Michelangelo, though he could not possibly have seen this work, must have had it in mind when he sculpted Ramses' rival. In the statue of Ramses there is a perfect equilibrium: neither time nor movement have any place here. Michelangelo's Moses, on the other hand, is all flow and fury. Here is the wanderer, the man who knows no rest until he dies of God's kiss. Momentarily I imagined these two grand works together, Pharaoh staring stonily ahead, Moses turning stormily leftward to face him, a wordless exchange passing between them.

9

Here I must say a few words about restlessness. I once read somewhere that a certain Hasidic tsaddik, I forget who, was asked why it is written in the Book of Psalms, "May God bless the house of Israel, may God bless the house of Levi, may God bless those who fear the Lord," rather than "May God bless the house of those who fear the Lord." His answer was that those who fear the Lord have no house. In all likelihood he meant that those who fear the Lord are so destitute that they never know from day to day if they will have a roof over their heads, but a second interpretation is possible. In the Bible there is an expression "to come to rest and to estate," a phrase which suggests that the two are connected; that is, that he who has an estate, a house, has rest. If it is not written of those who fear the Lord that they have a house, therefore, this must mean that they can have no rest. There is nothing restful about the fear of God. On the contrary, it must lead to restlessness, which is the true religious state.

The God of Israel is the Lord of Hosts. He is not like the gods of India, whom man perceives by staring at his navel until ultimate peace descends on him. He is a God of wandering and travel. A God who comes from the desert. A God of trial and contention. A God of conflict between opposites. A God who hides, and reveals Himself in the bush, and hides again.

10

The story goes on to tell how Moses brings the children of Israel out of Egypt and conducts them across the Red Sea while their pursuers drown. As soon as they reach the desert, they begin to complain: "Would that we had died in the Land of Egypt, where we sat by the pots of flesh!" Had these words been written in sand, they would have vanished long ago, but they remain in the book that I held as a distasteful memorial. Yet Moses continues to lead the rabble through a chain of forsaken places whose very names ring strangely in our ears: Sin and Dophka and Alush, Rephidim and Sinai and Kibroth-hattaavah (which means the Graves of Lust). And from Kibroth-hattaavah they journeyed to Rithmah, and from there to Rimmon-perez, and from there to Libnah. And from Libnah to Rissah, and from Rissah to Kehalah, and from Kehalah to Har Shefer, and from Har Shefer to Haradah (which means Anxiety). And from Haradah to Makheloth, and from Makheloth to Tahath (which means Bottom), and from Tahath to Terah, and to Mithkah, and to Hashmonah, and to Moseroth, and to Bene-jaakan. And from Bene-jaakan to Hor-haggidgad. Thus, slowly, the wanderers reach the fringes of civilization. From Hor-haggidgad they move on to Jotbah, and from Jotbah to Abronah, and from Abronah to Ezion-geber, and from Ezion-geber to Kadesh and the border of Edom. In this way they gradually approach the land of Canaan.

Perhaps—for who can say?—all these descents and foulings, these peregrinations from the Graves of Lust to the Bottom of Anxiety, are necessary. Perhaps one has to touch the bottom of the abyss before beginning the ultimate ascent, as a Polish Jew, Jacob Frank, was to declare some three thousand years later. Still, the story in the Bible is an obscure and tedious one—in spite of which, in the third month after leaving the land of Egypt, the Israelites reach the desert of Sinai, and camp opposite a mountain there while Moses ascends to God.

11

For forty days and forty nights Moses remains by himself with God. When he descends, the two tablets of the Law in his hands, he finds the people prostrating themselves at the foot of the golden calf, and is consumed by wrath. In a paroxysm of fury he takes the tablets, which are said to be God's own work, and smashes them on the ground. Moreover, we read that he assembles the Levites at the edge of the camp and commands them, "Let each of you fasten his sword on his hip and slay each his kinsman, his friend and his neighbor." And about three thousand of the people fell on that day.

What is it that arouses such wrath in the prophet that he breaks the tablets of the Law and seeks to slaughter his own people, or calls down destruction on the land it inhabits? What is it that makes him go bitterly in aggravation of the spirit, or sit catatonically among his countrymen, or take refuge in the desert, or lie for days on his side like a city under siege? It is the power of disgust. He, who has just come down from forty days and nights on the mountain, looks and sees the people wallowing before the golden calf, and cannot believe what he sees. He has seen the brevity of life, like a twinkle in an infinity of time, the terrible, stupendous riddle of man's existence; and he sees now how the common people are sunk in the fetid bog of their petty lies and concerns, their cowardice and obsequiousness, their trivial views and idiotic amusements, their sterile fulsome culture and corrupt, sophisticated wisdom, their loathing for whatever is pure and sublime. And so disgust fills his soul. He has seen the necessity in all things and the flow in them; he has experienced pure, wild, cosmic joy; he has known the love that is in everything and the fear and death that are in everything; and he cannot fathom the distance between all this and the sneaking, insensate, vainglorious human existence that he sees. Disgust fills his soul. Yet still Moses does not abandon the people. When his anger is appeased, we read, he carves new tablets of the Law and ascends the mountain with them again. And he is there for forty days and forty nights, and he writes upon the tablets.

12

We read, too, that Moses says to God at this time, "Show me Thy glory." And God says, "You cannot see my face, for man cannot see me and live." And He says: "Here is a place by me. Station yourself on the rock; and when my glory passes by, I will put you in a cleft of the rock, and cover you with my hand until I pass by; then I will take away my hand, so that you may see my back; but my face may not be seen."

Moses wishes to see the combined profile of the compassionate and the jealous God, of the God of love and the God of death, of Him who speaks from the splendor of the bush and of Him who attacks in the solitary night. Not that either of these aspects is untrue in itself, but to man they seem contradictory. Oppressively so. The rabbi of Kotsk once said: "Whatever is contradictory or paradoxical is called the back of God. His face, where all exists in perfect harmony, cannot be seen by man."

In order to enhance God's standing with the intellectuals of his age, Moses ben Maimon, commonly known as Maimonides, rigorously denied Him any possibility of assuming material form or shape. Perhaps he thought that he was doing God a favor. Moses ben Amram of the Bible thought differently. More than once, in defiance of all intellectualization, he saw God explicitly, in the flesh.

13

I read on about how, before they have gone very far from Mount Sinai and the events that occurred there, the children of Israel burst out crying: "O that we had flesh to eat! We remember the fish that we used to eat for nothing in Egypt, the cucumbers, the melons, the leeks, the onions, and the garlic; and now our souls are dry." Hardly have they done quarreling with Moses over the spiritual dehydration brought on by lack of garlic when his sister Miriam and his brother Aaron begin maligning him for having married a Negro woman. Yet all this contention, strife, backbiting, and stupidity notwithstanding, the people keep moving through the desert until they reach Kadesh. Here great weeping and wailing break out when the twelve spies return from Canaan. "Let us turn around and go back to Egypt," the people say to one another. At the very height of all this hatred, this despair and futility, when the people are on the verge of rising up and stoning Moses to death, the glory of God, we are told, appears again. And God says to Moses, "Tell them that their corpses shall fall in this desert."

Still the living corpses move on, driven by their leader's restlessness, by his dream, by his God. At some unspecified place in the desert, Korah and his backers stage an insurrection and charge Moses with being a mountebank who is leading them to disaster. And Moses is exceedingly wroth. In the desert of Zin his sister Miriam dies, she who stood by the Nile as a young girl to see what befell his cradle of reeds. How many years have gone by since then! Thence they journey to Hor Hahar, where his brother Aaron dies too, close to the land of Edom. Of Tsippora, Moses' first wife, we hear nothing; perhaps she too is long dead. Nor are Moses' sons ever mentioned. He is now an utterly lonely man, as perhaps he has always been by nature. Nowhere do we read of his ever having had a friend or a lover; his only converse is with God. He is old now too, fantastically old.

14

Still the people continue to wander, through complaints that the bread is bad, through wars with the Midianites and the Amorites, with the king of Arad and the king of Bashan. Roundaboutly, indirectly, they approach the land of Canaan. In one of their resting places, Moses has a wondrous vision of that land.

The land to which you are coming, Moses says, is not like the land of Egypt. What is the land of Egypt? It is a land where "You sowed your seed and watered it on foot like a garden by your house." In contrast, says Moses, the Promised Land is one that drinks rainwater from the sky, "A land for which the Lord your God cares, the eyes of the Lord being always upon it."

When Rabbi Simha Bunim of Pszyscha was asked what kind of curse it was for the serpent to have to eat earth, since this was a food that would always be available, he answered: "Man is condemned to eat bread by the sweat of his brow, so that if he wearies of his labors he will cry out to God. Woman is condemned to bring forth children in hardship, so that if her pain proves too great she will weep before God. Especially in their distress they remain linked to God. But God has given the serpent everything it needs, so that it will never turn to Him again."

The land of Egypt is the land of the serpent. The Promised Land is the land of man. It is the land of his true condition, which is always a religious one. This is the whole Torah in a nutshell.

15

The sky is still dark in my window. Distant stars twinkle placidly. The houses are indistinct forms. Silence. A streetlight shines quietly at the corner. I sit staring into the darkness.

Whom am I writing this for? The paper I write on is white, yet the universe answers in black. The earth answers with silence.

Only death is worth writing about. To ask, to explain. But these aren't the words.

God. But these aren't the words. I have no words.

16

The sky has turned gray. Dawn. The antennas on the rooftops reach up like crosses. The treetops nod slowly in the dawn breeze. Birds. One, very close, calls something that sounds like "jug, jug." "Jug jug jug jug jug."

I must have fallen asleep at my desk. I must have dreamed. I was in a strange land, at night. Perhaps in a small hotel, which was empty and deserted. Not a soul was in the rooms except for a young girl who sat in one of them alone. In my own room, an oil lamp hung from the ceiling. The oil was running low and I was afraid the wick would go out. I climbed on a chair to add oil. It was difficult because the ceiling was so high.

There was a second dream, too. I was in a strange cellar. Next to me, by a small window, sat an unfamiliar girl spinning on a staff. A pure, white light fell delicately through the window onto a square of bright fabric. I think now that there must have been something pagan about her. She told me that she liked to spin.

17

Morning light. A bright sky. I returned to my book and reached the end of the tale. At that time, says Moses, "I entreated the Lord saying, 'My Lord God, thou hast only begun to show thy servant thy greatness. . . . Pray let me go over and see the good land that is beyond the Jordan, those fair mountains and the Lebanon.' But the Lord was angry with me on your account and would not listen. And the Lord said to me, 'Enough, say not to me another word about this matter.'

"Then from the steppes of Moab Moses ascended Mount Nebo, the headland of Pisgah, which faces Jericho, and the Lord showed him all the land—Gilead as far as Dan, all Naphtali, the territory of Ephraim and Manasseh, all the territory of Judah as far as the last sea, the Negev, and the valley of Jericho, the city of palms, as far as Zoar. . . . And Moses, the servant of the Lord, died there in the land of Moab by the mouth of the Lord. And he was buried in the valley of Moab opposite Beth-peor; but to this day no one knows where."

Not long ago, some 3,500 years later, I, a fortuitous and unknown man, stood on the plateau above Jericho and looked down on the badlands of Moab to the east of the Jordan, and at the mountains of Edom and Moab and Gilead, and at Mount Nebo. I turned around to look at the mountains to the west, and for a moment I could scarcely believe that I was standing on the land to which Moses wished to come and could not. For who was I? The earth I stood on was hard and dry. It was flowerless, unattractive, untouched by any green; yet it was the earth which Moses loved and to which he wished to come. I didn't think then of the thousands of dead Israelites who had fallen in the desert before him; I thought only of him. For a few minutes I stood in the sun by myself until something told me to bend down and scoop up a bit of hard soil. I looked at it. I wanted to see what he, in his love for it, had so pleaded to come to. I put it to my lips and kissed it, for him.

18

When I first read Moses' plea and God's harsh answer, the thought occurred to me—and I was taken aback by the strangeness of it—that perhaps God was in trouble. Perhaps, I reflected, God had known some kind of love, and His trouble was that He had met with disappointment.

In the tenth chapter of Deuteronomy, Moses says: "Yet the Lord set His heart on your fathers to love them, and choose their descendants." He speaks of love in the preceding verse too, when he says, "And now, O Israel, what does the Lord your God require of you but to stand in awe of the Lord your God, and to walk in all his ways, and to love him. . . ." A few verses further on, he puts the demand of love first: "So you must love the Lord your God, and keep all His statutes, ordinances and commandments." Moses often calls God a jealous God—and jealousy, too, we know, is a sign of love. For according to Moses, who is (if such a person can be said to have existed at all) the most competent of all human experts on God's being, God wishes to be loved back in requital for His love. Five hundred years later, with unequaled clarity, the prophet Hosea makes the same point: when the people whore after strange gods, he declares, it is exactly the same as when his own wife betrays him with other men. Indeed, when a son is born to him, God commands him to call it Lo-ami, "Not-my-people," and explains that "you are not my people and I will not be your God." God's disappointed love, the polluting of the trust between Him and His people, causes a rupture of the relationship. Yet one day, the prophet asserts, God will fall in love with His people—beloved all over again. "And I will betroth you forever; and I will betroth you in justice, and in lovingkindness, and in mercy; and I will betroth you in faith, and you shall know the Lord." Of all these expressions of love, the last is the most pregnant with meaning. Love that is unaccompanied by knowledge of the beloved, of his existential dilemma, has no lasting value. Love cannot do without knowledge. Fourteen hundred years and many historical metamorphoses afterward, another Israelite, the apostle

John, points out in an epistle, "In this is love, not that we loved God, but that he loved us." We love Him back *because* He loved us first.

This mystic sense of divine love was not born with Christianity. It was always at the heart of the biblical concept of God. Jesus, in the mystery of his suffering and of his vision, understood what Moses had been through.

19

In fact, all human history may be viewed as a story of God's disappointment in love.

As far as the human understanding can grasp it, the prophets understood this. For what does a prophet's appearance signify? He cannot be understood until we understand how he understood God. And the prophet is the man who senses God's tragic dilemma. Hosea arrived at this sense of God as a result of his own wife's infidelity. Others did so not from personal analogy, but from a primal, cosmic intuition. In Moses' case, this developed into an almost human friendship, for we read that "No prophet has ever appeared in Israel like Moses, whom God knew face to face." No prophet whom God so chose, so loved, so frightened when He came to kill him, so repeatedly spoke to, so harshly rejected, and so utterly kept for Himself in the end, making even of his burial place a secret, a crypt forever apart from the wretched, senseless whirlpool of time and men.

In his innermost being, the prophet does not exist for the people. The people are the stage on which the mystery play of God's unrequited passion is acted out among men. The people are God's disappointment. In vain are all His signs and miracles, in vain His display at Mount Sinai, in vain Nebuchadnezzar and Auschwitz. The prophet exists for God, as though—if such a thing is conceivable— by means of an inner identification with Him, of an empathy with His sorrow and disappointment. As though to show Him that He is not alone.

20

What, then, is the prophet to do? The life of each prophet has something sacrificial about it. At the same time, each speaks with loathing of ritual sacrifice and burnt offerings, because such things have nothing to do with true sacrifice of self, which alone can lead to contact between the human and the divine. The sacrifices in the

Temple seem to them a cheap joke—a joke aimed not so much at themselves and at the sacrifice they have made as at something infinitely greater, at the mysterious tragedy of God.

Few men in human history have understood this as well as the Galilean who offered himself up in fulfillment of the Psalmist's words, "Sacrifice and offering thou dost not desire, burnt-offering and sin-offering thou dost not demand, so lo, said I: here I come." Paul, in his Epistle to the Hebrews, comments, "He entered into the Holy Place, taking not the blood of goats and calves, but his own blood."

21

The Law states that the adulterous woman must die. "And you shall be holy unto me," God says through Moses, "because I am holy." One must understand these words not only as a commandment but as a plea. As the woman who cheats strikes at the roots of her husband's existence, so the people that cheat strike at the roots of God's holiness, which is essential to His being. Only this mystery, which cannot be grasped with the intellect, explains the thought of the prophets, who perceived a connection between the pollution of life and its destruction. The adulterous woman must die. Yet the blood price is not necessarily paid by those who are least worthy or most evil. Perhaps this is because, as the Bible tells us, a sacrifice is invalid when the body of its bearer is imperfect. Whoever belongs to the people that God, for mysterious reasons of His own, chose for Himself in antiquity, is equally responsible; yet this responsibility rests most heavily on the best and most highly endowed. This is why Moses must die in distress without reaching his destination, why the prophets are always the victims, why Akiva was martyred by the Romans, why Jesus must be crucified. Perhaps this is why six million men, women, and children who bore no personal blame of their own, but nevertheless bore the consequences of God's ancient choice, were burned alive in the furnaces of Europe.

Some 160 years ago, Rabbi Nachman of Bratislav dreamed a dream. "In my dream," he relates, "I saw that it was the Day of Atonement. And I understood right away that on each Day of Atonement one person is picked to be sacrificed by the high priest. And since they were looking for that person, I volunteered to be him. And I was asked to put it in writing, and I did. Yet when they wished to sacrifice me, I repented and sought to hide. How could I hide, though, when that great crowd of men was around me? I managed to escape from the city; yet no sooner had I done this than I returned to it again, and behold! here I was in the city once more. Then I sought to hide among the nations of the world, though I knew that if anyone came to demand me from their hands they would surely yield me up. In the end, someone was found to be sacrificed in my place. Nevertheless, I fear for the future."

Jerusalem

1. *Back to the Goldin house in a dream*
Last night I returned to the Goldin house in a dream.

Over the years, I revisited it several times while awake. The look of the neighborhood hadn't changed. Neither had the street I once lived on. There were still ten houses on it, two of them synagogues, all pretty much the same.

I never entered the Goldin house itself during these visits, nor did I climb the winding wooden staircase to the roof, under which was hidden the small room I had lived in for a while when I was young. I simply stood on the sidewalk and looked up at it. For a long time. And then went my way.

Who knows, perhaps I held back because there had been changes in the house itself. In my own time it had been anonymous. The late Mr. Goldin was a jeweler. Among his tenants were a baker, a carpenter, a shopkeeper, and a *yeshiva* student. All of them still lived on the second floor, but the ground floor, to my surprise, had become institutionalized. A small sign above a doorway informed me that here were the offices of the Charitable Souls Society, while another sign announced that soon, with G-d's help, a medical clinic for the needy would be opened here.

Charitable institutions are a fine thing. Still, I couldn't help remembering a story I once read about a young man who left his father's house and, after much wandering, succeeded in becoming an author of books. One day he returned to the place of his birth and found that it had been made into a public library. The sad mockery of it did not escape him.

Last night, then, I dreamed that I returned to the Goldin house.

I returned at sundown, on a Friday, on the eve of the sabbath. I entered the courtyard, climbed the stone stairs to the second floor, and then the wooden stairs to the roof. I encountered no one, and before I knew it dusk had fallen. My small room was exactly as I had left it years before. There was the same wobbly table by the light of whose kerosene lamp I had written my first poems, the same primus stove on which I used to make tea, the same dilapidated sofa with bits of seaweed sticking out through the ripped upholstery. A page of poetry I had once wanted to write and never did lay on a chair. Now it was written, but I didn't touch it. A thick film of dust covered everything.

I stood in the darkness leaning against the railing of the roof. In the synagogue below, a crowd of men had assembled for the sabbath eve prayer. A light shone through a transom window in the house across from me.

Behind that window lived a young woman who was tall and white. I didn't know who she was, and all I could see of her face was its whiteness. Her hair was black, and her lips were the color of mulberries.

Every sabbath eve at this time she took a bath. The lighted transom was the window of her bathroom.

I saw steam. Hot water started filling the tub. A white mist covered the window. In its vapors stood the white woman.

She started taking off her dress. In the candlelit synagogue below, the first half of the sabbath eve prayer began. I could hear the voices of the men singing: *O let us give joyous praise to the Lord, let us lift our voice to the rock of our salvation . . .*

She let her dress drop. Only her head and shoulders were visible in the steam. Then these vanished too, and I knew that she was in the water.

I stood in the darkness, listening to the cantor below. *To greet the sabbath let us rise. For there our chiefest blessing lies.* And the congregation answered him: *Come, O come ye by my side. Come to greet the sabbath bride.*

The cantor's voice rose a pitch: *To the holy palace of the king. Rise, beloved, rise, take wing.* I could tell the words by the melody, and I knew that the white woman was stretched out in the water.

I waited for her to reappear, but there was only steam. I knew she must be soaping her white body.

The cantor's voice rose from below: *Shake off the dust thou slumb'rest in. Put on thy bridal diadem.*

And the congregation answered him: *Come, O come ye by my side. Come to greet the sabbath bride.*

Above me, as on the nights when I stood here awake, stretched the deep sky. One window alone was lit in the darkness, and I knew that soon I would see her.

Be not ashamed, O be not ashamed. For soon the king shall call thy name. . . . Come, O come ye by my side. Come to greet the sabbath bride.

She rose from the water and stood drying her hair. Her two breasts quivered slightly.

In the synagogue the song gathered strength. *Then all thy haters shall be hated. And thy beraters be berated. The Lord shall come to thee, elated. As cometh the bridegroom to the bride.* And the congregation answered: *Come, O come ye by my side. Come to greet the sabbath bride.*

She stood drying her breasts and her back in the steamy light, and I stood in the quiet quiver of the dark. She raised one long white leg and began to dry it, slowly, and then, through the steam, against the whiteness of her skin, I saw something like a patch of black grass. At that moment the quiver overcame me, and some stupendous being spread its wings inside me and took off and was gone, and I shut my eyes, and from below came the voice of the cantor beginning the second half of the sabbath eve prayer: *Bless ye the Lord who is blessed.* And the congregation answered him: *Blessed be the Lord who is blessèd for ever and ever.*

2. Mount Zion

After many years I ascended Mount Zion again. The old dirt track was overgrown with weeds, and I took the stairs instead. Various signs greeted me, some with verses from the Bible, others announcing institutions and shops. A guard stopped me at the entrance to King David's tomb and lent me a skullcap. Four men were reciting psalms by the catafalque. Tourists of both sexes circulated through the dank interior beneath massive Gothic vaults. I climbed the minaret outside. A wind was blowing. Across from me, its tombstones gleaming whitely, was the Mount of Olives, and beyond it the mountains of Moab, screened by blue haze. When I looked at the nearby church steeple I saw that the holes from the shells that had hit it during the 1948 war, when I was first here, were still visible. Doves of peace were roosting in them now.

I climbed back down. I had time on my hands, and so I lingered for a while in the crypt beneath the vaults. Next to me sat a man behind a small table, selling certificates in testimony that the bearers thereof had trod in this holy place.

There was nothing to make me feel that this was really David's grave—nor had there been anything back then, during the war. At the time, it was true, I hadn't known that the tradition was a late one, originating apparently with the medieval traveler Benjamin of Tudela. The biblical City of David, in a corner of which the king no doubt lies, was hundreds of meters northeast of here. The Christian tradition that the Last Supper took place on this site, where the Church of the Dormition now stands, is undoubtedly much older, for the writings of St. Epiphanus and, after him, of St. Cyril date it back to as far as the third century. Then, though, I knew nothing about this either. No one had told me about it, nor had I encountered it in any book.

Throughout those days and nights, however, I had sensed something primeval, dark, about the place.

The wall of the Old City had loomed grayly before me by day, blackly at night. An Arab sniper lurked behind its apertures. No one dared set foot in the narrow lane between the church and the wall. It was enchanted ground. Whoever infringed on it paid with his life.

I used to stare at the wall from our firing positions in the church as though bewitched. Only a few dozen paces lay between me and it, yet they led through the gates of death.

Sometimes, at night, I would sit by one of the windows in the church and send long bursts of fire from my machine gun at the wall, like a jackal howling at the moon. Invisible in the darkness, the mouths of the wall lit up in return each time the hidden machine gun opposite me flashed quickly back. The sound of my own gun, though deafening, was like a musical drumroll, and I liked the smell of the burned powder.

I saw no newspapers, had no radio, read nothing, heard nothing. I knew nothing about the conduct of the war, about where it was being fought or who was winning or losing it. Nor did I waste my time thinking about it. It had simply fallen on me from out of the blue, and I accepted it for what it was.

Forgotten fragments, like scenes from a dream, came back to me now.

When the fighting began, before I was sent to Mount Zion, I spent

a few days in an Arab neighborhood of Jerusalem called Musrara, in a
rear position near the broadcasting station. There had been a piano
in one of the studios there, and I used to shut myself up in the dark,
soundproofed room and hammer away on it, though I knew nothing
about music at all.

All the houses of Musrara had been abandoned, as though in a
dream. In some of them, food was still left on the tables, yet you
couldn't find a living soul in them. From time to time Jews would
come, soldiers or civilians, to loot what rugs, furniture, or radios
were left. What they wanted any of it for was beyond me. The world
was totally spiritual then, totally religious: all its conventions and
givens had melted away, shells whistled through the air like flying
angels of death, and one could have really died at any minute. Yet
even I made off with something, a small reproduction of Van Gogh's
Sunflowers that I found on somebody's wall. It cheered me to have
it, because Van Gogh and Gauguin were my two favorite painters in
those days. I can still remember that yellow.

Afterward, in Abu Tor, a neighborhood separated from Mount
Zion by hell on earth, I found an abandoned house with a room that
was empty except for an armchair and a large mirror. I used to sit for
hours in the depths of the chair, opposite the mirror, writing poems
on a pad of stationery that bore the letterhead of an Arab commercial
firm.

I liked best climbing at night onto the roof of that house in Abu
Tor, a neighborhood named after a comrade-in-arms of Saladin, and
throwing hand grenades from it at the Arab position down the street.
It didn't accomplish much, but I had a weakness for the sudden
flash, and for the thud of the explosion that followed.

Later, on Mount Zion in the Church of the Dormition, from which
the Virgin Mary supposedly ascended in her sleep to heaven, I used
to sit for long periods in the forsaken cells of the monks. Thus I
managed to live in a variety of times at once, among them my own
and the Middle Ages.

Now and then I would descend into town. The connecting pas-
sageway was a low, narrow tunnel that had been dug to the Jewish
neighborhood of Yemin Moshe. You had to traverse it doubled over,
like a worm burrowing through the earth. Once in the city, I went to
see two girls I knew, Hava and Ada. Sometimes, walking along a
deserted street, it would occur to me that I was living to see the
fulfillment of Nietzsche's words that man's destiny in life was to be a

warrior and woman's to be his paramour. The thought amused me, since—with a helmet shaped like a chopping bowl on my head and army pants a size too big for me that kept threatening to fall off—I looked like anything but a prophetic vision of the Übermensch. In general, though, those walks were a strange hallucination of empty city blocks, bloodstained sidewalks, suddenly shrieking shells, thirst, and a smell of sperm and sweat.

Those days were distant. Now I stood on the mount by the Old City wall, opposite Zion Gate, but neither mount, wall, nor gate was what it had been. Those days belonged to such another world and such another time that I could almost have believed that the war I took part in had been fought in crusader times, or back in the age of Joshua.

3. *Me'a She'arim*

The streets are narrow here. They wind among the columns of the houses like the spaces between the lines of a page of the Talmud.

Small, crooked alleyways, like letters of Rashi script.

Me'a She'arim, Bet Yisra'el, Batei Ungarn, Sha'arei Hesed.

How many nocturnal hours I spent wandering through these alleys during the years I lived in the area. Deathly silent hours of the night, when you could hear a pin drop. When the only sound was the echo of my footsteps on the cobblestones.

In the houses, behind latticed windows, Jews were covered by slumber as the fallen Israelites in the desert were covered by sand.

Sometimes I would pass a house of study. Through the window, by the light of a feeble, yellowish electric bulb, I would see two or three young students bent over their books, rocking softly back and forth while they chanted the ancient Aramaic words of the Gemara in a melancholy murmur: *Thus say the rabbis . . . wherefore Rabbi Levi bar Hama differs with Rabbi Hanina . . . on the one hand, this one says . . . and on the other hand, this one . . .* the torts and case laws of the Talmud . . . the world of Rava and Abayei, of Rav Ashi and Rabbi Abahu. . . .

Sometimes I would stop to read one of the placards affixed to the walls. Proclamations, prohibitions, excommunications. "In the name of our rabbis and officers of the Law, may they live in peace, amen. . . . Be it hereby made known . . . For as when the time of the Messiah grows nigh, heresy and apostasy stalk the streets. . . . And whereas on account of our innumerable sins the wicked thrive and prosper . . . Wherefore the Holy One Blessed Be He bestows on them success that we may be brought into temptation and withstand it. . . . May the Compassionate One have mercy on us and save us. . . . For Thou alone, O Lord our God, shall rule over us. . . . And may it be granted us to see the coming of the Redeemer. . . ."

Today I have come here on a workaday afternoon. Women are shopping in the market. Men are about their business. My eye is caught by a large notice on the wall. "Help!!!" it says. Its contents are trivial, but I know that all such cries here are essentially addressed to God.

Nearby stands a pretty boy with a proud, wise look on his face. A little scholar of the Law.

To tell the truth, I could never identify with these people (for if I could, I would have come to live with them as an observant Jew) who live by the rule of the Torah and its codes. To be religious, in my terms, means to understand that life is a parable of which God is the meaning—that is, to live life as a struggle to make contact with the divine. Somewhere else I have written about the instructive historical fact that the official codification of the Bible in the days of Ezra the Scribe was accompanied by the cessation of prophecy—in other words, by the drying up of the previously renewable source of human contact with God.

And yet still I feel close to them, these people who live as though in a fortress under siege, surrounded by a secular world they disdain and by a "culture" that revolts them. Their life is without compromise, without concessions. It is a waiting for the Messiah.

When I was called to the army to fight in the War of Independence, it grieved me to think that I might have to die defending the Hebrew University, or the bourgeoisie of Rehavia, or the offices of the press. These and many other things meant nothing to me then and mean nothing to me now, nor do I hesitate to say so. But the Torah is something else. I have no difficulty understanding that whoever believes in it must be ready to die for it. One must never refuse to be a martyr for God. There can be no other significance to life beside worshiping Him. The rest is simply a question of how one understands this worship—that is, of how one understands God.

Worshiping God, as the phrase suggests,* has nothing to do with pleasure or cultural frills. It is work, hard work, like paving a road, or

* In Hebrew the word for "Worship," *avoda*, is the same as the word for "work." *Translator*.

farming land, or building a house. In general, I don't believe that the purpose of life in this world is to snatch a little pleasure here or there. If it were, we might as well have been born bedbugs. In whatever we live and do—in our happiness, our suffering, our love, our hate, our passions, our thoughts—we must live and do it not just for itself, but as a parable, as a question, as a war. As work. As worship.

What is man? Man is a question. God is the answer. If the answer were available here, in this life, the question would be unnecessary. The painful tension between the two gives life its energy.

4. *Snow*
It is snowing on Jerusalem. It is snowing on its walls.
Snow falls on the Temple Mount. Snow falls on the Dome of the
    Rock.

Snow falls on Mount Zion. And on the Holy Sepulchre.
Snow falls on Sheikh Jarrah and on Al-Ghazali Place.

Faces of snow peer through the windows on the Via Dolorosa:
Faces of priests and of Levites and of *yeshiva* boys in black hats.

Beneath a sky of snow he walks slowly by himself.
Snowflakes in his hair, his head sunk on his chest.

Only women follow him, white women in dresses of snow:
Mary Magdalene who loves him, weeping tears of snow as she walks,

And Mary his mother, and Mary the mother of James, and that other
    Mary, the Mary of snow.
Follow him, dear women, for he is cold by himself in the snow.

Through the Gate of Ephraim they pass, onto a field that is shrouded
    in snow.
There in the snow will rise the cross which he will ascend with
    outstretched arms.

Drops of sweat will drip from his brow that is covered with thorns of
    snow
As into his hands and feet are driven four nails of snow.

Snow falls on Jerusalem. It is snowing on all the mountains.
On the Temple Mount and Mount Zion, on Sheikh Jarrah and Wadi
     Joz.

And the women at his feet can see in sunlight of snow
How slowly he melts before their eyes, like a man made of snow.

With him melt the white women, Mary Magdalene who loves him,
And Mary his mother, and Mary the mother of James, and that other
     Mary, the Mary of snow.

—translated by Hillel Halkin

UTAH DIED FOR YOUR SINS

fiction by MAX ZIMMER

from QUARRY WEST

nominated by Raymond Carver and QUARRY WEST

You MAY HAVE HEARD this way to hunt deer: take a double-edged razor blade, embed one edge in a salt block and leave the other edge in the air, and place the salt on a deer trail. A deer comes to it out of the hills on its way to water after sunset and begins to lick the block. The first lick slices its tongue. As the deer repeatedly cuts its tongue, it begins to get the better taste of licking its own blood with the salt. It will stand over the block and lick at it until the animal neatly bleeds itself to death. This method has an advantage over the killing of a deer with a rifle. First of all, the traditional hunt has as a part of itself a chase. When a deer is shot at the end of such a chase, its muscles are pumped full of blood. This gives the meat too rough, almost too alive a taste. This blood, when it is cooked in the meat, creates indigestion in some people. There is an unpalatable sense of thickness about it. On the other hand, when a deer licks at a razor blade in a block of salt, licks the salt away from around the blade so that the blade rises higher into the flesh, the animal is calm. There is a minimal flow of blood through its muscles. It has probably just eaten; its blood is concentrated in the inedible organs around its stomach. And it will die only after the heart has pumped the muscles and organs out, after the meat has been bled thoroughly by the tongue. Venison is a wild meat; blood carries the taste of bark and harsh grass; the absence of blood minimizes this wild aspect of its flavor.

Second here, a gunshot from a modern rifle is designed to kill or significantly maim a deer with little regard to where it strikes. Someone has the story that three legs have been amputated from a deer in a forest at the knees with a solitary shot. A complaint against a gunshot is that it inevitably ruins, in its method of mushrooming into a round plow, a part of the flesh. A razor blade in a block of salt costs only the tongue. It does not shred or hack at anything else. Some people prefer to eat tongue; I have no argument with them; let them carry their rifles after a deer, and aim customarily away from the head.

And at last, there is a humane and pastoral element to a deer that is dead as if it had slept there, after filling its belly with blood that will not be digested. Such a deer is easier to butcher than a deer that has been, perhaps, gutshot; a gutshot deer has lost the heterogeneity of its organs. There is nothing to be learned about how the human body functions in the butchering of a gutshot deer.

So: there are razor blades that never shave an armpit or a face or a leg. There are razor blades that never graze the skin, and instead of that, wait for animals that graze on high slanted meadows. There are razor blades that never slice an apple on Halloween.

Consider this. If you had an automobile in 1959, and held your cigarette in the palm of your hand at night at a hamburger drive-in and looked out at the street, you would not be bored with your automobile. You would have a friend with a 1940 Ford, and he would have cherried it thoroughly out. Your 1951 Olds looks like a hundred relatives have aged it when the Ford is around. You choose to customize your Olds. This is how you do it.

Appletons are shells that resemble spotlights. They attach to the posts of the windshield, and have the shape of small brilliant warheads on your fenders. You purchase a pair from Western Auto. You make, from quarter-inch plate, a set of shackles to bolt into the A-frames behind your wheels, and lower the front of your Olds by four inches. You dismantle the exhaust, and rebuild it with scavengers that hang out under your axle, two or four flared tubes. You remove all the trim from the body, remove the hood ornament, remove the trunk ornament, and push putty into the resultant holes. You flush the putty with the contour of the body; you paint your Olds with metalflake or fishscale mixed into any of the spectrum of Fuller automotive paints. Or you paint it candy apple red. You hang a tie or your high school tassle on the rear-view mirror. You fix a hula dancer that has a pair of eyehooks for a pelvis, or a dog with imitation ruby eyes that are wired to your brakelights, in the rear window.

There is an old round refrigerator in your garage. Random cans of Olympia and Coors rattle on the shelves when you smack the refrigerator door shut, and you have a habit now of looking out the window at the asphalt as you drink half the can. If you took an Olympia, you scratch the label in half and look at the dots on the back. There are from one to four of them, in a short brown row. One dot is to find her. Two are to find her and feel her. Three are to do these, and fuck her, and with four you forget her. You replace your rockerarm covers and air cleaner with chrome accessories, and tap a wolf whistle you ordered from J. C. Whitney into the intake manifold, and force the wire that controls the whistle through the firewall. You weld a row of razor blades inside the lip of the hood. Your customary dots are two.

At last you have the spinner hubcaps. They are round pressed plates as all hubcaps are; they have two raised bars that cross one another and span the plate. They are four thick spokes that knife out from the center of the hubcap in four directions. You press the spinners into the wheelrims because alloy wheels have not occurred yet at the accessory shops. Also, your Olds is used, one that you bought when it was seven years old, with the spots where you would not have worn them, with crumbs and french fries that are rough on your fingertips when you push your hands into the fat cloth crack between the bench and the backrest. And you look across the black metal dashboard that is laced with the transparent stains of drinks that perhaps are seven years old; some of the stains are indelible, and the windshield there ahead of you has been starred in four places by rocks. The splines of the stars are edges of split glass, and they catch the light and make fiery spears of it when you yaw the Olds back and forth. The front left wheel sets an annoying tremor at sixty-five mph that the Olds amplifies with rattles you think it has always had.

And you resent that your Olds has a history without you. I will tell you that it belonged to a basketball coach at Bountiful High, and what will that mean. So you modify it, to avoid this discomfort, rather than join histories with it. This is no ordinary luck. And now.

You sit with your date in your automobile much as you would sit with her in a restaurant. On one side of a booth together, and look at the side where you chose not to sit; there are the same coronas of those unknown drinks on the table as on your dashboard. You, this is more obscure: she is how she is because you have chosen her to sit in your customized Olds, spinners and all. She is not opposite you. She knows the Olds is yours for what she wants. She shaves her legs with her father's safety razor, she says, as high as her knees. The Olds is no longer yours. She lets your blood, not hers, when you feel the hot Kotex in her crotch. At dawn, if you have a rooster in your rear window, its crow will have the sound of a woman with a knife in her throat sobbing.

Because with the advent of alloy wheels, the spinner is a style of hubcap that has been defunct for twelve or so years, except in remote areas of Utah, where alloy wheels are still unheard of. There the accessory shops still have spinners. There you look at a 1940 Ford with its spinners twisiting the lights at midnight into cellophane-spangled toothpicks, and three probabilities occur to you. That the rear axle is locked, so the rear wheels never deviate from one another in rate of revolution, so rubber is laid whenever the Ford rounds a curve. That its spinners will rotate on who knows what automobile in another month. That your next hamburger will be speared with that kind of toothpick, when you raise it in that kind of night to your teeth.

And this, because spinners are as easy as silverware to steal. You wrap your hands around the spokes, and with Midnight Auto you transact four sharp yanks. Or your friend has installed valve stem locks. These are heavy and complicated knobs that would require you to rebalance your wheels, as he has; you would have to steal his weights as well. Or he has etched his name into a hidden place, and let it be spread that his spinners are marked and registered. Or he takes the law into his own hands. The spokes of his spinners are hollow. He has pushed putty into the spokes from the rear. He has cut a number of razor blades halfway into the putty. He has left you with your fingers pointing off your hands in eight directions at once. Each direction is an escape route.

And take the chariot races. Honed spikes that are fastened to the hubs of your chariot, to saw the legs from your opponent's horse at the knees. Such is the origin of the ornamental hubcap.

And take masturbation. Your fingers hang like castenets from your hands, and your hands try and no longer imitate a vagina. You only have the act as a memory, and to reinvigorate your memory, you walk into a river and try to hold handfuls of mud, as if your castanets were shells.

To masturbate is to yearn to be self-held, to be hermaphroditic. It has been rewarded by amputating the hands at the wrists. Look who you are, without your hands. You run your Olds out to have your spinners pluck at the neon curliques up and down the straight hard street where hamburgers are sold in sacks. Look who you are.

And once you are without your hands, a friend delivers a candle she has molded of paraffin and aluminum foil into the shape of a hexagonal nut. You write a letter to her. You read your letter aloud.

It has been my experience, you read, with the candle you gave me, that aluminum foil does not burn; therefore, I am using the candle as an ashtray. Imagine how long it will take a candle to burn away because of the cigarettes I happen to stub out around its wick.

But here you are let off the hook: here you hit four dots. The name at the end of the letter is not yours. It is Seymour Utah. Suppose he has hands. He then is the friend with the 1940 Ford. Now, more than thirty years old, he has a motorcycle. It is a 360 Bultaco, manufactured for riding in the hills; this is a ready-to-ride dirt bike. He has added the equipment to enable himself to ride it on the street as well.

He had the motorcycle the afternoon he rode it to The Ratskeller for an eight-inch venison pizza. The place made venison pizza available during the deerhunt in October. Utah liked to leave his helmet with his bike, and he had already had two helmets stolen. So he had made a band of steel that fit behind the padded headband in his helmet, and had welded seventeen razor blades around the band. He inserted the band into his helmet whenever he left the bike. If a thief had no knowledge of it, the band would treat his head like a Vegematic. Utah kept the headband in the compartment beneath his seat when he rode the Bultaco. He looked over the counter where the cook sliced a razor-sharp handheld wheel across his pizza four times, without having it fall apart. He ate the pizza clearheaded enough for anybody.

He had the motorcycle also on the day four miles along a deer trail where he had gutshot a deer. It had begun to blizzard. He had run the slurry of the deer's guts out onto the sparse snow. Then he had set it on its hooves and held it with his knees. This had enabled him to reach around the chest and spread the ribs apart. He had staggered around and fit the animal down over his Bultaco. Its rear legs had hung out over the handlebars; its head had swung in the mud of the knobbed rear tire. He had ridden the deer and the bike the four miles on the slippery trail back to the highway, like a child on a mechanized animal. He had become covered with mud. When he had pulled the deer from the bike, mud had sloughed out of the ribs. Mud had covered him and the deer and the bike in a communal hide. He had long ago unlocked the rear axle of the Ford; it had been on the shoulder where the mud road rose to the highway. He had bought bumper racks for his Bultaco. The Ford had been no more now than an old automobile. He had pulled the mud out of the deer and pushed the mud off his arms. He had looked up the highway to where the mud ran into the sky. The animal had been folded into the trunk and driven the thirty miles to Kearns. The wipers had not worked in the snow.

A razor blade is honed to enough of an edge that the first recognition of having been cut is not a result of pain. Utah was first aware of what he had forgotten to do, and done, when he thought that it was too red and early in the afternoon for a sunset. He was amazed at the beauty, first of all, of what he had thought was a sunset. The beat of the Bultaco on the highway became hard to distinguish from the taste of the pizza at The Ratskeller. Both perceptions ran down his throat. He headed his dirt bike west on the Bingham highway. The helmet covered his head completely, except for the region of his face where he had to shave. The wind dried the blood there, as it ran down the slant of his cheeks one layer after another, like thin red frosting on his whiskers. He pushed the helmet off his head while he rode. He began to look for a familiar dirt road around Cedar Fork. His hand reached out to turn the bright ring of the rearview mirror up until he could look at his face. The mirror shook from the

resonance of the engine. In the mirror his head shook. For a moment, while his hand worked at the final adjustment of the mirror,
and before he turned it rapidly downward again, his hand held this
pocket-sized, shaking portrait of himself: a huge rotting tomato in
the wind, or a heart that oozed blood onto his shoulders. He was
most astonished at how calm his hands were on the handlegrips, how
logically they hooked to the handlebars, how logical it was to have a
tachometer and a gray gasoline tank and the gray rumbling smudge
of the highway all between his knees. It all worked. He was an
extension of all this logicality He turned it all off the highway and
onto the dirt road. He could feel himself sweat more than he could
feel himself bleed. His left hand pulled the clutch lever and his right
hand twisted the accelerator grip as calmly as gloves that have just
been tossed onto a fire, that always look for a moment, before they
tremble and crack apart at their kindling temperature, as if they are
there to calm the flames. His shoe operated the gear pedal.

The road hurried him up toward the cedar. He scratched the
blood from his eyes. The mirror struck him as a circular, bouncing
postcard of the country he had come across and left orange with dust.
He ignored the notion of sending the postcard anywhere. It would
not hold still enough to sign; he liked postcards of wildlife; at a Union
76 truckstop, he had once bought eleven postcards of a jackelope,
depicted in a butchered photograph as a jackrabbit with antlers. He
turned the Bultaco up a deer trail, hoping to put an animal onto the
mirror. He followed his hands; all he knew about was how thirsty he
was, after the pizza, and how a deer trail, if it did not lead to water,
went on into the hills until it did lead to water. Utah had no idea that
it was an old deerhunter's joke. How many miles is unclear when he
laid his head in the trail, and his Bultaco rushed out from under him
at full throttle, and writhed in the dirt like

Like? This is complicated. A half-eaten grasshopper. A spider
bereft of its legs on the left side. A jackrabbit speared to the earth. Or
a rattlesnake, broken almost in half with a stone.

Then here is this. Does it coil or uncoil or recoil from this wound.
Does it rattle. Do its two halves coil and uncoil simultaneously, or
(one coiling the other uncoiling from the node originated by this
stone) in syncopation. Who knows. The hardship here is that animals
and insects abound. You think of your own. Remember only: it has to
do with nodes. You take the node of something and relocate the
node. The node of the Bultaco (about which all else revolves) is the

naugahyde seat. The node of the human is the crotch. The node of the razor blade is the place where you hold it.

Leftovers Utah had not known:

That alloy wheels had lately come on the market for motorcycles as well.

That the node of an animal is its tongue; nor that a deer, having drunk enough of its own blood, will become a carnivorous animal, and for how long is conjectural.

TO DANCE

fiction by MARY PETERSON

from FICTION INTERNATIONAL

nominated by DeWitt Henry

THE WOMAN WHO can't dance moves in with the Arthur Murray Studios dance instructor. When he learns of her affliction he misunderstands her motives in wanting to live with him. She reminds him they met quite by accident at the counter in Grant's, and that she was drinking a root beer and minding her own business. He addressed her first, wanting a light for his cigarette. This alone would not have been enough, except that half an hour later while he was having his picture taken in the little booth with the grey floral curtain over the door, she poked her head in thinking it was empty.

"Neither meeting," she reminds him, "had anything at all to do with dancing."

He is reassured, and, convinced that love can conquer, resolves to teach her to dance.

"You won't believe this," she tells him, "but it is absolutely impossible to teach me to dance. I have never been able to dance. Never, never."

"Can you tap your fingers to a record?" he asks her.

"Not if I'm listening to the words of the song."

"You can walk, can't you?"

"I didn't walk until I was seven years old."

"You can run."

"Well," she says, "that came later."

"The human body operates according to rhythms," he says. "We learn to carry a beat while we are still curled under our mother's heart."

"I think," she says, "that I learned the sound of my mother's spaghetti dinner and it had no rhythm at all."

"When did you discover the problem?" he asks kindly. She notices the way he strokes his chin, like a doctor. They are lying in bed and he has the other hand on her thigh.

She tells him she was in college and they were required to take a physical education course. She had never wanted to learn to fence, and tumbling seemed somehow immature. Then, she says, she was invited to the Senior Gala. But she tells him when she was small it took three years to learn the moves for hopscotch. "How far back do you want me to go?" she asks.

"I don't want the story of your life," he says.

"No?"

"I want to create you myself."

"I've been trying to do it for years," she says. "It can get very dull."

"But you never danced in high school?"

"My religion forbade it," she says, so well he believes her.

"It seemed to me," he says by way of explanation, "it was time I moved in with somebody. I'm twenty-two years old and I've never lived with a woman before. That can get to you, you know?"

She stands in the doorway to the bathroom watching him shave. The bathroom mirror is steamy from his shower and the one window is made of gritty frosted glass. The shower curtain has lily pads and goldfish on it. He bought it at a second hand store, he said, because it was "campy."

"I'm older than you," she says.

"I know." He turns and grins; she begins to wonder what he wants. "But don't tell me how much. I like there to be mystery between people."

"My college major was philosophy," she says.

He splashes water against his face and reddened neck. "What?" he says, reaching for the towel.

That evening he brings home some Studio records and says she will have her first lesson. He opens a paper packet in which there are many yellow gummed feet marked R and L. Kneeling, he places these on the floor in a pattern.

"L is for Left, and R is for Right."

She has been watching and has already figured this out.

"The waltz is perhaps the easiest dance to learn," he says. "We usually start there and work up to more difficult ones. You'll get the idea."

"I doubt that," she says.

The stereo is playing a very elementary waltz. Listening, he begins to count. "ONE-two-three, ONE-two-three. You got it? ONE-two-three." He snaps his fingers on the ONE.

She remarks that he looks very much like Lawrence Welk.

"Beat the time with me," he orders. "Think of your mother's heart."

One-two, she beats with her hand against her thigh. But delays before the three.

"You're putting me on."

"I tell you," she says, her eyes filling up, "that I can't keep a beat. My mother was a smoker and her heart was irregular."

He opens his arms and asks her to come stand on his feet.

They go around the room this way for a while, and he marks a deliberate, caricatured beat with his feet while her own feet slide off his and find themselves tangled between his ankles. She spends most of the time trying to get her feet on top of his again.

When the waltz finishes they are both exhausted.

The next day when she wakes at noon he has already left for the Studio, and she finds the little yellow feet glued carefully to the floor in the diagram of the waltz. The record jacket sits ostentatiously against the stereo. The apartment is very quiet. She holds her breath until she thinks she is having an anxiety attack.

She goes into the kitchen and puts coffee on the stove. From the kitchen she can see all the way past the stereo into the bedroom, where her two baby blue suitcases lean against the door. His telephone is in the bedroom. She thinks of making a phone call, but how can a woman tell her mother she wants to come home from a man with whom she has lived for only two days, who is trying to teach her to dance? That taxes, she thinks, the natural endurance of any mother.

The yellow feet show clearly on the living room floor against the stained walnut boards.

Later she sits on the couch with a book. She suspects he will be home soon. The book is one chosen from his shelf, a cheap edition of a spy thriller. Such a book, she reasons, should hold one's interest from the very first page, become gripping within the first chapter, entangle one in speculation and intrigue by the middle, and rivet one to the couch for the startling and improbable climax. She finds that the book does none of the above. The main character is soggy and badly-drawn. The plot is elementary. Nobody loves anybody. The murder on page seven is not credible. The drawing on the dust jacket does not enhance one's image of the action.

Closing the book, she thinks about her life. She, too, has not had a lover for a long time. Too long. However, she did once live with a man. It lasted several months. He worked as a bus boy and later she found out he was playing the numbers. When it ended she decided she would not do that again with any seriousness, since one could be damaged. Then she thinks this reasoning is just equivocation. The real reason is that she is chronically unable to see life except as a series of ironies, and in this context one decision seems as good as another.

Take this young man, for example. For a dance instructor, he is not very attractive. Oily, she could call him. She realizes she might have as easily bought a parakeet, as moved in with him. The choices that day were utter—large and small options. Anything was possible.

Now there is the problem of deciding whether moving in with him constitutes a large option.

One doesn't move in with a man one hardly knows.

Or one does.

She realizes her view of the world has been amoral for a long time and that she is surprised by nothing.

"Didn't you ever watch American Bandstand?" he asks her over their Hamburger Helper.

"Didn't you do the chalypso and the lindy with your friends while the TV was on?"

"No."

"I dated a girl who was a Girl Scout once," he says, "and she told me how they'd have club meetings and spend the whole time dancing with American Bandstand. It was in Philadelphia, you know?" He closes his mouth over the hamburger.

"I was a Brownie," she says.

"Maybe the waltz is too hard," he says. Inspired, he picks up the plastic knife from beside his plate. He asks her to hold the knife in her right hand, and he runs to the living room to put the record on. "Beat time!" he says when he comes back. "Against the table!"

The classic strains of the waltz reach from the living room into the kitchen. She closes her eyes and imagines a ballroom in Vienna. Then she sees the Studio. He is bending and gliding over the polished floors with the lovely girls who enroll with Arthur Murray. At a distance he looks very sophisticated. Never mind the cha-cha, she thinks—the rhumba, the calypso, the samba. Never mind the mad erotic dances of the steamy equatorial regions. This is just the waltz. The good old waltz. Simple beat, nothing to it, it will do. *And I can do it*. She raises the knife and brings it down on beat two.

"ONE," she says loudly.

"That was two."

"I'm sorry," she says, opening her eyes.

"Don't be sorry, for God's sake. Try it again! ONE-two-three. ONE-two-three."

"What's the name of this waltz?" she asks him.

"The Blue Danube."

"Don't you have something more modern?" She glances into the living room. The lights are out—except for the occult blue of the tuner—and she can't see the yellow feet any more.

The next afternoon he stands in the living room wearing bullfighter-tight pants with scarlet and gold spangles down the sides, and a silky black shirt with full sleeves. He clicks his heels together and snaps his fingers. "Today," he proclaims, "we learn the rhumba!"

"Oh God," she says.

"I mean at the Studio. Want to come watch?"

"Please," she says. "Don't." And retires to the bathroom.

She realizes she wants to give him a gift but is absolutely without a sense of what might please him. Finally she goes to a record store and buys a recording of the minuet. When she returns home this album looks absurdly out of place in his collection, and she puts it at the back of the stack where he may never find it.

"How did the dance start?" she asks him that evening.

"Which dance?" He is getting a carton of chocolate milk from the refrigerator.

"All dances."

"How should I know?" he says. "I'm only an instructor with Arthur Murray."

She tries to identify how she feels in this apartment. A guest? A friend? His lover?

"I passed through his life like a kidney stone," she says aloud, making words to formulate the experience. She wishes they were more funny than they are.

She goes into the bathroom and stands before the mirror, leans over his shave cream, his acne pads, his brush and comb, his squeezed tube of toothpaste. Reminds herself that they have certain things in common. For one thing, they both live in the same city. For another, they were both at the counter in Grant's on a Saturday morning. That says something, she reminds herself.

That evening over hot dogs they have a lengthy discussion about talent, in which he tells her of all the minor talents he has never yet explored. Photography. Calligraphy. Block printing. Pastels. The recorder. Poetry. And he has always wanted to learn serious acrobatics.

"You must have some too," he says encouragingly. "Aren't there disciplines you've always wanted to take up?"

"No," she says.

"What do you do with your free time?"

"I masturbate."

"Don't be cute," he says.

"I'm off to the Studio!" he says the next afternoon. He wears a black tuxedo with smooth satin lapels. In his buttonhole there is a little plastic white carnation. He spins and dips to his knees, stands again. "Voila!" he says.

"Marvy," she says. She is standing in the bedroom door still wearing her bathrobe. She notices that the yellow feet have been removed from the floor. Some floor wax has come off with them and there are dry ghostly marks of feet dancing the waltz.

"I may be late tonight," he says calmly. "Don't bother with fixing dinner."

After he has left she finds herself immersed in major problems of ethics and free will. She paces through the rooms. Stops to look at the uninteresting black and white prints he has framed and hung in uninteresting ways on the three white walls. She notices the imbalance between the geometric black and white curtains and the very obvious decorator fake fur yellow pillows on the white corduroy couch. Somebody sometime must have told him these arrangements were artistic. The plant in the window is an air fern because these require no care. It is too green. Probably, she thinks, they dye air ferns.

Something, she thinks, has been missing in my education to be an adult human person capable of reasoned choice. Some urgency. A vision of her mother and father comes to her, the photograph of them before the old frame house on Birch Street. They look like *An American Gothic*. Except that her father holds a garden hose and her mother wears a Villager blouse with small tea roses on it. They seem wrong to her. Not stalwart enough. Lacking Christian and Patriotic fibre. A life that should have been easy and filled with guidelines for right behavior has instead been given to her full of inconsistency and chance and improbable turnings. The old values were better, she thinks. Now we don't know anything. She wishes her friend had a recording of John Philip Sousa.

Meanwhile her friend is at work in the Studio she has never seen, retracing with his slim young body all the traditional gestures of movement. It seems to her he has unconsciously fitted himself to a system of values that she has always lacked, always wished for. To

dance, she thinks, is to return to the old forms. They were something to count on.

She pulls the bathrobe tighter around her waist and looks out the
plate glass window at the brick wall of the next apartment. All this
intellectualization becomes finally a waste of time, she thinks. Turning one's wheels. The reality is that here I am in the city in his
apartment, and the window is dirty.

Choice comes to us unbidden. We know which way to go. In his
dresser drawer she finds an extra set of the yellow feet and takes
them with her into the living room. She goes to the stereo and puts
on the recording of the waltz. Carefully she sorts the feet, putting all
the Right ones into a separate stack. When she kneels to the floor she
folds her bathrobe back from around her legs.

Her skin is white from no sun. She frowns at her legs, at the
loosening flesh of her thighs. Already middle age is setting in,
middle age and its complexities. Somewhere along the pike, she
thinks, I should have gained more ease in living than I have. At
thirty-three, she thinks, I don't even know how to pass the cheese.

Not that he notices. His needs are relatively simple. He makes
love like a man performing a function, a man reading on the toilet.
She would not believe him to be a dance instructor. But he told her
he learned to walk on tip-toe. "How nimble," she said, thinking of
the nursery rhyme.

Kneeling, she peels the brown backing from the Left paper feet
and arranges them one by one in a deliberate fashion going straight
toward the door. In the bedroom she can see her opened suitcases.
The waltz blares against the apartment walls; the waltz climbs the
striped paper on the window wall and clumps itself up under the
ceiling joint, pulsing.

"It is important to find the beat," he said. And she asked, "Why?"
He told her to think of riding the subway. If you don't have the
rhythm of commuting, the air doors will close before you've entered. But she argued that the crowd moved her faultlessly into the
train and the doors closed neatly on everybody; she argued that it
was easy when you were pushed by a mob. "You only think so," he
said. "Think again."

She thinks of rhythm. Lies back and wonders whether she will
follow the feet out the door. Wonders whether or not she loves him.
Love should be easy; it should be instinctual; it should make its own

new patterns each time. It has never been this way for her. The garage mechanic was enthusiastic but mentally dull—he made noises that sounded rehearsed. The accountant looked at his watch. The insurance broker wouldn't stop talking. The whole world seems to be a nightmare of indifference, of missed connections.

She raises her legs and observes how the flesh loosens down against her hips. When her legs are raised they are almost lovely— slim calves, after all, and good firm ankles. The thighs are a problem, but when they make love he doesn't notice.

The waltz blares through the room; it sidles along the varnished floor and clasps itself around her shoulders. Her bathrobe slips sideways. She extends her white arm. Runs a hand down her leg and pinches the skin—like a chastising parent, like an eager lover. Vienna and the Grand Ballroom enter her from the top, find the way to her hands. Her tiara glistens, spins points of light. She speaks softly to her partner: Oh, a marvelous time, of course I am beautiful. Her nipples are Renaissance spires. ONE-two-three she forgets him. The sun is on her legs. Her fingers believe they could waltz along forever.

𝄐 𝄐 𝄐

MONSTERFEST

fiction by "H. BUSTOS DOMECQ"

from FICTION

nominated by Joyce Carol Oates

editor's note: 'H. Bustos Domecq" is a pseudonym for the team of Jorge Luis Borges and Adolfo Bioy Casares. Written in local slang, the story is a parody of Argentina's political life during World War II—at the time of Peron's first government—when corruption, brutality and anti-Semitism were rampant. After years of underground circulation in Argentina, the story first appeared in the Uruguayan weekly *Marchá* in 1955.

> *Here begins your sorrow.*
> —Hilario Ascasubi, *The Blood Bath**

I'M TELLING YOU, Nelly, it was a regular civic demonstration. Me with my flat feet trouble and with my breath that gets blocked in my short little neck and with my hippo tummy, I had a real opponent in fatigue, specially when you think that the night before I thought I'd hit the sack early, I mean, who wants to look like a jerk on your day off with a big show coming up, you know? This here was my plan: show up in person at the committee at eight-thirty, at nine hit the sack like a sponge, and with the Colt under my pillow, take off on the Big Sleep of the Century, and be up and at 'em with the first cockadoo-dledo, when the guys in the truck would come pick me up. But tell me something, don't you think luck is like the lottery, and that somebody else is always winning? On the little plank bridge there that leads to the sidewalk I almost took a swimming lesson in the water flooding there 'cause of the surprise of running into my buddy Milk Tooth, one of those guys you meet once in a while. Soon as I saw his expense-account face, I knew he was going to the committee too, and just in the way of getting a view of the latest developments, we got to talkin' about the distribution of heaters for the great parade and about a Jew, who no questions asked, would take 'em for scrap iron over in Berazategui. While we got on line we struggled to tell each other in Pig Latin how once we got hold of the firearms we'd get 'em over to Berazategui, even if we had to carry each other pig-gyback, and there, after we pumped a little pasta into the guts, paid for with the weapon money, we'd buy—to the surprise of the ticket seller guy—two tickets back to Tolosa! But we might ay well have been talkin' French, 'cause Milk Tooth didn't catch any of it, me neither, and the fellows on line lent their services as interpreters, they almost busted my eardrums, and they passed us the ball-point to jot down the Jew's address. A lucky thing Mr. Marforio, who's skinnier than the slot you put the nickel in, is one of them old-timers that while you think he's just a pile of dandruff, he's really in touch with the inside feelings of the masses themselves, so you shouldn't be surprised that he stopped the whole shebang there, putting off the handouts till the big day, with the excuse that there was a delay in the Police Department about giving out the guns. We'd been standing on that there line for an hour and a half, something I wouldn't even do for cooking gas, when from Mr. Pizzurno's very mouth we heard the order to get out of there on the double, which we did cheerin', so full of spirit that even the cripple who works as doorman for the committee couldn't break it up with his raving brooms.

At a safe distance the gang got together again. Loiácomo started talkin', man, worse than the radio of the lady down the hall. The thing about these fatheads with the big mouths is that they get you going and then the guy they get going—the undersigned, follow?—don't know what's hit him, and they got you playing blackjack in Bernardez's store, and maybe you figured I was having a

Translators' note: *Hilario Ascasubi, Le Refalosa: a poem by the nineteenth-century poet Ascasubi, is a dramatic monologue spoken by one of the torturers working for Argentina's nineteenth-century dictator Rosas. Directed toward the poet himself, it describes the ritual awaiting him: "la refalosa," in which the tortured men with their throats cut slip in their own blood.*

good time but the sad truth is that they skinned me out of my last token, without even saying thanks for the memories.

(Take it easy, Nelly, now that the switchman's finished eatin' you up with his peepers and he's takin' off on the dray like a big jerk, let your little ol' Donald Duck give you another pinch on the cheek.)

When I finally crawled into the sack, my feets were giving off such tired signals that I knew right away that restful sleep was mine for the taking. What I didn't figure on was that member of the opposing team, healthy patriotism. All I could think of was the Monster and that the next day I would see him smilin' and talkin' like the great Argentine worker he is. I swear I got so worked up that I threw off the covers so I could breathe, just like a baby whale. Just about the time the dogcatcher comes around I got to sleep, what turned out to be as exhausting as not sleeping, 'cause I dreamt first about an afternoon when I was a kid, when my dear departed mother took me to a farm. Believe me, Nelly, I hadn't never thought about that afternoon, but in the dream I realized it was the happiest in my life, and all I really remember is some water with leaves shining in it and a very white and very gentle dog who I patted on the back; luckily I got out of that kid stuff and dreamt about more modern things, stuff on the big agenda: the Monster made me his mascot and, later, his Great High Priest Dog. I woke up and it'd taken five minutes to dream all that crazy stuff. I decided to turn over a new leaf: I gave myself a rub-down with the kitchen rag, I stuck my corns into my Buster Browns, I got all tangled like a squid in the sleeves and legs of my suit—my trusty overalls—I put on the wool tie with the cartoon characters you gave me the day of the other demonstration, and I went out sweatin' grease 'cause some big car came down the street and I thought it was the truck. With every false alarm what could of been a truck or not I popped out like a cork, trottin' like in gym class, covering the sixty yards from the third courtyard to the street entrance. With youthful enthusiasm I sang the march song which is our flag, but at ten of twelve I lost my voice and the millionaires from the first courtyard stopped throwing everything they had at me. At one-twenty the truck came, early, and when the comrades of the crusade were happy to see me, and I didn't even eat the bread the cleanup lady leaves for the parrot, they all voted to leave me, with the excuse that they were riding on a meat truck and not on a crane. I played along and hung on and they told me if I promised not to have a baby before we got to Ezpeleta they would carry me like a sack, but finally they gave in and sorta helped me up. The truck of the country's youth took off like a mad swallow and before it went half a block it stopped in front of the Committee. A gray-haired Indian came out,and it was a pleasure how he bossed us around, and before they could give us the complaints book, we was already sweatin' in the clink, like we had necks like grated cheese. A heater per head in alphabetical order was the way it was; meditate on that, Nelly; for every revolver there was one of us. Without even a time limit enough for us to line up outside the GENTLEMEN, or even to try to sell off a pistol in good shape, the Indian put us back into the truck which we couldn't escape without a letter of recommendation for the truckdriver.

Just sittin' there waitin' for the command, "Forward, march!" they had us standin' in the sun for an hour and a half, in plain sight of our beloved Tolosa, and as soon as the police went after them, the kids had us in slingshot range, as if what they appreciated most in us wasn't our selfless patriotism but our bein' blackbirds for the pie. When half of the first hour passed there prevailed in the truck that tension on which all social gatherings is based, but later the gang put me in a good mood when they asked me if I had signed up for the Queen Victoria Prize,* you know, an indirect way of referring to this base drum here in front, you know, they always say it ought to be made out of glass so that I could see, even if it was only the toes, of my size fourteens. I was so hoarse that it looked like I had a muzzle on, but in an hour or so I got back my silver tongue[1] a little, and shoulder to shoulder with the comrades in the breech, I didn't want to hold back my participation in a stereophonic singin' of the Monster's march, and I tried till I sorta croaked, somethin', honest, like a hiccup, that if I didn't open the umbrella I left home I'd have been like in a canoe with all the spit flying around, you'd have took me for Vito Dumas, the Solitary Sailor. Finally we got goin' and then the air started to flow, it was like takin' a bath in a soup pot, and there was a guy eatin' a sausage sandwich, there was somebody else with a salami, another guy with a loaf of bread, another guy with a half a

*Translators' note: Popular belief in Argentina: a prize for the first man to give birth.
1. While we was recuperating our energies with the help of some buns, Nelly told me[2] the poor sap stuck out the aforementioned tongue. (Note supplied by Young Rabasco.)
    2. She told me first. (Supplemental note by Nano Buttafuoco, Sanitation Dept.)

bottle of chocolate milk, and a guy in back with an eggplant parme-
gian', but maybe I'm thinkin' of another time when we went out to
the Ensenada, but since I didn't go I'm better off not talkin'. I
couldn't stop thinkin' about the fact that all those modern healthy
boys thought everything just like me, 'cause even the laziest has to
hear the official radio announcements 'cause that's all you can hear
even if you don't want to. We were all Argentines, all young, all from
the Southside and we were all rushin' to meet our twin brothers,
who, in the same kind of trucks, was comin' from Fiorito and Villa
Dominico, from Ciudadela, from Villa Luro, from La Paternal, but
over in Villa Crespo there's too many Jews and I say it would be
better for us to say we live in North Tolosa.

What team spirit you missed, Nelly! In every run-down
neighborhood a real avalanche, excited with the purest idealism,
wanted to come along, but the *capo* of our truckload, Garfunkel,
knew how to get rid of the miserable bunch of bastards, specially
when you think that in all those bums there could hide a fifth column
just like that, guys who could convince you before you go around the
world in eighty days that you're a certified jerk and that the Monster
is a tool of the Telephone Company. I wouldn't tell you too much
about more than one chicken who tried to take advantage of those
purges to slip away in the confusionism and get home just like that;
but admit it, some guys got it, some guys don't, 'cause when I've
tried to slip out of the truck it was a kick from Mister Garfunkel that
restored me to the bosom of those valiant heroes. At the beginning
we was received with an enthusiasm that was frankly contagious, but
Mister Garfunkel, who don't use his head just to hold up his hat,
forbid the driver to slow down so that no wise guy would try to bug
out. Another end of the stick was handed to us in Quilmes, where
the jerks got permission to flatten out their calluses, but at that
distance from home, who was goin' to leave the group? Till that very
second, as Zoppi or his mother is my witness, everything went like a
charm, but nervousness spread over the gang when the boss, Garfunkel to you, set us to shaking like jello when he ordered us to write
the Monster's name on all the walls and to jump back on the truck as
fast as a dose of castor oil before somebody took a swing at us. When
the moment of truth arrived, I grabbed my heater and got out, ready
for anything. Nelly, even for sellin' it for three bucks. But not even
one customer stuck his nose out so I had some fun scribblin' some

letters on a wall, and if I'd have spent another minute there, the truck would have gone around a corner and the horizon would have swallowed it up on the way to civic pride, togetherness, brotherhood, the Monsterfest. The truck was set for togetherness when I got back sweatin' like a pig with my tongue hanging out. They had on the brakes and the truck looked like the picture of a truck. Thank God that guy Tabacman, the guy who talks through his nose, the guy they call the Endless Screw, was with us, 'cause he's an ace with engines and after a half hour looking into the engine and drinkin' all the soda in my camel stomach, that's the nickname I gave to my canteen, he stood up and said, "Beats me," 'cause Ford turned out to be a mystery name for him.

I think I read on a wall somewhere that we should always look for the silver lining, 'cause just then Our Father presented us with a bike left in a vegetable garden, and it looked to me like the owner was gone for a new tire 'cause he didn't show his nostrils when Garfunkel himself hit the seat with his rear end. Then he took off like he smelled a whole block of sausages, like as if Zoppi or his mother shoved a firecracker up his ass. Not a few guys had to loosen their belts from laughin' so hard seeing the guy peddle like that, but after keepin' up with him for four blocks they lost sight of him, 'cause your pedestrian even if he's got Keds on his hands can't keep the victor's laurel when he's up against Mr. Bicycle. The enthusiasm of conscience on the march, in less time than it takes you, pudgy, to gobble up everythin' in front of you, made that guy disappear into the horizon, home to Tolosa, to hit the sack, the way it looked to me.

Now your little Porky's goin' to get confidential, Nelly: he was goin' like mad, runnin' from the Great God Fear, but like I always say whenever a fighter looks like he's sinkin' and the bleakest predictions pile up, suddenly the centerforward kicks a good one and makes a goal: that's the way the Monster does it for the Fatherland; and for our bunch that was scatterin' around, the truckdriver. That patriot, I take my hat off to him, took off like a shot and stopped the one who got farthest, right in his tracks. He slipped him a message so that the next day, 'cause of the bruises, everybody took me for the bread man's pinto horse. From down on the ground I gave such loud cheers that the locals had to stick their fingers in their ears. Meantime the truckdriver put us patriots in Indian file and if anybody

tried to get away the guy behind had carte blanche to ascribe him a
kick in the backside so that it still hurts me to sit down. Figure it out,
Nelly, what luck the last guy had, with nobody takin' shots at his rear
guard! It was—you guessed it—the truckdriver who drove us like a
bunch of flatfooted recruits to a place that I wouldn't hesitate to
characterize as the vicinity of Don Bosco, I mean, the Wilde. There,
chance put into our hands a bus headin' for Black Lady's Rest, as if
made to order. The truckdriver, who had the bus driver's number—
they both, in the heroic days of the Villa Dominico People's Zoo,
worked as halfs of the same camel—asked that Catalonian guy to
take us down. Before you could say go! to Gofreddo, we was already
added to the passenger list, laughin' till we showed our tonsils at the
impotent jerks waitin' on line that didn't get into the vehicle, bein'
left you might say, with a clear pat to go back, with no ill-feelin', to
Tolosa. I exaggerate, Nelly, that we was like in a bus, why we was
sweatin' like a can of sardines, that if you took a good look, the
LADIES over in Berazategui would've looked small. What stories of
mediocre interest ran around! And I don't have to say nothin' about
the beauty broadcast by Potasman the wop, right by Sarandí, and
right now I'd applaud the Endless Screw with my four hands 'cause
he was right in there winnin' his metal for bein' a comedian by
makin' me, after threatening me with a shot in the nuts, open my
mouth and close my eyes: a joke where he took advantage by
immediately stuffing my mouth with dust balls and other stuff from
the seats. But even suckers get tired and when we didn't know what
to do any more, a guy slipped me his penknife and we all used it to
make the seat covers look like strainers. To throw suspicion off us, we
all laughed at me; and later, sure enough, there was one of those wise
guys who jumps like a flea and ends up stuck in the asphalt, tryin' to
get out of the bus before the driver spots the damage. The first to hit
the ground was Simon Tabacman, who landed right on his ass; right
after, Noodles Zoppi or his mother; finally, even if you split open in
anger, Rabasco; then Spatola; *doppo*, Speciale the Basque. Meantime, Morpurgo got down and got papers and paper bags together,
obsessed with the idea of startin' a true-blue bonfire that would burn
up the Brockway bus with the intention of drawin' attention away
from the marks left by the penknife. Pirosanto, that nasal, mother-
less punk who has more matches than dirt in his pockets, took off on
the first turn so he wouldn't have to loan me a Luckie, almost tippin'

a hand, but at the same time with a Kool he grabbed out of my mouth. Me, without tryin' to show off, but tryin' to show a little style, was just about pullin' my mouth into shape for the first drag when Pirosanto, with a grab, kidnapped the cigarette and Morpurgo, as if he was sweetening the medicine, grabbed the match that was toasting my warts and set fire to the papers. Without even taking off his skimmer, lid, or hat, Morpurgo hit the street, but me, pot and all, beat him out and jumped first, so I was set up as a mattress for him, so I broke his fall and he almost broke the bottom out of my gut with his two hundred pounds. Jeez, when I pulled Manolo M. Morpurgo's boots, which was up to his knees, out of my mouth, the bus was burnin' in the distance, like Rome itself, and the guard-ticket-taker-owner was cryin' like mad about his investment turnin' to black smoke before his very eyes. The guys, tougher than him, was laughin', but we was still ready, I swear by the Monster, to run if the guy got really mad. Screw, the economy-sized joker, thought up a joke that while you're listening there with your mouth open you'll turn to jello from laughin'. Listen, Nelly. Clean out your ears 'cause here it comes. You said—but don't get distracted by that asshole over there you're makin' eyes at—that the bus was burnin' like Rome. Ha ha ha.

I was as cool as a cucumber, but turnin' yellow inside. You, who should be engraving every word that drops from between my teeth in your brain, maybe you remember the truckdriver who was half a camel with the bus guy. If you get me, we figured that he would get together with that crybaby and punish us for our bad conduct. But don't worry about your little bunny; the truckdriver took it all calmly and figured out that the other guy, without his bus, wasn't no oligarch you had to worry about no more. He smiled like the good-hearted slob he is; just to maintain discipline he nudged a couple of guys in a friendly way (here's the tooth he knocked out that I bought off him later for a souvenir) and then: Close ranks! Double time, march!

What a thing togetherness is! The proud column was advancin' through the backed-up sewers or the piles of garbage that mark the entrance to the capital, with no defections except maybe a third of us guys that started out from Tolosa. At least one incorrigible dared, with the approval of the truckdriver, to start to light up a Kent. What

a picture to color in: Spatola carried the colors, wearin' his T-shirt*
over his wool clothes; Screw and the rest followed him in ranks
of four.

It was probably around seven when we finally got to Mitre Avenue.
Morpurgo laughed like hell to think that we was already at Avel-
laneda. The playboys laughed too, almost fallin' off the balconies, out
of cars and open buses, they all laughed to see us on foot with no cars.
Luckily, Babuglia thinks of everything, and on the other side of the
Riachuelo some trucks was rustin' away, Canadian trucks that the
Institute, always on the alert, got as puzzles from the Demolition
Section of the American Army. Like monkies we scrambled up into
the khaki-colored one, and harmonizing, "Farewell, for I depart
weeping," we waited till a loon from the Autonomous Unit, super-
vised by Endless Screw, got goin' on installin' the engine. Lucky that
Rabasco, despite the backside face he got, made a deal with a guard
from the Monopoly, and after payin' for the tickets we filled up a
trolley that made more noise than a bagpipe. The trolley headed
bangity-bang downtown; it went along proud as a young mother that
under the eyes of Granpa carries in her tummy the modern generations that tomorrow will claim their place in the snack bars of life.
. . . In its bosom, with one ankle in a stirrup and the other with no
legal residence, went your dear clown, me. An innocent bystander
would've said that the trolley was singin'; it cut through the air,
pushed on by song; we were the singers. Just before Belgrano Street
the speed stopped dead after twenty-four minutes: I sweated to
understand and also because of the crowd, like ants of more and
more cars, that didn't let our means of locomotion take a single step.
    The truckdriver shrieked out the word, "Out, you bums!" and·
then we got out at the intersection of Tacuari and Belgrano. After two
or three blocks on foot, a question came out in the open: our throats
was dry and demanded liquids. The Puga and Gallach Emporium
and Dispensary of Beverages presented a means to resolve the
problem. But now tell me, bright boy: How was we goin' to pay? At
that junction the truckdriver came up with a plan. With the sense
and patience of a bulldog, which ended up seein' things the other
way, he tripped me up in front of the amused gang, then he stuck a

---

*Translators' note: Sacarse el saco—to take off one's coat—was a ritual act of humiliation
forced on professional groups to make them show their solidarity with the proletariat, known in
Peron's Argentina as descamisados—men in shirt sleeves.

screen over my head like a hat down to my nose, and out of my vest
spilled the dough I had, so I wouldn't look so bad when the hot-dog
stand came around. The purse went into the common fund and the
truckdriver, havin' taken care of me, switched to Souza, who's the
right-hand man of Gouvea, from Caravel Caramels—you know, the
guys that set themselves up as the Technical Tapioca Corporation.
Souza, who lives for Caramels, is paymaster over there, and it's for
sure that he's put into circulation so many bills—of up to fifty
cents—that not even Crazy Calcamonia had seen so many, and he'd
been pulled in for doctorin' up the first bank note he'd ever seen.
Souza's, natch, weren't fakes, and they paid in cold cash for our
consumption of Virginia Dare, and we went out like you do when the
jug's dry. Bo, when he's got the guitar, thinks he's Gardel.[1] He even
thinks he's Gotuso.[1] He even thinks he's Garofalo.[1] He even thinks
he's Giganti-Tomassoni.[1] There was no guitar in the joint, but Bo gave
out with "Farewell My Beloved Pampa," and we all sang the chorus
and the juvenile column was like a single shout. Each guy, in spite of
his youth, sang what his body told him to, till we was distracted by a
kike that came by lookin' so respectable with his beard. We let that
one off with his life, but a smaller one, easier to handle, more
practical, handier, didn't get off so easy. He was a miserable four-
eyes, without the muscles of an athlete. He had red hair, books
under his arms, the studious type. He barely noticed, he was so
distracted that he almost knocked over our color guard, Spatola.
Bonfirraro, who's a bug for details, said he wasn't goin' to let go
unpunished such irreverence for the banner and the picture of the
Monster. Right then and there he signaled to Ten-Ton Baby, whose
name is Cagnazzo, to go ahead. Ten Ton, always the same kidder, let
go of my ears, which he'd rolled up like peanut shells and, just to be
nice to Bonfirraro, told the Jew to show a little more respect for the
picture of the Monster. The guy answered with some nonsense
about havin' his own ideas. Baby, who gets bored with explanations,
shoved him with a hand that if the butcher sees it, the shortage of
steak is over. He pushed him into a vacant lot, the kind that one of
these days'll get turned into a parking lot, and backs the guy up
against a nine-story wall without windows. Meantime, the guys in
the back was pushin' us out of curiosity to see, and the guys in the
front ended up like a salami sandwich, between the nuts who wanted

[1] The most popular singer of that season.

a panoramic view and the jerks who was surrounded, who, God knows why, was gettin' mad. Ten Tons, aware of the danger, backpedaled, and we opened up like a fan making a semicircle, but with no exit, 'cause we was all along the wall. We was yellin' like the bears' cage and our teeth was chattering, but the truckdriver, who never missed a single hair in his soup, figured that more or less than one of us had in mind a plan for escape. Everybody was whistlin, then he set us up on a pile of rubble, which was there for anyone to see. You remember that that afternoon the thermometer hit soup temperature, and you're not goin' to argue that a percentage of us took off our coats.* We made the Saulino kid our coat guard, so he couldn't take part in the stonin'. The first shot got him right in the head—Tabacman—and it split his gums, and the blood was a black stream. I got hot 'cause of the blood and I hit him with a chunk that smashed his ear and then I lost count of the hits, 'cause the bombardment was massive. It was a riot; the Jew went down on his knees and looked at the sky and prayed in his broken speech like he wasn't there. When the bells of Monsterrat rang, he fell down, 'cause he was dead. We kept it up a little more with shots that didn't hurt him any more. I swear, Nelly, we left the body in a hell of a mess. Then Morpurgo, to make the guys laugh, made me stick the penknife in what used to be his face.

After exercisin', what gets you warmed up, I put on my jacket again, a move to keep me from catchin' cold, that could cost you a fortune in aspirins. Then I tied the scarf that you embroidered with your fairy fingers around my neck and accommodated my ears under my homburg, but the great surprise of the day came from Pirosanto, with the idea of settin' fire to our bleedin' rock pile, after auctioning off his eyeglasses and clothes. The auction wasn't a success. The glasses was covered with the slime from the eyes and the suit was sticky with blood. The books too was a bust, saturated as they was with organic remains. Luck had it that the truckdriver (who turned out to be Graffiacane) managed to salvage a seventeen-jewel Bulova, and Bonfirraro snagged a Fabricant watch that had up to three bucks in it and a snapshot of a lady piano teacher, and that sap Rabasco had to be satisfied with the Bausch glass case and a Plumex fountain pen, not to mention the ring from Poplavsky's old shop.

*See previous translators' note.

Pretty soon, pudgy, that street episode was relegated to oblivion. Banners fluttering, trumpet blasts excitin', the masses all around, great-arino. In the Plaza de Mayo, the great electric shock that signs his name Dr. Marcelo N. Frogman harangued us. He put us in shape for what came after: the words of the Monster. These very ears heard him, pudgy, just like the rest of the country, 'cause the speech was on national broadcast.

—Translated from the Spanish by
Alfred J. MacAdam with
Suzanne Jill Levine and
Emir Rodríguez Monegal

♨ ♨ ♨

THERE IS A DREAM DREAMING US

by NORMAN DUBIE

from PORCH

nominated by PORCH

for Thomas James

> *Every little chamber was one reed long*
> *from the gate to the roof of a chamber*
> *to the roof of another, and door against*
> *door. —found in a jar outside Cairo*

We are seven virgins. Seven lamps.
Each with a different animal skin on our shoulders.
We had crowns made of black mulberry with the pyracantha,
Its white flowers in corymbs spotted with yellow fruit.
On my forehead, in charcoal, is the striking digit
Of an asp, and with all of this we were nearly nude.

The procession to the pyramid began at the pavilion
At the very edge of the thirteen acres that were sacred.
We walked ahead of everyone with our priest,
But we are the last to leave this world for the portico
And the first gallery which is dark and cold.

We stood on the terraced face of the pyramid witnessing
The long entrance of the king's family.
The queen carried a lamb made of papyrus: its eyes
Were rubies. The Queen's brother was dressed

In little rattles made of clay.
Even the King's nursery followed him with two slaves
To the Chamber where we would all stay.

The sun no longer touched us on the plateau. It was lost
Making the sand dunes beyond the cataract rise and fall
Like water rushing toward us.
The glass doll was smashed above the portico,
And the doors began to close! We were inside the galleries
Of sun and flour and our seven lamps guided us
To the underground chamber. We could no longer hear
The drums leaving the inner acre.
I am the initial lamp and so I broke the last bottles

And from the bottles sand poured:
This last gate had two flanking chambers full with sand
And on the sand was the weight of marble columns,
Columns that joined the limestone slab that was
The last seal lowering now as the sand spills
Into two fern boxes on the floor.

The children had all been smothered and washed in oils,
All of the family is poisoned.
They sprawl around the sarcophagus which is open.
The priest has stabbed my six companions—it is
A noise like a farmer testing river soil.
I'm to drain the cup of wine that the King's mother
Handed me before dying. I was the *first lamp*, but

This is my story. I spilled the wine down my leg
And pretended to faint away. The priest thinking everyone
Had crossed from his world stopped his prayer. He walked
To the girl with the third lamp.
He kissed my dead sister on the lips. He ripped the silk
From her breasts. And then he fell on her.
Her arms were limp, I imagine even as they would be
If she were alive doing this with him.

The heat must have been leaving her body. He finished
And turned to me: what I saw was the longest

Of the three members of an ankh, all red, and from it
Came a kind of clotted milk.
But his strength was leaving him visibly; he put his
Dagger in his neck and bled down his sleeve.
I don't understand. But now

I am alone as I had planned.
I'm a girl who was favored in the market by the King.
I've eaten the grapes that the slaves carried in for him:
If someone breaks into this tomb in a future time how
Will they explain the dead having spit grape seeds
Onto a carpet that was scented with jasmine?
The arrogance of the living never had a better monument

Than in me. I am going to sleep
In a bed that was hammered out of gold for a boy
Who was Pharoah and King of Egypt. My father died free.
My mother died a slave, here, at this site after being
Whipped twice in a morning. In the name of Abraham

I have displaced a King. I picked him up
And put him in the corner, facing in and kneeling.
He would seem to be a punished child.
What he did? I will tell you; you will be told many times again:

He killed four thousand of my people
While they suffered the mystery of this mountain appearing
Where there was nothing but moving sands and wind!

🔥 🔥 🔥

THE BREAKER

by NAOMI CLARK

from BURGLARIES AND CELEBRATIONS (Oyez Press) and
SOUTHWEST: A CONTEMPORARY ANTHOLOGY (Red Earth Press)

nominated by Red Earth Press

Maria we called you:
a Spanish mare, they said, up from Mexico—
born to the saddle, but skittish, liable to panic.
We were not, anymore, the kind of family to keep saddle horses.
Straddled bareback, past dry holes and dry grey slush pits, past the
    mound where
we buried the cows, I'd stolen time from field and chickens
to ride low, nag transformed, under the scrub oak branches,
through darkening johnson grass where puma screamed, out onto
    the Great Staked Plains.
You sold cheaper than a nag,
kicked out the end of the trailer, the gate off the horselot.
All night I heard you circling the barbed wire, stamping.
All night I rode through the sky.
You were a small, dark mare, Spanish, bought for a plowhorse.

> I remember you in chains, Maria, the day he broke you to
>   plow-harness.
> Tied to a post, you drag the heavy iron beam, the heavy log
>   chains,
> twist and kick, whipped, driven round
> and round. Foam flies, and blood, with the broken har-
>   ness,
> with the tangled harness, the slipped chains. Your eyes
>   turn white.
> Only when you both fall does it end. Next day
> you plow ten rows before it starts.

You come to me now, Maria,
in so many dreams: your mad eyes,
your flinches, your broken stance, the slouch in the heavy harness,
your bowed head blindered, the break into frenzy.
My hands burn to heal you, to gentle you, to gentle your eyes.
Maria, you lift strong black wings,
rise free over the mesquites and the prickly pear, over the Caprock,
over the untrampled high grass of the Llano into the age of
    Comanche, Apache.

    And the man who broke you?

How shall I heal him, how stretch out my hand
in healing, my cold hands in healing
and warmth, how gentle?
O father, how shall I heal you?
What wings from the fire where you burn, and I the breaker?

THE DREAM OF MOURNING

by LOUISE GLÜCK

from SALMAGUNDI

nominated by Carolyn Forché, Karen Kennerly and Joyce Carol Oates

I sleep so you will be alive,
it is that simple.
The dreams themselves are nothing.
They are the sickness you control,
nothing more.

I rush toward you in the summer twilight,
not in the real world, but in the buried one
where you are waiting,
as the wind moves over the bay, toying with it,
forcing thin ridges of panic—

And then the morning comes, demanding prey.
Remember? And the world complies.

Last night was different.
Someone fucked me awake; when I opened my eyes
it was over, all the pain gone
by which I knew my life.
And for one instant I believed I was entering
the stable dark of the earth
and thought it would hold me.

VESUVIUS AT HOME: THE POWER OF EMILY DICKINSON

by ADRIENNE RICH

from PARNASSUS: POETRY IN REVIEW

nominated by PARNASSUS: POETRY IN REVIEW *and June Jordan*

I AM TRAVELLING at the speed of time, along the Massachusetts Turnpike. For months, for years, for most of my life, I have been hovering like an insect against the screens of an existence which inhabited Amherst, Massachusetts, between 1831 and 1884. The methods, the exclusions, of Emily Dickinson's existence could not have been my own; yet more and more, as a woman poet finding my own methods, I have come to understand her necessities, could have been witness in her defense.

"Home is not where the heart is," she wrote in a letter, "but the house and the adjacent buildings." A statement of New England realism, a directive to be followed. Probably no poet ever lived so much and so purposefully in one house; even, in one room. Her niece Martha told of visiting her in her corner bedroom on the second floor at 280 Main Street, Amherst, and of how Emily Dickinson made as if to lock the door with an imaginary key, turned and said: "Matty: here's freedom."

I am travelling at the speed of time, in the direction of the house and buildings.

Western Massachusetts: the Connecticut Valley: a countryside still full of reverberations: scene of Indian uprisings, religious revivals, spiritual confrontations, the blazing-up of the lunatic fringe of the Puritan coal. How peaceful and how threatened it looks from Route 91, hills gently curled above the plain, the tobacco-barns standing in fields sheltered with white gauze from the sun, and the sudden urban sprawl: ARCO, MacDonald's, shopping plazas. The country that broke the heart of Jonathan Edwards, that enclosed the genius of Emily Dickinson. It lies calmly in the light of May, cloudy skies breaking into warm sunshine, light-green spring softening the hills, dogwood and wild fruit-trees blossoming in the hollows.

From Northhampton bypass there's a 4-mile stretch of road to Amherst—Route 9—between fruit farms, steakhouses, supermarkets. The new University of Massachusetts rears its skyscrapers up from the plain against the Pelham Hills. There is new money here, real estate, motels. Amherst succeeds on Hadley almost without notice. Amherst is green, rich-looking, secure; we're suddenly in the center of town, the crossroads of the campus, old New England college buildings spread around two village greens, a scene I remember as almost exactly the same in the dim past of my undergraduate years when I used to come there for college weekends.

Left on Seelye Street, right on Main; driveway at the end of a yellow picket fence. I recognize the high hedge of cedars screening the house, because twenty-five years ago I walked there, even then drawn toward the spot, trying to peer over. I pull into the driveway behind a generous 19th-century brick mansion with wings and porches, old trees and green lawns. I ring at the back door—the door through which Dickinson's coffin was carried to the cemetery a block away.

For years I have been not so much envisioning Emily Dickinson as trying to visit, to enter her mind, through her poems and letters, and through my own intimations of what it could have meant to be one of the two mid-19th-century American geniuses, and a woman,

living in Amherst, Massachusetts. Of the other genius, Walt Whitman, Dickinson wrote that she had heard his poems were "disgrace-
ful." She knew her own were unacceptable by her world's standards
of poetic convention, and of what was appropriate, in particular, for a
woman poet. Seven were published in her lifetime, all edited by
other hands; more than a thousand were laid away in her bedroom
chest, to be discovered after her death. When her sister discovered
them, there were decades of struggle over the manuscripts, the
manner of their presentation to the world, their suitability for publication, the poet's own final intentions. Narrowed-down by her early
editors and anthologists, reduced to quaintness or spinsterish oddity
by many of her commentators, sentimentalized, fallen-in-love with
like some gnomic Garbo, still unread in the breadth and depth of her
full range of work, she was, and is, a wonder to me when I try to
imagine myself into that mind.

I have a notion that genius knows itself; that Dickinson chose her
seclusion, knowing she was exceptional and knowing what she
needed. It was, moreover, no hermetic retreat, but a seclusion
which included a wide range of people, of reading and correspondence. Her sister Vinnie said, "Emily is always looking for the
rewarding person." And she found, at various periods, both women
and men: her sister-in-law Susan Gilbert, Amherst visitors and
family friends such as Benjamin Newton, Charles Wadsworth,
Samuel Bowles, editor of the Springfield *Republican* and his wife;
her friends Kate Anthon and Helen Hunt Jackson, the distant but
significant figures of Elizabeth Barrett, the Brontës, George Eliot.
But she carefully selected her society and controlled the disposal of
her time. Not only the "gentlewoman in plush" of Amherst were
excluded; Emerson visited next door but she did not go to meet him;
she did not travel or receive routine visits; she avoided strangers.
Given her vocation, she was neither eccentric nor quaint; she was
determined to survive, to use her powers, to practice necessary
economies.

Suppose Jonathan Edwards had been born a woman; suppose
William James, for that matter, had been born a woman? (The invalid
seclusion of his sister Alice is suggestive.) Even from men, New
England took its psychic toll; many of its geniuses seemed peculiar
in one way or another, particularly along the lines of social inter-
course. Hawthorne, until he married, took his meals in his bed-

room, apart from the family. Thoreau insisted on the values both of solitude and of geographical restriction, boasting that "I have travelled much in Concord." Emily Dickinson—viewed by her bemused contemporary Thomas Higginson as "partially cracked," by the 20th century as fey or pathological—has increasingly struck me as a practical woman, exercising her gift as she had to, making choices. I have come to imagine her as somehow too strong for her environment, a figure of powerful will, not at all frail or breathless, someone whose personal dimensions would be felt in a household. She was her father's favorite daughter though she professed being afraid of him. Her sister dedicated herself to the everyday domestic labors which would free Dickinson to write. (Dickinson herself baked the bread, made jellies and gingerbread, nursed her mother through a long illness, was a skilled horticulturalist who grew pomegranates, calla-lillies, and other exotica in her New England greenhouse.)

Upstairs at last: I stand in the room which for Emily Dickinson was "freedom." The best bedroom in the house, a corner room, sunny, overlooking the main street of Amherst in front, the way to her brother Austin's house on the side. Here, at a small table with one drawer, she wrote most of her poems. Here she read Elizabeth Barrett's "Aurora Leigh," a woman poet's narrative poem of a woman poet's life; also George Eliot; Emerson; Carlyle; Shakespeare; Charlotte and Emily Brontë. Here I become, again, an insect, vibrating at the frames of windows, clinging to panes of glass, trying to connect. The scent here is very powerful. Here in this white-curtained, high-ceilinged room, a redhaired woman with hazel eyes and a contralto voice wrote poems about volcanoes, deserts, eternity, suicide, physical passion, wild beasts, rape, power, madness, separation, the daemon, the grave. Here, with a darning-needle, she bound these poems—heavily emended and often in variant versions—into booklets, secured with darning-thread, to be found and read after her death. Here she knew "freedom," listening from above-stairs to a visitor's piano-playing, escaping from the pantry where she was mistress of the household bread and puddings, watching, you feel, watching ceaselessly, the life of sober Main Street below. From this room she glided downstairs, her hand on the polished bannister, to meet the complacent magazine editor, Thomas Higginson, unnerve him while claiming she herself was unnerved. "Your scholar," she signed herself in letters to him. But she was an independent scholar, used his criticism selectively, saw him rarely and always on *her* premises. It was a life deliberately organized on her terms. The terms she had been handed by society—Calvinist Protestantism, Romanticism, the 19th-century corseting of women's bodies, choices, and sexuality—could spell insanity to a woman genius. What this one had to do was retranslate into a dialect called metaphor: her native language. "Tell all the Truth—but tell it Slant—." It is always what is under pressure in us, especially under pressure of concealment—that explodes in poetry.

The women and men in her life she equally converted into metaphor. The masculine pronoun in her poems can refer simultaneously to many aspects of the "masculine" in the patriarchal world—the god she engages in dialogue, again on *her* terms; her own creative powers, unsexing for a woman, the male power-figures in her immediate environment—the lawyer Edward Dickinson, her brother Austin, the preacher Wadsworth, the editor Bowles—it is far too limiting to trace that "He" to some specific lover, although that was the chief obsession of the legend-mongers for more than half a century. Obviously, Dickinson was attracted by and interested in men whose minds had something to offer her; she was, it is by now clear, equally attracted by and interested in women whose minds had something to offer her. There are many poems to and about women, and some which exist in two versions with alternate sets of pronouns. Her latest biographer, Richard Sewall, while rejecting an earlier Freudian biographer's theory that Dickinson was essentially a psycho-pathological case, the by-product of which happened to be poetry, does create a context in which the importance, and validity, of Dickinson's attachments to women may now, at last, be seen in full. She was always stirred by the existences of women like George Eliot or Elizabeth Barrett, who possessed strength of mind, articulateness, and energy. (She once characterized Elizabeth Fry and Florence Nightingale as "holy"—one suspects she merely meant, "great.")

But of course Dickinson's relationships with women were more than intellectual. They were deeply charged, and the sources both of passionate joy and pain. We are only beginning to be able to consider them in a social and historical context. The historian Carroll Smith-Rosenberg has shown that there was far less taboo on intense, even passionate and sensual, relationships between women in the American 19th-century "female world of love and ritual," as she terms it, than there was later in the 20th century. Women expressed their attachments to other women both physically and verbally; a marriage did not dilute the strength of a female friendship, in which two women often shared the same bed during long visits, and wrote letters articulate with both physical and emotional longing. The 19th-century close woman friend, according to the many diaries and letters Smith-Rosenberg has studied, might be a far more important figure in a woman's life than the 19th-century husband. None of this was condemned as "lesbianism." We will understand Emily Dickinson better, read her poetry more perceptively, when the Freudian imputation of scandal and aberrance in women's love for women has been supplanted by a more informed, less misogynistic attitude toward women's experiences with each other.

But who, if you read through the seventeen hundred and seventy-five poems—who—woman or man—could have passed through that imagination and not come out transmuted? Given the space created by her in that corner room, with its window-light, its potted plants and work-table, given that personality, capable of imposing its terms on a household, on a whole community, what single theory could hope to contain her, when she'd put it all together in that space?

"Matty: here's freedom," I hear her saying as I speed back to Boston along Route 91, as I slip the turnpike ticket into the toll-collector's hand. I am thinking of a confined space in which the genius of the 19th-century female mind in America moved, inventing a language more varied, more compressed, more dense with implications, more complex of syntax, than any American poetic language to date; in the trail of that genius my mind has been moving, and with its language and images my mind still has to reckon, as the mind of a woman poet in America today.

In 1971, a postage stamp was issued in honor of Dickinson; the portrait derives from the one existing daguerrotype of her, with straight, center-parted hair, eyes staring somewhere beyond the camera, hands poised around a nosegay of flowers, in correct 19th-century style. On the first-day-of-issue envelope sent me by a friend there is, besides the postage stamp, an engraving of the poet as popular fancy has preferred her, in a white lace ruff and with hair as bouffant as if she had just stepped from a Boston beauty-parlor. The poem chosen to represent her work to the American public is engraved, alongside a dew-gemmed rose, below the portrait.

> If I can stop one heart from breaking
> I shall not live in vain
> If I can ease one life the aching
> Or cool one pain
> Or help one fainting robin
> Unto his nest again
> I shall not live in vain.

Now, this is extremely strange. It is a fact, that in 1864, Emily Dickinson wrote this verse; and it is a verse which a hundred or more 19th-century versifiers could have written. It is undistinguished language, as in its conventional sentiment, it is remarkably untypical of the poet. Had she chosen to write many poems like this one we would have no "problem" of non-publication, of editing, of estimating the poet at her true worth. Certainly the sentiment—a contented and unambiguous altruism—is one which even today might in some quarters be accepted as fitting from a female versifier—a kind of Girl Scout prayer. But we are talking about the woman who wrote:

> He fumbles at your Soul
> As Players at the Keys
> Before they drop full Music on—
> He stuns you by degrees—
> Prepares your brittle Nature
> For the Ethereal Blow
> By fainter Hammers—further heard—
> Then nearer—Then so slow
> Your breath has time to straighten—
> Your brain—to bubble Cool—
> Deals—One—Imperial—Thunderbolt—
> Then scalps your naked Soul—
>
> When winds take Forests in their Paws—
> The Universe—is still—

(#315)

Much energy has been invested in trying to identify a concrete, flesh-and-blood male lover whom Dickinson is supposed to have renounced, and to the loss of whom can be traced the secret of her seclusion and the vein of much of her poetry. But the real question, given that the art of poetry is an art of transformation, is how this woman's mind and imagination may have used the masculine element in the world at large, or those elements personified as masculine—including the men she knew; how her relationship to this reveals itself in her images and language. In a patriarchal culture, specifically the Judeo-Christian, quasi-Puritan culture of 19th-century New England in which Dickinson grew up, still inflamed with religious revivals, and where the sermon was still an active, if perishing, literary form, the equation of divinity with maleness was so fundamental that it is hardly surprising to find Dickinson, like many an early mystic, blurring erotic with religious experience and imagery. The poem I just read has intimations both of seduction and rape merged with the intense force of a religious experience. But are these metaphors for each other, or for something more intrinsic to Dickinson? Here is another:

> He put the Belt around my life—
> I heard the buckle snap—
> And turned away, imperial,
> My Lifetime folding up—
> Deliberate, as a Duke would do
> A Kingdom's Title Deed
> Henceforth, a Dedicated sort—
> Member of the Cloud.
>
> Yet not too far to come at call—
> And do the little Toils
> That make the Circuit of the Rest—
> And deal occasional smiles
> To lives that stoop to notice mine—
> And kindly ask it in—
> Whose invitation, know you not
> For Whom I must decline?

> (#273)

These two poems are about possession, and they seem to me a poet's poems—that is, they are about the poet's relationship to her own power, which is exteriorized in masculine form, much as masculine poets have invoked the female Muse. In writing at all—particularly an unorthodox and original poetry like Dickinson's—women have often felt in danger of losing their status as women. And this status has always been defined in terms of relationahips to men—as daughter, sister, bride, wife, mother, mistress, Muse. Since the most powerful figures in patriarchal culture have been men, it seems natural that Dickinson would assign a masculine gender to that in herself which did not fit in with the conventional ideology of womanliness. To recognize and acknowledge our own interior power has always been a path mined with risks for women; to acknowledge that power and commit oneself to it as Emily Dickinson did was an immense decision.

Most of us, unfortunately, have been exposed in the schoolroom to Dickinson's "little-girl" poems, her kittenish tones, as in "I'm Nobody! Who Are You?" (a poem whose underlying anger translates itself into archness) or

> I hope the Father in the skies
> Will lift his little girl—
> Old fashioned—naughty—everything—
> Over the stile of "Pearl."

(#70)

or the poems about bees and robins. One critic—Richard Chase—has noted that in the 19th century "one of the careers open to women was perpetual childhood." A strain in Dickinson's letters and some—though by far a minority—of her poems was a self-diminutization, almost as if to offset and deny—or even disguise—her actual dimensions as she must have experienced them. And this emphasis on her own "littleness," along with the deliberate strangeness of her tactics of seclusion, have been, until recently, accepted as the prevailing character of the poet: the fragile poetess in white, sending flowers and poems by messenger to unseen friends, letting down baskets of gingerbread to the neighborhood children from her bedroom window; writing, but somehow naively. John Crowe Ransom, arguing for the editing and standardization of Dickinson's punctuation and typography, calls her "a little home-keeping person" who, "while she had a proper notion of the final destiny of her poems . . . was not one of those poets who had advanced to that later stage of operations where manuscripts are prepared for the printer, and the poet's diction has to make concessions to the publisher's stylebook." (In short, Emily Dickinson did not wholly know her trade, and Ransom believes a "publisher's style-book" to have the last word on poetic diction.) He goes on to print several of her poems, altered by him "with all possible forbearance." What might, in a male writer—a Thoreau, let us say, or a Christopher Smart or William Blake—seem a legitimate strangeness, a unique intention, has been in one of our two major poets devalued into a kind of naivêté, girlish ignorance, feminine lack of professionalism, just as the poet herself has been made into a sentimental object ("Most of us are half in love with this dead girl," confesses Archibald MacLeish. Dickinson was fifty-five when she died.)

It is true that more recent critics, including her most recent biographer, have gradually begun to approach the poet in terms of her greatness rather than her littleness, the decisiveness of her choices instead of the surface oddities of her life or the romantic crises of her legend. But unfortunately anthologists continue to plagiarize other anthologies, to reprint her in edited, even bowdlerized versions; the popular image of her and of her work lags behind the changing consciousness of scholars and specialists. There still does not exist a selection from her poems which depicts her in her fullest range. Dickinson's greatness cannot be measured in terms of twenty-five or fifty or even 500 "perfect" lyrics, it has to be seen as the accumulation it is. Poets, even, are not always acquainted with the full dimensions of her work, or the sense one gets, reading in the one-volume complete edition (let alone the three-volume variorum edition) of a mind engaged in a lifetime's musing on essential problems of language, identity, separation, relationship, the integrity of the self; a mind capable of describing psychological states more accurately than any poet except Shakespeare. I have been surprised at how narrowly her work, still, is known by women who are writing poetry, how much her legend has gotten in the way of her being re-possessed, as a source and a foremother.

I know that for me, reading her poems as a child and then as a young girl already seriously writing poetry, she was a problematic figure. I first read her in the selection heavily edited by her niece which appeared in 1937; a later and fuller edition appeared in 1945 when I was sixteen, and the complete, unbowdlerized edition by Johnson did not appear until fifteen years later. The publication of each of these editions was crucial to me in successive decades of my life. More than any other poet, Emily Dickinson seemed to tell me that the intense inner event, the personal and psychological, was inseparable from the universal; that there was a range for psychological poetry beyond mere self-expression. Yet the legend of the life was troubling, because it seemed to whisper that a woman who undertook such explorations must pay with renunciation, isolation, and incorporeality. With the publication of the *Complete Poems,* the legend seemed to recede into unimportance beside the unquestionable power and importance of the mind revealed there. But taking possession of Emily Dickinson is still no simple matter.

The 1945 edition, entitled *Bolts of Melody,* took its title from a poem which struck me at the age of sixteen and which still, thirty years later, arrests my imagination:

> I would not paint—a picture—
> I'd rather be the One
> Its bright impossibility
> To dwell—delicious—on—
> And wonder how the fingers feel
> Whose rare—celestial—stir
> Evokes so sweet a Torment—
> Such sumptuous—Despair—
>
> I would not talk, like Cornets—
> I'd rather be the One
> Raised softly to the Ceilings—
> And out, and easy on—
> Through Villages of Ether
> Myself endured Balloon
> By but a lip of Metal
> The pier to my Pontoon—
>
> Nor would I be a Poet—
> It's finer—own the Ear—
> Enamored—impotent—content—

The License to revere,
A privilege so awful
What would the Dower be,
Had I the Art to stun myself
With Bolts of Melody!

(#505)

This poem is about choosing an orthodox "feminine" role: the recep-
tive rather than the creative; viewer rather than painter, listener
rather than musician; acted-upon rather than active. Yet even while
ostensibly choosing this role she wonders "how the fingers feel /
whose rare-celestial—stir— / Evokes so sweet a Torment—" and
the "feminine" role is praised in a curious sequence of adjectives:
"Enamored—*impotent*—content—." The strange paradox of this
poem—its exquisite irony—is that it is about choosing not to be a
poet, a poem which is gainsaid by no fewer than one thousand seven
hundred and seventy-five poems made during the writer's life,
including itself. Moreover, the images of the poem rise to a climax
(like the Balloon she evokes) but the climax happens as she describes, not what it is to be the receiver, but the maker and receiver
at once: "A Privilege so awful / What would the Dower be / Had I the
Art to stun myself / With Bolts of Melody!" —a climax which recalls
the poem: "He fumbles at your soul / As Players at the Keys / Before
they drop full Music on—" And of course, in writing those lines she
possess herself of that privilege and that "dower." I have said that
this is a poem of exquisite ironies. It is, indeed, though in a very
different mode, related to Dickinson's "little-girl" strategy. The
woman who feels herself to be Vesuvius at home has need of a mask,
at least, of innocuousness and of containment.

On my volcano grows the Grass
A meditative spot—
An acre for a Bird to choose
Would be the General thought—

How red the Fire rocks below—
How insecure the sod
Did I disclose
Would populate with awe my solitude.

(#1677)

Power, even masked, can still be perceived as destructive.

> A still—Volcano—Life—
> That flickered in the night—
> When it was dark enough to do
> Without erasing sight—
>
> A quiet—Earthquake style—
> Too subtle to suspect
> By natures this side Naples—
> The North cannot detect
>
> The Solemn—Torrid—Symbol—
> The lips that never lie—
> Whose hissing Corals part—and shut—
> And Cities—ooze away—
>
> (#601)

Dickinson's biographer and editor Thomas Johnson has said that she often felt herself possessed by a demonic force, particularly in the years 1861 and 1862 when she was writing at the height of her drive. There are many poems besides "He put the Belt around my Life" which could be read as poems of possession by the daemon— poems which can also be, and have been, read, as poems of possession by the deity, or by a human lover. I suggest that a woman's poetry about her relationship to her daemon—her own active, creative power—has in patriarchal culture used the language of heterosexual love or patriarchal theology. Ted Hughes tells us that

> the eruption of (Dickinson's) imagination and poetry followed when she shifted her passion, with the energy of desperation, from (the) lost man onto his only possible substitute,—the Universe in its Divine aspect . . . Thereafter, the marriage that had been denied in the real world, went forward in the spiritual . . . just as the Universe in its Divine aspect became the mirror-image of her "husband," so the whole religious dilemma of New England, at that most critical moment in its history, became the mirror-image of her relationship to him, of her "marriage" in fact.*

*A Choice of Emily Dickinson's Verse, p. 11.

This seems to me to miss the point on a grand scale. There are facts we need to look at. First, Emily Dickinson did not marry. And her non-marrying was neither a pathological retreat as John Cody sees it, nor probably even a conscious decision; it was a fact in her life as in her contemporary Christina Rossetti's; both women had more primary needs. Second: unlike Rossetti, Dickinson did not become a religiously dedicated woman; she was heretical, heterodox, in her religious opinions, and stayed away from church and dogma. What, in fact, *did* she allow to "put the Belt around her Life"—what *did* wholly occupy her mature years and possess her? For "Whom" did she decline the invitations of other lives? The writing of poetry. Nearly two thousand poems. Three hundred and sixty-six poems in the year of her fullest power. What was it like to be writing poetry you knew (and I am sure she did know) was of a class by itself—to be fuelled by the energy it took first to confront, then to condense that range of psychic experience into that language; then to copy out the poems and lay them in a trunk, or send a few here and there to friends or relatives as occasional verse or as gestures of confidence? I am sure she knew who she was, as she indicates in this poem:

> Myself was formed—a carpenter—
> An unpretending time
> My Plane—and I, together wrought
> Before a Builder came—
>
> To measure our attainments
> Had we the Art of Boards
> Sufficiently developed—He'd hire us
> At Halves—
>
> My Tools took Human—Faces—
> The Bench, where we had toiled—
> Against the Man—persuaded—
> We—Temples Build—I said—

> (#488)

This is a poem of the great year 1862, the year in which she first sent a few poems to Thomas Higginson for criticism. Whether it ante-dates or postdates that occasion is unimportant; it is a poem of

knowing one's measure, regardless of the judgments of others.
    There are many poems which carry the weight of this knowledge.
Here is another one:

> I'm ceded—I've stopped being Theirs—
> The name They dropped upon my face
> With water, in the country church
> Is finished using, now,
> And They can put it with my dolls,
> My childhood, and the string of spools,
> I've finished threading—too—
>
> Baptized before, without the choice,
> But this time, consciously, of Grace—
> Unto supremest name—
> Called to my Fill—the Crescent dropped—
> Existence's whole Arc, filled up
> With one small Diadem.
>
> My second Rank—too small the first—
> Crowned—Crowing—on my Father's breast—
> A half unconscious Queen—
> But this time—Adequate—Erect—
> With Will to choose—or to reject—
> And I choose—just a Crown—

(#508)

Now, this poem partakes of the imagery of being "twice-born" or, in
Christian liturgy, "confirmed"—and if this poem had been written
by Christina Rossetti I would be inclined to give more weight to a
theological reading. But it was written by Emily Dickinson, who
used the Christian metaphor far more than she let it use her. This is a
poem of great pride—not pridefulness, but *self*-confirmation—and
it is curious how little Dickinson's critics, perhaps misled by her
diminutives, have recognized the will and pride in her poetry. It is a
poem of movement from childhood to womanhood, of transcending
the patriarchal condition of bearing her father's name and "crowing
—on my Father's breast—." She is now a conscious Queen,
"Adequate—Erect/ With Will to choose, or to reject—."

There is one poem which is the real "onlie begetter" of my
thoughts here about Dickinson; a poem I have mused over, repeated
to myself, taken into myself over many years. I think it is a poem
about possession by the daemon, about the dangers and risks of such
possession if you are a woman, about the knowledge that power in a
woman can seem destructive, and that you cannot live without the
daemon once it has possessed you. The archetype of the daemon as
masculine is beginning to change, but it has been real for women up
until now. But this woman poet also perceives herself as a lethal
weapon:

> My life had stood—a Loaded Gun—
> In Corners—till a Day
> The Owner passed—identified—
> And carried me away—
>
> And now We roam in Sovereign Woods—
> And now We hunt the Doe—
> And every time I speak for Him—
> The Mountains straight reply—
>
> And do I smile, such cordial light
> Upon the Valley glow—
> It is as a Vesuvian face
> Had let its pleasure through—
>
> And when at Night—our good Day done—
> I guard My Master's Head—
> 'Tis better than the Eider-Duck's
> Deep Pillow—to have shared—
>
> To foe of His—I'm deadly foe—
> None stir the second time—
> On whom I lay a Yellow Eye—
> Or an emphatic Thumb—
>
> Though I than he—may longer live
> He longer must—than I—
> For I have but the power to kill,
> Without—the power to die—

(#754)

Here the poet sees herself as split, not between anything so simple as "masculine" and "feminine" identity but between the hunter, admittedly masculine, but also a human person, an active, willing being, and the gun—an object, condemned to remain inactive until the hunter—the *owner*—takes possession of it. The gun contains an energy capable of rousing echoes in the mountains and lighting up the valleys; it is also deadly, "Vesuvian;" it is also its owner's defender against the "foe." It is the gun, furthermore, who *speaks for him*. If there is a female consciousness in this poem it is buried deeper than the images: it exists in the ambivalence toward power, which is extreme. Active willing and creation in women are forms of aggression, and aggression is both "the power to kill" and punishable by death. The union of gun with hunter embodies the danger of identifying and taking hold of her forces, not least that in so doing she risks defining herself—and being defined—as aggressive, as unwomanly, ("and now we hunt the Doe") and as potentially lethal. That which she experiences in herself as energy and potency can also be experienced as pure destruction. The final stanza, with its precarious balance of phrasing, seems a desperate attempt to resolve the ambivalence; but, I think, it is no resolution, only a further extension of ambivalence.

> Though I than he—may longer live
> He longer must—than I—
> For I have but the power to kill,
> Without—the power to die—

The poet experiences herself as loaded gun, imperious energy; yet without the Owner, the possessor, she is merely lethal. Should that possession abandon her—but the thought is unthinkable: "He longer *must* than I." The pronoun is masculine; the antecedent is what Keats called "The Genius of Poetry."

I do not pretend to have—I don't even wish to have—explained this poem, accounted for its every image; it will reverberate with new tones long after my words about it have ceased to matter. But I think that for us, at this time, it is a central poem in understanding Emily Dickinson, and ourselves, and the condition of the woman artist, particularly in the 19th century. It seems likely that the 19th-century woman poet, especially, felt the medium of poetry as dangerous, in ways that the woman novelist did not feel the medium

of fiction to be. In writing even such a novel of elemental sexuality
and anger as *Wuthering Heights*, Emily Bronte could at least
theoretically separate herself from her characters; they were, after
all, fictitious beings. Moreover, the novel is or can be a construct,
planned and organized to deal with human experiences on one level
at a time. Poetry is too much rooted in the unconscious; it presses too
close against the barriers of repression; and the 19th-century woman
had much to repress. It is interesting that Elizabeth Barrett tried to
fuse poetry and fiction in writing "Aurora Leigh"—perhaps apprehending the need for fictional characters to carry the charge of
her experience as a woman artist. But with the exception of "Aurora
Leigh" and Christina Rossetti's "Goblin Market"—that extraordinary and little-known poem drenched in oral eroticism—Emily
Dickinson's is the only poetry in English by a woman of that century
which pierces so far beyond the ideology of the "feminine" and the
conventions of womanly feeling. To write it at all, she had to be
willing to enter chambers of self in which

> Ourself behind ourself, concealed—
> Sould startle most—

and to relinquish control there, to take those risks, she had to create
a relationship to the outer world where she could feel in control.

It is an extremely painful and dangerous way to live—split between a publicly acceptable persona, and a part of yourself that you
perceive as the essential, the creative and powerful self, yet also as
possibly unacceptable, perhaps even monstrous.

> Much Madness is divinest sense—
> To a discerning Eye—
> Much sense—the starkest Madness.
> 'Tis the Majority
> In this, as All, prevail—
> Assent—and you are sane—
> Demur—you're straightway dangerous—
> And handled with a chain—

(#435)

For many women the stresses of this splitting have led, in a world so ready to assert our innate passivity and to deny our independence and creativity, to extreme consequences: the mental asylum, self-imposed silence, recurrent depression, suicide, and often severe loneliness.

Dickinson is *the* American poet whose work consisted in exploring states of psychic extremity. For a long time, as we have seen, this fact was obscured by the kinds of selections made from her work by timid if well-meaning editors. In fact, Dickinson was a great psychologist; and like every great psychologist, she began with the material she had at hand: herself. She had to possess the courage to enter, through language, states which most people deny or veil with silence.

> The first Day's Night had come—
> And grateful that a thing
> So terrible—had been endured—
> I told my soul to sing—
>
> She said her Strings were snapt—
> Her Bow—to Atoms blown—
> And so to mend her—gave me work
> Until another Morn—
>
> And then—a Day as huge
> As Yesterdays in pairs,
> Unrolled its horror in my face—
> Until it blocked my eyes—
>
> My Brain—begun to laugh—
> I mumbled—like a fool—
> And tho' 'tis years ago—that Day—
> My brain keeps giggling—still.
>
> And Something's odd—within—
> That person that I was—
> And this One—do not feel the same—
> Could it be Madness—this?

(#410)

Dickinson's letters acknowledge a period of peculiarly intense personal crisis; her biographers have variously ascribed it to the pangs of renunciation of an impossible love, or to psychic damage deriving from her mother's presumed depression and withdrawal after her birth. What concerns us here is the fact that she chose to probe the nature of this experience in language:

> The Soul has Bandaged moments—
> When too appalled to stir—
> She feels some ghastly Fright come up
> And stop to look at her—
>
> Salute her—with long fingers—
> Caress her freezing hair—
> Sip, Goblin, from the very lips
> The Lover—hovered—o'er—
> Unworthy, that a thought so mean
> Accost a Theme—so—fair—
>
> The soul has moments of Escape—
> When bursting all the doors—
> She dances like a Bomb, abroad,
> And swings upon the hours . . .
>
> The Soul's retaken moments—
> When, Felon led along,
> With shackles on the plumed feet,
> And staples, in the Song,
>
> The Horror welcomes her, again,
> These, are not brayed of Tongue—
>
> (#512)

In this poem, the word "Bomb" is dropped, almost carelessly, as a correlative for the soul's active, liberated states—it occurs in a context of apparent euphoria, but its implications are more than euphoric—they are explosive, destructive. The Horror from which in such moments the soul escapes has a masculine, "goblin" form, and suggests the perverse and terrifying rape of a "bandaged" and powerless self. In at least one poem, Dickinson depicts the actual process of suicide:

> He scanned it—staggered—
> Dropped the Loop
> To Past or Period—
> Caught helpless at a sense as if
> His mind were going blind—
> Groped up—to see if God was there—
> Groped backward at Himself—
> Caressed a Trigger absently
> And wandered out of Life.
>
> (#1062)

The precision of knowledge in this brief poem is such that we must assume that Dickinson had, at least in fantasy, drifted close to that state in which the "Loop" that binds us to "Past or Period" is "dropped" and we grope randomly at what remains of abstract notions of sense, God, or self, before—almost absent-mindedly—reaching for a solution. But it's worth noting that this is a poem in which the suicidal experience has been distanced, refined, transformed through a devastating accuracy of language. It is not suicide that is studied here, but the dissociation of self and mind and world which precedes.

Dickinson was convinced that a life worth living could be found within the mind and against the grain of external circumstance: "Reverse cannot befall/ That fine prosperity/ Whose Sources are interior—." (#395) The horror, for her, was that which set "Staples in the Song"—the numbing and freezing of the interior, a state she describes over and over:

> There is a Languor of the Life
> More imminent than Pain—
> 'Tis Pain's Successor—When the Soul
> Has suffered all it can—
>
> A Drowsiness—diffuses—
> A Dimness like a Fog
> Envelopes Consciousness—
> As Mists—obliterate a Crag.

> The Surgeon—does not blanch—at pain
> His Habit—is severe—
> But tell him that it ceased to feel—
> That creature lying there—
>
> And he will tell you—skill is late—
> A Mightier than He—
> Has ministered before Him—
> There's no Vitality.

(#396)

I think the equation surgeon-artist is a fair one here; the artist can work with the materials of pain; she cuts to probe and heal; but she is powerless at the point where

> After great pain, a formal feeling comes—
> The nerves sit ceremonious, like Tombs—
> The stiff Heart questions was it He, that bore,
> And Yesterday, or Centuries before?
>
> The Feet, mechanical, go round—
> Of Ground, or Air, or Ought—
> A Wooden way
> Regardless grown,
> A Quartz contentment, like a stone—
>
> This is the Hour of Lead
> Remembered, if outlived
> As Freezing persons, recollect the Snow—
> First—Chill—then Stupor—then the letting go—

(#341)

For the poet, the terror is precisely in those periods of psychic death, when even the possibility of work is negated; her "occupation's gone." Yet she also describes the unavailing effort to numb emotion:

Me from Myself—to banish—
Had I Art—
Impregnable my Fortress
Unto All Heart—

But since Myself—assault Me—
How have I peace
Except by subjugating
Consciousness?

And since We're mutual Monarch
How this be
Except by Abdication—
Me—of Me?

(#642)

The possibility of abdicating oneself—of ceasing to be—remains.

Severe Service of myself
I—hastened to demand
To fill the awful longitude
Your life had left behind—

I worried Nature with my Wheels
When Hers had ceased to run—
When she had put away her Work
My own had just begun.

I strove to weary Brain and Bone—
To harass to fatigue
The glittering Retinue of nerves—
Vitality to clog

To some dull comfort Those obtain
Who put a Head away
They knew the Hair to—
And forget the color of the Day—

Affliction would not be appeased—
The Darkness braced as firm
As all my strategem had been
The Midnight to confirm

No drug for Consciousness—can be—
Alternative to die
Is Nature's only Pharmacy
For Being's Malady—

(#786)

Yet consciousness—not simply the capacity to suffer, but the capacity to experience intensely at every instant—creates of death not a blotting-out but a final illumination:

This Consciousness that is aware
Of Neighbors and the Sun
Will be the one aware of Death
And that itself alone

Is traversing the interval
Experience between
And most profound experiment
Appointed unto Men—

How adequate unto itself
Its properties shall be
Itself unto itself and none
Shall make discovery.

Adventure most unto itself
The Soul condemned to be—
Attended by a single Hound
Its own identity.

(#822)

The poet's relationship to her poetry has, it seems to me—and I am not speaking only of Emily Dickinson—a twofold nature. Poetic language—the poem on paper—is a concretization of the poetry of the world at large, the self, and the forces within the self; and those forces are rescued from formlessness, lucidified, and integrated in the act of writing poems. But there is a more ancient concept of the poet, which is that she is endowed to speak for those who do not have the gift of language, or to see for those who—for whatever reasons—are less conscious of what they are living through. It is as though the risks of the poet's existence can be put to some use beyond her own survival.

> The Province of the Saved
> Should be the Art—To save—
> Through Skill obtained in themselves—
> The Science of the Grave
>
> No Man can understand
> But He that hath endured
> The Dissolution—in Himself—
> That man—be qualified
>
> To qualify Despair
> To Those who failing new—
> Mistake Defeat for Death—Each time—
> Till acclimated—to—
>
> (#539)

The poetry of extreme states, the poetry of danger, can allow its readers to go further in our awareness, take risks we might not have dared; it says, at least: "Someone has been here before."

> The Soul's distinct Connection
> With immortality
> Is best disclosed by Danger
> Or quick Calamity—
>
> As Lightning on a Landscape
> Exhibits Sheets of Place—
> Not yet suspected—but for Flash—
> And Click—and Suddenness.
>
> (#974)

Crumbling is not an instant's Act
A fundamental pause
Dilapidation's processes
Are organized Decays.

'Tis first a cobweb on the Soul
A Cuticle of Dust
A Borer in the Axis
An Elemental Rust—

Ruin is formal—Devil's work
Consecutive and slow—
Fail in an instant—no man did
Slipping—is Crash's law.

(#997)

I felt a Cleaving in my Mind
As if my Brain had split—
I tried to match it—Seam by Seam—
But could not make them fit.

The thought behind, I strove to join
Unto the thought before—
But Sequence ravelled out of Sound
Like Balls—upon a Floor

(#937)

There are many more Emily Dickinsons than I have tried to call up here. Wherever you take hold of her, she proliferates. I wish I had time here to explore her complex sense of Truth; to follow the thread we unravel when we look at the numerous and passionate poems she wrote to or about women; to probe her ambivalent feelings about fame, a subject pursued by many male poets before her; simply to examine the poems in which she is directly apprehending the natural world. No one since the 17th century had reflected more variously or more probingly upon death and dying. What I have tried to do here is follow through some of the origins and consequences of her choice to be, not only a poet but a woman who explored her own mind, without any of the guidelines of orthodoxy. To say "yes" to her powers was not simply a major act of nonconformity in the 19th century; even in our time it has been assumed that Emily Dickinson, not patriarchal society, was "the problem." The more we come to recognize the unwritten and written laws and taboos underpinning patriarchy, the less problematical, surely, will seem the methods she chose.

THE UNITED STATES

fiction by ROBLEY WILSON, JR.

from FICTION INTERNATIONAL

nominated by FICTION INTERNATIONAL *and DeWitt Henry*

LATER WE WILL TELL how we happen to be here in the first class lounge of the *United States*, but for the time being: there are three of us, and we are, incredibly, the only persons seated in a space that is at least fifteen meters wide and perhaps twenty-five meters long. At this moment a steward is coming to our table with a tray of martinis, two up and one on the rocks. Even after last night, Patricia and I are too effete to sip our drinks around ice; Donald believes that a drink on the rocks lasts longer and is less debilitating than a drink served without ice in a stemmed glass—he truly *thinks* about such things—while I am presently far more concerned for the textures and warmths slightly above Patricia's shapely knee; this sort of thing is a constant preoccupation with me, ever since Patricia's husband sailed for America on board the *Olympia*, three months ago. And now the steward is beside our table, arranging the drinks before us; each martini costs one dollar US. All of us are offended by the price.

I wonder if we remembered to tell you that the year is 1953.

We have driven to the ship in Patricia's husband's Jaguar Mark VII Saloon—a quite remarkable machine, perhaps a trifle short on headroom, but lovely nevertheless. The motorcar is a deep burgundy in color, it has wire wheels and those wide whitewalls hardly anyone will know in twenty years, until all at once they begin to "come back," and its interior appointments (as they say) especially include tan leather upholstery whose odor is in its way as heady as the scent Patricia is wearing, and whose appearance is as rich but understated as the white linen suit she has chosen to wear today. It's a hell of a car, really. The speedometer changes colors in ascending kilometer ranges, turning from green to soft orange to a suffusion of anxious red. Donald and I have been driving the Jaguar for the past two months—Patricia is afraid of motorcars and cannot drive—and just last week we reached 180 kilometers per hour on the *autobahn* from Bremen to Hamburg. God, what a car it is. Then, as now, Patricia huddled against me in the back seat and helped me place my hands so the outrageous speeds would make neither of us nervous.

Did we say the ship is docked in Bremerhaven? During the summer months—the "Season"—the *United States* docks here every two or three weeks. If I am not mistaken, she stops at Le Havre inbound and Southampton outbound—or it may be the other way around. In any event, her sister ship, the *America*, docks here all year. Whichever ship you choose, the tourist class passage to New York costs 186 dollars US.

In 1953 a great many things seem possible. We are all young: Patricia is 24, Donald is 23, I am 23; our best estimate at this moment of a humid afternoon in July is that the English-speaking world is just our age, and that it is careless, unencumbered, bright, in superb good health, ready to try anything at least twice, and well-enough-off to afford anything genuinely worth the purchasing. Nothing will change our minds. Once, in a pellucid instant, Patricia has suggested to me that we shall for the rest of our lives retain this judgment of the world, and that whatever happens we will hug to ourselves our faith in our own *rightness*, our own *worthiness*. This extraordinary wisdom while she was teasing me and giggling at the shock on Donald's face. In fact, our world-view is somewhat blurred as we leave from Patricia's apartment and set out to the Columbus Quai. There has been a farewell party; it began the afternoon of the day before, and it was a proper affair—with a guest list, formal invitations written out in Patricia's artful little hand, a time span (3:30 to 5:30) specified, and a gorgeous subtle punch concocted mostly from champagne and vodka. Some twenty-or-so guests: A/2C and Mrs. Bradley Archer, whose mutual ambition is to enter the diplomatic service; A/2C James Neubauer and the Fräulein Ingeborg Theisse; S/Sgt Stanley ("Stosh") Borzyskowski; A/1C Mark Greenawald, who has dedicated his life to finding and marrying the richest girl in the Cincinnati-Covington area; A/B Gerald Barker, a gambler (poker, especially seven-card stud); three Special Services hostesses—Jean, Virginia, and Constance Elaine—; Carlotte and Heinz Schmitt, the German nationals who own the building, who are Patricia's landlady and landlord, whose punch recipe it is that we have followed and praised, and (finally) a German girl no one seems ever to have met before whose full name is Gertrud Maria Magdalena Schüssler, and whose unclothed body will some time be described—by Greenawald—as "purest gold."

And for all our mutual worthiness, the American air force is the sole deep occasion for our meeting here on Burgomeister-Schmidt-Strasse 29, Bremerhaven, Bremen Enclave, West Germany, on Saturday the 11th of July, in the Year of our Lord Nineteen-Hundred-and-Fifty-Three.

Pros't, Schatz.

This scene: It is the day before the sailing of the *United States*, about half-way through the farewell party at Patricia's apartment. The heat in the apartment is beyond endurance; on the hall staircase leading upward to the Schmitt rooms we are strewn like toys, sweating, nursing our drinks. No one left at 5:30; at seven, Neubauer and Fräulein Theisse flagged a Mercedes taxi and directed its driver to the Butterfly Bar, where they bought a quantity of hot *bockwurst*, then returned to the Burgomeister-Schmidt-Strasse address at about 8:15. Neubauer claims to have made love to Fräulein Theisse three times during the errand—once going and twice returning—and he has marched the taxi driver upstairs as witness. Neubauer is a short man, Fräulein Theisse is a plump lady; anything is possible. We are all grateful for the *wurst*.

This scene: We are sprawled on the staircase, sweating and belching. Someone at the top of the stairs has actually fallen asleep. We hear him snoring; we hear the punch glass topple out of his grasp and roll down two steps before Mrs. Archer, Caroline, pushes it through the balustrade uprights with her elbow. The glass bounces before it breaks in front of Patricia's open door. An odd sight; it is as if the glass has levitated from the hall floor and burst in mid-air. At the sound of the breaking, Constance Elaine rushes out to ask what the noise is. She is barefooted, and when we finally get her to the military hospital a bemused German doctor has to take seven stitches in her foot.

Finally, this scene: The staircase is like the vanes in some sort of vertical heat duct, and we are half-lying, half-fainting against varnished surfaces. Patricia is on the fifth step, sprawled, leaning against the wall, her eyes half-closed and gazing—apparently—at the light fixture above us. She is humming; in her left hand is a nearly empty champagne glass, the bowl cradled in her fingers, the stem free and swaying like a pendulum. It is Patricia who once explained that you tell whether a woman is married or unmarried by the way she holds a stemmed glass. If she has anything to explain to me now, or if she is even *thinking* of anything, no evidence presents itself. I can see in her half-hidden eyes the reduced reflections of the light bulb overhead, can make out the tune she is humming—"You Belong to Me," an out-of-date Jo Stafford song—can assume from the looseness of her wrist that she is only floating down the long staircase into her concealed world of memory and idle daydream. I am seated below her, on the second step. I have laid my head back between her thighs, my left temple resting against the bare flesh above her stocking-top and below the white (silk?) panties she wears, the back of my head pillowed on her belly. In my left hand I hold what remains of a water glass of punch, my right arm is laid along Patricia's right leg, my hand stroking her ankle. I cannot begin to describe how drenched with sweat I am, how lethargic I feel. If the world ended now, if the sky fell, if the Russians attacked . . . it would all be one and indifferent. The heat between Patricia's legs is like the sun's, the softness of her thighs is clouds and flowers; against the back of my head is the throbbing of a secret engine waiting to drive the world wherever it desires. I imagine her sheer sexual energy directed toward no end, and idling, a dim green light in our shared darkness. I say to Patricia:

"the punch is drunk up."

She stirs; I ride, giddy, with her small movement. "Oh, I know," Patricia says. "This bunch of people. . . ." She shifts the champagne glass to her right hand, strokes the stem between the thumb and fingers of her left. I am looking up at her, my head far back; I see her face through the curve of her glass, and I feel the hem of her skirt over my right ear. The hot odor between Patricia's thighs is the ozone of that obscure engine driving us, driving me.

But we are all under inhuman pressures. In the spring a British Lancaster was shot down by MIG-17's of the Soviet—Air Army (Rostock) in the corridor between Hamburg and Berlin. Soon after, two American jet fighters were intercepted and destroyed along the Czech border by MIG's of the—Air Army (Zwickau). We monitored both incidents, in each case listening to the Soviet ground controller vector his fighters to the target, hearing the command to open fire, startled to realize—because the appropriate code words are so rare—*the attack is real, people are dying.* We sit in our barracks rooms all through the wet spring months, drinking Tuborg beer and talking of war—of pre-emptive nuclear strikes, of our closeness to the enemy zone (ten air minutes), of our own importance, of whether we are interested in dying. From Rotenburg, in the British Zone, where our officers go to record the flying time necessary to keep their flight pay, it is said that both the British and American pilots in their ray-shaped Hawkers fly hedgehopping missions across the zonal border to provoke the Soviet radar; we find this an exciting notion, fun. We are all Romance, espionage, cloak-and-dagger, ready to have the life coaxed out of us. If the tanks roll in East Berlin, may we not someday march with the citizens against them?

What is immediate, of course, is that we finish the farewell party for Patricia. She is returning to the States, to her husband, and Donald and I must drive her in her husband's Jaguar to the Columbus Quai. Our lives have a particular purpose.

I say this ("Our lives have purpose.") to Patricia in the living room of her apartment. It is exceedingly late—actually Sunday morning,

the day of her departure, around three o'clock. We are lying on the
floor together; I cannot tell where the others are, though in some
dim corner of my brain I must know they are still in the building, in
the hallway, probably even in the room with us. The truth is that we
have all drunk so much—first the punch, and then a putting-
together of all the wines, whiskies, aromatics, liqueurs, and mixes
left in the apartment, all poured mindlessly into the emptied punch
bowl and then parceled out among the party—we have all drunk so
much, we are deep inside ourselves and scarcely able to connect
with a world discrete from us. When I say "Our lives have purpose,"
Patricia says "Mmm," and turns her face toward me; I touch my lips
to her forehead and taste sweat, delicately salt.

Somewhere in time she has changed her clothes. As I touch her it
seems to me she is wearing only a robe, a black robe with red and
orange appliqué flowers patterned on the lapels, a robe tied at her
waist by a black slender belt frayed at the ends. I put one hand
against the robe—is it silk?—and feel her breasts beneath the
smooth fabric; they are unexpectedly soft, as if she were older, as if
she were someone's mother. She raises her left hand and rests it on
the back of my fingers—not to take my hand away, but neither to
encourage me. I kiss her eyes, the closed lids; I kiss her cheeks, the
corners of her mouth. Now I kiss her full on the mouth, open her
lips, insist my tongue between her teeth.

She bites my tongue.

When I pull my head back, startled, she opens her eyes to read my
face. What she sees makes her laugh, and no matter what I do or say I
cannot stop her laughing.

Patricia's husband is one of those who had no dealings with the city's
whores, who visited the bars rarely, who lived even under the
obligations of a military occupation (and a military presence looking
ahead) as if the barracks were a row of brownstones and the par-
queted floors of our modest rooms were aglow under the reading
lamps of The Club. Before Patricia flew to Germany to marry him,
he was my roommate and tried to teach me grace, to encourage me
to recognize style. Every afternoon at four—unless we worked the
day shift out at Squadron Operations—he mixed a pitcher of martinis; we sat, like two gentlemen of Cambridge, sipping our drinks,
listening to Barbara Carroll or Mabel Mercer or Hugh Shannon or

the most-prized Greta Keller, not so much weighing the problems of our world as settling them.

Once in a great while Donald joined us for cocktails, and it was Donald who, only a week before Patricia's arrival at the Bremen airfield, innocently brought her bridegroom into the Butterfly for his famous encounter with Ingeborg Theisse—plump ripe Ingeborg, with the reddest hair, the best English, of all the prostitutes in the Enclave.

"They say he's cherry," we told her.

"Now wait a second." said the groom.

"I can give you advice," Ingeborg said. "Always ride high; the woman has more sensation high."

"I'll remember."

"But honestly, you never touched a woman?" Ingeborg took his hand and drew it under her skirt—a black skirt, long, but slit at the sides. He tried to pull away, but she is a woman of great strength and held him; she pressed his hand up between her legs—he blushing, she smiling—and rocked against him. All of us looked part-wise, part-perplexed.

Then: "God, please! Please leave me alone!"

He startled us, there was such pain in the words, and when we looked at his face we saw tears bright in his eyes and wet on his cheeks. Ingeborg stopped moving, stopped smiling. She backed away from him and slid his hand out from under her clothes; he held the hand up as if it were hurt. No one said much, and poor Donald looked like death.

Later it was Donald who took Ingeborg to her room—no ships were in port—and the rest of us, Stanley and Gerald and Mark, went back to the barracks. In the room—it was after midnight; we were having a last beer while the phonograph played *One Touch of Venus*—Patricia's husband said to me:

"Don't ever tell Patsy."

So. Just a few weeks ago his father died and he took an early discharge to go home to Kansas City to manage a packing house.

Years from now, when we hold reunions or meet accidentally at an air terminal or bump into one another at conventions, we will sit in a dark corner of some barroom nothing like the Butterfly and talk about Bremerhaven—though it is impossible, in 1953, to know what

our recollections will come to. Will we remember our first days in
the city: October, rain blowing in off the North Sea (a Sea that is
invisible to us beyond the great mounded-earth dikes), a cold whose
dampness seeps to the very marrow? The rubble, seven and eight
years after the end of the war, pulled to the sides of streets only
beginning to be repaved, and the first new, raw apartment houses
rising beside basements reeking of brown water? Or the stories we
hear from everyone, American and German, about the retaliation
bombing of the city after Coventry—how the British Havilands
strafed and bombed from less than a hundred meters of altitude,
leveling the Hafenstrasse, wasting most of the residential city, leaving wholly untouched the port facilities and the Marine Barracks
where all of us came to live? The foresight of the Allies: it makes us
proud. Surely we will remember the whores—Inges and Margots
and Karlas and Erikas—who drink and laugh with us, who know our
secret projects better than our officers, who charge for their favors
300 marks when the merchant ships are in, 20 when they are not?

This scene, the last with Patricia ashore: It is shortly after dawn, a
windless morning, gray from a fog that will not burn away until
nearly noon. The apartment is emptied of revelers—except for
Donald, asleep on a sofa under the bay window. Everything is a
shambles. Glasses are on all the furniture surfaces—chair arms,
table tops, bookshelves, hassocks—and on floors and carpets. A lot
of things, liquid and not, have been spilled; if you look out the
doorway into the hall you see glassware, paper plates, crumpled
napkins, as if someone had overturned a trash barrel at the head of
the stairs; the air is heavy with stale cigarette smoke, the odors of old
perfume and fancy drink.

Patricia is awake first, and rouses me out of a heavy-headed sleep;
my body has settled into some shape that has no life of its own—a
piece of sod, a stone, a rug rolled for storage. I groan and, groaning
and hearing myself, open my eyes to see where the sound comes
from. Patricia and I are still joined, our bare legs stuck together with
sweat, the two of us even holding hands like children on a hayride.
Her robe is open and twisted under us; I am in my blue shirt, my
black socks, but the rest of my uniform is in a heap in the seat of a soft
chair near the kitchen door. My tongue hurts me. I remember being
bitten, I remember Patricia laughing, I remember nothing else.

"What time is it?" I try to find my watch, but it is on my left wrist, and my left wrist is under Patricia's back. I try to move her, and as she rolls away from me it is like adhesive tape being ripped off my skin. Our bellies and thighs are red, our hair drenched. She reaches out to me, leans over and kisses me.

"What a hellish country this is," she says hoarsely.

We help each other to stand. We bathe and dress. We wake Donald.

We forgive ourselves everything, though we have endless parties, drink too much, make frequent fools of ourselves in the eyes of the German nationals. Sometimes we have fistfights with the infantry—our barracks neighbors, our comrades-in-arms. Other times we quarrel with the naval detachment nearby. Mostly we tyrannize over the civilians; we say things like "Who won this war?" (though we were far too young to have fought it) and we sell cigarettes and coffee and sometimes currency on the black markets. Also we travel. We go to Amsterdam and smoke marijuana for the first time in our lives. We go to Copenhagen, spend a lot of time and money in the after-hours clubs, and stay at the Roxy Hotel because the girls are lovely and speak English. Are we not the perfect ambassadors of freedom?

The worst times are political—the rumors that our Squadron will be the first evacuated in the event of war, that if there is no time for evacuation our officers have orders to shoot us. It is a glamorous notion. We argue by the hour: Would you let yourself be shot? Would you surrender? If you were tortured would you reveal military secrets? Then our lives seem rich but desperate. It is said that Lieutenant Wieczorek, the watch officer when an orange alert was called during the defection of a Polish fighter pilot, suffered a nervous breakdown and tried to kill himself.

The best times are parties on shipboard—but not American ships, whose liquor prices are too high. The ships of German, Greek, Swedish, Canadian registry—these are fine. Some ships become traditions; the North German Lloyd's liner *Berlin*, the old *Gripsholm*, is a regular—about 12 cents for the finest Scotch whiskey, always crowded, plenty of "nice" local girls. For all departure parties you only need to arrange a visitor's pass with a member of the ship's crew. That is simple, and it is the least the crewman can do after inflating the economy hereabouts.

The three of us sit in the barren first class lounge of the *United States*, drinking our expensive martinis and finding it difficult to make conversation. I am amazed at how lovely and rested Patricia looks after last night, and I have said so; Donald agreed with me. Donald has promised we will be most careful with the Jaguar until we bring it to be shipped aboard the *America* next week, and I have seconded the promise; I have reminded her that we shipped home her husband's MG-TD without mishaps two months ago. Patricia has confided that in an odd way, much as she loves her husband and much as she is looking forward to Kansas City and the nice new home now being built for her, she will miss dirty old Bremerhaven and all the good friends—she squeezes my hand—left behind. She says that at the very least she will try to make the people back home understand that even if we are not dying in Korea, we are all doing an important job—we are in Europe for a *purpose*. I look at Donald; he is making a face, a horrible face. "You are all preventing a *big* war," Patricia says.

An hour later we are standing on the cobbled Quai, waving up at Patricia as the *United States* slowly pivots away from shore, the German tugs nudging her into the brown waters that flow from the North Sea. It has gotten very warm, and Patricia has taken off the long-sleeved jacket of her suit; the ruffles of her white blouse—is it silk, in this weather?—flutter as she waves down to us. There is so much noise, so many voices, music so loud to our left, that to shout more goodbyes would be useless. We only watch, and as the image of Patricia slowly diminishes in my sight I remember just for an instant what she was saying over martinis. Did she mean it? Could anyone?

A week later Donald and I drive the Mark VII Saloon back to Columbus Quai; it is going aboard the *America* for New York, where Patricia's husband will meet it and drive it to Kansas City. What a shame—I say this to Donald just after we have handed the car over to the dispatcher—what a terrible shame Patricia's husband will never be able to drive the car on U.S. roads at the speeds permitted on the new Bremen-Hamburg *autobahn*. Yes, says Donald, this motorcar is too good for him—too fast, too temperamental for the ZI. Sometimes Donald himself is too military, as when he adopts such jargon as ZI—for "Zone of the Interior"—when he means home, the States. Greenawald concurs. "A Chevy would satisfy that phoney," he says. Greenawald has hung around with us since the

United States sailed, boring us endlessly with the precious golden
skin of Gertrud Maria Magdalena Schüssler. We walk away from the
car, preoccupied by speed and beauty, and drift up a flight of steps to
the restaurant overlooking dockside.

The restaurant is crowded, but we find a table near a window. We
order a Beck's and two Karlsbergs. "Really," Greenawald is saying,
"when she took off her clothes I felt like King Midas; she was purest
gold." Donald glances at me; I shrug. For myself, Patricia has been
in and out of my head since the tugs pushed her ship into the channel
of the Weser. Her languor, her textures, perhaps her wealth. . . .

We sit, drinking the beer, talking hardly at all. Once Donald
points out the window, and I turn to see the Jaguar, cradled in raw
wood, suspended from the cable of a crane slowly swiveling toward
the *America*. I feel an odd, momentary churning in my stomach, and
I hope they know to be careful. The auto looks like a plum, rounded
and vulnerable, dangling from an artificial branch. In ten minutes it
is out of our sight.

On the way to the center of the city I am absorbed in 1953 and our
curious lives away from the familiar—what serious things concern
us, what friends we have met, what confident future we look ahead
to. I believe I have become, like Donald, too solemn for my own
good, and when the yellow streetcar passes the Butterfly I motion
the others to get off and follow me into the bar. I want to look for
Ingeborg; I think I want to make fun of Greenawald's golden
girlfriend with all her pretentious saintly names.

THE OTHER FACE OF BREAD

by "The Workers' University"

from CROSS CURRENTS

nominated by CROSS CURRENTS

Note: the following document, which first appeared in the Italian monthly *Humanitas*, has no particular author. It represents communal reflections and subsequent plan of action by a group of poor Italian immigrants working and living in Brussels. The "university" is not merely a minority living within an affluent dominant culture, but a community living in diaspora. In his introduction to what follows, translator Emmanuel L. Paparella says: "Perhaps the sort of popular culture that we see incarnated by the Workers' University in a brave attempt at genuine community may have something to teach many of us who have grown complacent with our advanced degrees. It may mercifully begin to strip us of the illusion of knowing all there is to be known about *culture, liberation,* and *schooling.* It certainly has much to offer us in the way of *simplicity, courage* and *compassion.*"

EXCLUSION IS THE EVIL from which the emigrant dies. A death occurring too far away to be noticed, and which is announced in a foreign language. The reality of this exclusion has become a geographical fact. We have progressively been excluded from education, from language, from politics, and finally from our own land. Our dignity as sovereign citizens has vanished little by little; with emigration it no longer exists, even on paper. "To be excluded" is a passive verb, but the phenomenon is equally betrayed in the infinitive "to emigrate"; more appropriately, one should speak of a deportation.

Since exclusion is a mechanism which in successive circles touches almost all Italians, we have asked ourselves what and who presides over this sinister phenomenon. We have come to the conclusion that what's at play here is a sort of logic—the logic of private interest. He who succeeds (well, or even not so well) in possessing something becomes a carrier of such logic. And as one climbs up the ladder of possessions, one becomes not only a carrier but a guarantor. He who has more to defend also possesses sufficient means to organize the complex structures of consent and to become a leader. It is therefore things (*la roba*, as Verga used to say) which decide if one is "in" or "out."

When one possesses a great deal of *roba* (property), however, one naturally lacks both the time and the opportunity to work all of it, and therefore decides not to work it at all. The burden of work (contact with things) is then put entirely on the shoulders of those who possess nothing. Proprietors have the leisure to fly off to the Olympus of abstraction, to school and politics, while the proletariat is more and more sucked in by things and matter. It is not by chance that in Greece slaves were "ilioti"—that is, those "immersed in matter."

Made sick with all kinds of distinctions, Western civilization has fallen under the influence of a manichean concept of culture: spirit and matter, free men and slaves, philosophers and "cafoni" (farmers), good and bad. On one side you havé "liberal arts," on the other, manual arts. The former is conceived as the kingdom of the spirit, freedom and knowledge; the latter is the dark region of matter, slavery and ignorance. On the level of cultural praxis the differences have been settled even more quickly. Since he who deals with spirit receives prestige and splendor from the subjects he treats, it was highly fitting to signify this with a series of symbols acquirable with money. Money, therefore, is on the side of spirit and nobility is the guarantor of exclusivity, which is assured by the mathematical law that if one wants to have much it is necessary that the whole be divided among the few.

"Aristocracy" can be defined as a group of indolent persons, all of whom know the same things, tell them to each other, congratulate each other about them, and invent the game of "exquisite corpse" to convince themselves they are alive. Among such people the question of for what and to whom such knowledge is useful is altogether secondary.

Such culture suffers from a loss of reality, and has become asphyxiating and delirious. We are reminded of a famous philosopher who, when confronted with the objection that reality was different from the way he was celebrating it, answered: "So much the worse for reality."

We, however, feel solidly anchored in reality. For us, therefore, the answer of the philosopher, in concrete terms, means: "so much the worse for Rosario, Calogero, Salvatore"; in other words, reality leaves us "so much the worse," after passing through our bones and bruising our knees. Philosophy manuals define as an idealist a scholar who specializes in spirit. To us Angelo seems much more of an idealist; despite having been brutally excluded, he still hopes to lend a helping hand to changing the world. The philosopher's response, on the other hand, is both delirious and cynical, but such cynicism too often becomes political praxis.

Exclusion is a history and a logic. A schizophrenic history and a logic crystallized in the "wisdom" of a prophet which, for modesty's sake, we quote in Latin: *Mors tua, vita mea*. The fact that emigration is a way of dying was not invented by us. Concretely, exclusion begins with little elbow kicks, each innocuous in itself, but which in the long run put one "out of the game." And the name of the game is: "a few play on the skin of many."

The place where our exclusion is consummated is called Cureghem, a neighborhood of Anderlecht, one of the nineteenth municipalities of Brussels, the capital of Europe, something of which we were never aware. As far as we were concerned, it could have been the capital of Becinania.

Cureghem has precise borders. On one side, there is the stench of the canal; on the other, a generous supply of pornographic moviehouses. Within this slaughter-house are rows of buildings, nine out of ten put up before 1914. Italians, Greeks, Spaniards, and North Africans live here, making up a world that would be interesting if it did not also bring together the contradictions and angers of all these separate groups. The few Belgians there are themselves foreigners in their own country, a remnant of the same process of exclusion. In such a situation the adults try to keep up some sort of continuity with their background, calling each other *paesano* in a rather empty spirit, while the young desperately try to shed even this symbolic tie. Ultimately, neither approach is successful. While the world of the excluded may be able to organize a rudimentary form of survival, it is condemned right from the start to a pathetic sub-culture. The dominant culture, the emanation and legitimation of economic and political power, possesses the necessary power to impose itself as "exemplary." However, this culture, which is vain and arrogant in its natural environment, becomes ridiculous and even farcical here.

Popular culture is all too often understood as simply colonization. As in any such process, it is useful in unloading the surplus, enlarging the market, and setting up areas of pseudo-philanthropic tourism for bored people in search of a good conscience. TV, films, and reading courses directed by various agencies are mostly given over to indoctrinating the passive with a pretentious and useless veneer. Such "education" is designed to enlarge the market for cultural sub-products created by a "cultured" class who wish to acquire the pitiful savings of poor workers in order to re-affirm the primacy of spirit. If people are scandalized by the popularity in our neighborhood of magazines devoted to scandal, sex, and celebrities, the scandal is not to be found where most of them will look for it. We need to analyze its source, that cultural manicheanism with which the official culture is sick, and the whole process of exclusion which derives from it.

A genuinely popular school begins, then, with the will to liquidate this manichean dualism and all the "natural" implications it legitimizes. Rather than limit oneself to containing the damages (though this is morally praiseworthy), it is a rule of efficiency and a verification of the seriousness of one's intervention to attack root causes. The therapy of dealing with symptoms hides a plan of conservatism, while the attack on causes shows a will for renewal. It seems to us that the cultural poverty of our world derives mainly from the age-old and open split between reality and word, and the subsequent subordination established by those who pretend to cultivate the word against those who deal with reality. In such a system it is only natural that reality seems to offer no light, and the corollary is that thought is seen to be without content.

From these general considerations we can derive two precise guidelines for a serious practice of popular education:

1. To commit oneself entirely to the environmental conditions of the people with whom one wants to grow. In other words, choose, even geographically, the side one wants to take: the habitat gives evidence of exclusion or belonging, and is also a means of socialization. As for those teachers who occasionally descend on us from the consulate office, we don't know where they're from, and they remain strangers to all our problems. They teach us words out of their vocabulary, not syllables and numbers from our life. They rub elbows with us without in the least getting to know us; they even smell different. Why don't they bring along small groups of European students and show them where they'll end up if they don't study? There would no longer be any need of preaching to encourage them to be diligent and studious.

2. "To teach Latin to little Peter, it helps if one knows Latin, but above all, one must know little Peter." The truth is that we don't think you can teach us anything. We have an experience of life, suffering, and work that is in no way inferior to yours. Our life, suffering, and work unite us to three billion others across the world, so our experience is historic. Of course, if you wanted to, you could get us to talk; we could meet as equals and compare notes in order that the reality which we live—so full of contradictions—might be replaced by a different and better organization of the world. Instead, we are objects of discussion in official places; officials whom we have never met are making decisions that affect our lives. University graduates recite statistics about us from memory. They have learned all about us in classrooms, along with "scientific" formulas that yield the best profits and allow them to rationalize power. Sociology majors come to inquire about our exclusion and to measure the state of our resignation. Results and proposals are then discussed in graduate seminars, and it all ends up in some social drinking at a bar near the university, a kind of students' picnic.

Someone who settled in the neighborhood and had a serious commitment to reality would begin by listening. Such a listening, active, patient, and stimulating, would unearth the *petit-bourgeois* aspirations which grow up also among those who have been excluded, who often seek for identifications foreign to their condition. Sometimes we forget that we cannot escape exclusion all by ourselves, on tip-toe, via individualistic "emergency exits." Even if, for example, someone wins at the numbers, it doesn't really change anything for the winner and means even less for the rest of us. It is the neighborhood that is sick rather than its inhabitants, and the sickness consists in the logic of exclusion we have described. Unless we are convinced of this, each intervention will end up either by expropriating the moral resources of the excluded, or provoking the type of rebellion described by Franz Fanon when he says, "When a white man talks of culture, the North African makes sure he has his knife on him." Active listening will ultimately discourage the instinct to beg for welfare and the habit of waiting for the benevolence of the rich. Such an attitude, archaically anti-democratic, shows to what extent the excluded have been stopped cold at the doors of the modern era. To educate while listening means to set up relationships among equals, and to learn to interpret discomfort, shame and fear in the categories of cause and effect. Only in this way can we abandon the state of object and enter that of a political subject.

This analytical and active listening begins our long march toward trust, which does not conceal contradictions, false myths, and counterfeits, but passes over them with the delicacy and precision of a surgeon. Trust is not abandoning oneself to someone else's hands, but the verified conviction that the other wants what you want, and wants it in terms of your specific situation—without illusions, without holding back. Trust is also born by demonstrating that one is not furnishing service but creating a conscience. A service presupposes clients; helping to create a conscience presupposes only the conviction that one is confronting real people. This is especially true when the notion of school as a service is not seen as indispensable; it then becomes doubly important to create a conscience.

Beginning with the above principles, we have opened a type of school which could be defined as the other face of bread, in the sense that it prepares the individual to become a "user" of his humanity and therefore to make social and political realities his own. A night school. A poor school. Because of this, the word "school" seemed inadequate to us. School was born far away from the stench of the canal and reflects a parasitic reality which had first made slavery possible, and later the subjugation of serfs and of the proletariat. *Schola* was the *otium* of those who disdained the neg-*otium* from whose proceeds they lived. For us, who are immersed in neg-*otium*, knowledge coincides with an active intervention in the world in order to render it a home for men and women. "University," therefore, seemed to be a better word for what we were trying to accomplish; it promises a universality of participation and the acceptance of a universe of research which could very well be found between the canal and the railroad station. Despite its present connotation, "university" was not repugnant to us.

Nobody donated the Workers' University to us: we built it with our own hands. The municipal administration rented us an old ramshackle house destined for demolition after being abandoned five years ago. At the end it had been a bar, but we didn't mind that; it meant one less place of alienation and one more possibility for conscience. The first month of our university was dedicated to manual labor. We dismantled the old signs, moved the old furniture, and fought a brave battle against the perennial dust; then we painted and prepared everything as if we were expecting a baby. In the main lobby we hung signs that indicated a few guidelines:

> — If you are planning for a year, plant some rice
> If you are planning for ten years, plant a tree
> If you are planning for one hundred years, open a school.

> — Do not forget that you learn from your comrades when they learn from you.

> — School is not a personal fact
> but the occasion to fulfill a duty—
> the duty of teaching and learning.

The first inscription is a Chinese proverb; the next two were rules in the campaign against illiteracy conducted by FRELIMO (Front for the Liberation of Mozambique). On one of the walls we hung a large statue of Christ without a cross and without arms; next to it, we put this sign: "I have no other hands but yours." This was not done to introduce a confessional aspect to our enterprise but as a declaration of the responsibility of everybody for everything.

After laying this groundwork, we organized our first year of life. The unit of didactic measurement was the week, which was divided in the following manner:

Monday: 6:30-8:30 p.m. Reading about a political-social event in the editorial section of two newspapers at opposite ends of the ideological spectrum. Comparison and analysis of ideological assumptions.

8:30-9:30 p.m. Italian language—beginning with the prose of the article discussed in previous class.

Wednesday: 6:30-8:30 p.m. Analysis of the event previously discussed, from a political point of view. Search for appropriate categories.

8:30-9:30 p.m. Principles of mathematical reasoning.

Friday: 6:30-8:30 p.m. Economic categories, and analysis of the same event from the angle of economics.

8:30-9:30 p.m. French language, beginning with the text of a French newspaper referring to the event under observation.

Saturday: 2:00-4:00 p.m. Analysis of the same event in sociological categories.

4:00-6:00 p.m. Interdisciplinary confrontation and first critical evaluation.

(Tuesday and Thursday night—Italian and French for comrades who have recently joined.)

After four months of this schedule, we made a first survey of the principles that had emerged from these economic, political, and sociological analyses. The reading of Italian and French continued. After this first systematic review of our program, we substituted psychological for political analysis, and continued with this method for the rest of the year.

In this way we gradually became aware of how many Cureghems there are in the world, who our friends are, and where they live. We have begun to understand that the most important pages of a newspaper are not about sports or the latest divorces of movie stars. When we read about sports or crime now, we try to understand their socio-political implications. Above all, we are no longer afraid of words, white collars, beautiful houses, luxury cars, and bank accounts: we know who pays for all these symbols and we are able to measure the boredom and egotism that they conceal.

One evening toward the end of the year, we received a visit from about fifteen students from the Jesuit college of Namur. As part of their spiritual "retreat" they are giving themselves a sensitivity-excursion in the poorest sections in the city. This time it was our turn. They arrived while we were still in the midst of one of our learning periods, and had to wait. When we finished, they came in, elegantly dressed and chatting easily with each other; one could smell the perfume of letters and spirit. A few months previously, we'd have been intimidated by their presence and their words, but by this time we were aware of being their equals. We asked them the reason for their visit and they answered that they had come to "become aware" of our problems; it ended up with us showing them *theirs*. We told them we didn't have any problems except the ones given us by the society of exclusion; then we asked them why they were students. The most intelligent answer took refuge in a sort of blind obedience to parental wishes. Others were even more banal, and some cannot be repeated; none even hinted at the kind of analysis that for us is now normal and familiar. We left them on good terms, but more aware than ever of the difference between knowledge as a weapon and knowledge as a hobby.

We have to admit that we ourselves are not completely healed of the kind of egotism which is the premise of a discriminatory logic, and which, in a world which practices exclusion, seems to be the only way to salvation. Nevertheless, we know quite well that this represents the great force of division among the excluded, and is one of the biggest factors in maintaining the *status quo*. Some of us, in fact, have been unable to remain faithful to a commitment which does not promise a career or money, or the opportunity to escape individually from the condemnation of exclusion. Those few have left us and have not come back.

But the group as a whole has held together quite well. In addition to feeling comfortable with each other, little by little it has internalized a strong sense of solidarity. The differences which we had inherited from structures alien to our world have fallen away and we have witnessed the birth of a common will to make life something worthwhile. In such a context everybody is indispensable, just as in a life-and-death situation. In our first year we learned to manage words, to measure the effects of the process of exclusion on a world scale, and not to feel alone when confronting the powers that dictate division and prosper on distinctions. In the second year we decided to commit ourselves to our specific reality as immigrants and its daily implications, implications which define our condition of exclusion. While a new group began the work of conscientization and acquisition of language skills with the method of the first year, we have begun to understand our reality as a word to be interpreted and to be acted upon in communion with the present effort of world liberation.

To work on the particular with one's heart open to the whole is the necessary precondition for getting beyond resentment and beginning to plan. So, we have dedicated ourselves to an analysis of emigration, beginning with ourselves, our families, and our neighborhood. Each has prepared an "identity card" of his own condition as one of the excluded. This was done to make sure that learning did not lead to a rejection of one's own world. When we reduced these personal notes to a common denominator, we became aware that the areas of exclusion most crucial for us were work, housing and education. We then divided ourselves into study groups according to our professional occupation: the workers dealt with work, technical students with education, and a mixed group with housing. Each sub-group was to deal with the problem from a different angle and with different instruments: brief questionnaires, in-depth questions to friends and comrades, systematic readings. Every two weeks during a common meeting each sub-group reported on the difficulties encountered and results obtained. When we thought it useful, someone with special competence on a particular subject would be invited.

In this way we have become conscious of numerous situations which we had once thought of as natural, and which we now see as the outcome of irresponsible choices destined to perpetuate exclusion. As a result, our neighborhood now appears to us like a transparent word, pregnant with suffering and hope. We would like to humanize and activate this suffering so that hope may become a place of encounter. This seems to us a good starting point for next year's plan of action.

In the face of obvious difficulties and limited results, some may ask: why lose time taking up such enormous problems when there are so many immediate concerns that remain unresolved? The answer is simply because we believe this is the entrance to (and exit from) the world of exclusion, where the other vital problems live and fester. Of course, there are actions with a more immediate and pragmatic goal, but until they are invested with a new consciousness they will remain ambiguous. Even if we understand their urgency, it does not follow that we will be able to legitimize the way they are carried out. The same action may have a particular content and significance for the one who organizes it, and a different significance for one who participates in it. And it can very well happen that the workers are once more excluded from actions that are carried out with them, and (presumably) for them. All participation in our planning is welcomed by us, since this represents a way of continuing the program of *conscientization*. Once the word is learned, it renews itself and spreads by its contact with everyone's reality. Only in this way does it become intelligence and life.

We mentioned Europe some pages back—Europe, a new reality, in whose creation we are participating. A reality that could be different, if it is not born under the curse of exclusion. The Europe of today is foreign to us, with its egotism, provicialism, and the accumulated hates of its individual nations. It is burdened with all the contradictions that dozens of wars, hundreds of false starts, and centuries of repression have created. Having been excluded from the old structures, we cannot accept or allow new ones to be announced without us and against us. If Europe is an historic occasion, we insist on a different history. There are many things to be worked out in regard to the new Europe that is being prepared, but it should at least be obvious that it must be a Europe of all Europeans. And it stands to reason that the first Europeans are those who, for reasons of work—in other words, in order to build this Europe—find themselves outside their own country. There are now millions of workers like ourselves involved in an anarchic and insecure diaspora.

We have the modest presumption of believing that we have begun a path leading to the utopia of human community. We say utopia because, between the possible and the real, there will always be a creative tension, stimulating new projects and new generosity. But it seems to us that commitment to the word is a practice of charity which, as immediate injustices are eliminated, prepares a dialogue pregnant with the hesitations and hopes of those who are sensitive to the reality of evil. This is the only "social love" we understand—a love that doesn't limit but renews, that doesn't merely restrain the effects of evil but denounces the root causes and fights against the mentality that generates it. We don't know if all this will eliminate confrontation, but we are convinced that if such confrontation becomes necessary it will be positive, responsible, and able to generate history. Such a clash will predispose each individual, as Gandhi used to say, "to ally himself with the better part of his enemy against his worse part." The word and the understanding of life have taught us trust in people and a fundamental optimism. To paraphrase an affirmation of Mitterand, we can safely state that, although the excluded may not always be in the right, the society that punishes them is surely always in the wrong.

Translated by Emmanuel L. Paparella

LETTER FOR A DAUGHTER

by LORRIE GOLDENSOHN

from PLOUGHSHARES

nominated by Maxine Kumin

Put it this way, lovey, some people
stab themselves with their own strength:
stubbornly clinging, when all the best
of collective wisdom, not just your parents,
but your friends, too—calls up the feral
outline of a lover that love for yourself
should let you let go.

Thinking about it, I had it all
so clear in my mind, as placed above you
on this northern map, I wrote you good advice—
but the lines have wavered, and fallen short;
failing to touch that adolescent pride,
still hammer-firm in a southern city.
What lover could clear,

or should, the blackness from those eyes . . .
Wednesday, the pig came; we stacked it in boxes
by the door; the weather turned cold enough
to keep anything we wanted stiff. As in mute
promise, the pieces of the pig lay wrapped,
lay waiting for the festival of the returning child.
You didn't come.

By Thursday, hinting at spoils,
the massed disordered meat still lay
in its blood-stained papers, two greasy boxes
to be rendered into lard. At nightfall,
all of the burners covered with the big black
kettles and pots, we did it; swept up the floors
and put the cans away, warm oil

oozing in every crack of the littered stove,
as the large cans held their snowfall of fat
like deferred pleasure. His hair,
strained of color, holds you: the round, full
throbbing of that muscular neck, as it turns
in its senseless activity, the large hands
with the light blond fur, the blunt

nails knotting in the thickness of your hair,
quick and light in their ambiguous caresses,
hold you; tease and deploy us with the hopeful
possibility of our mistake—as nothing can be done—
our stomachs full of the veteran pig, the six months
since we saw you. The river in back of the house
clarifies. Slowly and carefully, the snow

thins from the winter-scabbed path. All things
drive to their opposite number. My life
hunkering down in your youth, as absently,
you blur towards a stale body—fresh error—snow
gives way to the black slick mud, and the sky
lightens. Sunday, that bald signal, augmenting,

reaches round for its repeating self again.

"TALK TO ME, BABY"

by MICHAEL DENNIS BROWNE

from THE IOWA REVIEW

nominated by THE IOWA REVIEW *and Mary MacArthur*

1

A friend at a cocktail party tells me
of being on a fishing trip up North
and meeting some men from Illinois
who showed him how to clean and filet a fish properly;
and of how, when one particular pike
was stripped almost clean, almost all of him gone,
the jaw with the razory teeth opened
and some kind of cry came from the creature,
that head on the end of almost no body;
and the man with the knife said:
"Talk to me, baby."

2

Up in the Boundary Waters last weekend
I hooked a trout, my first, and played him.
I got him to the shallows
and tried to raise him. And the girls
got down into the water with my leather hat—
we hadn't brought a net—and I was yelling
"I've got a fish! I've got a fish!"
out into the evening, and the girls
tried to get him into the hat, and did once,
but then he was out again—a wriggle, a flap—
that fish jumped out of my hat!
and the line, gone loose, jerked, snapped, and he was back
in the water, the hook in him.

And he didn't turn into
a glimmering girl, like he did for
young Willie Yeats,
nor was he a Jesus, like for Lawrence;
he just drifted head down near the shallows,
huge, the huge hook in him.
And Louis and Phil came up in the other
canoe, and we got the flashlight on him,
and tried to get hold of him. But then, somehow,
we lost him, drifting about, he was not there
but gone somewhere deeper into the water,
every minute darker; my hook in him.

I hooked five or six snags after that, yelling
each time that each one was a fish, bigger
than the last. But I brought nothing living up.
And the other canoe went ghostly on the water,
silvery, like a dish with two quiet eggs in it;
and the pines were massed, dark, and stood and smelled
strong, like a bodyguard of dried fish.

3
Breathing, my brother in my house,
and breathing, his wife beside him.

Breathing, my brother in America,
his body in my bed, her body.

Their tent the color of the sun in my garden.
And they are riding West.

And both of us riding West, brother,
since we swam out of the father,

heading, six years apart,
the same way.

The dog stares at me, not knowing
why I have not fed him.
The cat crying to come in.

Whom we feed, sustain us.
Who need us, we keep breathing for.

I have seen you, at supper with friends,
put your hands to the guitar strings

and bring strong music out, seen you
sit and pick out

a tune on the piano,
on a friend's penny whistle.

To hold an instrument, to play.
To hold a pen, to write.

To do as little harm as possible
in the universe, to help

all traveling people, West, West;
you are not traveling alone,

not ever; we all go with you;
only the body stays behind.

4

When I stand on my island, a Napoleon,
one hand nailed to my chest,
the writing hand;

when I can only *stare*
at the ocean, at the birds
running and turning against the light . . .

When I am
the Illinois man and his kind,
"Talk to me, baby,"

the one with the knife inside, sometimes,
the one you may meet on your travels,
the one behind you in the line to get on the bus,

the one arranging a deal in a phone booth
as you drive past,
when I become that thing I sometimes become,

I will go into
the green of this visit, the green
you asked me to try to see

after my earlier, darker poems for you—
and this, the fourth one, darker
than I meant, since the man with the knife

swam into it—O when that killer
stands over our city, our sleeping and loving places,
tent, canoe, cabin of sweet people—

I will hear with your ears
the songs of the birds of the new world
that so quicken you, and look for

their wings that flame and flash—there! there!—
among the leaves and branches . . .

5

Too often I have wanted
to slip away, the hook in me,
to roll off the bed
and into the dark waters under it;
to drift, head down,
hide, hide, the hook in me;
to roll
in the wet ashes of the father,
wet with the death of the father,
and not try
to burn my way upward; the son, rising.

I swear to you now, I will survive,
rise up, and chant my way through these losses;

and you, you, brother, whatever that is,
same blood, you who swim
in the same waters,
you promise me to make your music too,
whatever the hurt;

O when we are almost only
mouth, when we are almost only a head
stuck on the pole of the body,
and the man says "Talk to me, baby,"
let's refuse him, brother, both, all of us,
and striking the spine like an instrument, inside,
like birds, with even the body broken,
our feathers fiery—there! there!—among
the leaves and branches, make
no sounds he will know;
like birds, my brother, birds of the new world, *sing*.

MEETING COOT

by WILLIAM PITT ROOT

from COOT AND OTHER CHARACTERS (Confluence Press)

nominated by Tess Gallagher and Colleen McElroy

Nope not hardly local.
                    Buggywhip
in a world of powerbrakes,
that's me. Unplucked old coot
in a world of sitting ducks
and pumped-up turkeys. Me,
I'm crazy. Crazy like that loon
who spends the livelong night
trying to decide which moon
to court—the far one in the air
or the nearer one in water—
so it clammers back and forth

and back and forth it yodels
while the brightmouthed fox
stands baffled on the shore.

Nope not these parts.

🔥 🔥 🔥

HORST WESSEL

fiction by C.W. GUSEWELLE

from THE PARIS REVIEW

nominated by THE PARIS REVIEW

I AM NOT A LUCKY traveler. Business has taken me often to the far parts of the world and on these journeys I have made it unhappy practice to fall ill in the place I am visiting. This time it is nothing more sensational than an infected tooth, and in so prosaic a place as Bad Godesberg. Tomorrow I will need to find a dentist and have the tooth looked at and treated—or more likely taken out. Which is a nuisance, because it will surely set back my entire schedule of appointments by a full day.

But if sickness is never convenient, other times the infirmities have at least been more interesting—not only clinically, in themselves, but for what they have allowed me to learn *en passant* about the nature of those societies in which I have been stricken.

Once among some Berber people at an oasis south of the Atlas Mountains in the Sahara a kidney ailment felled me suddenly, terrifyingly. I was in indescribable pain, but by the greatest luck there was a doctor in the place, a Dutchman. The people brought him to me and he injected me with two syringes of morphine—the maximum sublethal dose.

More than a day later I awoke in a ward of a little desert infirmary where I had been taken—formerly a French colonial clinic, staffed now by the Dutchman and several half-trained Moroccan assistants.

There were on the steel cots in that room, besides myself, seven young Berber men, all sufferers of trachoma, a fly-borne disease of the eyes which is common to the region and very often blinding. The method of treatment there—and for all I know everywhere— required that the eyes be kept continually open. At the desert infirmary that was accomplished by passing a thread through each eyelid, then rolling back the lids and taping the ends of the taut threads to the upper forehead. Waking there, floating up like a drowned swimmer from the depths of the morphine stupor and seeing my roomfellows asleep—the seven of them with lids open and eyes rolled up whitely in their sockets—and finding moreover that my own pain was entirely gone, for some time I believed that I was in a morgue.

In fact the crisis had passed. Presently the Berber boys woke and as my head cleared we talked, in my pidgin French and theirs. That happened to be the day of the first rain in that place in two years. We stood at the windows, all of us invalids together, and watched it fall for perhaps thirty minutes. Outside no one took cover. The people stood fully in the open, looking up, becoming wonderfully wet in the sharp winter morning of the desert. And then the sooty little cloud passed northward, dragging its skirts up the flank of the high Atlas, and the rain stopped for another year or two.

The treatment of trachoma requires time. Just how much I didn't ask, but some weeks at least. My wardmates said that it was possible, surprisingly soon, to become used to sleeping with the eyes open and that at any rate it was easier than going blind.

The Dutch doctor I never saw again, but his Moroccan aides were wonderfully considerate and kind. They discharged me late that same day, still a bit trembly in the knees but otherwise recovered. In the only store in the village I found some Swiss chocolate bars and

took them back that evening and passed them through the window
to my colleagues in the ward.

That morning's shower, where it had crested the barrier range,
had become briefly a real storm. We looked at the African moon on
the new snow mantle of the mountains and ate chocolate and discussed whether the high pass would be open so that I could get out to
the north by hired car. Then we shook hands under the raised screen
of the window and I went on about my life and they remained there
in theirs.

And as you can see, had it not been for the sickness, all of that I
would have missed.

That adventure is one among many. There have been formidable
dysenteries: from a plate of raw shellfish in Venice in a more trusting
time; from a sugar bun bought, in deliberate madness, from a vendor
in Oaxaca; from the mayonnaise on the Salad *National* in the street
cafe of the hotel of that name in Moscow.

Now certainly the pain of a tooth is not to be compared to the
episode with the kidney. Nor is it as degrading as an ungovernable
bowel. Still, in this moment, it is unpleasant enough. The tooth is
the farthest one back on the right side. The least pressure sets it
aflame. To chew on it is unimaginable. Today is Thursday. In the four
days from Monday morning in Cracow until arriving on this afternoon's plane I have eaten, in total, one bowl of beetroot soup and
three dishes of ice cream.

Because the wisdom tooth and the molar next to it on that side
already have been lost, the tooth in question is of functional importance. I would have liked to save it if at all possible and have eaten
aspirin and waited for it to subside. That has happened in the past a
time or two. Yesterday, however, a great knot rose up beside the
tooth on the inner gum. As I touch that now lightly with the side of
my tongue it seems immense. The swelling has even spread to the
soft tissue beneath the tongue itself, so that to speak or even to
swallow is unpleasant. Not agonizing, but distinctly uncomfortable.
This development I will admit has a bit alarmed me. I recall
stories—or seem to—of the poison from abcessed teeth going directly to the brain. Or possibly it was to the heart. In any case, of
people being overwhelmed by massive corruption. My Polish
friends advised, since it was only a further wait of a day, having it
looked after in Germany.

This afternoon I fell asleep on the plane to Frankfurt and dreamed first that the rot had spread to the tooth next to the hurting one, so that it had to be removed, too. Then it was decided that the matter had been so long neglected it would be necessary to take the whole side of the jaw. The dentists—for in my dream there were armies of them—said that they could rebuild the jaw with bones from my foot, but that the foot would have to be sacrificed. I could choose: a plastic foot or half a face.

I flung myself back and away from them and struck the swollen side of my face against the airplane window and awoke with a scream. The stewardess came and I took a complimentary double whiskey. So this is the illness of this trip; always there is something. The point, then, is to see what can be learned from it.

This hotel is the one in which I always stay. There are other, more elegant ones here, but this one is pleasant and I am used to it. The concierge is very sympathetic. By the time I arrived the dentists all had left their offices, so he will ring one the first thing in the morning. Meantime I have eaten another six aspirin and will hope that on waking the problem will have disappeared. Unlikely, but possible of course. My room faces out on the small park with its ancient trees and, on the far side, a tennis club. It is very deep twilight now, and still the figures of the tennis players in white can be seen gliding soundlessly in the distance. They will hit the ball as long as it can be seen, or after.

Sleep is out of the question.

There is a drinking hall that fronts on the street below the hotel, just under my window. The constant roar of shouting and singing is unbelievable. I telephoned the night man on the hotel desk but he said that there was no help for the noise in such weather. It is uncommonly hot for the season and the windows of the stube must be kept open. Doors, too.

Mine is a corner room, so I have tried shutting the street window and opening the one over the alley to the rear. But there are some men down there—Greeks or Yugoslavs or Turks of some sort—sitting among the cans and beating out rhythms on wooden sticks. The rattle of that penetrates directly to my tooth. Even the din from the drinking hall is preferable.

One time in Leopoldville when it was still the Congo I came down with malaria and was immediately put out of my hotel room for no better reason than that the bastard of a manager—a Belgian—knew how desperately I needed it. Another bed wasn't to be had anywhere in that wretched town, so I sat burning and chattering by turns, through all of two nights and part of a second day, at a table in a street cafe, my bags beside me, a figure of pity and curiosity, watching the sun wheel across and the heat lightning rise north of the Stanley Pool at evening and seeing men carry up butchered pieces of crocodile through the mist from the river at first light and skinned monkeys hung by their wrists from sticks for the market. Until a plane delivered me out of there to Nyasaland.

In bad times it is always reassuring to remember worse.

A sudden cool breath of wind just came through the window. Maybe the weather will change. Below, young men come out of the drinking hall and go lurching across the street, arms flung around each others' shoulders, trumpeting like bulls. They have no regard for the traffic, which is mostly trucks at this hour. The trucks come up soundlessly, Mercedes-Benz trucks—tires just hissing on the pavement—forty miles an hour at a minimum. Trucks and men on foot pay absolutely no attention to one another. The men start into the street. The truck goes past with a rush of wind. The men are gone. Not mashed on the street, just *vanished*. How many such miracles can there be? I cannot watch any longer.

The wind comes more strongly now. There is rain in it. I think I hear the banging of windows being closed, the slamming of doors. I know they must still be singing fiercely below, but I cannot hear it. The Turks have gone in from the alley.

The pain seems less. I can let my mouth close until the teeth touch without crying aloud. But the protuberance beside my tongue, the pocket of infection, is enormously larger, so I know there has been no improvement.

This morning the concierge found that his own dentist was in Switzerland on holiday. The dentist of the dining room manager was, himself, ill. But the concierge assured me there were many others in the town, and he consulted the directory. I was sent finally to an office over a wine and spirits shop, just on the Theaterplatz behind the hotel. The dentist was large and pink, like a grocer, and he ran a pink finger slyly back beside my tongue, investigating the great lump.

A woman assistant appeared. He took a scalpel from her and tried to open the abcess. He jiggled his wrist in fine little aiming motions, like someone about to throw a dart. Then jumped forward—and recoiled just as quickly with a sad cry, face pinched up in anger and regret.

"The incision is not satisfactory," the assistant explained. "The swelling is too hard. So Herr Doktor will rub a substance on it and perhaps in the afternoon, when you come again at thirteen o'clock, it will have softened."

The dentist took down a drill and without anesthesia, with hot bone smoke rising, drilled out entirely a filling on the top of the tooth. I screamed and tried to bite his hand. He clucked reproachfully, but the drill stopped. He gave me a pat of reassurance and selected an instrument with a delicate wire hook on its end and probed inside the tooth until he found the nerve. Then, quite deliberately, he took up the nerve on the point of the hook and tugged at it, lifted, so that I was in fact levitated from the chair and hung writhing like a worm on the hook point.

There was a milk glass light fixture on the ceiling, filled with the brown shapes of dead millers. How they got inside the globe was a mystery that I tried to solve while hanging there on the hook point. Then he let go of the nerve and I dropped a long distance back into the chair.

There is an American military hospital at Wiesbaden two hours or less from here by electric train. I remembered that there was a morning express, so I ran out of the Theaterplatz and across the street, only just being missed by a truck, then the four blocks to the station. I have not run so fast in years. A train was leaving, its last coach just bending out of view. I asked, and it was the train to Wiesbaden.

I sat for a while on a bench on the station platform, watching other trains arrive and leave. The through freights came flashing past, a blur of metal and sucking wind, the face of the driver up behind his window an iron mask, just as he would surely look to someone on the track.

On the opposite platform was an interesting group. Some young people in their twenties, away early for a weekend of climbing or hiking. There were maybe a dozen of them, lean boys and square-shouldered girls, in lederhosen or bluejeans, all with rucksacks. And others: a young couple holding hands; a father alone with an infant in a carriage; a student late to his studies; an old man sitting bolt erect, both palms resting on the silver handle of a cane standing vertical before him. All these in tableau, like sparrows on a wire.

I noticed then a fine cinematic effect. The liquid voice on the platform speaker would announce the scheduled arrival, and on the very instant—as the minute hand of the clock made its final quick advance—the train would slide in and stop, somehow impatient in repose, a band march playing from the open windows of the coaches. Only a moment it would hesitate, then it was gone—and in its going was like a curtain drawn back to reveal a whole new set of people: a long-haired youth in sunglasses; two somber Chinese; an unkempt laborer, some Balkan type; an old couple with matching umbrellas. All already frozen in position as if they had been there forever.

It was wonderful, almost magical, the way the curtain of the train endlessly closed and opened to change the players. I sat for some minutes watching that. The group of young hikers still was on the platform, talking, laughing. An old man listening at one side intruded finally to say something that must have been purposely or accidentally funny because the young people erupted in whoops of joy. And encouraged by that inclusion he offered more, talked louder, forced himself upon them. Until finally, incredibly, he was doing little jumps—waving his cane, jumping straight up stiff-legged off the ground and making quarter-turns in the air.

The young people had lost interest, were not even looking any more. They were talking about something among themselves and had forgotten him quite completely. *Jump, turn.* He abased himself a while longer, and finally crept off ducking and swaying with humiliation. Then a train came and took them all away.

The lump is by now even larger. It is like a turnip filling the lower right side of my mouth. Swallowing is harder as well, even the swallowing of spit. The danger of suffocation briefly occurred to me.

I have just come from the tennis club in the park. There are seats for the public outside the screens, in the shade of the old trees. One player interested me especially. He was a youth of twenty or perhaps a little more with a long, misshapen sickle of a jaw, a helmet of yellow hair and a gangling, bowlegged, hollow-chested child's body—except that he was easily six and a half feet tall. What struck me was the combined impression he conveyed of stupidity and ferocious power.

Last week, from Cracow, I took the excursion to Auschwitz. In the museum of the place there are pictures, made by some of the few

who survived, showing scenes of daily life in the camp. The great
dumb blond child on the tennis court reminded me of the S.S.
warders in those paintings. The racquet was a toy in his fist. He was
not particularly skilled, but when it happened that he did hit the ball
fairly it was *always* unplayable. When he blundered, which was
often, he stomped about the court in an elaborate public show of
rage. Once, after some glaring stroke of ineptitude, he flung his
racquet with such force that it stuck handle-first so high in the fence
around the court that a ladder had to be brought from the club house
to get it down. And in the end, after all of this, the blond brute won
his match easily from a more practiced but smaller, older and
thoroughly frightened opponent.

There is nothing to do now except lie here in the room until the
hour of thirteen, which is of course 1 p.m. Watching the tennis took
my mind briefly off of my predicament. But it is hot again today and
because it has become all but impossible even to drink a glass of
water the possibility of dehydration must be considered. So I have
come indoors to conserve my fluids. These are the last six aspirin in
the bottle. I can't for the life of me imagine why the son of a bitch had
to drill the filling out of the tooth.

I have given the concierge a list of names and telephone numbers
so that he may reschedule my appointments for Monday, with
apologies.

The damned tooth is now broken off a fraction above the gum. Not
broken cleanly—shattered off. It was with my consent, so I am the
fool to blame.

The old dentist was very positive that the thing could not be
saved, and I have passed nearly beyond caring. Just to be rid of it is
now my main hope. But I am *half* rid of it instead. And I must be
careful how I place my tongue. The stump is like broken glass.

He tried to take the tooth, but it was lodged there some way and
he hadn't the strength. So the girl added her weight to his. Finally
they called the man from the store below, to hold my head and
shoulders back against the chair. And it was with the three of them
working that it happened. I was looking at the millers in the milk
glass ceiling globe when there was such a great resonant *whonnnnng*
of a sound that I thought something had struck the building. I looked
down from the light globe and fixed a picture, like a photograph—
first of the storekeeper, his face inverted above me, mouth open

empathetically, then of the doctor and his aide frozen together in midfall, the glass-topped cabinet also falling, the dozens of little implements caught motionless in flight.

My next memory is of being alone in the room some time later. How much later I can't say. For a giddy moment I thought the tooth was gone, for I felt the vacancy plainly. But then I felt also the broken remnant and, with my forefinger, found that the tooth missing was the one *forward* of the diseased one. I sprang up with a cry and, hearing me, the assistant came and drew a crude picture on a scrap of paper, giving me to understand that the root of the abcessed tooth had been hooked under the sound one, so that there was no choice but to remove the impediment. The way was now clear, she said, to complete the extraction. But first the doctor instructed that I go to the hotel and regain my strength and return still again in the evening, when it was cooler. I don't know what the temperature has to do with it. Or, for that matter, what I am to need my strength for. That has an unsettling sound to it.

Outside it occurred to me to hail a taxi and ask advice at the embassy. Even in such a simple thing as the cab I had difficulty making myself understood. And it was no use anyway. The embassy had closed early because of a terrorist threat. Volkpolice had cordoned off the compound. I waved my passport and shouted mushy sounds at them through the taxi window, but the blond corporal just spoke to the driver who backed and turned the Mercedes and took me straight to the hotel.

Here I am, then, and without aspirin the pain is nearly unbearable. One would have thought it might reach a level beyond which there was no increase.

Alternately I lie here on the bed and sit in my chair beside the window. Only a few moments ago, while sitting, I saw three men and two girls come out of the beer stube directly into the path of a silver and purple tandem truck. The truck did not stop or even slow. Other people came out of the drinking hall and stood looking down at the corpses. I wanted to see the conclusion of it, but my pain made me light-headed and I had to come to the bed. Someone must have collected the bodies because the racket of singing has begun again below.

This last was worst. Still the stub of the tooth will not yield. He has given up pulling it out. He tried with a chisel and then a saw—a little whirring circular blade for cutting bone. The saw caught once and leaped to the side and bit into my tongue. There was no pain. My tongue has almost no feeling now. But there was very much blood. So he took a penlike electrical instrument with a glowing white-orange filament to cauterize the the wound.

His window looked down on the Theaterplatz, and during all of this a bus arrived and a great many people got out and set up a portable stage with tent. A crowd began to gather, pulling up benches and shoving for seats.

The old man's hand shook as he started to cauterize. He held his wrist with the other hand to steady it, but both shook the same. The tool rattled against my teeth. He burned my mouth terribly, and seeing that he began to cry and left the instrument smoking in my mouth and turned away in regret.

I took the thing out of my mouth and got out of the chair and with great clarity of mind looked through his cabinet until I found surgical gauze, which I tore off the roll and wadded in my shattered mouth. Then I went to stand at the window while he composed himself.

On the far side of the Theaterplatz people were sitting at cafe tables eating ice cream and drinking expresso. The ones from the bus unfurled a star of David flag and erected a placard that read, "Israel, 28 Years of Independence." Then they began to dance, all of the young Jews looking like Arabs. The Germans were clapping and stamping their feet to the music. A stone flew out of the crowd and I cried a warning, which came out only a weak grunt against the glass. The stone was a flower snatched up quickly with a blown kiss. Then another blossom came flying and one of the dancers dropped without a twitch.

The old man, having dried his eyes, brought soap and towels for us both. The soap had a greasiness and an odd smell, the towel a hairy feel. We stood looking out silently together. Tomorrow, sometime, I will go back to him. I understand that. So does he. We both have invested much and there is a kind of communion between us.

Walking to the hotel I saw my face reflected in a shop window and it is most arresting. Hugely distorted, discolored, the mouth cracked and blistered. The swelling is like a goiter, now, filling the entire space between ear and shoulder. It is fearful to look at and the concierge, when I entered, leaped up in astonishment. I tried to communicate to him my full resignation, but he turned immediately away and pretended not to understand.

Now I am in my room, my head swaddled in the dripping folds of a cool towel. A few minutes ago I went down to the drinking hall to ask—just politely to *ask*—if perhaps they could temper their racket, and they beat me. The Jews are still dancing in the Theaterplatz. Actually their music with the beer songs from the stube make a not unpleasing combination.

The Turks in the alley have stacked boxes on which they can stand to look in at my incredible face. Across the way, in the darkening park, there is some terrible commotion. With a snapping of branches and eruption of shredded leaves a tennis racquet comes exploding up through the trees—and I know that it is only the young *stürmer* late at his play.

HEY, IS ANYONE LISTENING?

by STEPHEN MINOT

from THE NORTH AMERICAN REVIEW

nominated by THE NORTH AMERICAN REVIEW *and DeWitt Henry*

WHEN A TROUPE of actors discover they are playing to an empty house, they cancel the show. Oh, there may be some muttered obscenities, some shuffling of feet, some half-hearted talk about the show going on, but it won't. Actors are a dedicated lot, but they aren't crazy.

When poets and writers with high literary standards discover that they have no readers out there, their first move is to deny the facts. Earnestly. Then they run to a foundation for support.

This is a difficult statement to make not only because it describes some of my best friends but because it applies to me as well. In fact, I am presently the grateful—truly grateful—recipient of a grant from the National Endowment for the Arts. It's paying the mortgage and a hunk of the fuel bill while I teach part time, write fiction, and take time to study the great American tradition of grant-giving.

There's certain logic here: at least my views can't be written off as sour grapes. They are not steeped in bitterness. I'm appreciative. I'm also uneasy.

It has been four years since Harvey Swados wrote that grim article which appeared shortly after his death in the *New York Times* Book Section, January 21, 1973. It should be required reading for all writers, poets, teachers of writers and poets, and foundation personnel.

He laments the fact that his students do not read little magazines. What fiction they do see is in anthologies and paperbacks. And where do they plan to publish?

> . . . in the quarterlies and little magazines which few read regularly and to which none subscribes. One gets the impression that for them these periodicals exist, not because of any intellectual or spiritual commitment on the part of their editors or readers, but rather as a kind of neutral repository for creative efforts. . . .

Now, four years later. I see no change. Here are some solid— though admittedly non-statistical—facts which I consider each time another story of mine appears in a little magazine.

—I have not met an undergraduate student in the past decade who has ever subscribed to a little magazine before taking my writing courses.

—I have not discovered a single colleague in the English Department of the college at which I teach who has ever subscribed to a little magazine publishing fiction or poetry.

—The city of Hartford, Connecticut, has a population of 158,017, is the state capital, is the home of more than five colleges and universities, and does not have a single bookstore or newsstand which will sell a single literary quarterly on a regular basis.

—Although colleagues and students assure me that they make use of the periodical room of our library, and although our library subscribes to every periodical I have appeared in, not once in eighteen years has anyone on this campus ever said, "Hey, I saw your story in. . . ."

Odd.

I am reminded of a television panel discussion I took part in one Sunday morning. It was a taped, professionally produced, publicized production on a commercial station. I was brazen enough to poll a large number of my colleagues the next day. "Oh, by the way. . . ." No one had seen it. Even my wife missed it. My two sons. As for me, something came up and I just forgot.

So much for television's Sunday-morning intellectual ghetto. It has no audience. Zero. Zilch. The cameras grind on, the airways are filled, "culture quotas" are met, but the sets are turned off.

So I learned my lesson. Never again. But I do go on appearing in little magazines. Why? Because, I tell myself, sometimes these stories are reprinted in *Best Stories of*—or in anthologies for college use which real people read. And at least once a publisher took a chance with my little-magazine fiction and printed a paperback collection.

This is what I say when pressed, but my real motivation is less defensible than that, less rational. I do it because except in rare moments of lucidity I convince myself that little magazines have an audience.

They do, of course, in a manner of speaking. Three-thousand for this one, fifteen-hundred for that. Mostly writers like myself, I suspect. A few junior editors. Scattered across a nation, this may mean that for any one magazine there will be five readers in my home state of Connecticut and another seven in an adjoining state. We'll never meet. We'll never discuss what we read, never share our reactions.

We few subscribers are reduced like whales to scattered pods; we are no longer a viable population. We may call out across spaces as I am doing now, but we do not enrich each other. It is a large and chilly sea.

Such is the state of affairs for most writers of fiction. What's life like for the poet?

Feeling strong? Read *Coda*. Read *what*? *Coda* is the most informed, most carefully researched newsletter for poets and writers. It covers contest deadlines, publication statistics, grants, information on little presses and little magazines. Its May 1976 issue reported that the Walt Whitman Award competition received 1,475 manuscripts from which one collection of verse was selected. With odds like that, how could they miss? Yet the sales of the winning collection, excepting libraries, came to a stunning 1,500. In that case, for every practicing poet who put together a decade or more of work there was one—count them, *one*—reader.

That's the sound of one hand clapping.

* * *

Another statistic: *Field: Contemporary Poetry and Poetics* is reported by *Coda* as having received 10,500 individual poems from 1,875 contributors in 1975. And how many subscribers? Just 520. Three submitters for every subscriber.

This isn't tragic, it's crazy. Writers of "serious," "literary" fiction and poetry are guilty of some astonishing delusions about which they are very reluctant to talk. The plain fact is that there's more of us up here on the stage than there are out there in the audience.

* * *

Like paranoids everywhere, we have our list of little green men who are masterminding this whole evil plot. We expose them endlessly and on every possible occasion—in class, in print, at writers' conferences. Indeed, this may be the primary function of writers' conferences. Here is a partial list:

1. Claim: It's the fault of publishers. If they were intelligent, educated men they would publish good fiction and poetry. (Haunting reminder: intelligent, educated publishers of subsidized presses like Illinois and Pittsburgh do publish good fiction and poetry and they lose a bundle. Whose fault is that?)

2. Claim: It's the fault of magazine editors. How come you can write good stuff for a decade and still not place it? (Late night second thought: how many people do I know who would read it if it were accepted? Let's see now, how many of my friends actually subscribe to more than one literary magazine? How many do *I* subscribe to? Well, I just don't have time.)

3. Claim: It's all the fault of high printing costs and high retail prices of books and magazines. (Sobering fact: the relative cost of a hardcover book and a fifth of good Scotch has remained more or less constant over the past three decades.)

4. Claim: The National Endowment ought to hand out more money for us ignored writers. (Counter-question: You want to

increase the number of poetry manuscripts submitted each year from 3,250 to 6,000? To 50,000?)

I too have mouthed these complaints, but they just don't make sense. The absurdity of it all struck me while I was attending the Book Affair in Cambridge last year. It was a great gathering and display of little magazines and little presses put together through the backbreaking, unpaid, selfless efforts of dedicated men and women. It was an enormous act of faith. Yet there was something sad about the sight of table after table of publications which would never reach as many as 400 people—some fewer than 50. All of these were either surviving on grant money or waiting for it. Only a handful of publications represented there had managed to win enough of a following to survive as a self-supporting entity.

There were, of course, stellar exceptions. *Ploughshares* was kept afloat with foundation money and now has a fighting chance of being a viable and significant force on the literary scene. *Fiction International* was there and it certainly has hewed out an exclusive domain for itself not filled by any other publication. Other live-and-well publications included NAR and the *Massachusetts Review*. But the great bulk of magazines there were so minor as to have no real following, no real public need for existing. Most were the private hobbies of their editors. Not one published work which cried out for national distribution. Yet most of these editors expected public aid in the form of grants. And some were very impatient.

I was reminded of the Indian Thoreau writes about in *Walden*. He was furious because no one would buy the baskets he made.

> Thinking that when he made the baskets he would have done his part, and then it would be the white man's to buy them. He had not discovered that it was necessary for him to make it worth the other's while to buy them, or at least make him think that it was so.

Doesn't sound like Henry? Well, he went on to say that he himself had decided not to get into the selling business. His choice. But every editor I spoke to at the Book Affair *was* concerned with sales and most, like the Indian, were indignant that the public had not come running to buy their wares.

The heart of the problem as I see it is this: We who take literary creativity seriously have put the bulk of our efforts into producing

more and better fiction and poetry; we have ignored to an astonishing degree the task of establishing an audience for that work.

The fault lies both with the universities and the foundations. We
in the United States invented the phenomenon of the creative
writing class. There were none at the turn of the century; they are
now an almost required portion of every U.S. college curriculum.
There are more M.A. programs in writing in 1977 than there were a
decade ago and they are presently undergoing a dramatic increase in
popularity. No national commission has determined that we need
more writers and poets; the growth is internal and self-perpetuating.
We are turning out more and more skilled literary craftsmen and
craftswomen—an ever expanding tribe of basket weavers in a nation
which at present prefers plastic.

As for the foundations, I cannot fault them for financing hard-
pressed writers and poets, but they are generating a backlog of
hostility as these subsidized work-wizards discover that there is no
market for their wares. What if we quadruple the number of poetry
manuscripts submitted to the University of Pittsburgh Press each
year? What have we done but quadruple the number of frustrated
and embittered unpublished poets? How can we defend that kind of
program to a tax-weary public? How can we defend NEA's budget
against, say, HEW's?

The real risk, of course, is that the absurdity of subsidizing un-
wanted literary productivity will finally be made known to the wider
public. What if these same doubts are raised in the pages of *Play-
boy*? We may find the foundations under attack even before we can
effect a change in policy. There is a pressing need for a change in
policy *before* the wider public begins asking the same questions
Thoreau did of his Indian.

There is, I think, a reasonable solution. It is a ten-year plan. It
would cost no more tax dollars. It could start next year.

The National Endowment for the Arts could establish this policy:
That for a decade at least two-thirds of all foundation grants must be
justified by a credible claim that such payments will create a wider
audience for the arts.

Who loses? It means, first, a reduction of grants for individual
writers and poets. No grants whatever for new magazines or insol-
vent old ones. The thrust of this policy is toward establishing a new
and wider need for both fiction and poetry; eventually both writers
and magazines will benefit.

How do we establish this need? There are a multitude of possible programs some of which are now in effect in small measure. Here is a sample of what could be a long list of proposals:

1. Subsidize classroom use of little magazines in high schools and colleges. This will require supporting those magazines which are at least willing to cooperate. I selected three of the top literary magazines for classroom use this year and only one (NAR) was interested. One of the others waited a month and then demanded pre-payment (as if the college would skip the country to save $18); the third couldn't bother to locate 15 copies. Some editors have the survival instincts of lemmings. To hell with them. These grants would go only to those publications which demonstrate a clear interest in survival by offering special rates for students, desk copies for instructors, and something resembling prompt response. Such magazines deserve a bonus grant—not merely enough to cover administrative costs, but enough to serve as a reward for finding new readers.

2. Subsidize in-class distribution organizations. Recently into the business of distribution is The Plains Distribution Service (Box 3112, Fargo, ND 58102) which in addition to serving as an outlet for Midwestern small press books has begun putting together classroom-use packages of as many as six literary magazines, themselves primarily Midwest based.

And most recent of all, CCLM (Coordinating Council for Literary Magazines) has begun exploring "cluster" distribution schemes with help from a private foundation grant.

3. Heavy subsidy of bookmobile programs. So far, only one such bus travels about, bringing little magazines and small-press publications to campuses. If we in Hartford have not been able to buy a copy of the *Virginia Quarterly Review* or the University of Illinois short story collections or the Fiction Collective novels, that means that no one outside of New York, Cambridge, and San Francisco has. There should be a bookmobile in every state covering each campus twice each term. And they need ample funds for publicity.

4. Increase the ongoing Poets-in-Schools program. Real live poets and authors in the classroom suggest that language is something we can all enjoy and share. The present program is excellent, but it is only a start. These students are most likely to be the ones who will voluntarily buy and read the little magazines of the 1980s.

5. Support cooperatives such as the one called *Magazine*. This

group has been running joint ads in the *Nation* and the *New Republic*, dividing the cost among six member-magazines. They have also been working on joint problems of distribution. Many such groups are needed to solve a variety of shared needs.

6. Support any group which is willing to present a display of literary magazines at the annual Modern Language Association regional meetings. It is simply astonishing that these gatherings which bring together tens of thousands of intelligent teachers of English had never until 1976 (when CCLM, an offshoot of the NEA, tried it in New York) been used to present journals of contemporary fiction and poetry. Scholars and writers do, after all, share the same language.

The lack of such a display to date may not be entirely accidental. Last year I was asked by the University of Illinois Press to arrange an informal display of four of their short-fiction collections at the NEMLA (New England M. L. A.) meeting in Burlington, Vermont. Since I was a member of NEMLA and was giving a paper, and was also one of the authors represented, I was sure there would be no problem. A matter of common courtesy, I thought. I was naive. All four books were promptly discarded and when I tried, unsuccessfully, to retrieve them, I was reprimanded at some length for "illegally displaying wares without paying the proper fee." Textbook publishers had paid hundreds of dollars for the privilege and who did I think I was?

7. If existing little magazines are to receive any support at all during this ten-year test period, grants should be limited to those publications which, without reducing quality, have been able to increase their circulation by 20% in any given year. Such awards should be based on their operating budget since flat grants always favor the smallest publications. Another method is to offer a matching grant of 50% of each new subscription gained during a 12-month period. In either case, awards would be restricted to those who are willing and able to find new readers.

Such a policy would bring cries of protest from some of the older publications which have grown used to the comfort of regular subsidies. But these are often the magazines which have acquired over the years an editorial arrogance which is inexcusable. One of our oldest and formerly most distinguished publications now regularly takes six months or longer to read submissions. Another describes its function in *Writer's Market* as "Mostly for academics . . . and friends and family of the editor." Such publications have renounced all claim to public support.

8. Flat grants to libraries which are willing to put on displays of little magazines complete with readings by some of the contributors.

9. Grants to daily or weekly newspapers which are willing to run short short stories of quality, as have many Italian newspapers for decades. Papers like the *Boston Globe* are already moving in this direction and need only an encouraging nudge.

10. Support for a full-time advisory finance-and-distribution team of individuals with magazine experience, the group to study the particular problems and needs of individual magazines and help editors to broaden their appeal and increase their circulation.

Doubtless there are many more routes, but the goal should be the same: establishing and maintaining a wider audience for the good fiction and poetry which we are now producing.

There is no possibility that such a program would lead to commercialism. Editors who volunteer their time to manage little magazines are not going to turn into Rupert Murdochs at the scent of grant money. For one thing, there just isn't enough. NEA's budget will always be modest by European standards. More than that, the literary community has its own well-formed values and will not sacrifice them. Change will be slow. But change is possible if leadership is provided.

I am convinced that the shift in emphasis which I have been describing can in a decade produce a dramatic revitalization of our national literary scene. I see no reason why we cannot create a literary audience which will treble the readership of existing little magazines, make it possible to publish books of poetry on a break-even basis, and provide a market for those publishers willing to present collections of short stories. To achieve these goals we have to create a national interest in contemporary literature and build from that a genuine community of readers and writers.

I envision a great range of publications, each with its own special character—not the "neutral repository for creative efforts" but publications with active, enthusiastic support. I see no reason why we cannot one day expect students entering our writing classes to have been subscribers to little magazines since their high-school years, to be aware already of what is being published and to be able to support with enthusiasm their favorite periodicals and writers. Is it so fantastic to imagine students and even a few colleagues discussing the fiction and poetry of little magazines as naturally as literate adults now talk about what has just appeared in the *New Yorker?*

I am not describing a vast cultural revolution. Such a group will always be a minority within a society which is concerned with other values; but I can visualize this minority becoming a genuine community, sharing a body of contemporary literary works and a familiarity with living authors and poets, sharing also a vocabulary and a set of values, differing sharply in their preferences, taking pleasure both in the agreements and the disagreements, and exploring avenues of growth which are essential for creative development.

We are years from this right now. What's worse, we aren't moving toward it. Like composers of non-popular music, we are in stasis. Almost no one is listening. We're crazy if we claim we don't care. And we're myopic if we can't see what direction we must take. It does no good to pay us to produce more fiction and poetry if there is no one who wants to read it.

EVERYONE KNOWS
WHOM THE SAVED ENVY

by JAMES GALVIN

from ANTAEUS

nominated by Carolyn Forché

It isn't such a bad thing
To live in one world forever.
You could do a lot worse:
The sexual smell of fresh-cut alfalfa
Could well be missing somewhere.
Somewhere you'd give in to some impetuous unknown,
And then stand guilty, as accused, of self-love.
It's better not to take such risks.

It's not as if we had no angels:
A handful remained when the rest moved on.
Now they work for a living
As windmills on the open range.
They spin and stare like catatonics,
Nod toward the bedridden peaks.
They've learned their own angelic disbelief.

The mountains still breathe, I suppose,
Though barely
The prairie still swells under a few small churches.
They are like rowboats after the ship's gone down.
Everyone knows whom the saved envy.
Runoff mirrors the sky in alpine pastures;
Imagine how quickly one's tracks unbloom there.
This world isn't such a bad world.

At least the angels are gainfully employed:
They know where the water is,
What to do with wind.
I try not to think of those others,
Like so many brides,
So many owls made of pollen
Wintering in a stand of imaginary timber.

♨ ♨ ♨

SWEENEY ASTRAY

by SEAMUS HEANEY

from ARMADILLO

nominated by ARMADILLO

This run of verses occurs about half-way through a Middle-Irish work known as BUILE SHUIBHNE, or SWEENEY ASTRAY, as I have rendered it, astray in his mind and in his own country. It is the story, in prose and verse, of a king from the north of Ireland called Sweeney who is cursed by one St. Ronan and turned into a bird at the Battle of Moira. Sweeney had gone there to fight on behalf of another king called Congal. The main body of the work is an account of his subsequent woes and wanderings, such as his residence in a madman's glen called Glen Bolcain; his pursuit by a posse of kinsmen headed by Lynchseachan; his hunger and exposure to the elements; his various guilts; and his foreknowledge of his own death by the spear at St. Mullin's church in Carlow.

Readers of Flann O'Brien's AT-SWIM-TWO-BIRDS will be familiar with Sweeney as part of the comic apparatus of that novel. My sense of him is more elegiac. His experiences are purgatorial. He physics his pomp, takes protective colouring from the landscape itself, becomes its tongue. He is Lear and Poor Tom at once, a type of the poet as inspired madman, paranoiac, schizophrenic, totally sympathetic.

Some of the verse reworks older traditional material, such as the "tree alphabet" at the beginning of this extract. It is composed in strict bardic forms, whose metronome I do not try to follow. Instead, I have let the stanzas wear out a metrical or free shape for themselves in response to the feel and sense of the original material.

Seamus Heaney

Suddenly a clamour
and belling in the glen!
The little timorous stag
like a wild musician

saws across the heartstrings
a high homesick refrain
of deer on my lost hillsides,
flocks on my native plain.

Here bushy, leafy oak trees
climb up to the daylight,
the forking shoots of hazel
divulge their musky nut.

The alder is my darling,
all thornless in the gap,
some milk of human kindness
coursing in its sap.

The blackthorn is a jaggy creel
stippled with dark sloes;
green watercress is thatch on wells
where the drinking blackbird goes.

Sweetest of the leafy cliques,
the vetches strew the pathway;
the oyster-grass is my delight
and the wild strawberry.

Ever-generous apple-trees
rain big showers when shaken;
scarlet berries clot like blood
on mountain rowan.

Briars insinuate themselves,
arch a stickle back,
draw blood and curl up innocent
to sneak the next attack.

The yew tree in each churchyard
wraps night in its dark hood.
Ivy is a shadowy
genius of the wood.

Holly rears its windbreak,
a door in winter's face;
life-blood on a spear-shaft
darkens the grain of ash.

Birch-tree, smooth and blessed,
delicious to the breeze,
high twigs plait and crown it
queen of trees.

The aspen pales
and whispers, hesitates:
a thousand frightened scuts
race in the leaves.

But what disturbs me
more than anything
is an oak rod, always
swinging its thong.

*

Ronan was dishonoured,
he rang his little bell;
he clapped me in a labyrinth
of curse and miracle;

and noble Congal's armour,
that tunic edged with gold,
swathed me in doomed glory
with omens in each fold.

His lovely tunic marked me
in the middle of the rout,
the host pursuing, yelling,
—That's him in the gold coat.

—Get him, take him live or dead,
every man fall to.
Draw and quarter, pike
and spit him, none will blame you.

The horsemen still were after me
into the north of Down,
my back escaping nimbly
from every javelin thrown.

I fled, I must confess,
like a spear's trajectory,
my course a whisper in the air,
a breeze flicking through ivy.

I overtook the startled fawn,
outstripped his dainty toe,
I caught, I rode him lightly—
from peak to peak we go;

from Inishowen's hilltops
I scorched along so free,
mountain after mountain
until I'm at Galtee

and from Galtee up to Liffey
I'm skipping terrified
and reach, towards evening,
Ben Bulben, where I hide.

Who on the even of battle thought
with me so puffed in pride
that I would spin off fortune's wheel
to scour that mountainside?

       *

And then Glen Bolcain was my lair,
my earth and den;
I've roamed those slopes contented
by star and moon.

I wouldn't swap a hermit's hut
in that dear glen
for a world of mountain acres
or spreading plain.

Its waters' flashing emerald,
its wind so keen,
its tall brooklime, its watercress's
luscious green.

I love the ancient ivy-tree,
the merry sallow,
the birch's sibilant melody,
the solemn yew.

And you, Lynchseachan, can try
disguise, deceit,
the liar's mask, the shawl of night:
I won't be caught

again. You managed it the first time
with your litany of the dead:
father, mother, daughter, son,
brother, wife—you lied

but when you come the next time
Clear the Way!
Or face the heights of Mourne
and follow me.

*

I would lodge happily
in an ivy bush
high in some twisted tree
and never come out.

The skylarks'
unexpected treble
sends me pitching and tripping
over stumps on the moor

and my hurry
flushes the turtle dove.
I overtake it,
my plumage rushing,

am startled
by the startled woodcock
or a blackbird's sudden
volubility.

Think of my wild career,
my coming to earth
where the fox still
gnaws at the bones—

then away I go again
eluding the wolf in the wood,
athlete of air,
lifting off towards the mountain,

the bark of foxes
echoing below me,
the wolves howling
my send off,

their vapouring tongues,
their low-slung speed
shaken off like nightmare
at the foot of the slope.

Hobbled to the past,
I show my heels
and breast into guilt,
a sheep without a fold.

In the old tree at Killoo
I sleep soundly
dreaming back prosperous days
with Congal in Antrim.

A starry frost will come
dropping on the pools
and I'll be astray here
on the unsheltered heights:

herons calling
in cold Glenelly,
flocks of birds quickly
coming and going.

I prefer the elusive
rhapsody of blackbirds
to the garrulous company
of humans.

I prefer the squeal of badgers
in their sett
to the tally-ho
of the morning hunt.

I prefer the re-
echoing bellow of a stag
among the peaks
to that arrogant horn.

Those unharnessed runners
from glen to glen!
Nobody tames
that royal blood,

each one aloof
on a summit,
antlered, watchful.
Imagine them,

The stag of high Slieve Felim,
the stag of the steep Fews,
the stag of Duhallow, the stag of Orrery,
the fierce stag of Killarney.

The stag of Islandmagee, Larne's stag,
the stag of Moylinny,
the stag of Cooley, the stag of Cunghill,
the stag of the two-peaked Burren.

The mother of this herd
is old and grey,
the stags that follow her
are branchy, many tined.

I would creep beneath the grey
hut of her head,
would roost among
her mazy antlers,

would be dissembled
in this thicket of horns
that come sloping at me
over the belling glen.

I am Sweeney, the whinger,
the scuttler in the valley.
But call me, instead,
Peak Pate, Stag Head.

      *

The springs I always liked
were the fountain at Dunmall
and the spring-well on Knocklayde
that tasted pure and cool.

Forever mendicant,
my rags all frayed and scanty,
high up in the mountains
like a crazed, frost-bitten sentry

I find no bed nor quarter,
no easy place in the sun:
not even in this reddening
covert of tall fern.

My only rest: eternal
sleep in holy ground
when St. Moling's earth lets fall
its dark balm on my wound.

But now that sudden clamour
and belling in the glen!
I am a timorous stag
feathered by Ronan Finn.

DAVID

by DAVID McCANN

from POETRY

nominated by POETRY

The Guildmaster, Brunelleschi, had him, and after
that he was glimpsed in a litter emerging from the
palace of the Fool, who would buy anything. No one
knew whether the boy was an Egyptian or a Greek, nor
when he first came to spend afternoons in the dim
courtyard at Number 64 Via delle Caldaglie. The boy
never spoke, only smiled and in the evenings coolly
acquiesced. It was a blessing, that day Brunelleschi
came and drew him away. The work had lain still for
weeks. Donatello bowed with grace to the inevitable,
then cast the head of that master thief beneath the
upturned heel of his April love. The mob roared at
the joke. Brunelleschi himself, it was said, was torn
in half by pride. The boy went north at summer's end,
where Giangalleazo kept him one year. Much later he
returned, bigger than life. At the warm stone of his
flesh he made the whole city kneel.

🔥 🔥 🔥

PARTING SHOT

fiction by WALTER ABISH

from STATEMENTS 2 (Fiction Collective)

nominated by Raymond Federman and Ronald Sukenick

1.

I RETURNED FROM MOROCCO in September in time for my exhibition of photographs at the Light Gallery on Madison Avenue. Most of the exhibition was devoted to photographs I had taken of the Mosque of Kairouan, and of the city of Kairouan which is surrounded on all sides by desert. At the very last moment, before the exhibition was to open, I decided to include a photograph I had taken of Irma on the West Side pier a week or two before my departure for North Africa. I was fully aware that the photograph was out of context with the exhibition, and might even be disconcerting to a viewer looking at the Great Mosque, and the innumerable shots I had taken of the shrouded women in the city. I included the photograph of Irma for no particular reason that I can understand. I had invited her to accompany me to Morocco and Tunis, but she couldn't make up her mind, and I finally left without her. I worked in my darkroom on the print of Irma in her one-piece bathing suit only after my return from North Africa. At the opening the gallery was packed with people, and in general the show was well received. I sold about a dozen prints the first night. In all I sold eight prints of the photograph of Irma sunning herself on a bench at one hundred and twenty-five dollars each, but of the eight buyers only Gregory Brinn called me to invite me to his place on Central Park West for a drink. I remember looking everywhere for Irma at the opening, but apparently she never made it.

A friend of mine informed me that Gregory Brinn was an authority on Guy de Maupassant, who incidentally had visited and admired the Great Mosque of Kairouan in 1889. Brinn was also a literary critic, and his wife was the daughter of Emmanuel F. Hugo, a well-known and extremely popular writer. Somehow, I had not expected to be the only guest invited that afternoon; however, both Gregory Brinn and his wife, Maude, were extremely cordial. Somewhat furtively I looked around for the photograph he had bought, and finally located it on a bookshelf in his study. The photograph was inside a Kulick frame.

From his desk Gregory Brinn had a superb view of Central Park eighteen floors below, and, whenever he chose to turn his head slightly to the left, a view of Irma in her one-piece bathing suit. I must admit I was somewhat disappointed that he had not picked one of the photographs of the Great Mosque. As an authority on Maupassant who had written with great eloquence of the latter's visit to the Mosque, Brinn's failure to choose one of the Kairouan photographs struck me as odd. She has a striking face, he said, referring to Irma. He then asked me if I was attracted to the kind of cold sensuality Irma exuded. I couldn't think of an appropriate answer.

What makes you decide to photograph someone, Gregory asked me just before I left. I walked out of their apartment with a vague sense of having been used. I felt that I had been asked over in order to supply Gregory Brinn with information regarding the woman on the photograph he had bought. Perhaps he felt that for the price he had paid I should provide the information. When I had said that I knew Irma quite well, he had promptly asked me if I ever had an affair with someone simply as a result of having taken their photograph. Well, Irma is always photographically available, I replied, expecting him to laugh. With no change of expression on his face, he stared at me, apparently trying to evaluate what I had said.

The following day his wife went to the gallery and bought one of the photographs of the Great Mosque, one that had two men in white cloaks standing in the background. She paid with her own personal check. I think she bought the print purely as a way of apologizing for her husband's behavior. I had been invited over on a false pretense, and she knew it. My first impulse was to ring her up and thank her for buying the print, but then realized how awkward and stilted the conversation would be, since her purchase had only been a gesture, and what I was thanking her for as a professional photographer was her supposed good taste, and her admiration for my work.

Months later I ran into her on Madison Avenue. She was looking at a blue blazer on display in one of the shopwindows at Triplers. Do you like it, she asked anxiously, momentarily leaving me with the impression that she intended to buy it for me. It's very handsome, I said. I'm so glad you like it. I intend to get it for Gregory. He looks so good in a blazer. I could tell that she was very much in love with him.

By the way, what's the name of the woman in the photograph you took?

Irma, I said reluctantly, Irma Dashgold.

She's awfully attractive. I believe Gregory's fallen in love with her. Do you see her often?

Now and then.

You must come and see us again, she said politely. Gregory and I enjoyed your visit immensely. I wanted to thank her for buying the print of the Great Mosque, but didn't.

I fell in love with Irma the first time I saw her. I was much younger, and it was easy to fall in love with her, or perhaps I should correct that and say, that she made it easy for one by treating love the way she treated everything else, with a kind of elegant casualness.

What does she do? Maude asked.

Who?

Irma.

I really don't know.

She said goodbye, and then entered Triplers, I assume to buy the blazer. I hoped I would not run into her again, since the encounter had made me remember her gesture, it also reminded me of her husband, and their very beautiful apartment on the eighteenth floor. I remembered the view from the apartment, as well as the gleaming parquet floor, and the way each object in the apartment appeared to have been carefully placed where it was in order not to detract from the beauty of another object. Visiting their place was a little bit like going to a museum. Although Gregory Brinn was successful, it was mostly if not entirely her money, or more precisely, her father's money that had paid for everything in the apartment. I could not efface the photograph of Irma sitting on his bookshelf within close proximity of his desk. It may have been the reason why I never displayed Irma's photograph in my place, although I was greatly tempted to.

2.

The large plate glass windows of the stores on Madison Avenue are there to protect the intrinsic value of the plaid suit, of the houndstooth hunting jacket, of the blue blazer, the purple polo shirt, the polka dot scarf and what are essentially tastefully arranged objects in the shopwindow, without for a second depriving the passerby of the perfection of the merchandise.

Does the accumulation of what is perfect indicate wealth. The large plate glass windows are always clean. They not only permit a viewer to see what is inside the shopwindow, they also reflect what stands and moves outside the store. It is not entirely uncommon to see a man wearing a blue blazer stop to look at what appears to be the exact replica of his jacket in a shopwindow. It is, in fact, wealth that permits the easy replication of what is perfect, despite Whitehead's admonition: *Even perfection will not bear the tedium of indefinite repetition.*

Did Whitehead know that wealth enables people to acquire the perfect apartment, the perfect country house, the perfect haircut, the perfect English suits, the perfect leather and chrome armchair, the perfect shower curtain, the perfect tiles for the kitchen floor, and a perfect quiche available only from a small French bakery near Madison Avenue, and the perfect Italian boots that look like English boots but are more elegant, and the perfect mate, and the perfect stereo, and the perfect books that have received or undoubtedly are just about to receive a glowing review in the *Saturday Review*. Wealth makes it so much easier to have the perfect encounter with a stranger, enjoy the perfect afternoon, make perfect love, a sexual encounter that is enhanced by the objects that are in the room, objects that may at one time have attracted a good deal of attention while on display in a Madison Avenue shop window.

I do not feel well, said Maude. I distrust Gregory with all my heart. I also distrust my own acquisitiveness, and my occasional generosity. Why on earth did I buy Gregory that 200 dollar jacket? What I really would like is to spend my life somewhere in the country, away from the stores. I would like to stroll down a country lane, surrounded by horses and whitewashed barns, and wave to friendly yet aloof farmers with weatherbeaten faces. I do not feel that the perfection of anything in this apartment has enriched my life in the slightest. All it has done is to protect me from what I consider garish and crude. I walk around in the nude to combat the incipient coldness of Gregory. How easy it is to give in to his remoteness and to surrender and embrace his sexual indifference . . . We no longer make love. We occasionally fuck . . . two collectors of perfect experience, assessing the degree to which we have arrived at the state of perfection.

3.

Gregory does not know where in the city I had taken the photograph of Irma. It will take him some time to find the pier with the double row of benches on either side. People who visit the pier walk up one side and then return by the other. When I took the photograph early in the morning most of the benches were not occupied. I let Irma pick one. What do you want me to do. Anything you like, I said. She wearing her one-piece bathing suit. Her feet resting on the bench in front of her, she leaned back, and shut her eyes. She was posing, she was also trying to decide whether or not to accompany me to North Africa.

Everyone who enters Gregory's study, comments on the photograph.

Isn't that a Kulick frame?

Yea.

Who is she?

I saw the photograph at a gallery on Madison. She possesses a certain almost undefinable sensual coldness that I find attractive.

They stare at Irma. Their eyes dissect her. I see what you mean.

I wonder what she does, Maude remarked to Gregory.

Why don't you ask the photographer.

She smiled. I will, the next time I see him.

Why don't you give him a ring? He's in the book.

4.

Don't you think you ought to put on a robe instead of parading naked around the house, said Gregory. There are people out there. Gregory pointed at the houses on the other side of the park. You may not know it. It may not occur to you, but anyone looking into our apartment must get a curious impression of the way we live.

We're on the eighteenth floor, she reminded him.

I still wish you wouldn't walk around in the nude.

I wonder if you have the vaguest idea of how irritating you are, said Maude.

I merely suggested that you put on a robe. People talk. The doorman has been giving me the strangest looks for the past month.

People talk. Is that what you would say to that glorious beauty in your study. You'd be off like a shot if you had the teeniest chance of fucking her.

Oh well, said Gregory, I better take a walk. I don't want to stand in the way of one of your little melodramas.

From their apartment on the eighteenth floor Maude can see the buildings on Fifth Avenue across the park. Using Gregory's binoculars, she can make out Gregory's tall figure in his blue blazer as he heads for the other side of the park, turning occasionally to look at someone who has attracted his attention. Once he turned around, as if sensing that he was being observed, and shading his eyes against the sun with one, stared at their building, at their floor, at her standing naked at the window. But at that distance she could not make out the expression on his face. There really was no need to see his expression. It never changed. He was going over to the Madison to look at the latest exhibition of photographs at the Light Gallery.

5.

Maude called her closest and dearest friend Muriel. Tell me, she asked impulsively. Have you and Gregory ever fucked? I won't be mad if you say yes.

So you take me for some kind of shit, said Muriel. I don't screw around with married men if I happen to know their wives.

Then what about Bob?

But that's different. I can't stand Cynthia. Look, why don't you come over and talk about it?

What's there to talk.

Whatever's on your mind. Whatever made you pick up your phone.

I can't make it today, said Maude firmly. Maybe tomorrow.

Not before eleven, said Muriel.

Do you ever sunbathe on a park bench?

Never, said Muriel emphatically. I can't bear the sun.

Maude studied Irma's photograph, and realized that Irma resembled her slightly. Yes, there was a distinct resemblance. One of these days, she decided, I'll go to a park or to one of those piers on the West Side wearing only my skimpiest bathing suit, and then, among all the freaks and weirdoes with their Great Danes, I'll stretch out on a bench, my eyes shut, soaking in the sun, oblivious to everything and everyone around me . . .

When Gregory had stepped out of their apartment to walk across to the Light Gallery he was wearing a blue gingham shirt she had bought him for his thirty-eighth birthday, and the blue blazer she had bought him at Triplers. She had spotted it in the shopwindow. She had not even intended to buy him anything that day. Yes, he said, when he tried it on. It's a nifty jacket. She had also bought him three silk shirts, two ties, and a belt. Seeing him for the first time, a woman, any woman might think that Gregory was a really sexy sort of guy. He loved to leave women with that impression.

6.

Maude is quite prepared to acknowledge that the instability of every object around her, the instability of her vision, the instability of her fragile demands upon herself and others may have paved the way to what had happened, at the same time that it steeled her for the eventuality of Gregory's abrupt departure. Perhaps *unannounced* was the word for which she was searching, not *abrupt*. His departure being unannounced appeared as abrupt. He left saying that he was going to take in a show at the Light Gallery. The mere mention of the gallery brought to mind the acquisition of the photograph, and then the presence of the photographer in their apartment, a somewhat hostile presence, she felt.

She watches Gregory leave, and with the aid of his binoculars follows his progress across the park. Most likely he will proceed straight to the Light Gallery, but the possibility that he will fail to return cannot be ruled out . . . He'll do anything to demolish her, destroy her, intensify the agony she suffers daily at the instability, the fragility, the ambiguity, the indirectness of everything that is said and done.

But despite the aforementioned instability of her vision, she can easily run up a flight of stairs,
    she can also sew on a button,
    prepare a mushroom omelette,
    calmly undress in front of an open window,
    grip a head between her thighs,
    turn her head ever so slightly to the left and then to the right at the dinner table and gravely listen to what the men on either side of her are saying.
    What else can she do?
    Afflicted with the grave insecurity that measures the exact, the precise breaking point of every object, she can also muffle her screams.
    She can wait in a panic for Gregory's return.
    She can kill some time by writing a letter to her father who is spending the summer as usual in his rundown country place.

7.

This is an introduction to the father. His left eye twitches at what appear to be regular intervals. But his handwriting is quite controlled, quite steady, almost appearing confident and overbearing. Wherever he happens to be, he is waiting for the mailman, waiting for the envelope bearing her nervous scrawl.

Why am I writing this letter to my father, Maude asks herself. I am writing this letter to cause him pain.

It is one of those beautiful days in early June or late August. In one week Maude has received half-a-dozen picture postcards from friends vacationing abroad. Most of the postcards show a good deal of blue sky, an excessive amount when you come to think of it. It is the color so dearly loved by the suntanned men and women stretched out on the white beach, their blank-looking faces turned skywards. The postcards she receives are all cheerfully cryptic. If you only knew who is screwing Lou. P and S have separated again. He is trying to persuade me to leave F. Who is Lou. Who is P and S. and who is F? The postcards allude to exotic Persian rituals in the caves. The cards are all addressed to her and Gregory, it being taken for granted that they, for the time being at least, are still sharing the same perfect apartment overlooking Central Park. That they are still sharing the same magnificent blue tiled bathroom with the sunken tub, and that occasionally, when the situation demands it, they compare each other favorably to someone else, someone who may have suddenly cropped up in their life, someone who smiled at one of them invitingly, a smile that could not have been mistaken for anything else . . . For all Maude knows, everyone who has been writing and calling her on the phone may know more about the woman in the photograph than she does. For all she knows, Gregory may at this moment be seeing the woman. It might have been he who requested the photographer to take the photograph of her in the black bathing suit. Nothing could possibly surprise her now.

All the same, despite her almost detached awareness of Gregory's ongoing unfaithfulness (what an old-fashioned word) she is mistaken in her belief that anything she might write her father could possibly cause him pain. He is inured to her attempts to cause him pain, because he recognizes her intent to do so. No, her letter will not cause him pain. When someone stole his new bike, that caused him pain, and whenever he misses a train back to the city, it causes him a terrible and agonizing pain.

What is her father doing at this precise moment. He is working on his eighteenth novel. His principal character, Agnes, a divorcee, is walking along Madison Avenue, musing to herself as she glances at the more attractive shopwindows. It would never, for instance, occur to Maude's father to question the fragility of glass, or ponder the intrinsic function of the large plate glass windows in a post-industrial society. Not unlike his daughter, his character Agnes can run up a flight of stairs,
    sew on a button,
    prepare a spinach pie for seven,
    toss a vase across the room,
    set the dial correctly on the small washing machine in the kitchen,
    and determinately search for a specific word in the dictionary, a word that would spell a certain release, that would indicate a lightening of the burden some people suddenly, when they least expect it, feel in their hearts, or roughly in the area where they suspect their heart to be, somewhere below the left shoulder, and a bit to the right.

Like his daughter, his character, Agnes, can lightheartedly chat for hours on the phone with her best friend. It is part of the novel's format. The conversation may appear banal. But it is pertinent to the novel's development. Still, Maude's father is terribly selective in his choice of details he wishes to magnify and details he wishes to omit. If the doorman is about to collapse, and if Agnes, his character, mistakenly presses the wrong elevator button, he neglects to mention it. He glosses over the universal dread people have that someone may change the locks on their doors while they are out. All his male characters are somewhat heavy-handed but brave. They seem to show a marked preference for fur collars on their wintercoats, and stare expectantly at the naked woman in their bedroom. The woman, in this case, is Agnes. She is standing proudly (?) erect, her legs slightly parted. All the men agree that she has superb legs. Fleshy calves. In chapter three of his eighteenth novel Agnes is about to be screwed. This she knows. She anticipates it. One might say she was aware of it the moment she woke up that morning. It will happen today, she said to herself. Not that she could possibly anticipate it all in its minute details, but only in a broad sense that did not, however, diminish the clarity of her vision of the event that was to take place. It could happen at any moment. She may, for the duration of the climactic encounter, lie on her back, or sit on a tabletop, or crouch on the floor. The positions, for that is what they are called, are as recognizable as the objects that are so carefully and meticulously displayed in any one of the shopwindows on Madison Avenue. A woman can easily spend an hour selecting a blouse, asking herself: shall I buy this one or that. A woman can always recognize a beautiful blouse. A woman can also recognize a prick, even in its flaccid state. Each recognition presents a different problem to the mind. What is my correct response, asks the character in her father's novel. Clearly it is to arouse the man. In doing do, the man, as it were, recedes into the background, becoming one with the wallpaper, as Agnes concentrates her entire attention on the man's prick.

If only all my father's female characters did not resemble me, sighed Maude.

As stated previously, the unreliability of Maude's vision, the unreliability of each telephone conversation she has, the unreliability of every encounter with a friend, acquaintance, or past lover, has prepared Maude for Gregory's disappearance. It was really astonishing, when she thought of it, that his disappearance had not occurred at an earlier date. That he had waited five-and-a -half years to disappear. A few characters in her father's novels had on one occasion or another dropped out of sight, but they were all minor characters, and never missed by the reader. Evidently her father had no use for disappearances. He did not care to create ambiguous situations that required a great deal of explanations. Instinctively, he understood the readers' distaste for the gratuitous act. He knew his women readers, and his readers were predominantly women. He interviewed them in the supermarket. A woman was not bewildered when she saw a naked man in front of her. She can readily grasp in a man's excitement the great need that manifests itself daily in all human beings. A woman can to a great extent determine her own response to that need.

She can run up a flight of stairs,
undress,
examine herself in the mirror with narrowed eyes,
and ask herself: Will they like me?

before entering the adjacent room where the two men she had met an hour earlier are waiting.

It is taken for granted that a woman has certain preferences.

She prefers one bedspread to another,

one man to another,

one position to another,

one picture frame to another,

although at times all things tend to blur, to become indistinct, so that each choice becomes increasingly difficult.

What would Maude say if asked, what is it that you now want most?

8.

Are you aware, Gregory had told Maude shortly after they were married, that all the women in your father's novels are exact replicas of you? They're all highly sexed women with splendid legs who tend to be nearsighted. They all seem to spend a good deal of time writing lengthy confessional letters to their fathers. She hadn't noticed until Gregory brought it to her attention. If not for Gregory she would still be reading her father's novels without a clue as to the true identity of his principal female characters. In her father's latest novel, Agnes, the ash blonde divorcee was gazing raptly at a shopwindow on Madison Avenue when a young athletic-looking man with a slightly protruding cleft chin stopped at her side, to comtemplate the objects that were on view behind the thick plate glass window. She felt her pulse quicken. The two of them stared at the imported leather suitcases, the leather briefcases, the leather handbags, the gloves, hats, slippers, all of leather, and all imported. She could see his face reflected on the shopwindow. The protruding cleft chin was a minor flaw, easily overlooked. He wore a winter coat with a fur collar. The coat was unbuttoned, and she could see the vested plaid suit he wore. Cooly he studied her reflection on the plate glass window, debating whether or not to speak to her.

At night, alone in bed, Maude tosses about in her sleep. Whose head is she gripping between her thighs. Is it Gregory's or is it the head of the man in the winter coat with the fur collar?

Although the world is filled with doubtful and dubious information, a woman can tell at once when a man is trying to pick her up. A woman, by the time she reaches thirty, has seen her share of men, dressed and undressed, singlemindedly striding towards her. It is consistent with this singleminded sexual pursuit that a woman will daily, sometimes hourly, examine herself in the bedroom or bathroom mirror with narrowed eyes, asking herself: Will he like me?

Everytime we fuck, Gregory once confided to Maude, with a slight almost imperceptable grimace of distaste, I feel as if I am one of the characters in your father's latest novel.

Why the detestation, Maude asks herself. Does he dislike me, or does he merely dislike the women in Dad's novels, in which event I could try to persuade Dad to alter them somewhat, to make them less demanding.

9.

Please do not be distressed by this letter, she wrote her father. I really expect Gregory to return within the hour. He went to look at the latest photographic exhibition at the Light Gallery on Madison. An hour after he left I fixed myself a light lunch. Tomato soup with an egg in it, and a tuna sandwich on rye bread. At four in the morning I called Muriel. I had to speak to someone. I would have preferred to speak to you, but I know how you hate to have anyone call you when you are at work . . . and I can never tell when you're not either at work on your novel or asleep.

Gregory left Maude on a Tuesday. He walked out of the apartment just as she was getting ready to plan her day. He looked his usual unconcerned self as he stepped out of their eight-room apartment on the eighteenth floor, an apartment containing two color tv sets, approximately eight thousand books and two thousand records. Most of the books had been signed by their authors. To Gregory with the deepest gratitude, and such shit.

When Maude runs into an acquaintance in the park who inquires what she has been doing with herself, Maude replies: I am presently working on a long letter.

10.

Writers receive long letters with grave misgivings, particularly when the letter appears to have been written by a close member of the family. Lengthy letters have a way of becoming books. They are a pretext to enable the letter's author to enter the combative world of literature. How many people have squeezed their unwelcome presence into literary history just by writing a long revealing letter to their father.

I fully comprehend, wrote Maude to her father, that when Gregory went off to see the exhibition at the Light Gallery, it may not yet have dawned on him that he might not return. I clearly recall saying: Give me half-an-hour, and I'll get dressed and come with you. No, no, he said. He was only going to take a quick look at some photographs. On his way back he would pick up the *Times*. I never saw the *Times* that day. I was so certain he would get it. The next day I couldn't get a copy of Tuesday's *Times*, for love or money. When I called Muriel, she at once asked me what's wrong. I asked her if she had Tuesday's Times. She said no.

I think you are well rid of Gregory, Muriel had said. What you need is a stable, strong, and emotional man.
No, said Maude. What I now need is a smaller apartment.

What I now need is a smaller apartment, she writes her father. I also need a place to store the books and records. Could you possibly take a few days off and drive over in the station wagon? You always wanted that entire set of Maupassant. Remember?

How odd, thinks Maude, that under the circumstances I am not discontent. How odd that I did not become a prisoner of my marriage to Gregory. How bizarre that he should have walked out on my life on a Tuesday before breakfast. How fortunate I am not to have any children to worry about. The oddest thing of all was the fact that she could no longer remember his face. It worried her. Poor Gregory's face had been effaced from her memory. Try as she did she could not put Gregory's handsome face together in her mind. She managed the lips and eyebrows and even the hair, but she could not assemble the total face. The total face escaped her. She succeeded, however, at the first try with the face of the young photographer, thinking to herself, what a sweet face. I bet he's an awfully sweet guy.

11.

This is an introduction to the nervous handwriting of Maude. She is sitting at her little writing desk, writing a long letter to her father. She can see her father in his large rather neglected country house impatiently waiting for the mailman, impatiently waiting for her letter. Her father is wearing his old Harris Tweed. He and the mailman go through their familiar routine, speaking about the weather, the crops, the livestock, before the mailman reluctantly hands over the mail.

She could have typed her letter, but she preferred to write it by hand, infecting the desperate message her letter conveyed with the angular nervousness of her handwriting. Her handwriting accentuated the intensity of her feelings. It clamored for attention. It also demanded an immediate sympathetic response.

Everything that you see and hear is plausible, her father had once said. At the same time, it can also remain highly questionable. All the things in this house, the house included, more or less reflect a certain taste. Is it my taste? Take this couch, for instance. Why is it still here when it should have been sitting in the garbage dump years ago? If I were to sit down and write about the couch I would probably write that I was attached to it, in order to make plausible its presence in my study.

In her letter Maude casually mentions that Gregory had briefly stepped out to see an exhibition at the Light Gallery two weeks ago. She had intended to accompany him, but he had reminded her that she owed her father a letter. If not for the letter she might have accompanied Gregory to the gallery. In the late afternoon, when Gregory failed to return, she called the gallery, identifying herself as the lady who some time ago had purchased a print of the Great Mosque of Kairouan. She wondered if there were any other prints left of the Mosque, and incidentally, had her husband, Gregory Brinn, been in that day to purchase another photograph of the lady in the one-piece bathing suit sunning herself on a park bench?

12.

Every evening Maude walks naked to the window and takes a deep breath. She is relaxing. She is also asking herself: What will I do tonight? She can always take in a movie, or go to a concert, or see a play, or read a good book, or watch an old movie on TV, or do some Yoga exercises, or bake a cake. She can also, on the spur of the moment, invite someone to dinner.

Are you free tonight she asked me on the phone. I thought you might like to come over for dinner. I know this is terribly impromptu. You can bring your friend. The woman in the photograph. Oh, by the way, Gregory is away on business. It'll just be the two or three of us.

She can also go to one of the neighborhood bars and strike up a conversation with a stranger, someone who will undoubtedly have read one if not more of her father's eighteen books. Whenever she mentions her maiden name, the response is immediate: Good God, you're the daughter of Emmanuel F. Hugo. I firmly believe he's the greatest writer since Maupassant. She used to have her father read Maupassant to her when she was a child. The mere mention of Maupassant makes her weep.

She can also, just to show that she doesn't give the slightest damn, throw a gigantic party, inviting all her friends and their friends, and just people her friends may know or run into. I've been looking for you, she said severely. I was afraid that you mightn't show up. I don't know half of these people. Did you bring her along? I introduced Irma to Maude.
Why did I bring Irma along?
Did I want her to see her photograph in Gregory's study?
Did I want her to see the view from the eighteenth floor?
Did I want her to savor the perfection of the apartment? The perfection of every object in the apartment? The perfection, consequently, attained by her photograph in being in such close proximity to the other carefully selected objects in the study.

Goodnight. Maude kissed me on the lips. I left without Irma. I couldn't locate her in the dense crowd. Thank you for bringing her, said Maude.

13.

On the spur of the moment I decided to throw a large party, Maude writes her father. It may cause him pain. It is intended to cause him pain. She describes the people who came to her party, she also describes Irma, describes her in a way to cause her father anguish.

Maude likes to write letters. She's quite an accomplished letter writer. The letters are breezy, informative and even witty. She likes to make fun of herself. She writes of the time she and Gregory spent a week in Jamaica. They had been making love when the door of their hotel room was opened by the chamber maid. Just put it on the table, said Gregory without even turning around. The maid placed his polished shoes on the table and quickly stepped out of their room. They burst out laughing hysterically as soon as the maid had left, but when her father made use of the incident in one of his novels, Gregory actually threatened to take him to court. He's really totally humorless, said her father. My poor child, married to a humorless man.

She married a man who was an authority on Maupassant, and who was also a book reviewer for one of the major journals in the country, because it was so refreshing to have someone who could analyze so thoughtfully all the women characters in her father's books. Of course, that one is you too, Gregory would say. Can't you see how your father is trying to disguise her to lead us astray? That first year she spent with Gregory was the most exciting time in her life. Suddenly she was able to cope with her fear of the elevator going out of control, and plunging eighteen floors to the ground floor.

I wonder what I should do with all the books the publishers keep sending to Gregory, she asked me. I didn't feel like inquiring if she had seen Irma since the party. It wasn't any of my business. I realized that for the second time I was the recipient of an invitation from one of the Brinns that was given in bad faith. Maude had wanted me to bring Irma to her, and I had complied.

Why? Why? Why?

14.

Without the slightest trepidation Maude enters the room in which
the two men are sitting on the couch with Irma. No one prevents her
from walking to the window and looking at the West Side Drive, as
she pretends not to notice that the two are quite openly caressing
Irma's small white breasts, breasts that resemble her breasts. In
order not to see the the men and Irma, Maude is compelled to partly
close her eyes, or focus them elsewhere, on the wallpaper for
instance. It is a pity about the wallpaper. The wallpaper destroys the
room. It makes the room smaller and less attractive. Obviously Irma
had little sense for color or design. Maude would have suggested a
bolder pattern. But Irma had an incredible body. Most men noticed
her body. Irma, at their first encounter had quite casually mentioned
that her legs were her best feature. What an amazing thing to say,
Maude had thought at the time. For some reason the two men were
not touching Irma's legs. Perhaps, it occurred to Maude, they were
saving Irma's legs for later. Perhaps they were satisfied to look at the
legs while concentrating on other parts of Irma's anatomy. Who can
say? Who can tell what is on the mind of a man who is caressing a
woman? One of the two men was rather attractive. He had bony
hands and blue eyes. For no discernable reason he looked at Maude,
and said: I expect to make a lot of money next year. At least twenty
thousand. Maude was not impressed. Her father made eight times
as much after taxes each year. She watched the two men who might
easily have stepped out of one of her father's novels strip Irma
naked. She had expected Irma to offer a certain amount of resistance. A certain struggle was called for, Maude felt. Instead, all she
saw was total compliance. It is depressing, she thought, to see an
attractive woman give in so easily. In her father's books the women
always put up a certain struggle. Even in Maupassant it was not
merely, one, two, three. Is Irma, she wondered, without backbone.
She tries to stiffle a yawn. Her yawn is an unabashed admission that
she is becoming bored by the spectacle and by her role as captive
audience. She is thirty-five and easily bored, but she makes no move
to leave the apartment. Having read the *Story of O*, she knows what
would happen if she did. She knows how the men would respond.

I can take a taxi home, thinks Maude. She is disconcerted to find
Irma staring at her. It's not more than ten, at the most fourteen steps
to the door, another twelve to the elevator.

She would describe what had taken place in a letter to her father. She would go into great detail to cause him anguish. I was afraid, she would write, I was so afraid, and yet, I was so excited, so excited.

Her father wrote big fat American books. At this moment he is sitting at his typewriter turning out beautiful books for America. He is a man of letters. He is a man America respects. He is a man who understands the quintessential American need for friendship. It is this fundamental understanding that has enabled him to sell his books in the hundred thousands. People crave friendship, not sex. Her father's face is recognized by millions. Each time he takes the BMT he is besieged by the readers of his books. She adores her father. She adores the poignant titles of his books. Books, in which all the principal female characters resemble her. It is only to be expected, she thinks. She can also recognize the figure of her father in his books: Her father at the age of four, seven, eighteen, twenty-two, forty-nine, sixty-seven, eighty-one, one hundred and two.

15.

Maude is compelled to concede that one of the two men, the more agreeable-looking one, is screwing Irma in her presence. She stares at Irma's face in amazement. It is a face she can no longer recognize. It could be me, thinks Maude, how easily it could be me.

Where the hell have you been, shouted Gregory furiously when she got back to the apartment at four a.m. I've been going stark raving mad. He kept pounding the table as he spoke. She had never seen him looking so agitated. I want an explanation.

You . . . you . . . you dare ask me where I have been. Her voice was quivering with indignation. You've been gone for over two weeks.

Oh no, cried Gregory. Not again. It's going to be one of those long drawn out melodramas. I can't take it. I simply can't take it. Not at four in the morning.

16.

I really don't know why you wish me to take your photograph in a black bathing suit in a park, but if you insist, I will.

It's a going away present, Maude explained.

A parting shot, I said.

I like the view from the eighteenth floor. I like everything about this apartment. From my desk I can see Central Park, and when I turn my head slightly to the left sitting on the second shelf is a photograph I took some time ago. My father-in-law wants to use it on the cover of his next book. Sure, I said, if Maude doesn't object.

Maude, Naked as usual, enters my room.

𝕭 𝕭 𝕭

SNAKE

by ANNE HERBERT

from THE COEVOLUTION QUARTERLY

nominated by THE COEVOLUTION QUARTERLY

IN THE BEGINNING God didn't make just one or two people, he made a bunch of us. Because he wanted us to have a lot of fun and he said you can't really have fun unless there's a whole gang of you. So he put us all in this sort of playground park place called Eden and told us to enjoy.

At first we did have fun just like he expected. We played all the time. We rolled down the hills, waded in the streams, climbed the trees, swung on the vines, ran in the meadows, frolicked in the woods, hid in the forest, and acted silly. We laughed a lot.

Then one day this snake told us that we weren't having real fun because we weren't keeping score. Back then, we didn't know what score was. When he explained it, we still couldn't see the fun. But he said that we should give an apple to the person who was best at playing and we'd never know who was best unless we kept score. We could all see the fun of that. We were all sure we were best.

It was different after that. We yelled a lot. We had to make up new scoring rules for most of the games we played. Other games, like frolicking, we stopped playing because they were too hard to score. By the time God found out about our new fun, we were spending about forty-five minutes a day in actual playing and the rest of the time working out the score. God was wroth about that—very, very wroth. He said we couldn't use his garden anymore because we weren't having any fun. We said we were having lots of fun and we were. He shouldn't have got upset just because it wasn't exactly the kind of fun he had in mind.

He wouldn't listen. He kicked us out and said we couldn't come back until we stopped keeping score. To rub it in (to get our attention, he said), he told us we were all going to die anyway and our scores wouldn't mean anything.

He was wrong. My cumulative all-game score is now 16,548 and that means a lot to me. If I can raise it to 20,000 before I die I'll know I've accomplished something. Even if I can't my life has a great deal of meaning because I've taught my children to score high and they'll all be able to reach 20,000 or even 30,000 I know.

Really, it was life in Eden that didn't mean anything. Fun is great in its place, but without scoring there's no reason for it. God has a very superficial view of life and I'm glad my children are being raised away from his influence. We were lucky to get out. We're all very grateful to the snake.

"ALL DRESSED UP BUT NO PLACE TO GO": THE BLACK WRITER AND HIS AUDIENCE DURING THE HARLEM RENAISSANCE

by CHARLES SCRUGGS

from AMERICAN LITERATURE

nominated by Michael Hogan

It's all right to have the boom but are the people buying?
                    —Claude McKay to Walter White—June, 1925

Without great audiences we cannot have great poets.
                    —Walt Whitman

THE BLACK WRITER of the 1920's *knew* that more white people than black read his works. He often expressed the naive belief that black art was removing racial barriers. Yet he worried about his relationship to his own community, and he was sometimes puzzled and angered by the response of the black audience to his best efforts.

The anxiety that he felt on these occasions made him ask: who was his proper audience? Was it black? Could it be white? Or was art sufficient unto itself and the question of an audience unimportant? The issues raised during an historical period, Alfred North Whitehead has observed, tell us more about it than do its answers. The problem of a suitable audience for black writers preoccupied the best minds of that period in American literary history we now call the "Harlem Renaissance."

No one saw the issues more clearly than did James Weldon Johnson. In an article called "The Dilemma of the Negro Author," written in 1928 for H.L. Mencken's *American Mercury*, he noted that

> . . . the Aframerican author faces a special problem which the plain American author knows nothing about—the problem of the double audience. It is more than a double audience; it is a divided audience, an audience made up of two elements with differing and often opposite and antagonistic points of view. His audience is often both white America and black America. The moment a Negro writer takes up his pen or sits down to his typewriter he is immediately called upon to solve, consciously or unconsciously, this problem of the double audience. To whom should he address himself, to his own black group or to white America? Many a Negro writer has fallen down, as it were, between these two stools.[1]

According to Johnson, if the black writer fulfilled the expectations of the white audience, he outraged his black audience; if he satisfied the black audience, he bored the white audience. The white reader wanted the black character in literature to fit his conception of *the* Black Character in life: his nature was comic and his society was primitive. On the other hand, the black reader wanted a "*nice* literature," one which reflected the bourgeois aspirations of the race. "This division of audience," Johnson lamented, "takes the solid ground from under the feet of the Negro writer and leaves him suspended." In the future there might be a fusion of these two audiences, Johnson suggested, but for the present the situation looked rather bleak.

The *American Mercury* article was not Johnson's last word on the

[1]James Weldon Johnson, "The Dilemma of the Negro Author," *American Mercury*, XV (Dec., 1928), 477.

subject of audiences. He wrote an article for the *Crisis* six months later entitled, "Negro Authors and White Publishers." In it, he warned the black writer against making a "fetish of failure" as the result of believing the myth that white publishers only accepted works which degraded the Negro. He pointed to an enormous list of recently published books reflecting the "upper" levels of black society, noting as well that they were far more numerous than those dealing with Harlem lowlife. The gist of his essay was that all levels of black life should be open to the artist and that the talented black author has "as fair a chance today of being published as any other writers."[2] In short, Johnson urged the black writer to create art and to worry less about how he appeared to both black and white audiences.

Johnson's essays reveal an interesting contradiction. In the first, he made the assumption that an artist created a work of art for a specific audience. "It is doubtful," he said, "if anything with meaning can be written unless the writer has some definite audience in mind." In the second, he argued from another position: the sanctity of art is the artist's only concern, and white publishers judge a man's writing on the basis of its intrinsic merit.

Warner Berthoff has pointed out that this same confusion of attitudes had plagued the "new American renaissance" of the previous decade. *Seven Arts* magazine (1916–1917), a platform for young American critics such as Van Wyck Brooks, Waldo Frank and Randolph Bourne, had announced in its first issue that the time was ripe for a rebirth of the arts in America and in such an epoch, "the arts ceased to be private matters." American artists would now participate in a new fellowship to express the "national self-consciousness" of a people, perhaps even to create it. Yet Berthoff notes that even as this ideal relationship between artist and audience was being set forth, the magazine also asked the artist who contributed to its pages that he be true to *his own* artistic vision, to "self-expression without regard to current magazine standards."[3] This unconscious contradiction between the artist responsible to himself and the artist responsible to the *polis* was never resolved by American intellectuals in that period before the 1920's. In a sense, the Great War solved the

---

[2]James Weldon Johnson, "Negro Authors and White Publishers," *Crisis*, XXXVI (July, 1929), 227.
[3]Editorial in *Seven Arts* (Nov., 1916) as quoted in Warner Berthoff, *The Ferment of Realism* (New York, 1965), p. 290.

problem by removing it. The American intellectual simply lost faith in the American scene as a potential civilization and fled to Europe. In Paris he recreated the communal spirit of good fellowship he longed for in America, and from this vantage point, he even wrote about America, but he no longer had any hopes of expressing its "consciousness." Those writers who remained behind (and those who returned from Europe) may have continued to believe in the "new American renaissance," but the 1910–1917 ideal of "great audiences" supporting "great poets" got lost in the shuffle of other questions and other arguments.[4]

The writers of the Harlem Renaissance repeated the pattern of experience of 1910–1917—but with an important difference. They too hoped to express the communal consciousness of a people, and they too were undermined—but not by a great catastrophe (not even by the Great Depression of 1929), rather by the very audience which they hoped would sustain them. James Weldon Johnson put his finger on the mark when he said that the black writer felt "suspended," but the suspension he felt was the result of not being supported by what should have been the "great" audience. Ironically, the black writer often felt more comfortable with white publishers and white readers than he did with his own people, because at least he knew what they wanted. And yet, he knew that he was still a marginal member of American society and that, like it or not, his real community was black.

At one time or another, nearly every black writer or critic in the 1920's complained of this dilemma. Sometimes, not having a black audience, the black artist became insecure, and then self-conscious; he declared loudly that only "pure art" mattered, and he withdrew to Axel's Castle to create it. At other times, he illustrated James Weldon Johnson's thesis of the double audience by contradicting himself when he tried to describe who his audience was. But behind the disillusionment and confusion, the black writers of the 1920's

---

[4]See Berthoff, pp. 287–298. Berthoff suggests that the best writers of the 1920's freed themselves from the cultural provincialism of the previous decade. They no longer asked, "How can I be American and real?" but, "How would Flaubert have done it, or Balzac, or Jules Laforgue, or Mann or Joyce or . . . Dante or Shakespeare or Catullus. . . .?" (p. 298). In this sense, the Great War and the European experience liberated the American artist from being too preoccupied with his audience. On the other side of the ledger, Malcolm Cowley has amusingly described the aesthetic squabbles which followed in the wake of his generation's return from Europe. Instead of doing battle with the American public, they fought among themselves, often over petty principles of art. The "new American renaissance" had degenerated into a kind of bohemian Mannerism. See *Exile's Return* (New York, 1961), pp. 171–196.

wanted to believe in the Whitmanesque ideal. Aubrey Bowser, a black writer and publisher of the period, expressed it succinctly in an angry letter he wrote to Carl Van Doren in 1926. Irritated by a scene in Carl Van Vechten's *Nigger Heaven* (1926), Bowser pointed to the specious logic of an American editor in the novel. Editor Durwood, a thinly-disguised portrait of H.L. Mencken, tells Byron Kasson, the milksop black hero, to stop writing melodramatic stories about love affairs between white men and black women and start exploring the rich, untouched depths of Harlem: ". . . if you young Negro intellectuals don't get busy," says Durwood, "a new crop of young Nordics is going to spring up who will take the trouble to become better informed and will exploit this material before the Negro gets around to it."[5] The reason black writers don't write the truth about black life, Bowser told Van Doren, is that they have to cater to the whims of white publishers and the prejudices of the white public. "The Public!" he continued:

There's the key to the whole matter. All the great literatures, how-ever wide their final vogue, were written for local publics. The whole world reads Shakespeare, but he wrote for the English. Virgil wrote for a Roman audience, Homer for a Greek, Dante for an Italian. They had no other public than their own in mind. Imagine them fettered by the necessity of pleasing foreign editors and a foreign public! Imagine Dickens and Thackeray shaping their novels to conform to French or Italian ideas of what an Englishman should be. Thus the Negro, to write convincingly, must write with a Negro public in mind.[6]

[5]Carl Van Vechten, *Nigger Heaven* (New York, 1971), p. 223. Van Vechten had given that advice to black writers more directly through a symposium sponsored by the *Crisis* the same year his novel was published. See *Crisis*, XXXI (March, 1926), 219.

[6]Unpublished letter (September 4, 1926) to Carl Van Doran concerning a review of *Nigger Heaven* in the *New York Herald Tribune* (August 22, 1926) which Bowser thought Van Doran had written. Sending Bowser's letter to Van Vechten, Van Doran told Van Vechten that he had not written the review. See Carl Van Vechten Collection, New York Public Library Annex. That Van Vechten ignored the black artist's need of a Negro public is not surprising, since most white intellectuals of the period believed that art was all that mattered when black literature was the subject of discussion. Again, see *Crisis* symposium in 1926 on "The Negro in the Arts." When H. L. Mencken read Johnson's article on "Negro Authors and White Publishers," he made the observation to Johnson "that Negro authors now have nothing whatever to complain of. If they have anything to say, the chance to say it is wide open before them." Undated and unpublished letter, James Weldon Johnson Collection, Beinecke Library, Yale University. For Mencken, once the black artist was free to "do" black life, no other obstacle existed. Curiously enough, Mencken had recognized the need for a responsive audience when he discussed the plight of the (white) artist in America in "Puritanism as a Literary Force" (1917) and "The National Letters" (1920).

Great literature written for a local public: the spirit of the Harlem Renaissance is contained in this phrase, and it is repeated in different ways by Alain Locke, W.E.B. Du Bois, Sterling Brown, and other spokesmen for the "New Negro."

II

In 1926, Alain Locke wrote an article, "American Literary Tradition and the Negro," in which he tried to account for the American artist's recent but unexpected liberation from "stock Negro stereotypes" of the past.[7] He concluded that the "revolt against Puritanism" was responsible for this new honesty in Negro characterization. Locke was, of course, referring to the contemporary taste for the "pagan and emotional aspects of Negro life," but he was also aware of a larger literary and cultural revolt which had been going on for almost two decades.

Attacking Puritanism had been symptomatic of a general disgust with the hypocrisy of American life, but more specifically, Puritanism became a convenient whipping post for those who were demanding a new American literature soon after the turn of the century. Puritanism was associated with the "genteel" literature of an age which continued to exert its pernicious influence, making it impossible for a writer like Dreiser to gain an audience or even to get published.[8] Furthermore, to flagellate Puritanism became a way of dealing with those conservative critics—Paul Elmer More, Irving Babbitt, Stuart Sherman—who represented the literary establish-

[7]Alain Locke, "American Literary Tradition and the Negro," *Modern Quarterly*, III (May-July, 1926), p. 221.

[8]For example, see Mencken's essay in *Seven Arts*, "The Dreiser Bugaboo," (Aug., 1917). Mencken was one of the leading attackers of Puritanism. In the *Smart Set*, he waged war against the narrow-minded morality of most Americans. See "The American: His Morals" (July, 1913); "The American: His Ideas of Beauty (Sept., 1913); "The American: His New Puritanism" (Feb., 1914). Also, see "Puritanism as a Literary Force" in *A Book of Prefaces* (1917) in which he linked the moralist with the philistine, the pagan artist with the truly civilized man. Mencken continued to use these catagories in his famous attack on Southern culture, "The Sahara of the Bozart" (*Prejudices: Second Series*, 1920). Here he blamed Puritanism for making the South an intellectual wasteland after the Civil War; the arts could not flourish in an atmosphere of moral fervor. He hoped that "the new school of Aframerican novelists" would give the South the artistic treatment it deserved. See "Letters and the Map," *Smart Set* LXIII (Nov., 1920), 139–140—as quoted from Fred C. Hobson, *Serpent in Eden: H. L. Mencken and the South* (Chapel Hill, N.C., 1974), p. 26. Not enough attention has been given Mencken's writings as a direct influence upon the philosophical basis of the Harlem Renaissance.

ment and who, it was felt, hid their moral near-sightedness behind the mask of Humanism.

While the critics of Puritanism gathered like a crowd to a public hanging, the intellectuals who most interested Locke—Van Wyck Brooks and Randolph Bourne—attacked Puritanism with the hopes of overhauling the very foundations of American civilization. To these men, Puritanism consisted of a set of attitudes which have persisted throughout our history and which have prevented Americans from experiencing a sense of national community. Bourne was to call the dominant Puritan attitude "the will to power."[9] Individual aggressiveness and greed defined the American character, and even self-abnegation became a means to self-exaltation. Brooks, Bourne, and Waldo Frank (*Our America*, 1919) located the battleground in terms of the antinomy: Puritan versus *Polis*. The Puritan was moralistic, egocentric, and life-denying; the *Polis* was pagan, social, and life-affirming.

Brooks first defined the issues. In *The Wine of the Puritans* (1908), written when he was twenty-two, certain ideas were introduced which he fully developed in his more famous treatises on American life—*America's Coming-Of-Age* (1915) and *Letters and Leadership* (1918). He complained that America, unlike other nations of Western Civilization, had no childhood and consequently had never matured. Faced with a wilderness which had to be conquered, the Puritans felt they could not afford the luxury of leisure. At the very outset of their history, Americans behaved like serious adults, and, Brooks believed, they have never outgrown this survival ethic, have never gone beyond "the idea that sustaining the machinery of life was a kind of end in itself."[10] For not only do they distrust beauty and pleasure, but they exist as a collection of isolated, striving, self-reliant individuals whose only "culture" is something borrowed, as one would gather pieces of art on a tour of the continent. Brooks expressed for his generation this gap between the floating Faustian spirit and the viable community which could have supported him:

The vague ideal of every soul that has a thought in every age is for that communion of citizens in some body, some city or state, some Utopia,

[9]See Randolph Bourne: "The Puritans's Will to Power," *Seven Arts*, II (April, 1917), 631–637.
[10]Claire Sprague, ed., *Van Wyck Brooks: The Early Years* (New York, 1968), p. 4, All references to Brooks are from this edition.

if you will, which the Greeks meant in their word πολιτεια [commonwealth]. Those artificial communities—Brooks Farms and East Auroras—are so pathetically suggestive of the situation we all are in! "We get together" (What an American phrase that is!) because we *aren't* together, because each of us is a voice crying in the wilderness, individuals, one and all, to the end of the chapter, cast inward upon our own insufficient selves. . . . (p.55)

In *America's Coming-Of-Age*, Brooks developed an idea he had mentioned in passing in *The Wine of the Puritans*. Puritanism, he argued, led to a strange bifurcation in the American character between the lowbrow, acquisitive business man who could not rise above his business and the highbrow intellectual who lept to the Ivory Tower in order to escape being overwhelmed by amorphous American life. Here, in short, was the tragic lot of the American artist: unable to plant himself in the rich soil of a community, he spoke in windy abstractions to a non-existent "ideal" audience.

But despite this stringent criticism of America's past and present, Brooks often spoke optimistically of America's future. Both *America's Coming-Of-Age* and *Letters and Leadership* ended with the hope that the American artist would become the legislator of his people, that he would give shape to the formlessness of the American experience, for "after all," Brooks said, "humanity is older than Puritanism" (p. 158). And in a 1918 essay in the *Dial*, he coined what was to be his most memorable phrase, "a useable past," which the artist must find, or invent if need be, to fulfill America's dream of becoming a civilized community.[11]

A young disciple of Brooks, Randolph Bourne, further refined his mentor's notion of the organic *polis* which gave ballast to a people. Bourne had, quite early, singled out the theme of youth as his special province. The youth of any society, he said, was its lifeblood. Its fresh thoughts kept a culture from decay and, in fact, became the

[11]Sprague, p. 223. After the Great War, Brooks lost confidence in the American scene until the 1930's when his books began to celebrate America's literary past. In Harold Stearns's infamous *Civilization in the United States* (New York, 1922), he published an essay called "The Literary Life" in which he specifically attacked the American reading public whose unimaginative and unsympathetic response forced real artists into mediocrity. He quoted Dreiser's rebuke of Jack London, who never wrote to excel but to sell, because "he did not feel that he cared for want and public indifference (p. 182)." In 1920 Brooks illustrated his theme of the American artist compromised by his public in his literary biography of Mark Twain. Twain played the fool and jester out of the same fear that drove London to write pulp.

basis for the future. A culture died when its young people were denied a voice.[12]

After he visited Europe in 1914, Bourne's conception of culture as a living continuity began to take shape. He saw that in France older members of society listened to young people because even their radicalism sprung from the roots of a unified community. By contrast, Americans were "culturally humble." The older generation clung to the pious platitudes of Western Civilization and gave these the name of "culture." To Bourne, this definition indicated a failure of nerve, a self-abasement; it was an open admission that Americans could not find the seeds of culture from within.[13]

Bourne searched for a source of cultural strength in ethnic background. He argued that America had never been a "melting pot," for if this had been the case, our specific identities would be dead and buried, forsaken for a merger into a common ideal. Assimilation had resulted not in a common consciousness but only in a tasteless, colorless "culture" represented by the "cheap newspaper, the 'movies,' the popular song, the ubiquitous newspaper."[14] There was nothing distinctive about the American people. Fortunately, said Bourne, this anti-culture had a weak hold on Americans; America still remained a "federation of cultures." Cosmopolitanism was our real virtue, and our real culture lay in the future, in the total contribution to be made by each ethnic group to the larger living community.

Bourne saw further that the city, with its diffuse population in a single geographical space, would become the center of American civilization, just as the city-state had been the center of Greek civilization. Within the walls of the *polis*, the "Beloved Community" would be created.[15] Artists like Whitman would sing its praises and celebrate the common bond which knit American to American. Bourne died of influenza, at thirty-two, in the same year that the Great War ended, but his dreams for America died before he did. America's entry into the war and the intellectuals' support of it

[12]Randolph Bourne, *Youth and Life*, Boston, 1913. See especially "Youth," "The Two Generations," and "The Virtues and The Seasons of Life."

[13]See Randolph Bourne, "Maurice Barrès and the Youth of France," *Atlantic Monthly*, CXIV (Sept., 1914), 394–399. Also, "Our Cultural Humility," *Atlantic Monthly*, CXIV (Oct., 1914), 503–507.

[14]Randolph Bourne, "Trans-National America," *Atlantic Monthly*, CXVIII (July, 1916), 86–97—as quoted from *The History of a Literary Radical & Other Papers*, ed. Van Wyck Brooks (New York, 1956), p. 270.

[15]Sherman Paul, *Randolph Bourne* (Minneapolis, 1966), p. 35.

shattered his optimism, and he was remembered in the 1920s not as a harbinger of glory but as a martyred hero who had courage to attack the shallowness of American jingoism when everyone else had jumped on the bandwagon.

The Brooks-Bourne program was tailor-made for the Harlem Renaissance. Negro youth as Prophetic voices, Harlem as the "Beloved Community"—these ideas were sung in a new key by Alain Locke in *The New Negro* (1925). Locke especially singled out the city as a cause of a new "race welding," a new feeling of community among black people: ". . . American Negroes have been a race more in name than in fact, or to be exact, more in sentiment than in experience. The chief bond between them has been that of a common condition rather than a common consciousness; a problem in common rather than a life in common. In Harlem, Negro life is seizing upon its first chances for group expression and self-determination."[16] Now black men could see their lives as united by a shared experience, which was different in kind from that caused by their former common condition. The advantages of this communal situation for the Negro artist were obvious: if the great Greek dramatists were nurtured by Athens and, in turn, wrote great plays to sustain its spirit, the Negro artist might recreate this perfect symbiotic relationship between artist and community in Harlem. Even now, Locke argued, the younger generation was expressing this "life in common." Throwing off the "trammels of Puritanism," it refused to depict black people as victims, the community of black people as the oppressed (p. 50). Young people were investigating their Negro heritage in the hope of creating art rather than propaganda. Through living together in Harlem, Negroes were a people in more than just name; they were experiencing a "spiritual Coming of Age (p. 16)."[17] Soon the black audience would recognize its face in the mirror of art, no longer seeing the gross distortions as in the imperfect mirrors of the past, and it would applaud and support the artist.

[16] Alain Locke, "The New Negro," appearing in *The New Negro,* ed. Alain Locke (New York, 1969), p. 7. All references to *The New Negro* are from this edition.

[17] The association of the city with "Coming of Age" is the theme of more than one essay in *The New Negro.* See Charles S. Johnson, "The New Frontage on American life," pp. 278–298; and James Weldon Johnson, "Harlem: The Culture Capital," pp. 301–311. For a different interpretation of Locke as a black Van Wyck Brooks, see S. P. Fullinwider, *The Mind and Mood of Black America* (Homewood, Ill., 1969), pp. 115–122. Fullinwider does not concern himself with the theme of community in the work of either Brooks or Locke; rather he focuses upon the desire of both men to find viable "myths" in the modern world.

III

Alain Locke was later to meet opposition from black writers on certain specific issues, but in 1925, he had given a voice to their highest aspirations. Furthermore, he had placed the writer within a recognizable tradition. The ideals of the Harlem Renaissance echoed the actual accomplishments of 5th century Greece, not to mention the more recent developments in the Ireland of Synge and Yeats. And, best of all, the New Negro wished to bring to fruition, both for his own people and America, the dreams of Walt Whitman, who had prophesied an organic society in which artists and audience would live in harmony.

But as the decade progressed, it became increasingly evident that something was missing: the black audience. In fact long before 1925, Jean Toomer had privately expressed the same aspirations as Locke and had come to reject them.

Like Alain Locke, Jean Toomer was influenced by the American critics of the pre-war era, especially Waldo Frank. In an unpublished letter, written in 1922, he described the opposition the black artist faced in his own community as a latent effect of the Puritan ethic. Using the vocabulary and framework of Brooks, Bourne, and Frank (especially *Our America*), Toomer traced America's indifference to art to the Puritans. Repressing all emotional energy as they exploited the material world, the Puritans had condemned art as sinful because it was useless. Such an attitude, denying so much, could not last forever, and now that the "gods of Industry" had been appeased, a new age had begun, enriched by art. White artists, Toomer said, were transcending the anglo-saxon ideal by finally expressing their buried emotional life, by searching for beauty within whatever color ethnic group it was found. But those "of the darker skin" were still slaves to the attitudes of their former owners: "we who have Negro blood in our veins, who are culturally and emotionally the most removed from the Puritan tradition, are its most tenacious supporters. We still believe, in fact we believe it now more so than ever, that a man's worth should be gauged by material possessions. . . . We are sceptical of the value of art. We are suspicious and often ashamed of our emotions."[18] Furthermore, Toomer

[18] Unpublished letter to Mae Wright, August 4, 1922, Toomer Collection, Fisk University, Box 10, Folder 10.

continued, Negroes were ashamed of the color of their skins. Black artists must make black people proud of themselves, must make them see the beauty of themselves, of their lives: "Their eyes must open to the charm of soft full lines. Of dusk faces. Of crisp curly hair. Their ears must learn to love the color and warmth of mellowed cadences, of rounded southern speech." In December, 1922, Toomer wanted to start a literary magazine "that would function organically," he told Sherwood Anderson, "for what I feel to be the budding of the Negro's consciousness." Yet, while he realized there was a "tragic need" for a magazine to encourage and to provide "creative channels" for young black talent, he also knew that black people generally would not respond to it. "In fact," he said, "they are likely to prove to be directly hostile."[19]

Toomer's imaginative work at this time also revealed an underlying pessimism. In an unpublished play he titled "Natalie Mann," he depicted the black artist victimized by his audience. The artist, Nathan Merilh, dares to create a new art form—dramas written around Negro folk songs. By digging into his racial past, he aspires to give black people a sense of themselves. The good society people of Washington want nothing to do with Merilh's art, so he flees to New York, accompanied by Natalie Mann, who also wishes to liberate herself from the stuffy black bourgeoisie. Another friend, Etty Beale, is a dancer. She is thwarted by her audience: "I quit dancing for churches and community centers because I couldn't stand the people," she explains. She now dances in cabarets: "Cabareting is killing all the finer stuff in me, but in most of them they're honest."[20]

This theme of the isolated artist was shown less melodramatically, but more effectively, in *Cane* (1923), a collection of stories, poems and sketches. In "Box Seat," Toomer satirized the black middle class through the character of Muriel. Having come to the Lincoln Theater for a jazz concert, she is embarrassed by a farcical interlude consisting of two boxing dwarfs. After the match, one dwarf offers her a bloody rose but, disgusted and afraid, she rejects it. In the context of the scene, the rose symbolizes the grim but magnificent heritage of the Negro past, and in rejecting it, Muriel also rejects the Negro artist who is committed to celebrating that past no matter how

[19] Unpublished letter to Sherwood Anderson, December 29, 1922, Toomer Collection, Fisk University, Box 1, Folder 1.
[20] "Natalie Mann," Toomer Collection, Fisk University, Box 49, Folder 9.

ugly it may appear to others. From Toomer, what is positive in the black experience is inextricably welded to the grotesque.

In "Theater," another short story in *Cane*, meaning grows out of a different kind of artist-audience confrontation. John watches a rehearsal of chorus girls. One, Dorris, stands out from the rest and seems to dance for him. Her movements suggest the rich, fecund, canebrake world of the South, but the intellectual John, lost in his own fantasy, fails to respond to her passion. The weeping Dorris at the end of the story is also the weeping artist. *Cane* ends with "Kabnis," the long tale in which both Kabnis and Lewis are writers visiting Georgia. Toomer has Kabnis working as a schoolteacher who destroys himself through his inability to accept the rural community on its own terms. On the other hand, Lewis, Toomer's version of the healthy black artist, can respond to the raw beauty of the South, yet he seems strangely detached from the black community he admires. It accepts him, but it does not understand him, and at the end of the story he seems almost as lonely a figure as Kabnis.

It is no surprise that Toomer finally turned to the white literary world for his own identity as an artist. Waldo Frank, Paul Rosenfeld, Gorham Munson, Hart Crane, Kenneth Burke—these became his circle of friends, and in time he would decide to write as an "American" for other Americans. Such a literary philosophy was in character, it is true, but one wonders how much the absence of a black audience had to do with his decision not to be known as a "Negro artist."[21]

Ironically, Toomer had pointed to a spectre in the woodpile as early as 1922, three years before *The New Negro* and Locke's declaration of independence from the burdens of the past. And it was not long after 1925 that other black critics began to echo Toomer's criticism. W.E.B. Du Bois, who consistently argued for a black literature freed from the whims of white publishers and directed to the needs and reality of black life, nevertheless attacked black readers for allowing their minds to be shackled. Du Bois had his own version of the "Beloved Community," and it focused upon the idea of freedom and responsibility. He complained in the *Crisis* (1926) that "the young and slowly growing black public still wants its prophets

---

[21] See my article, "Jean Toomer: Fugitive," *American Literature*, XLVII (March, 1975), 84–96. Toomer was ultimately dismayed by the parochialism of the Harlem Renaissance; and his own attitude toward himself as a "Negro" was ambiguous, resolved only, if then, by adopting the mask of the "American" artist.

. . . unfree."[22] Talk of sex frightened it; religion confined it; its worst side had been shown so often "that we are denying we have or ever had a worst side." He urged "that catholicity of temper which is going to enable the artist to have his widest chance for freedom. We can afford the truth." As things stood, a white jury passed down its judgments *ex cathedra*, and black readers nodded in agreement.

Sterling Brown was to repeat this attack upon black cowardice several years later in a brilliant essay called "Our Literary Audience." According to Brown, black readers lacked "mental bravery."[23] Taking his cue from Whitman's famous statement—"without great audiences we cannot have great poets"—he bitterly noted that those who ought to be the black artist's proper audience were "fundamentally out of sympathy with his aims and his genuine development." Sensitive because of past literary distortions of the race, black readers demanded that they be depicted as black knights in shining armor. No race ever became great through avoiding the truth, he said: "And now, if we are coming of age, the truth should be our major concern."

As if to illustrate Du Bois's criticism and to anticipate Brown's, Claude McKay wrote a letter to James Weldon Johnson in the same year his novel, *Home to Harlem*, was published (1928) in which he complained that his only audience was a certain segment of the white population. Radical leftists did not like his novel becuase it was not propagandistic; the Negro middle class did not like it because it showed the realities of lowerclass existence, which embarrassed them: "We must leave the real appreciation of what we are doing to the emancipated Negro intelligentsia of the future, while we are sardonically aware now that only the intelligentsia of the 'superior race' is developed enough to afford artistic truth."[24] By the word "sardonically" McKay implies that no white man, however intelligent, can replace the black writer's rightful audience. In short, it takes *two* to make a New Negro.

Perhaps the most curious case of being troubled by a "double audience" was that of black novelist Walter White. A close friend of H.L. Mencken, Carl Van Vechten, and Sinclair Lewis, White was also an important official in the NAACP. He moved in both white and

[22] W.E.B. Du Bois, "Criteria of Negro Art," *Crisis*, XXXII (Oct., 1926), p. 297.

[23] Sterling Brown, "Our Literary Audience," *Opportunity*, VIII (Feb., 1930), p. 46.

[24] Unpublished letter to James Weldon Johnson, April 30, 1928, James Weldon Johnson Collection, Beinecke Library, Yale University.

black literary circles and expressed his opinions freely to publishers about what he thought black readers would and would not buy. In 1924, the year Knopf published *The Fire in the Flint*, he wrote: "I have told several publishers . . . that the reason colored people do not buy books is because publishers have not brought out the right sort, i.e. they have published caricatures of the Negro like the stories of Octavus Roy Cohen, Hugh Wiley, and Irvin Cobb, or base libels on the Negro like the vicious novels of Thomas Dixon."[25] However, when he talked about his own novel, he claimed he wrote it for white people. George H. Doran and Company had first agreed to publish *The Fire in the Flint* in 1923, but had finally rejected it after consulting Southern author, Irvin Cobb. Frustrated and angry, White wrote H.L. Mencken for advice, and Mencken promptly suggested he send it to a black publishing house, pointing out that he would meet the same "difficulties" from other white publishers "as you encountered with Doran."[26] But White replied that he *wanted* a white publisher, the more established and conservative the better: "Colored people . . . know everything in my book—they live and suffer the same things every day of their lives. It is not the colored reader at whom I am shooting but the white man and woman who do not know the things you and I know."[27]

Now here was a strange paradox. White had complained to Eugene Saxton at Doran that no novelist in America's past had adequately portrayed "what an intelligent, educated Negro feels."[28] His novel, he argued, depicted the Negro in all his humanity. Surely, then, such a character as White's Dr. Kenneth Harper should appeal to black readers, yet he had said that he was "shooting at" a white audience. Why? He certainly wanted a black audience, for he told Mencken, who had indeed recommended his novel to Knopf, that he expected a huge sale from members of the NAACP.[29] I suspect, however, that White knew but would not admit that the black audience he had promised to white publishers was a myth. And, in fact, records in the Library of Congress indicated this to be the case. White did try to sell the novel for Knopf through the NAACP, and the results were disastrous. For instance, the Denver

[25] Unpublished letter to E. R. Merrick, May 8, 1924, NAACP Executive Correspondence Files, Manuscript Division, Library of Congress.
[26] Unpublished letter to Walter White, Oct. 16, 1923, ibid.
[27] Unpublished letter to H. L. Mencken, Oct. 17, 1923, ibid.
[28] Unpublished letter to Eugene Saxton, Aug. 19, 1923, ibid.
[29] Unpublished letter to H. L. Mencken, Oct. 17, 1923, ibid.

branch returned seventy-six of the hundred copies it was asked to
sell to its members, and since White had assumed financial responsibility, his royalty went toward paying for these copies.[30] Similar
situations occurred in Sioux City, Omaha, and Des Moines,[31]
but White never gave up hope. He kept insisting, as he said to
a friend, "If a novel as frank as mine goes over big . . . it will
mean that publishers will not only be willing to consider manuscripts by other colored writers but will be actively seeking
them."[32] Publishers continued to seek manuscripts after 1924, and
The Fire in the Flint went through several editions in two years,
yet it was clear that white people were the chief supporters of
the "boom."[33]

Once black writers became aware of their isolation from their real
audience, various attempts were made to encourage black people to
read and buy books. Walter White, for example, had a brief career as
a columnist with the *Pittsburgh Courier* where he tried to be a black
Samuel Johnson, "a rambler through the flood of books that deluge
us."[34] He not only discussed books by and about the Negro but

[30] Unpublished letter to L. Golden of Alfred A. Knopf, Inc., Sept. 26, 1925, ibid. Walter
White sent Knopf a check for $3.20, and told Golden to keep the $114.00 he had coming to him
from the sale of the novel. Thus his total loss was $117.20. In his other dealings with the
branches, he worked out an arrangement whereby he would not be liable if the novel failed to
sell.

[31] Unpublished letter to L. Golden, July 12, 1925, ibid. White told Golden that the only
thing to be done with the Des Moines branch was to turn its account over to an attorney. White
had written all three branches, asking them to pay for the copies they received but to no avail.
They simply could not sell White's novel even at the discount (50 cents off the $2.50 list price)
which Knopf gave them.

[32] Unpublished letter to Bishop Hurst, September 9, 1924, ibid. White often made this plea
to the NAACP branches. On December 9, 1924, he wrote James Tanter of the St. Louis branch
and told him that he was not exploiting the NAACP but "that the success of any novel by a
Negro will help open the way for other Negro artists." And he pleaded with Charles Howard
(March 28, 1925) of the Des Moines branch: "I am particularly anxious that all business
dealings in connection with this book be up to the mark for it is the first book by a Negro that
Knopf has ever published." He made the same point to W. B. Dabney of the Cincinnati branch
(April 2, 1925).

[33] It is clear too that the "boom" was more imaginary than real. In the 1920s, no novel, play
or book of poetry by a black author ever attained the popularity of Du Bose Heyward's *Porgy*
(1925), Carl Van Vechten's *Nigger Heaven* (1926), or Julia Peterkin's Pulitizer Prize winning
Scarlet Sister Mary (1928). Despite the hoopla surrounding the New Negro, white authors
writing about blacks often made the best-seller lists, but no black author in the 1920s wrote a
book that could be called a best-seller.

[34] I am quoting from his first column which I found in the NAACP Correspondence Files.
White wrote this column from March to October, 1926, at which time he resigned because the
newspaper had attacked some officers of the NAACP. Also, see his unpublished letter to F. R.
Inescort, March 10, 1926, NAACP Correspondence Files, Manuscript Division, Library of
Congress. He told Inescort of the Putnam publishing firm that he took this position with the
Courier in order to "increase the general reading public among black people."

urged black people to widen their horizons by reading Dreiser and Sandburg. Nella Larsen, author of two novels, *Quicksand* (1928) and *Passing* (1929), wanted to start her own bookstore in Harlem. James Weldon Johnson had told her, she wrote to Carl Van Vechten, that the publishers "all deplore the absence of a shop up there. . . ."[35] Black critic and poet, William Stanley Braithwaite planned to create a "Negro Book Week," during which Negroes would be urged to buy books by Negro authors. Such a plan would convince "the publishers that we have become a book-buying people."[36] Furthermore, it would "liberate the Negro writer from that handicap which exist [sic], and leave him free to express himself." The "handicap," of course, was the black writer's dependency on a white audience, the Gordian knot of the Harlem Renaissance upon which many a blade fell but which no one succeeded in cutting.

IV

Wallace Thurman—a novelist, playwright, and sometime editor—was a neurotic idealist who made himself miserable by comparing his work to the writings of Tolstoy, Proust, and Thomas Mann.[37] No doubt he would have been unhappy if he had been read by millions, yet he has left the most complete and outspoken record to date—in both his published and unpublished writings—of a black writer's conception of his audience.

Like others, he attacked black people for expecting their writers to spout "sociological jeremiads" or build "rosy castles around Negro society."[38] He shrugged off the middle class denunciation of *Nigger Heaven*, pointing out that those who believed all black people were

[35] Unpublished letter to Carl Van Vechten, Sept. 29, 1926, James Weldon Johnson Collection, Beinecke Library, Yale University.

[36] Unpublished letter to James Weldon Johnson, August 12, 1934, ibid. Throughout the 1920's, the *Crisis* ran a column called "Book Chat," written by white author Mary White Ovington, in which the major emphasis was upon making the black public familiar with books by and about black people. Similarly, Alain Locke wrote a yearly "Retrospective Review" for *Opportunity*, and throughout the 1920's and 1930's this magazine kept its readers informed as to what was being published. Sterling Brown wrote a literary column called "The Literary Scene—Chronicle and Comment"; Gwendolyn Bennett played "The Ebony Flute"; and Countee Cullen held forth in "The Dark Tower."

[37] Langston Hughes, *The Big Sea* (New York, 1940), p. 235.

[38] Wallace Thurman, "Negro Artists and the Negro," *New Republic*, LII (Aug. 31, 1927), 38.

like Anatole Longfellow would believe so even if Van Vechten had never written the novel.[39] The problem was, as he saw it, that both "sincere" artists and "insincere" artists had used material from low-life, and the black bourgeoisie was too sensitive to portraits of the past, yet not sophisticated enough to distinguish a Porgy from Florian Slappey.[40] Like McKay, he looked to a future in which the Negro audience would be free from cultural insecurity.

If Thurman distrusted his own middle class, he positively feared the "mob." "It was a matter of experience," he wrote in his unpublished autobiography, "that he had and would suffer from the hands of the black mob as much if not more than he had and would suffer from the hands of the lily whites."[41] And he illustrated this generalization in a letter he wrote to his white friend William Rapp: "I am fighting hard to refrain from regarding myself as a martyr and an outcast. I wish you could take my place in Negro society for about a week. Even on the train I was beset by a Pullman porter for my dastardly propaganda against the race."[42] No doubt he was referring to his novel, *The Blacker the Berry* (1929), in which he had satirized color prejudice within the race.

Thurman was equally contemptuous of the black writer's white audience. He complained that white critics considered the Negro artist "a highly trained dog doing trick dances in a public square." If he wasn't seen as a freak, he was lionized beyond his actual merits, so that all writers whose grandparents were slaves "befo' de wah" were naturally geniuses.[43] Also, the white audience had certain expectations from a book by a black author which, Thurman realized, he had unconsciously tried to fulfill while writing *The Blacker the Berry*. In his novel, he wanted, as he said in his autobiography, "to interpret some of the internal phenomena of Negro life in America," yet he saw later that all the references were still to outside conditions, to the racial prejudice which made prejudice within the race possible. In other words, he tried to create art but in reality stooped to writing propaganda that appealed to an audience he did not

[39] Wallace Thurman, "Mr. Van Vechten's Jurors," unpublished essay, James Weldon Johnson Collection, Beinecke Library, Yale University.
[40] Wallace Thurman, "Negro Artists and the Negro," p. 38.
[41] Wallace Thurman, "Notes on a Stepchild," James Weldon Johnson Collection, Beinecke Library, Yale University.
[42] Unpublished letter to William Rapp, July 1929, ibid.
[43] Wallace Thurman, "Nephews of Uncle Remus," *Independent*, CXIX (Sept. 24, 1927), 298.

respect, white people who wanted to read about the miserable darkies.[44]

Enfants of Spring, his satiric novel on the Harlem Renaissance published in 1932, is an appropriate conclusion to the entire period. Thurman called attention to the complete futility of an aesthetic movement cut off from communal soil, whose artists gather in a hothouse only to wither and die.

Euphoria Blake, a black Mabel Dodge, turns her house over to black artists, believing that Niggeratti Manor will fill "a real need in the community."[45] The artists, however, do everything but create—they throw parties, seduce women, and talk incessantly about art. Flattered by white society's temporary interest in the "New Negro," they think they need only live like artists to *be* artists. On the surface, Thurman's satire is obvious, but he strikes much deeper. He documents the tragic insularity of the black writer in the 1920's.

Raymond, a novelist (and a portrait of Thurman himself), and his white friend Stephen have platonic dialogues on the theme of isolation and community. Stephen leaves Niggeratti Manor, disgusted with the degenerate company in which he finds himself. He writes Raymond: "To have been surrounded by such a collection of whites would have driven me mad long ago (p. 191)." Raymond explains to Stephen that he needs the company of intellectually stimulating people, but lacking them he must make do with what he has: "I am forced to surround myself with case studies in order not completely to curdle and sour (p. 194)." But he *has* curdled and soured. Unable to relate to the black middle class, he finds bohemian life equally stultifying and debilitating. He is not only distracted by the dissipated lives of his fellow artists, but also the house itself, which was supposed to be a community in microcosm, seems only a collection of separate egos. Nothing brings this to the surface more than the soirée held by Doctor Parkes. The ideal community as envisioned by Alain Locke is parodied when Thurman refers to Dr. Parkes (Locke)

---

[44] Wallace Thurman, "Notes on a Stepchild," James Weldon Johnson Collection, Beinecke Library, Yale University. Thurman was not always above exploiting the taste of white people. He told Rapp that they should write a play about a ruthless woman who becomes the slave of a worthless character: "The morons should eat that up, especially in the movies, if given a great deal of darky dancing, nigger comedy, and coon shouting." No doubt he had these favorite elements in mind in his collaboration with Rapp on the hit play *Harlem*. Dramatically centered around a "rent party," the play treats all the bizarre aspects of Harlem which would interest a white audience: "numbers," the Bump (a dance), and black language.
[45] Wallace Thurman, *Enfants of Spring* (New York, 1932), p. 266.

as a mother hen hovering over her chicks (p. 180). The chicks are rebellious, each wanting his own aesthetic way. The "community" falls apart in argument, and the house is once again left to its old anarchic habits.

Raymond sets off in a new direction: "I'm going to write . . . a series of books which will cause talk but won't sell. . . . Negroes won't like me because they'll swear I have no race pride, and white people won't like me because I won't recognize their stereotypes (pp. 214, 215)." He is determined to penetrate at last the crazy quilt cabaret surface which white people define as Harlem and to smash the brittle bourgeois world which the black middle class calls "black life." Real rebellion, Thurman suggests, is for the artist to make contact with the audience of "a quarter-million Negroes" living in Harlem (p. 222).

But Thurman always remained an elitist, and this forestalled any possible affirmation we may have expected from Raymond's statement. The novel ends with another character's tragi-comic death, a character Thurman both sympathized with and disliked, written in Thurman's best "fin-de-siècle" manner. An egotistical young writer who models himself on Huysmans and Oscar Wilde, Paul Arbian illustrates the fact, as Raymond says, "that the more intellectual and talented Negroes of my generation are among the most pathetic people in the world today (p. 225)." As a grand finale, Paul arranges to commit suicide during a party, leaving his unpublished novel where it will be discovered by the guests. But the bathtub in which he dies overflows, the flood ruining his manuscript, making it unreadable.

Throughout the 1920's, "art" was the magical word. If only black writers would create art, and not propaganda, then and only then would they come of age. They strove to be cosmopolitan artists and not provincial hacks eternally bemoaning their bootless state as black people. The counterpart to the cosmopolitan artist is the audience whose taste is, to use Du Bois's word, "catholic." Once the black artist discovered the absence of an appreciative audience he often, like Thurman, adopted a "decadent" voice and loudly proclaimed that audiences did not matter, knowing all too well that they *did indeed* matter.[46]

---

[46] Even Langston Hughes, poet of the people though he was, talked sometimes as if he were an aesthete from the 1890's: "We younger Negro artists who create now intend to express our individual dark-skinned selves without fear or shame. If white people are pleased we are glad.

It took Richard Wright to point out, in "Blueprint for Negro Writing" (1937), that the Renaissance had got the issues all wrong.[47] The central concern of the black artist was not "art" but the total culture in which his people lived. Before he could create an art which truly spoke to *a black audience* (as opposed to the black bourgeoisie), he must comprehend the political system in America—the grim economic realities—which had made his people a nation within a nation. Thus the search for the artist's place within his own community continued in the 1930's, taking on a new responsibility. Now the artist was urged to shape not the "taste" of black people but rather their political consciousness.

If they are not, it doesn't matter. . . . If colored people are pleased we are glad. If they are not, their displeasure doesn't matter either." Langston Hughes, "The Negro Artist and the Racial Mountain,"*Nation,* CXXII (June 23, 1926), 694. This tendency of the black artist to leap to the Ivory Tower of Art when he sensed his audience deserting him caused W. E. B. Du Bois to issue a warning that the Harlem Renaissance was falling into an abyss of decadent aestheticism. See W. E. B. Du Bois, "Criteria of Negro Art," *Crisis* XXXII (Oct. 1926), 290–297.

[47] Richard Wright, "Blueprint for Negro Writing," *New Challenge,* II (Fall, 1937), 53–65.

WHILE
THE RECORD PLAYS

by GYULA ILLYÉS

from AMERICAN POETRY REVIEW

nominated by Teo Savory

They heated hatchet blades over gas fires in roadside workshops
and hammered them into cleavers.

They brought wooden blocks on trucks and carried them across
these new provinces grimly, quickly, and steadily: almost
according to ritual.

Because at any time—at noon or midnight—they would arrive at
one of these impure settlements,

where women did not cook nor make beds as theirs did, where
men did not greet one another as they did, where children
and the whole damned company did not pronounce words
as they did, and where the girls kept apart from them.

They would select from these insolent and intolerable people
twelve men, preferably young ones, to take to the
marketplace,

and there—because of *blah-blah-blah* and moreover
quack-quack-quack and likewise *quack-blah-quack*—would
beat and behead them,

of historical necessity—because of *twaddle-twiddle* and *twiddle-diddle*, and expertly, for their occupations would be different one from the other,

agronomist and butcher, bookbinder and engineer, waiter and doctor, several seminarists, cadets from military academies, a considerable number of students.

those familiar with Carnot, Beethoven and even Einstein, displaying their finest talents.

because, after all, nevertheless, *blah-blah-blah* and *twiddle-dee-dee*,
while through loudspeakers records played—music and an occasional gruff order, and they, the zealous ones, wiped their foreheads and turned aside every now and then to urinate since excitement affects the kidneys;

then having washed the blocks and hauled down the large tricolor which on such occasions always waved above their heads,

they too would march on into the broad future,

past the heads, carefully placed in a circle,

then out of the settlement where now also

and forever and ever,

reason, comfort, and hope would be no—

wrr-wrr-wrr—that is to say—*we-wp, wa-rp,* the sound (by now the only one

without music or words) that the needle makes as the record grinds on.

translated from the Hungarian by William Jay Smith

HOW THE HEN SOLD HER EGGS TO THE STINGY PRIEST

by NANCY WILLARD

from FIELD

nominated by FIELD

An egg is a grand thing for a journey.

It will make you a small meal on the road
and a shape most serviceable to the hand

for darning socks, and for barter
a purse of gold opens doors anywhere.

If I wished for a world better than this one
I would keep, in an egg till it was wanted,

the gold earth floating on a clear sea.
If I wished for an angel, that would be my way,

the wings in gold waiting to wake,
the feet in gold waiting to walk,

and the heart that no one believed in
beating and beating the gold alive.

THE ANGEL
AND THE MERMAID

by RICARDO DA SILVEIRA LOBO STERNBERG

from SMALL MOON

nominated by SMALL MOON *and DeWitt Henry*

An angel fell in love
with a mermaid.

A creature of little imagination,
the mermaid
rejected the possibility
of such a being
and when he hovered over her
so white against the blue
would turn quietly to her sisters
and ask
how is it that foam
has taken flight?

The angel grew sullen,
gained weight,
began to molt.

He was moved
further and further back
in the choir
but still his shrill lament
pierces the lovely melody
bringing a dark cloud
into the eye of god.

KOYUKON RIDDLE-POEMS

workings by RICHARD DAUENHAUER

after Fr. JULIUS JETTÉ, S.J.

from ALCHERINGA/ETHNOPOETICS

nominated by ALCHERINGA/ETHNOPOETICS

IN 1913, FATHER JULIUS JETTÉ, S.J. published a two-part article on the riddles of the Koyukon Indians, an Athapaskan group living on the Yukon and Koyukuk Rivers in the interior of western Alaska. [Jetté, "Riddles of the Ten'a Indians," *Anthropos* 8 (1913) 181–201; 630–651] The Jetté article contains 110 riddles, each presented in the original Koyukon accompanied by a literal interlinear translation, a free translation, explication, and commentary. The workings here are based on the Jett collection, to which the serious student of riddles is directed.

According to Jetté's introduction, the genre was associated with the return of light, and riddling was done only after the winter solstice. But even at the turn of the century, when Jetté was in the field, the riddle genre was on its way out as a viable medium of entertainment and verbal art. Today riddling is almost extinct in Koyukon, although it is still practiced by some tradition bearers, and has been experienced in context by some fieldworkers. [David Henry, Summer Institute of Linguistics, personal communication.]

The riddles in Jetté are a fine example of the highly developed verbal art of a tradition of poetic imagination which has declined and has in general been lost in the last 70 years—a period characterized by two generations of suppression of Native language and culture and by disruption of the language and intellectual community by the educational establishment and other government agencies, some of which continue to advocate and enforce total English replacement of Native languages rather than competence, comfort, and pride in both Native language and English. I hope these workings suggest that their Koyukon originals are hardly the creations of a conceptually and verbally impoverished people in need of intellectual transfusions from a paternalistic benefactor.

The riddles in Jetté exemplify the poetic use of everyday language and the imaginative juxtaposition of everyday images, of seeing something in terms of something else, and verbalizing that picture through manipulation of the wonderful and indefinite potential of language. With suppression and eradication of Native Alaskan intellectual traditions, and with the diminished possibilities for transmitting oral tradition because of language loss among the younger generations, a situation has developed in which even the average fluent speaker of Koyukon—though no fault of his or her own—is no longer familiar with riddles and riddle style.

For example, each riddle in the Jetté collection begins with the formula "tla-dzor-kara'ana" ("riddle me.") None of the younger speakers of whom I have inquired were familiar with the formula, even though they are fluent in Koyukon. Also, younger speakers (30-60 age group) find much of the grammar bewildering. For example, a verbal prefix indicating a tree-like object would logically never occur with a first person subject pronoun—unless, as in the riddle style, the speaker is a tree, and the grammatical manipulation is a clue. Such grammatical combinations seem to have delighted the old time riddle composers, but strike the younger speakers as totally non-sensical and incorrect. . . .   I have made one major change: I have treated the riddles as imagist poems, and have changed the riddle format to that of a poem, giving the clues in the first part of the poem, and the answer in the second.

from the introduction by Richard Dauenhauer

6/J7

Flying upward,
ringing bells in silence:
the butterfly.

9/J13

Far away, a
fire flaring up:
red fox tail.

12/J17

Someone's throwing
sparks in the air:
plucking the reddish feathers
of the grouse.

15/J20

Round and shiny
at the end of my spruce bough:
Lynx feet
or the great gray owl.

17/J27

At the water hole
the ice spear
trembles in the current:
a swimming otter's tail.

20/J34

We come upstream
in red canoes:
the salmon.

21/J35

Like a water plant:
floating salmon guts.

23/J39

The hilltop trail
running close beside me:
a thing on which
the wolf has peed.

25/J42

Like fine hair
on the penis of a squirrel:
veins in birchwood.

31/J62

Behind the woodpile
we lie in sheepskin blankets:
last year's
excrement.

32/J64

Like a herd
trailing up the hill:
the graveyard,
tombstones carved
with animal designs.

41/J106

I found my
last year's arrow:
using the same
song of mourning
twice.

WASTE OF TIMELESSNESS

fiction by ANAÏS NIN

from WASTE OF TIMELESSNESS AND OTHER EARLY STORIES
(Magic Circle Press)

nominated by Magic Circle Press and Ted Wilentz

editor's note: Anaïs Nin (1903–1977) was a Founding Editor of *The Pushcart Prize* series. This story is from a collection of her early and previously unpublished fiction, issued shortly after her death. Few people worked harder than Anaïs Nin to encourage new authors and small presses. We honor her memory.

IT WAS THE USUAL invitation to a usual houseparty, the usual people, and with her usual husband. Why must it be friends of the "great writer" Alain Roussel rather than Alain Roussel himself who invited them out for the weekend?

Besides, it was raining.

The first thing Mrs. Farinole said was: "It has not rained here all summer. What a pity it should today, of all days! It will be impossible for you to image how perfectly lovely this place can be."

"Oh, but I can very easily imagine," she answered and looked around appreciatively at the hills, the pines, the sea quite formally

© 1977 Anaïs Nin

framed to make a cozy windless nook. And then she imagined a gigantic gust of wind sweeping the whole place clean, and Mrs. Farinole saying: "I am so sorry, our house has flown away, and so I cannot ask you to spend the night. I shall have to telephone the carpenter. He must do something about it immediately."

And then Alain Roussel would happen to pass by in quest of material, carrying a crab net. Seeing her on the road he would say: "Will you come with me? We can spend the weekend on that old fishing boat on the beach. It is a grand place." (He would use another word, a better one than "grand" but she could not think of it just at that moment.)

Her husband would say: "Wait a minute then. I must get her raincoat. She is subject to neuritis."

"There is Roussel's house," said Mrs. Farinole. "He has painted his gate in turquoise green. It will soon turn grey with the sea air."

"Have you read all his books?" she asked.

"We will, by and by," said Mr. Farinole. "Did you know that he wrote the last three right here?"

"And while they were repairing his house, too," said Mrs. Farinole. "I don't know how he could do it."

"And his cook was ill—the house was terribly disorganized," added Mr. Farinole.

"He wrote something very extraordinary in a magazine," she said.

"He *is* a very extraordinary man," said Mr. Farinole. "Did you ever hear how he repaired his own oar when the mechanic could not make out what was the matter?"

"And here is our house," said Mrs. Farinole. "Henry, show her the stubborn wisteria."

They paused in front of the door.

"Do you see this wisteria? It was a stubborn plant—insisted on growing to the left for two years, and at last I got it around to the right, and over the door, where I wanted it."

During this story little Mrs. Farinole shone with pride. "That is just like Henry, to be so *beautifully* persistent."

"Do you think," she asked, "that he could make me grow to the right too? I would really like to grow to the right, and over the door, but it seems impossible."

Mr. Farinole laughed, "You have Irish in you, have you?"

"No, why?"

"Whenever Henry says something funny we said: 'You have Irish in you, have you?'"

"You do!"

"And he, invariably answers. 'And a little Scotch besides!' "

"Now," said Mrs. Farinole, "you know the family's pet joke."

"I think that is delicious," she said. For a little while she did not hear the rest of the conversation. She was thinking that she would like to ask Roussel what he meant by intuitional reasoning. "By intuitional reasoning," she thought, "I could be made to grow to the right, and over the door, but not by reasoning alone."

They walked to the end of the garden.

"What is that? A boat? A boat in this garden?"

"I will show you," said Mr. Farinole. "It was here when we got the house. It is an old Norman fishing boat, used as a tool house. See, it is black because they put tar on it to preserve it. What a shape it has eh? So deep, so fat, so comfy, so safe looking."

"May I look inside, oh, may I?"

"We put a bed there once for a little boy guest. He insisted on sleeping there. He got such a thrill out of it!"

The inside smelt of tar. There was a bed, several old trunks, garden tools, pots, seeds, and bulbs. There was a tiny square window on each side of the door. The roof sloped down squatly.

"Oh, I would like to sleep here too." she said.

"Have you Irish in you?" said Mrs. Farinole.

"Think of your neuritis," said her husband.

"Henry is awfully proud of that boat," said Mrs. Farinole.

"I hear the dinner bell," he said evasively and modestly.

It was all so much easier since she knew about the existence of the boat—so much easier to jump gaily from topic to topic, being always careful not to exceed a certain moderate temperature.

There was the boat waiting in the dark garden, at the end of the very narrow path, the boat with its little twisted doorway, its small windows, the peaked roof, its smell of pungent tar . . . the very old boat which had travelled far, now sunk in a quiet dark garden.

The atmosphere in the Farinoles' library was dense with laughter. She must not stop laughing. Her husband had said: "The Farinoles have the most delightful sense of humor." There was nothing to be done about it.

It was bedtime.

The Farinoles did not believe that she meant to sleep on the boat, not until she was half way down the path, with her nightgown under her arm. Then they shouted: "Wait! Wait! We'll walk down with you."

"I know the way," she called back, running faster.

"You will need a candle."

"Never mind, there is a sickly moon, it will do."

Then they called out something else but she did not hear them.

She walked around the boat. It was tied to an old tree. She unfastened the mildewed rope. "And now I am gone," she said, stepping into the boat and banging the little door after her.

She leaned out of one of the windows.

The sickly moon was covered by a cloud.

The wind rushed once through the garden.

She sat on her bed and cried: "I would really like to go away. I would like never to see the Farinoles again. I would like to be able to think aloud, not always in hushed secrecy." She heard the sound of water. "There must be a trip one can take and come back from changed forever. There must be many ways of beginning life anew if one has made a bad beginning. No, I do not want to begin again. I want to stay away from all I have seen so far. I know that it is no good, that I am no good, that there is a gigantic error somewhere. I am tired of struggling to find a philosophy which will fit me and my world. I want to find a world which fits me and my philosophy. Certainly on this boat I could drift away from this world down some strange wise river into strange wise places . . ."

In the morning the boat was no longer in the garden.

Her husband took the 2:25 train home to talk this problem over with his partner.

The boat was drifting down a dark river.

There was no end to the river.

Along the shores there were plenty of landing places, but they were very ordinary looking places.

Roussel had a house on the banks. When she made as if to pay him a visit he asked: "Do you admire me?"

"I love your work," she said.

"And no one else's?"

"I do care for Curran's poetry, and Josiam's criticisms."

"Don't stop here," said Roussel. And she saw that he was surrounded with ecstatic worshippers, so she pushed her boat away.

Along the shore she saw her husband one day. He signalled to her, "When are you coming home?"

"What are you doing this evening?" she asked.

"Having dinner with the Parks'."

"That is not a destination," said she.

"What *are* you headed for?" he shouted.

"Something big," she answered, drifting away.

More quiet shores unfolded. There was nothing resplendent or marvellous to see. Little houses everywhere. Sometimes little boats tied to a stake. People used them for small rides.

"Where are you going?" she asked them.

"Just resting from ordinary living," they said, "off for a few hours for just a little fantasy."

"But where are you going?"

"Back home after a while."

"Is there nothing better further on?"

"You're stubborn," they said coldly. She drifted away.

The river had misty days and sunny days, like any other river. Occasionally there was magic; moments of odd stillness when she felt the same intense exaltation she had experienced the first night on the boat, as if she were at last sailing into unutterable living.

She looked out of the little window. The boat was sailing very slowly and going nowhere. She was beginning to get impatient.

On the shores she saw all her friends. They called out to her cheerfully but formally. She could feel that they were hurt. "And no wonder," she thought, "they must have sent me many invitations and I have not answered them."

Then she passed Roussel's place again. Now she was sure she had travelled in a circle. He called out to her: "When are you coming home? The Farinoles need their garden tools, and the trunks, too."

"I would like to know," she called out, "what you mean by intuitional reasoning?"

"You can't understand," he called back. "You have run away from life."

"It was the boat which sailed away." she said.

"Don't be a sophist," he said. "It sailed away at your own bidding."

"Do you think that if I came ashore we could have a real talk? I feel then that I might not be wanting to travel."

"Oh," said Roussel, "But it might be *me* who would want to travel. I do not like perfect intimacy; you might write an article about it."

"You're missing something," she said. "It would be an interesting article." And she drifted away.

The shores still offered commonplace scenery, and there was no world beyond.

Her husband called out to her: "When are you coming home?"

"I wish I were home now," she said.

The boat was in the garden. She tied up the cord to the old tree.

"I hope that you had a good night," said Mrs. Farinole. "Come and see our wisteria. It has grown to the left after all, in spite of everything."

"During the night?" she asked.

"Have you Irish in you? Don't you remember how the wisteria looked twenty years ago when you first came to our house?"

"I have been wasting a lot of time," she said.

🔥 🔥 🔥

WOLFBANE FANE

fiction by GEORGE PAYERLE

from WOLFBANE FANE (The Kanchenjunga Press)

nominated by The Kanchenjunga Press

> *O mother, drive us out*
> *Of the throat of hell*
> *Where we are eaten and broken.*
>
> Jon Furberg, *The Wanderer*

ACROSS LOW, DULL SLOPES of the sea, Wolfbane Fane peers from the bow of his longship through mist toward the northernmost isles of Britain. He knows his eyes are green. Behind him, twoscore savages in furs oar silently. Only a squeak and a gurgle announce the approach of Fane's Wolf, long swansneck arching the carved head high into scrolls of mist. Too bland a wolf, Fane thinks. Religious. A spiritual wolf, carved likely by some secret Christian. Asger the Oak-beam, woodcarver to the Earl Furor of Fane—an unlikely Christian. But Christians, broods Fane, are unlikely entirely. A creeping chill of Christians inches up Fane's considerable back. Cold spider. And down hindwise through the tangled canyon of his arse.

The lookout mumbles something incomprehensible from the masthead and points. Fane growls. The spider reaches for the boulders of his groin. Fane crushes it and sees a glow in the dim lump of Britain. The kraken's eye. He motions to Skar, who passes the word: Head for the church and the mead hall. Don't fuck around. Kill anything that moves unless it's too much trouble or you want to bring it home.

Wolfbane squeezes the haft of his six-foot steel axe, grunting like a half-wet pump. A pent sea churns in Fane. His eyes glow. As his ship grinds onto the shingle Fane's eyes are green demons leaping for shore. Having grunted himself to a steady snarl, he runs through muddy paths and cart-tracks, the crest of his own wave, and falls upon a low, shapeless building emitting chinks of light. Bellowing "Wolfbane," he smashes through the door into a greasy flicker of spent drinkers who flounder in disbelief. The axe crushes heads and tables, scattering blood, brew and tallow. Trestles and drinking horns bounce from Fane's shoulders. Fane sees everything and nothing. A squat Celtish man in rough wool bashes him from behind with a stump. On his knees Fane already has swept an arc of shattered legs. Knives flash before him but Fane drinks his own blood, spins the steel haft as a staff, butts and flails, catches a screaming wench in the belly and rolls over her. Finding his rhythm, Fane whirls to cleave the broad Celt like a block of wood.

As his men flit past to plunder, Fane attacks the building's beams and earth. The roof caves in upon him. He hacks his way through to clear air. Surrounded by howls and hewing, he works a motley of huts and sheds toward the monastery on the hill, already taken. Fane slows in a tangle of slaughtered monks. After a few tentative whacks at the walls, he ceases. Silence. Only the tinkle of stray stars through thickening mist. Occasional screams from the cove. The odd groan. Soaked in blood, sweat and sperm, Fane shivers. Dry, dull pains wander in his spine.

"Waldo!"

Pale Waldo, Fane's gnome, peers from between the legs of a woman half-buried in bales of cloth under the stern decking.

"Hasn't she bit you to death yet?"

"She's out cold, chief."

"Hm. Find Skar. Church down the coast somewhere. Before morning."

Fane turns on his concupiscent Norsemen, flicking the axebutt at asses and heads. "Stir, you halfling whoremasters! If you can't take it along, break its neck."

Limping from a chance encounter with a panicked boar, Skar approaches.

"Wolfbane! You're wounded."

"By Thor's balls, I'm dead. Get the men moving."

"It's no good. We can't hit again tonight. The word'll spread."

"So we'll spread faster."

Some days later, Fane discovers a place called Lindisfarne, where he leaves a bell cloven that had rung once too many, and sacrifices fifteen monks on their own altar. He broods among lichen-mottled rocks near the sea. Skar approaches, hesitantly fondling his weapon.

"Wolfbane, maybe we should rest for a while. Find some women—"

Fane growls. Pale mutilated bodies stumble before his eyes among the waves and rocks. Drizzling dawn.

"You're shivering. A nice green cove. We've just been going from one place to the next . . . . The men're getting twitchy. Must be a village over there we could sneak into before noon. These women'll fuck anything."

Fane takes a sudden swipe at the boulder in front of him. Sparks and splinters. The steel axe hums. Fane shakes the jolt out of his arm and sucks throbbing teeth.

"Next thing, you'll wanta go home."

"Well why not? Pretty soon we'll have more than we can carry—"

"Fat. Go home and get fat! Sit on the vik and wait for your fat father to break his neck. No. We go back up the coast. Get what we missed."

"Then home?"

"Sheep tit!" Skar glimpses white water in Fane's eyes.

Fane's Wolf prowls up and down the east and west coasts of Scotland. Fane's eyes sink deeper into his skull. His crew see that the fever no longer leaves him after battle, and grow desperate. The haze of deadmen clears for Fane only when there is something to kill.

Standing to his knees in rubble and guts, Fane peers through the early light of one more sacked village. He sways, a failing bull shaking blood from his eyes.

"Skar! Where's the next town?"

"There is no next town. There aren't any more towns. We've had it. Let's go home."

Fane slogs toward Skar, his eyes old fires in their pits.

"No more towns, Skar. Nothing more." Wolfbane Fane wheezes, heaves, and flings up his axe into Skar's face, who falls. Fane's crew bunch like a pack of old and exhausted dogs. Fane blunders through them, felling bewildered men among their booty. Protests and irresolute arms rise against him, as though this must all momentarily be revealed as a berserker's jest. It is not.

Having laid waste his crew, Fane demolishes the Wolf, shattering planks and timbers. Up to his armpits in brine, he severs the stern with a last blow and stands sagging among debris.

Only Waldo survives, hidden in the stern, floating out to sea.

Fane stands alone. Among the shadowy horrors tumbling about him, he can see nothing to raise his axe against. The currents of his great body falter in confusion; his genitals sink like plumbs to some final uncertainty. He turns to the land. It rises upon his vision, dim but wastable.

Shouting his own name, Wolfbane attacks the landscape. His groans and pain hew forests, fens, sparks and showers of earth. For a day and a night and a day, Fane cleaves a swathe into the uplands, parting crags and lowering valleys, pissing horse-streams and sweat into mud of his own making until at last the sea floods through and in a great cry rolls over him.

WASHED OUT FANE, wrinkled and drained, lies stranded on a fresh shingle shore, steel axe clenched in his senseless fist. Curls of vapour unfurl from his furs and matted hair.

A young woman in white robes inches down the rocks to the water's edge. She looks out the glinting firth toward the sea, and stumbles on the bulk of Fane.

"Poor man. Shipwrecked in the storm."

She bends over him, searching for heartbeat and breath, finding little. Her pale hair falls over his eyes, the lids of which she parts with light fingers. Glassy. She fondles his balls. Nothing.

Seagulls mumble and wail in perplexed circles at this new development.

The woman clambers back over the boulders and up the ridge,

sweat beading on her pale-gold skin and trickling between her breasts to the tangled curls of her groin, which no one can see. She has left a troublesome white vision to lie bottomed in Fane's night.

Squat monks and peasants return with her to haul the bulk of Fane, axe and all, into a monastery cell.

Over a period of weeks the Christians refurbish him. They take his steel axe, place a silver bar, and mount it as a crucifix in the lower gallery, perhaps in anticipation of Loyola. Fane recovers strength and colour, but not memory or sense. The young woman comes to him bringing broth and delicacies and sits by him in the garden—a practice which he regards with as little apparent awareness as he regards everything else, and which the monks discourage against the day when he will become sensible. She accepts this as befits her humble nature. Her name is Caea.

As Fane improves, he is set to work in the fields, where he manages and manhandles vegetables. Finding him intelligent though uncommunicative and uninspired, the monks decide to scribe him. Apprenticed to an ancient priest intent only on illumination, Fane is discovered to have considerable scriptive talent and a certain austere taste. On the death of old Scrotus, Fane becomes a fully journeyman scribe. But his eyes remain clouded.

One morning after several years of this, the matin-bell awakens Fane with a momentous erection and longings to recall his dreams. He peers through gluey eyes and italic haze. Spider. Spinning from the roof of his cell. Fane trembles and slaps his crotch to crush the recollected crawler there. Christians.

Wolfbane Fane in skivvies leaps from his plank bed and, bellowing, charges to the lower gallery. He uncrucifixes his axe, cleaves the laybrother garbage disposer who chances upon him, and proceeds to matins with eyes like a clear morning in winter. Fane's eyes are fangs, starved animals leaping before him into the sheepyard.

Monks, priests, prie-dieus and lecterns scatter. The sibilant swoop of Fane's axe tumbles pillars and masonry. Among the wreckage, shredded manuscripts flutter like gilt-flecked butterflies.

Caea, in white, wreathed in her flying hair, struggles through the dust and falling stone.

"No, Fane! No! You mustn't—"

Fane halves her from the hairs of her head to the secret curls of her fork. He stumbles on her body, but continues, blundering through heather to sit and brood in a soggy fen.

Drizzled Fane chews grass ends, fearing the nameless dull pains lurking in his spine and the dark cavities of his bowel. In self-defence he envisages a plan. Stray Norsemen enserfed in upland villages, weapons, and boats to carry them to the West, which has since become Ireland. Fane foresees his kingdom. He proceeds, eating roots and moor hens, wiping his ass with heather.

At the side of a certain road, very much like any other Fane has come upon, a road leading down to a wooded and tilled valley, there sits a woman of indeterminate age braiding ox-hide into horsewhips. Fane eyes her suspiciously, hunching his stolen furs closer about his shoulders. It is her presence alone that makes the road remarkable.

She looks up at him with the maddening neutrality of old women. Her face resembles the leather she works. Fane contemplates twenty-foot whips, plaited from the hides of weather-beaten hags, to be employed in the flaying of Christians.

"So you're the demon."

Not knowing how to take this cryptic and familiar greeting, Fane pauses and scowls.

"My name is Wolfbane Fane. I'm a man."

She shrugs. "You slaughtered forty monks and a woman and de-molished a monastery. Don't complain if people call you a demon."

Fane growls and hefts his axe. "If you know all that, old woman, you should know to sit by the road and keep your mouth shut."

The woman shrugs again. "Your dreams trouble you. You will die."

"I know that already!"

"You will have disasters. I'll die soon, but before that you will have disasters."

"I make my own prophecies!"

Fane axes her, glowers for a time, then belabours her body with the horsewhips before hacking them to pieces. He goes on, jowls and entrails sagging like lead.

IN WOODLOTS AND FIELDS; creeping by night into their huts, he finds the men he wants. He enters drinking halls disguised as a goatherd and gathers Danes, Jutes and Norwegians over mead. Fane hears stories of an ancient Roman camp inhabited by ghosts. Marshalling his force there, he discovers a huge mass of iron nails buried in the earth. Impressed by his sagacity and the green lunacy of his eyes, Fane's men energetically prepare to conquer Ireland. They construct a forge. They fashion swords, axes and helmets from the Roman nails, and brew ale to banish whatever ghosts Agricola left to guard them.

On the coast, just before embarking for the West in stolen boats, Fane finds Waldo sitting on a rock at high-water line, eating raw fish. Waldo trembles but continues to chew.

"What're you doing here?"

"Waiting."

Fane grinds his teeth and glares.

"Can I come with you?"

"Waldo, you're a fool."

"I know, chief. Would you like a fish?"

Wolfbane's progress through Ireland outrages druids. The bulky Fane, singing his own name, refusing to lie down under a dozen mortal blows, threatens to become more potent than oak trees in the Westmen's imagination. The druids send their eldest to beguile the viking.

This druid, though blue and wrinkled, breathes with dignity.

"Mighty Wolfbane, has it come to this? Look how the Christians have done you—"

"What do you want, manpoacher?"

"I was about to ask a similar question. We have been sitting by, saddened to see you wasting yourself and your fellows, to say nothing of these," sweeping his arm at large, "your kith in the West—"

"Nearest I've got to kith are these savages that carry swords in my name."

"Surely, noble Fane, we are more your blood, of Yggdrasil, not that bent Christian tree, than the priests who have beguiled you. We share the Rune. Our gods are brothers—"

"My gods are the savages I slaughter."

"What does it gain you? You see what these priests have done to you? Make peace with us, and you shall be King. Where are your great carved chairposts, where are your proud women? You sit here on a stump surrounded by doggish men. What does it gain you?"

"Nothing. If I want to be King I can be King. I can split your skull for an alehorn. It gains me nothing. The Christians are savages, but womanish and crafty. Like you, priest. You want to snare me. You want to get my dogs out of your pigsty. You want me to go murder some Christians for you and come back to hear peasants gripe about the weather until you find some way to get rid of me. I'm sick of murdering Christians. You offer me nothing, priest, and I've got that already. It's what I understand. Now go away; you make me a talking fool."

"Forgive me. I didn't realize you are a reflective man—"

"Reflective my ass! You don't even offer me the relief of knocking your brains out. Get away! I'm a coward. I need something to kill. Do you have any blood?"

Fane seizes the druid by the throat and roars,

"Do you have any blood, you wormeaten rag? How dare you stand here listening as though I were a noddled old woman? Where's my friend Skar, where's the forty poor stinking armpits of barbarians that shipped south with me? Only Waldo, tame pup. . . .

"That's right, that's right, just stay right here where I've got hold of you and maybe I'll forget you're not worth butchering. I don't need flies and drooling old men, I need something with teeth, or something that screams and runs, a mountain, anything but this."

He pauses, panting, wafting the old man absently at arm's length.

"Any man must be a coward who can't get himself killed. Slinking Christ curse your blue bones!" Fane slings him in a blue heap to the floor. "If you've any blood, cut your throat and wet down the dust. A coward, you hear? I can't die!"

Various shaggy figures at the edge of firelight giggle furtively in their beards and ale. Fane glowers round.

"A dog. A good dog to kill. Where are my dogs!" The shadows diminish. In the stillness Fane turns again. "Or a magician. Tempt me, Druid! Make magic, so I can kill you."

A pause.

"Pah! Even a mad boar wouldn't confuse you with something alive."

The druid gathers himself, a bluish shade by the fire. His throat creaking like an old joint, he manages some crotchety resonance.

"Wise Fane, perhaps there is something more than I can say. Perhaps my daughter—"

He beckons. Caea steps from the shadows, tall in white robes and catching firelight in her hair, quite unhewn.

Fane regards her, looks about vaguely for his axe, and swoons face down in the dust, hair singed at the fire's edge.

The druids dose him with monk's hood, known as wolfbane, and bewitch him from his derelict vikings, who mill around like so many coracles in an eddying sea. Waldo pants after his master, but is waylaid by a hired wench and bamboozled in a root cellar.

Cunning, these druids. They fashion of Fane's axe a steel chain and bind him with it to cliffs where sea-eagles tearing at his eyes wake him from the bane.

Fane droops through hazes of poison, blood and spume. He thrashes and bellows into the wind whirling about him like the cries and talons of birds, until, dry crackles issuing from his throat, he droops once more. Wolfbane hangs in his lock and chains with a dull will, as though the determined weight of his bulk might of itself tear loose and plummet into the broken waves. Pale ghosts of nippled linen flicker in miasmad Fane. His spine, his thigh-bones and the marrow of his arms ache like one many-rotted and immensely diseased tooth.

Dimly clacking and chewing a parched tongue, he decides dying might well not be worth its end. Immediately despising himself for this thought, he swears to speak no more of anything to anyone, himself included. Settled there, bottomed in the vast cavern of his own darkness, Fane aches, harrassed by ill-humoured phantoms.

As the itinerary of his present disasters wanders in and out over the personal geography of Fane, his genitals weigh on him, sodden lumps jammed into his groin and likely to breed a plague of wormy conclusions there.

Thus firmly wedged between self-abnegation and exposure, Fane seems unaware of Caea, who picks her way toward him across the rocks. She sees him, head slumped, hanging as though all possible gravity gathered in him and pointed to the meandering white centre of water below his feet.

In the windswept, shadowless light something loose and shadowy stumbles behind the hard points of Caea's squinted eyes. She reaches under her blue cloak and withdraws a key, with which she unlocks Fane's prison. A hairy-balled boulder, he plunges into the sea.

Wolfbane slides back to consciousness smothered in bedclothes and down. This puzzles him as a recollection of death. He grunts experimentally, wondering if movement is a possibility still open to him, until he feels something tickle his organ. Caea is lying beside him. Fane decides that after a certain point, amazement profits a man nothing.

"I decided to choose my own regret," she says. "And so, as the Christians say, I committed an act of faith. My father wore the key around his neck; I cut his throat. Then I claimed you by the right of salvage."

It comes over Fane that she has done something on his behalf. That business in Scotland, plucking him from the dregs of his own disaster and feeding him soup—that had been merely Christian and untrustworthy. But this is something new in Fane's experience. Wed to a woman by salvage, handed the chains of his axe and the blood of her father. Fane takes pause.

Her brush is brown and highlighted gold. He chews there reflectively for a time, lunges into her, finds himself surrounded and exploded. Wolfbane Fane has awakened in a strange place, with the sense of a man who steps from a boat and finds his feet neither wet nor on land, but walking over water. In this Fane sees no credibility.

He excuses himself at a reasonable hour and seeks a bog, wherein he sits chewing mudgrass.

He searches out nude Waldo, still nibbling mushrooms from the groin of his root-cellar whore, and drags him forth by one buttock into the yard.

"Nodog! Half-whelped spawn of a sheep! How can you have less sense than your master?" Fane regards inverted Waldo with fierce, lunatic inquisition.

Waldo sensibly remains dumb and is dropped into the mud.

"Looks like we're staying. I will be a Lord and live in a stone house. Get some clothes."

Fane sits in a pigsty, thinking.

He decides that at times further stupidity is inexcusable.

Caea, as a result, becomes pregnant and Fane delighted.

When she tromples unclothed in a vat of grapes he falls upon her joyfully, ignoring the fact that never before in Ireland or elsewhere has he encountered grapes.

Fane encourages agriculture. When, on occasion, confronted by militant groups of Westmen, he goes forth with regret to crush them. He wears his chain for a belt and, axeless, swings it for a weapon.

Throughout, he buries implausibility in unfrequented corridors of his bowel, venturing only now and again, roughly at lunar intervals, to soothe whatever suspicious conscience lurks there—timorous, savage, and seeking blood-certainty to guard its back and defend its front. To accomplish this placation, Fane thrashes his breast with fists and stones, secluded by night in the bog.

The full octave of cries accompanying this exorcism arouses myth and terror among his subjects.

Caea awaits him one winter night wrapped in a wolfhide robe by the fire in his hall.

Enter Fane, solemn, stiff about the joints, and berimed. She smiles, shrugs the robe from her shoulders, and says, "Fane, beat mine too."

HIS SUSPENSION CONTINUES until Caea gives birth. Hearing the first cry of his new blood, Fane sweeps aside a herd of women to enter the room. He finds Caea swaddled, sweaty, drained to a fading sheen, and dead. Midwives and greybeards huddle behind him, saying nothing.

Fane lifts her body, meditatively tries the weight, and lays her down. He remembers deadmen and fish, the boiling down of corpses for soap. He takes the chain from his waist.

"The child, you ancient middens. Where is my child?"

Nothing.

Fane bellows like the bog at full moon and flails. One men and midwives fall broken, sheaves of an abandoned harvest.

"My child, I will have my child and make him no child again!"

Wolfbane blunders through doorways and furniture, a fuddled cry sailing full against a lee shore of his own making. After crashing for some time through whatever he encounters, Fane becomes methodical. He searches house to house, village to village, hut to hut, investigating barns and pigsties, bludgeoning whomever he suspects of hidden knowledge and hence leaving a trail of fractured thieves, druids and old peasants. Again, nothing.

At last, when the carcass of a newborn goat is flung anonymously at his feet, Fane rests. It occurs to him that all this is getting him nowhere.

He summons an artisan.

"We will build a monument." Fane unrolls a diagrammed parchment to all intents and purposes depicting Stonehenge.

"A circle of pillars. Beams across the top. No frills. An altar in the middle, arranged so the sun hits it at dawn on the first day of Spring and sunset the last day of Winter. When it's done, we'll bury the woman under the altar."

"What do you want to make it out of?"

Fane muses, surprised.

"Pine. Or oak maybe? Stone for the altar. What else?"

"Why not make the whole thing out of stone? Big, solid pieces. Lasts. Looks good."

"That would take a hell of a lot of stone! You can't move things that big."

"Get some strong men, some good white oxen, and a lot of time—you can do anything."

"How long?"

"Long."

Fane considers.

"Well, then I wouldn't be around to see it, would I?"

"No, more'n likely you wouldn't. But what difference does that make?"

A pause.

"I guess you're right. Yeah, I guess. . . . But look, by then no-body'd even remember what it was for. There wouldn't be anything much to bury, if anyone did."

"No. But what difference?"

Fane regards the artisan. He looks over the artisan's shoulder at the lowering sun. The phantoms of his eyes stagger.

"I suppose you're right. Why don't you do that. I'm going to build a ship."

In the west of Ireland, while his ship is being built, Fane walks down a road hoping to be set upon by bandits. By the side of the road, an old woman sits plaiting ox-hide into horsewhips.

She says, "You have had disasters. You will die."

Avalanches come loose in Fane. He waits for their dust to settle.

"You said that last time."

"Before you die you will have disasters."

Fane stands looking down at her, fingering his chain, thinking it would do little good for the mountain to fall on her.

Without looking up, she says, "But sometimes all a man can do is go find a new axe."

Fane, of several minds, continues down the road until he sees smoke, whereupon he seeks out and thrashes a shepherd.

Having selected his crew, Fane gathers them, points to the setting sun, and says, "We're going there."

"What do we do when we arrive?"

"Depends what's there, sheep dung. Don't think so much."

Fane's ship arrives in what might as well be Newfoundland. His crew find this congenial and virgin. There are trees, fish, land and no one to fight.

"How soon do we go home and get the women?"

"Idiot. Are you a goat? A cow? What does a dog want with pastures? We'll sail around this and go on."

"We can't sail around it. There's no more water—we're on the other side."

"There's always more water."

"No. We're going back for the women. What kind of chieftain are you anyway?"

Fane lays waste his crew and ship, except for Waldo who hides under a rock with crabs.

Travelling overland in a sense of vacancy sufficiently large to be invincible, solitary Fane realizes at length that he is being followed. His followers unobtrusively, and for the most part invisibly, herd him toward their village. Since their colour seems strange and their manner uninspiringly docile, Fane's curiosity and frustration impel him to suffer direction.

In the village he is surrounded by coppery savages who fall on their knees before him and raise a chant unmistakably religious. Disappointed of his assumption that they intend this as prelude to dismembering him, Fane, in exasperation, speaks.

"You senseless spawn of pigs, get off your knees! I'm just another funny-coloured savage. Can you row a boat?"

This produces no useful result. Wolfbane mimes a vessel, makes paddling motions, and points to the westering sun.

Wolfbane Fane peers through mist from the lean prow of his Wolf. Across long swells, light glows in the dark lump of Britain. Armed with a fresh axe of Damascus steel, hair streaked grey, ageing Fane crouches at the head of furred oarsmen and creeps in on the tide.

He leaves his men with the boat and hunches toward the light-chinked door, where he bursts in and stands watching drinkers, benches and tables swirl in confusion. Eerily, groundmist rising from his lower regions, Fane returns to his crew.

"It's no use," he says.

"What do you mean it's no use?"

"It's no use. Shove off. We're going home."

"What? It's just a village like any other village—"

"Do as I say. There's all these guys drinking in there . . . it's just no use."

"Old woman! You should have stayed home by the fire. Out of the way."

"Back in the boat, halflings, and watch your mouth!"

His crew advance on Fane.

"Get out of the way, old fool, no-one's grandfather. Old men should be fed to the wolves."

Fane shrugs, hefts his axe, and lays waste a final crew. He finds Waldo in an empty barrel, and says,

"It's no use, Waldo," and breaks Waldo's neck.

He destroys the ship, impatiently, and flings his axe into the sea. Throwing helmet, shield, belt and furs after it, he turns again toward the drinking hall, wearing only his woollens, carrying a piece of gold.

The place is dark and full of knives. Fane enters. He throws down the gold, asks for mead, and drinks. The darkness full of knives falls upon Fane and overwhelms him.

🔥 🔥 🔥

LOWELL'S GRAVEYARD

by ROBERT HASS

from SALMAGUNDI

nominated by Jonathan Galassi and Daniel Halpern

IT'S PROBABLY A HOPELESS MATTER, writing about favorite poems.
I came across "The Lost Son," "The Quaker Graveyard in Nantucket" and "Howl" at about the same time. Some of the lines are still
married in my head and they still have talismanic power: *snail, snail,
glister me forward; Mohammedan angels staggering on tenement
roofs illuminated; this is the end of running on the waves.* I see now
that they are all three lost son poems, but at the time I didn't see
much of anything. I heard, and it was the incantatory power of the
poems that moved me. Enchantment, literally. I wandered around
San Francisco demolishing the twentieth century by mumbling to

myself, *blue-lunged combers lumbered to the kill* and managed to
mix up Roethke's *ordnung! ordnung! papa's coming* with the Lord
who survived the rainbow of his will.

*

   You can analyze the music of poetry but it's difficult to conduct an
argument about its value, especially when it's gotten into the blood.
It becomes autobiography there. The other night in a pub in Cam-
bridgeshire (named The Prince Regent and built just before the
regency in the year when the first man who tried to organize a craft
union among weavers was whipped, drawn, quartered and disem-
bowelled in a public ceremony in London) the subject of favorite
poems came up and a mild-looking man who taught high school
geology treated us to this:

> For it's Din! Din! Din!
> You limpin' lump o' brick dust, Gunga Din!
> Though I've belted you and flayed you,
> By the livin' Gawd that made you,
> You're a better man than I am, Gunga Din!

And he began to talk about his father's library in a summer cottage in
Devon. I thought of how my older brother had loved that poem, how
we had taken turns reading Vachel Lindsay and Kipling aloud on
summer nights in California, in our upstairs room that looked out on
a dusty fig orchard and grapevines spilling over the wooden fence.
   Poems take place in your life, or some of them do, like the day
your younger sister arrives and replaces you as the bon enfant in the
bosom of the family; or the day the trucks came and the men began to
tear up the wooden sidewalks and the cobblestone gutters outside
your house and laid down new cement curbs and asphalt streets. We
put the paper bags on our feet to walk back and forth across the road
which glistened with hot oil. That was just after the war. The town
was about to become a suburb in the postwar boom. The fig orchard
went just after the old road. I must have been six. Robert Lowell had
just published in the *Partisan Review* a first version of "The Quaker
Graveyard in Nantucket."

*

Thinking about this a long time later made me realize that "Quaker Graveyard" is not a political poem. I had assumed that it was, that its rage against the war and puritan will and the Quakers of Nantucket who financed the butchery of whales was an attack on American capitalism. But a political criticism of any social order implies both that a saner one can be imagined and the hope or conviction that it can be achieved. I had by then begun to have a way of describing such an order, got out of a melange of Paul Goodman, Camus and *To the Finland Station,* but what lay behind it was an imagination of early childhood, dusty fig leaves and sun and fields of wild fennel. Nostalgia locates desire in the past where it suffers no active conflict and can be yearned toward pleasantly. History is the antidote to this. When I saw that my paradise was Lowell's hell, I was forced to see that it was not a place in time I was thinking of, but a place in imagination. The fury of conflict is in "The Quaker Graveyard" but I went back to the poem looking for the vision of an alternative world. There is none. There's grief and moral rage but the poem imagines the whole of human life as sterile violence:

> All you recovered from Poseidon died
> With you, my cousin, and the harrowed brine
> Is fruitless on the blue beard of the god . . .

and it identifies finally with the inhuman justice of God:

> You could cut the brakish waters with a knife
> Here in Nantucket, and cast up the time
> When the Lord God formed man from the sea's slime
> And breathed into his face the breath of life,
> And blue-lunged combers lumbered to the kill.
> The Lord survives the rainbow of his will.

There are no choices in this history of the experiment of evolution and so there can be no politics. "The Lost Son," all inward animal alertness and numbed panic, contains the possiblity of a social order by imagining return. And "Howl" wants to imagine a fifth international of angels.

It struck me then that the poem was closer in sensiblity to someone like Robinson Jeffers than to most of the poets that I had come to associate with Lowell. Both poets are forced to step outside the human process and claim the vision of some imperturbable godhead in which the long violence of human history looks small. But in "Quaker Graveyard" it is important to say that is the position the poem *finally* arrives at because it is a poem of process, and of anguish. Warren Winslow drowns, the Quakers drown, the wounded whale churns in an imagination of suffering and violence which it is the imperative of the poem to find release from, and each successive section of the poem is an attempt to discover a way out. When I was beginning to read poetry to learn what it was and what it could be, this seemed the originality of the poem and its greatness.

*

And it's still hard for me to dissociate it from the excitement of that first reading. The poem leapt off the page. Its music, its fury and grief, haunted me:

> where the bones
> Cry out in the long night for the hurt beast
> Bobbing by Ahab's whaleboats in the East

By that time Lowell was writing in the later, more influential style, then controversial, now egregious orthodoxy:

> These are the tranquilized fifties
> and I am forty . . .

But I didn't know that, and I still find myself blinking incredulously when I read—in almost anything written about the poetry—that those early poems "clearly reflect the dictates of the new criticism," while the later one are "less consciously wrought and extremely intimate." This is the view in which it is 'more intimate' and 'less conscious' to say "my mind's not right" than to imagine the moment when

> The death-lance churns into the sanctuary, tears
> The gun-blue swingle, heaving like a flail,
> And hacks the coiling life out . . .

which is to get things appallingly wrong.

*

Years later I heard a part of this judgement echoed in a curious way. I was listening to Yvor Winters, just before his death, lecturing on George Herbert. He was talking about Herbert's enjambments and, in one of his rare excursions into the present, he said in a bass grumble, "Young Lowell has got a bad enjambment which he got from Allen Tate who probably got it from Herbert." I thought of "The Quaker Graveyard":

>   Light
>   Flashed from his matted head and marble feet
>   Seagulls blink their heavy lids
> Seaward

It lit up the poem all over again. Lowell had just published this in one of the fashionable journals:

> Only man thinning out his kind
> sounds through the Sabbath noon, the blind
> swipe of the pruner and his knife
> busy about the tree of life . . .

Non est species, but plenty of *decor*. I'm still not sure what I think about these lines. There is enormous, ironic skill in the octosyllabic couplets, and terrible self-laceration in their poise. It is probably great writing in the sense that the state of mind couldn't be rendered more exactly. But I wondered about the state of mind and said a small prayer to the small gods—hilarity and carnality—that I could escape it. The writer, among other things, is getting a certain magisterial pleasure from seeming to be outside the picture. The writer of these lines is in it:

> And rips the sperm-whale's midriff into rags,
> Gobbets of blubber spill to wind and weather,
> Sailor, and gulls go round the stoven timbers
> Where the morning stars sing out together . . .

*

It is possible, I suppose, to object to the brilliance of the writing. Charles Olson is said to have complained that Lowell lacquered each of his poems and hung it in a museum. But this judgement, like the 'confessional' revolution envisaged by the professoriat, seems to be based on the sociology of Kenyon College or the fact of meter or Lowell's early models, on everything but a reading of the poems. Finish in poetry is, as Olson insisted, a question of form following function. "The Quaker Graveyard" is brilliantly written, and in a decade of amazing poetry: the *Pisan Cantos*, the first books of *Paterson*, *Four Quartets*, HD's *War Trilogy*, Stevens' "Credences of Summer," Roethke's "The Lost Son." But its brilliance seems neither dictated nor wrought; it is headlong, furious, and casual. There are moments that hover near grandiloquence—"Ask for no Orphean lute . . ." but they didn't bother me then and don't much now.

Everything about the sound of the poem seemed gorgeous on first reading. "A brakish reach of shoal off . . ." sounded like an impossible Russian word, sluggish and turbulent; the Indian-Yankee "Madaket" bit it off with wonderful abruptness. I still like to say it:

A brakish reach of shoal off Madaket,—

In the second line, the oddness of the sound, which is a substitution in the third foot, has a slightly startling effect:

The sea was still breaking violently . . .

The rhythm breaks "breaking," makes a violence out of slackness in a way that I had never seen before and it was clearly intended because *still* is an extra syllable:

The sea was still breaking violently and night

From here to the end of the stanza, the energy of the poem allows no rest—

Had steamed into our North Atlantic fleet,
When the drowned sailor clutched the drag-net. Light
Flashed from his matted head and marble feet,
He grappled at the net
With the coiled hurdling muscles of his thighs:

I loved the nervous restlessness of the rhyming, the way you accept
"net" as the rhyme for "fleet" and "Madaket", then get the off-rhyme
"light," so that when you arrive at "feet" it is hardly an arrival and
you are pushed toward "net" again. It's like a man shooting at a target
with such random desperation that the hits count for no more than
the misses. This effect, together with "young Lowell's bad enjambment," transmute an acquired skill into articulate rage. And the
colon after "net" is not a rest; it insists on the forward hurtle of the
lines:

                    The corpse was bloodless . . .

                              *

Warren Winslow or not, it has always seemed to me that Lowell
himself was the drowned sailor, just as Roethke is the lost son.
Otherwise the sudden moments of direct address make no sense:

                                   Sailor, will your sword
Whistle and fall and sink into the fat?
In the great ash-pit of Jehoshaphat
The bones cry for the blood of the white whale,
The fat flukes arch and whack about its ears,
The death lance churns into the sanctuary . . .

It is having it both ways to be the young man drowned in the "slush,"
in the "bilge and backwash," "the greased wash," "the sea's slime"
where "the whale's viscera go and the roll of its corruption overruns
the world" and to be at the same time the young poet who identifies
with the vengeance of the earth-shaker, "green, unwearied, chaste"
whose power outlasts the merely phallic brutality of the guns of the
steeled fleet, but the impacted writing permits this and it is
psychologically true. Distrust of birth is the beginning of one kind of
religious emotion.

In the speed of the writing, the syntax comes apart; it dissolves
into emotion, into music and the subterranean connections among
images. Throughout the poem it is characteristic that the important
associations occur in subordinate clauses or compounds so breathless that you have to sort your way back quite consciously to the
starting point. This resembles the syntactical strategies of the
French surrealists, particularly Desnos and Peret. The main clause
is a pushing off place and the poem makes its meaning out of its
momentum. It's a way of coming to terms with experience under
pressure and not some extrinsic decision about style. Even the lines
about the shark—

> Where the heelheaded dogfish barks its nose
> On Ahab's void and forehead

are not Clevelandizing; they are not even—in the period phrase—a
metaphysical image because their force is not intellectual. The lines
depend on our willingness to let barking dogs marry scavenging
sharks in the deep places where men void and are voided. To
complain about this is not to launch an attack on 'consciously
wrought' but the reverse.

The current taste is for the explicit, however weird. Surrealism
comes to mean the manufacture of peculiar imagery and not something in the sinews of a poem. The fish in "For the Union Dead" are a
midpoint in this levelling process. They are transformed into sharks
and then into cars as "a savage servility slides by on grease," but the
delivery is slower, the context narrative and topographical. It is
pretty much the same image as in "The Quaker Graveyard," but it
has been clarified like broth, a fish stock served up as clam chowder
to the peremptory gentleman in the cartoon who likes to see what
he's eating.

And this won't do for Lowell because the power of his imagery has
always been subliminal; it exists as the nervous underside of the
thing said. Look at this, for example, from "Fourth of July in Maine."
The poet is addressing Harriet Winslow:

> Dear Cousin, life is much the same,
> though only fossils know your name
> here since you left this solitude,
> gone, as the Christians say, for good,

Your house, still outwardly in form
lasts, though no emissary comes
to watch the garden running down,
or photograph the propped-up barn.

If memory is genius, you
had Homer's, enough gossip to
repeople Trollope's Barchester,
nurses, Negro, diplomat, down-easter,
cousins kept up with, nipped, corrected,
kindly, majorfully directed,
though family furniture, decor,
and rooms redone meant almost more.

How often when the telephone
brought you to us from Washington,
we had to look around the room
to find the objects you would name—
lying there, ten years' paralyzed,
half-blind, no voice unrecognized,
not trusting in the afterlife,
teasing us for a carving knife.

High New England summer, warm
and fortified against the storm
by nightly nips you once adored,
though never going overboard,
Harriet, when you used to play
your chosen Nadia Boulanger
Monteverdi, Purcell, and Bach's
precursors on the Magnavox.

This is affectionate, even cozy. And beneath that first sensation is
deep pathos; and beneath that is something like terror, so that the
force of the phrase "life is much the same" keeps changing—for the
worse—as you read. The imagery of a life with fossil memory, a
run-down garden, a propped-up barn, a devastated Troy and cursed
Mycenae, a Barchester that needs repeopling, people who need to
be nipped and corrected, or redone, a half-blind paralyzed woman
(the syntax has a way of paralyzing her objects as well), the need to be

fortified against summer (with nips: the carving knife lying suddenly across both the cozy drinking and the corrected behavior) all issue in, among time's other wreckage, a Magnavox, the great voice which reproduces a great religious passion in the form of a performer's art. Everything dwindles, is rendered. Boulanger's Monteverdi. Lowell's Harriet. It's easy to explicate poems and hard to get their tone. The tone here has one moment of extraordinary pathos which is deeper than the cat-like movement through entropy and corrosion:

> half-blind, no voice unrecognized,
> not trusting in the after-life,
> teasing us for a carving knife.
>
> High New England summer . . .

But in the end the tone has to do with rendering; the whole passage is majorfully directed. It is not the experience but a way of handling the experience. The imagery accumulates its desolating evidence, but in such a way that the terror in the poetry is perceived while the novelistic pathos is felt. The subterranean images, whether "consciously wrought" or not, are intellectual. In this way, it is exactly a metaphysical poem as nothing in *Lord Weary's Castle* is.

In the second section of "Quaker Graveyard" there's not much that could be called development. Four sentences, three of which use syntax only as a line of energy, do little more than elaborate an instance of what used to be called the pathetic fallacy, but they confront the experience of grief, of terror at the violence of things, directly:

> Whenever winds are moving and their breath
> Heaves at the roped-in bulwarks of this pier,
> The terns and seagulls tremble at your death
> In these home waters. Sailor, can you hear
> The Pequod's sea-wings, beating landward, fall
> Headlong and break on our Atlantic wall
> Off 'Sconset, where the yawing S-boats splash
> As the entangled screeching mainsheet clears
> The blocks: off Madaket, where lubbers lash
> The heavy surf and throw their long lead squids

For blue-fish? Sea-gulls blink their heavy lids
Seaward. The wind's wings beat upon the stones,
Cousin, and scream for you and the claws rush
At the sea's throat and wring it in the slush
Of this old Quaker Graveyard where the bones
Cry out in the long night for the hurt beast
Bobbing by Ahab's whaleboats in the East.

The effect here is not simple, but for me it is the most beautiful moment in the poem. The whole of that first sentence relaxes. The lines break deliberately as if they were trying to hold the emotion in place. But the content is terrible and the perception is extraordinarily intense. The feathers of the gulls ruffling in the wind are made to hurt. And it's such an ordinary perception. "Whenever winds are moving," to my Pacific grounding, is almost always, so that the image registers the steady pain of merely seeing. For some reason this connected in my mind with a thing Levi-Strauss says near the end of *Tristes Tropiques:* "What I see is an affliction to me, what I cannot see a reproach." The power of this image connects all the description in the poem with the eyes of the dead sailor and the gulls' eyes and the profoundly becalmed eyes of the Virgin of Walsingham. It connects the wind's breath with the breath of the poet which accelerates into violence again in the next sentence. And that sentence is a good example of the expressive power of syntax in the poem. In its fierce accumulation of images, you lose any sense that it began, rather gently, as a rhetorical question. This is a way of being lost, of drowning in the dissolution of syntax. Surrealism, I'm tempted to say, is syntax: not weird images but the way the mind connects them. Here they swell and gather toward violence, toward a continuous breaking like the breaking of waves on the shore and the effort of control is conveyed by the way "the entangled screeching mainsheet clears the blocks."

So the poem must slow down again: "Seagulls blink their heavy lids/Seaward." This fixity, the imperturbable consciousness of the gull whose feathers a moment before were trembling in "home waters," is an enormous relief. It is not the dead staring eyes of the drowned sailor and it is not yet the seeing of Our Lady of Walsingham. That heavy-lidded blinking of gulls seems to have a wonderful Buddha-like somnolent alertness when you look at it. It accepts things as they are. It's when gulls are perched on piers, heads tucked in a little, eyes blinking matter-of-factly, that I'm suddenly aware they have no arms, no hands. Even if they don't like what they see, they're not going to do anything about it. And this is the relief. But gulls are also scavengers. Their seeing doesn't hope for much, but it belongs to the world of appetite and their appetites are not very ambitious. That is why the sailors, grasping at straws in section IV, are only three-quarters fools. They want something, have heard news "of IS, the whited monster." So the lines accelerate again. The sea, godly in the first section is consumed in the general violence in this one and the section ends in a long wail for Moby Dick, the object of desire, monster and victim.

Almost all of "The Quaker Graveyard" works in this way. It's hard to get at without a lot of tedious explication, but look at the third section of the poem. If you ask yourself how the language or the thought proceeds, it's not easy to say. First sentence: All you recovered died with you. Second sentence: Guns blast the eelgrass. Third sentence: They died . . .; only bones abide. Characteristically, the Quaker sailors appear at the extremity of a dependent clause; then their fate is seized on, midway through the section, as a subject, and the stanza unravels again into violence as the sailors drown proclaiming their justification. And it does not seem arbitrary. It seems inevitable, because this hopelessly repeated unravelling into violence is both the poem's theme and the source of its momentum. Hell is repetition and the structure of anger is repetition. In this poem history is also repetition, as it is the structure of religious incantation. They are all married here, desperately, and the grace of the poem has to exist in modulation of tone. This modulation, like the different textures of an abstract expressionist painting or like the very different modulations that create the texture of Whitman's poems—"Song of Myself" comes to mind—is the grandeur and originality of "The Quaker Graveyard." Not theme, not irony or intimacy or the consciously wrought, but absolute attention to feeling at that moment in the poem's process.

*

"They died/When time was open-eyed,/Wooden and childish." It takes a while—or took me a while—to see that this is the one moment in the poem that reaches back into childhood. The image has about it the helplessness of childhood. Time here must be the

wooden, openeyed figureheads on old whaling ships, probably seen
in books or a maritime museum. The look of the eyes on those old
sculptures, their startled and hopeful innocence, dawns on you and
it creates the state of mind of the child looking up at them *Was* not
seemed. The verb makes the child's seeing sovereign and irrecover-
able. Lost innocence is not the subject of the poem. There is a kind of
pleading between the poet and the innocence of his cousin, the
ensign who went to the war and did his duty. "All you recovered . . .
died with you". But the innocence of the child, of the ensign, of the
figureheads is only one syntactical leap away from the stupidity and
self-righteousness of the Quaker sailors—"If God himself had not
been on our side"—who are swallowed up without understanding a
thing. Their eyes are "cabin-windows on a stranded hulk/Heavy
with sand."

*

Sections IV and V continue this riding out of violence but the
conclusions of both take a turn that brings us to the religious issue in
the poem. It didn't puzzle me much in that first excited reading
because I ignored it. I was living down a Catholic childhood and
religious reference in poetry seemed to me not so much reactionary
as fossilized and uninteresting. But it was surely there in a lot of what
I was reading. Robert Duncan's work was thick with religious imagery, & the "Footnote to Howl" exclaimed, "Holy! Holy! Holy!" I
didn't know Lowell was a convert to Catholicism or that this was a
momentous rejection of his heritage. For that matter, I didn't know
what a Lowell was. But I could see that the poem was not Catholic in
any sense that I understood. It is true that the implicit answer to the
question "Who will dance the mast-lashed master of Leviathans/Up
. . ." is Christ. Orpheus, the way of art, is explicitly dismissed at the
beginning of the poem. And the fifth section, the most terrible, the
one in which the whale receives the sexual wound of all human
violence, ends with a prayer: "Hide/Our steel, Jonas Messias, in
thy side."
   But the first of these passages is a question and the second is a
supplication, not a statement of faith. Insofar as the poem is Christian, it seemed to me to be a very peculiar Christianity. I was
prepared to grant that the killing of the Whale was also an image of
the crucifixion of Christ, but in the poem this act is the source and

culmination of evil. "When the whale's viscera go. . . . its corruption over-runs this world." There is no sense here of the crucifixion as a redemption. I can imagine that three or four pages of theological explication could put it there, but it isn't in the poem. Typologically the legal torture and murder of the man-god is not the fall; in the Christian myth it is not cruelty and violence but pride and disobedience through which men fell. One can make a series of arguments, threading back through the blasphemous pride of Ahab to the dominion given man by God in the epigraph to the poem, and emerge with a case for cruelty as a form of pride, but cruelty is not pride. They're different things, and it is cruelty and death, not pride and the fall, that preoccupy the poet, no matter how much of Melville or theology we haul in to square this vision with orthodoxy.

Reading Robert Duncan has given me a way to think about this issue in Lowell:

> There was no law of Jesus then.
>   There was
>   only a desire of savior . . .

Somewhere in his prose at about the same time Duncan had written that the mistake of Christianity was to think that the soul's salvation was the only human adventure. That was an enormously liberating perception. It put Christ on equal footing with the other gods. And the gods, Pound had said in a phrasing that seems now late Victorian, were "eternal moods," forms of consciousness which men through learning, art, and contemplation could inhabit. They were not efficacious. We were not Mycenean warlords, burning bulls and hoping the good scent of roast beef found its way to attentive nostrils; and the Mother of Perpetual Help did not, as my aunts seemed to believe, repair carburetors or turn up lost purses. But the gods were real, forms of imagination in which we could dwell and through which we could see. "The verb," Pound had said with the wreckage of his life around him, "is 'to see' not 'walk on'."

I got my Catholicism from my mother's side, Foleys from Cork by way of Vermont who drank and taught school and practiced law on the frontiers of respectability until they landed in San Francisco at the turn of the century. My father's side was Protestant and every once in a while, weary probably with the catechisms of his children, he would try to teach us one of his childhood prayers. But he could never get past the first line: "In my father's house there are many mansions . . ." He would frown, squint, shake his head, but that was as far as he ever got and we children who were willing to believe Protestants capable of any stupidity including the idea that you could fit a lot of mansions into a house, would return to memorizing the four marks of the true church. (It was one, holy, catholic, and apostolic.) But that phrase came back to me as a way through the door of polytheism and into myth. If Pound could resurrect the goddesses, there was place for a temple of Christ, god of sorrows, desire of savior, resting place of violence. I could have the memory of incense and the flickering candles and the battered figure on the cross with the infinitely sad and gentle face and have Aphrodite as well, "the fauns chiding Proteus/in the smell of hay under olive trees" and the intoning of Latin with which we began the mass: "*Introibo ad altare Dei.*" On these terms, Lowell's prayer moved me: "Hide our steel, Jonas Messias, in thy side." And I could accept cruelty as the first fall; it was truer to my experience than pride or disobedience which the violence of the state has made to seem, on the whole, sane and virtuous. Not the old dogma, but a piece of the unborn myth which American poetry was making. And this is the sense of things in the poem. There is no redemption promised in the prayer at the end of section V. There is only the god of sorrows and the receiving of the wound.

*

Sexual wounding: it is certainly there in section V, both in the imagery and in the way the section functions, literally, as a climax to the poem. This is the fall, the moment when corruption overruns the world. And the rhetorical question, "Sailor, will your sword/Whistle and fall and sink into the fat?" wants to make us all complicit. The passage is Calvinist in feeling; every day is judgement day:

> In the great ashpit of Jehoshaphat
> The bones cry for the blood of the white whale

In sexual imagery, not only the penetration by the death lance but the singing of stars, the dismemberment of the masthead, we are all judged:

The fat flukes arch and whack about its ears,
The death-lance churns into the sanctuary, tears
The gun-blue swingle, heaving like a flail,
And hacks the coiling life out: it works and drags
And rips the sperm-whale's midriff into rags,
Gobbets of blubber spill to wind and weather,
Sailor, and gulls go round the stoven timbers
Where the morning stars sing out together
And thunder shakes the white surf and dismembers
The red flag hammered in the masthead . . .

This needs to be seen straight on, so that we look at the sickening cruelty it actually describes. It's a relief and much easier to talk about myth or symbolic sexuality. This is an image of killing written by a pacifist who was willing to go to prison. It makes death horrifying; it makes the war horrifying, and the commerce of the Nantucket Quakers whom Melville reminded his readers to think of when they lit their cozy whale-oil lamps. "Light is where the landed blood of Cain . . ."

But, just as there is disgust with the mothering sea in the bilge and backwash throughout the poem, there is a deep abhorrence of sexual violence, of sexuality as violence. I'm not sure how to talk about it. There is Freud's gruesome little phrase, as gruesome in German as in English but lacking the pun: the sadistic conception of coitus. But calling it that doesn't take us very far. The fact is that there is an element of cruelty in human sexuality, though that isn't the reason for the Puritan distrust of sex. The Puritans distrusted sexuality because the sexual act dissolved human will for a moment, because—for a moment—men fell into the roots of their mammal nature. You can't have an orgasm and be a soldier of Christ. Thus *Samson Agonistes*. And the Puritan solution, hidden but real in the history of imagination whether in Rome or the Enlightenment, was to turn sex into an instrument of will, of the conscious cruelty which flowered in the writings of Sade. It is there in our history and Lowell is right to connect it with the annihilative rage of capitalism. Flesh is languor ("All of life's grandeur/is something with a girl in summer . . .") but it is also rage. It marries us to the world and the world is full of violence and cruelty. This is part of the bind of the poem which is also the Calvinist bind of determinism and free will. The way out is not-world, an identification at the end of the poem with the "unmar-

ried" Atlantic and the Lord who survives the rainbow-covenant of
evolution.

All of which would be pretty grim if it were not for "Our Lady of
Walsingham." It's a remarkable moment in the poem, the most
surprising of its modulations, a little tranquil island in all the fury. I
imagine that for a lot of younger writers it was the place where they
learned how far you could go away from the poem and still be in it.
Pound says somewhere, sounding like a surly Matthew Arnold, that
a history of poetry that's worth anything ought to be able to point to
specific poems and passages in poems and say here, here and here
are inventions that made something new possible in poetry. This is
one of those places.

Its occurrence makes emotional sense because it follows section V.
It is the peace of the satisfaction of the body's rage, a landscape of
streams and country lanes. The nineteenth century would have
described the writing as chaste or exquisite and I'm not sure we have
better words to praise it with. Its wonderfully plain and exact:

> Our Lady, too small for her canopy,
> Sits near the altar. There's no comeliness
> At all or charm in that expressionless
> Face with its heavy eyelids. As before,
> This face, for centuries a memory,
> *Non est species, neque decor,*
> Expressionless, expresses God: it goes
> Past castled Sion. She knows what God knows,
> Not Calvary's cross nor the crib at Bethlehem
> Now, and the world shall come to Walsingham.

This is another temple, not the god of sorrows but the goddess of an
almost incomprehensible peace. It appears to be the emphatically
Catholic moment in the poem (which adds a peculiar comedy to the
idea that "Lycidas" was somehow its model; I've just visited the
cathedral at Ely where Milton's friend Thomas Cromwell personally
beheaded all the statues in the Lady Chapel. If the setpiece digressions of Alexandrian pastoral taken over by Milton to scourge a
Popish clergy have really become a hymn to the Virgin Mary, it is the
kind of irony—funny, too elaborately bookish—that would please
the author of *History.*). But I don't think it is Catholic, or not
especially Catholic, and that is its interest.

The crucial phrase is "past castled Sion." Lowell is not after sacramental mediation but a contemplative peace beyond any manifestation in the flesh, beyond thought or understanding, and—most especially—beyond desire. This isn't incompatible with Catholic theology, but it's not central to its spirit which is embodiment: the Orphean lute and the crib at Bethlehem. This apprehension of God, of a pure, calm, and utterly clear consciousness, belongs equally to all mysticisms, Christian or otherwise, and it has always seemed to me that the figure of Our Lady here looks a lot like Guatama Buddha. It is the embodiment of what can't be embodied. This is a contradiction, but it is one that belongs to any intellectual pointing toward mystical apprehension. It is the contradiction that made the world-denial of Buddhists and Cathars at the same time utterly compassionate toward and alert to the world and the flesh and makes the Buddhist Gary Snyder our best poet of nature. This is not the rejection of the world which the last lines of the poem suggest; it's something else and for me it's something much more attractive as a possibility of imagination.

But how does it square with the last lines? I don't think it does. Nor does it contradict them. That's the aesthetic daring of this section. What the Lady of Walsingham represents is past contention. She's just there. The method of the poem simply includes her among its elements, past argument, as a possibility through which all the painful seeing in the poem can be transformed and granted peace. She floats; everything else in the poem rises and breaks, relentlessly, like waves.

*

I finally got to hear Robert Lowell read a couple of years ago in Charlottesville, Virginia—in Jefferson Country where the roadsigns read like a rollcall of plump Hanoverian dowagers and America comes as close as it ever will to a munching English lane. The setting made me feel truculent anyway and when he began by murmuring an apology for the earlier poems—'rather apocalyptic,' 'one felt so intense'—I found myself on the poems' side. And the voice startled me, probably because I'd been hearing the work in my own for so long. I thought it sounded bizarrely like an imitation of Lionel Barrymore. It was not a voice that could say, "Face of snow,/You are the flowers that country girls have caught,/ A wild bee-pillaged honeysuckle brought/To the returning bridegroom—the design/ Has not yet left it, and the petals shine," without sounding like a disenchanted English actor reading an Elizabethan sonnet on American television.

I had felt vaguely hostile toward Lowell's later work, though I admired it. I thought, for one thing, that the brilliant invention of "The Quaker Graveyard" had come about because he had nothing to go on but nerve and that, when the form cloyed in *The Mills of the Kavanaughs*, he had traded in those formal risks for the sculpted anecdote and the Puritan autobiography, a form about as original as John Bunyan's *Grace Abounding*. Out of the manner had come, not so much in Lowell himself as in the slough of poetry *Life Studies* engendered, a lot of narrative beginning "Father, you . ." or "The corn died in the field that summer, Mother/when . . ." It struck stances toward experience, as if Williams had said, "No attitudes but in things!" I wanted the clarity that "Our Lady of Walsingham" looked toward and in "Waking Early Sunday Morning" I thought he had come to something like that earlier insight and abandoned it too easily:

> I watch a glass of water wet
> with a fine fuzz of icy sweat,
> silvery colours touched with sky,
> serene in their neutrality—
> yet if I shift, or change my mood,
> I see some object made of wood,
> background behind it of brown grain,
> to darken it, but not to stain.
>
> O that the spirit could remain
> tinged but untarnished by its strain!
> Better dressed and stacking birch . . .

As if you had to choose between them or tarnishing were the issue. That glass of water interested me a lot more than the ironies about electric bells ringing "Faith of our fathers."

Anyway, when he began to read, all this buzzing of the head stopped. There was the sense, for one thing, of a body of work faithful to itself through all its phases (early, middle, and ceaseless revision). And there was the reading of "Near the Ocean." Hearing it, I began to understand the risks attendant on backing away from the drama and self-drama of *Lord Weary's Castle*. Pain has its own grandeur. This disenchanted seeing was not serene neutrality—it was not serene at all; it had the clarity of a diminished sense of things not flinched at. I thought it was a brave piece of writing and it revisits the territory of "The Quaker Graveyard," so it seems like a place to end:

> Sand built the lost Atlantis . . . sand,
> Atlantic ocean, condoms, sand.
>
> Sleep, sleep. The ocean, grinding stones,
> can only speak the present tense;
> nothing will age, nothing will last,
> or take corruption from the past.
> A hand, your hand then! I'm afraid
> to touch the crisp hair on your head—

CONVERSATION BY THE BODY'S LIGHT

by JANE COOPER

from WESTIGAN REVIEW OF POETRY

nominated by Hayden Carruth

Out of my poverty
Out of your poverty
Out of your nakedness
Out of my nakedness
Between the swimmer in the water
And the watcher of the skies
Something is altered

Something is offered
Something is breathed
The body's radiance
Like the points of a constellation
Beckons to insight
Here is my poverty:
A body hoarded
Ridiculous in middle age
Unvoiced, unpracticed

And here is your poverty:
A prodigality
That guts its source
The self picked clean
 In its shining houses

Out of my nakedness
Out of your nakedness
Between the swimmer in the skies
And the watcher from the water
Something is braided
For a moment unbalanced
Caught—the barest shelter
Lost but reoccurring:
The still not-believed-in
Heartbeat of the glacier

CHINATOWN SONATA

by YUKI HARTMAN

from FRESH PAINT (Ailanthus Press) and HOT FOOTSTEPS (Telephone Books)

nominated by June Jordan, Phillip Lopate, Ailanthus Press and Telephone Books,

IT has always been transcendental—I've always gone to Chinatown,
and had my fill
of everything. Flipping open Encyclopedia of New York City to
Food, I'm already faint with
the gullible bottomless appetite of Texan in the frail Japanese frame
devouring the Chinese sunrises.
Waiters are always smiling when I come in, cash registers light up
like the Christmas trees.
Like a civilzed iguana I'm so gentlemanly till the table is set with
Sizzling Rice Soup,
Clams Soaked in Black Bean Sauce, white flesh of chicken flash-fried
with wine and vinegar,

chestnuts, ginger, and cool Wine Chicken, Peking Duck, Aromatic
      Beef, shrimps scrumptious
in the red hot sauce, and more and more I can't help any longer,
      I sharpen my jaws like a
helpless crocodile and writhe on my seat like Nero starved for days,
      to the ocean of
feasts beyond my wildest dreams, even whopping down the
      chopsticks to finely carved toothpicks.
And how people jump back when I smile at them! Excuse me,
      you look so delicious in a sesame
colored dress and scallions splattered across your waist area,
      haven't I seen you before? In Shanghi Inn? At Setchuan
House? In Hunan? It doesn't matter. I'll see you somewhere.
      Don't be terrified. I would be
the gentlest crocodile you ever saw, when served properly. Be careful.
      And when I'm
finished, drinking lake after lake of Jasmin tea I'm glowing with the
      contentment of human condition,
I may feel heavenly too, and swallow clouds after clouds for dessert,
      what else can I eat?
All should be full: Bars full of students, pediatric wards full of
      babies and mothers and
fathers in hysteria, schools full of sloppy brats, sexy teachers,
      Chinatown full of
restaurants and gift shops, 20th Century would have been so dull
      without those cat eating
chefs behind the kitchens, protruding on the side streets, I thank
      you with my potbellied dizziness,
I think I'll lie down here in the booth of plastic covers and dream
      of a dragon accupuncturing my
saturated torso with their fine whiskers. The Year of Hare is
      approaching rapidly, and will the
wild flowers bloom again in the backyard of Li Po, sprouting up my
      message of another century,
that I'm a glutton, and a helpless harebrain lusting after women, too,
      will he, and other great ones,
write me a note of dismissal or let me stay with them like a kitchen
      boy, scooping up a soup
of heron's egg (eagle's heart), and turtles still swimming around in
      the fragrant leaves of some time ago?

SOME RECOGNITION OF THE JOSHUA LIZARD

by Robert Burlingame

from NEW AMERICA

nominated by NEW AMERICA

Van Densburgh, herpetologist of California
First catalogued him, in a green note of four pages—
This sleek saurian, this less than finger shape
Homesteading the wreckage beneath trumpeting Joshua.

He named the stealth gemmed inside that tense
Sanctuary, slight body gloved in round blackness—
Those scales of night overarched by swords,
By the uplifted arms, an Old Testament stance.

Love this creature, Van Densburgh so much as said:
He lives at peace with rat and wren, the flycatcher,
The sand—this chameleon faith solemn
At the foot of a desert king with God-shaggy head.

So love of God begins, once wrote Ansari, another
Wilderness lord—in the simple wish to live
Even beneath a saw-tooth sky—in harmlessness.
From such root we rise to love the different brother.

🔥 🔥 🔥

THE FAT GIRL

fiction by ANDRE DUBUS

from ADULTERY AND OTHER CHOICES (The Godine Press)

nominated by The Godine Press and DeWitt Henry

HER NAME WAS LOUISE. Once when she was sixteen a boy kissed her at a barbecue; he was drunk and he jammed his tongue into her mouth and ran his hands up and down her hips. Her father kissed her often. He was thin and kind and she could see in his eyes when he looked at her the lights of love and pity.

It started when Louise was nine. You must start watching what you eat, her mother would say. I can see you have my metabolism. Louise also had her mother's pale blonde hair. Her mother was slim and pretty, carried herself erectly, and ate very little. The two of them would eat bare lunches, while her old brother ate sandwiches and potato chips, and then her mother would sit smoking while

Louise eyed the bread box, the pantry, the refrigerator. Wasn't that good, her mother would say. In five years you'll be in high school and if you're fat the boys won't like you; they won't ask you out. Boys were as far away as five years, and she would go to her room and wait for nearly an hour until she knew her mother was no longer thinking of her, then she would creep into the kitchen and, listening to her mother talking on the phone, or her footsteps upstairs, she would open the bread box, the pantry, the jar of peanut butter. She would put the sandwich under her shirt and go outside or to the bathroom to eat it.

Her father was a lawyer and made a lot of money and came home looking pale and happy. Martinis put color back in his face, and at dinner he talked to his wife and two children. Oh give her a potato, he would say to Louise's mother. She's a growing girl. Her mother's voice then became tense: If she has a potato she shouldn't have dessert. She should have both, her father would say, and he would reach over and touch Louise's check or hand or arm.

In high school she had two girl friends and at night and on week-ends they rode in a car or went to movies. In movies she was fascinated by fat actresses. She wondered why they were fat. She knew why she was fat: she was fat because she was Louise. Because God had made her that way. Because she wasn't like her friends Barbara and Marjorie, who drank milk shakes after school and were all bones and tight skin. But what about those actresses, with their talents, with their broad and profound faces? Did they eat as heedlessly as Bishop Humphries and his wife who sometimes came to dinner and, as Louise's mother said, gorged between amenities? Or did they try to lose weight, did they go about hungry and angry and thinking of food? She thought of them eating lean meats and salads with friends, and then going home and building strange large sandwiches with Italian bread. But mostly she believed they did not go through these failures; they were fat because they chose to be. And she was certain of something else too: she could see it in their faces: they did not eat secretly. Which she did: her creeping to the kitchen when she was nine became, in high school, a ritual of deceit and pleasure. She was a furtive eater of sweets. Even her two friends did not know her secret.

Barbara was thin, gangling, and flat-chested; she was attractive enough and all she needed was someone to take a second look at her face, but the school was large and there were pretty girls in every classroom and walking all the corridors, so no one ever needed to take a second look at Barbara. Marjorie was thin too, an intense, heavy-smoking girl with brittle laughter. She was very intelligent, and with boys she was shy because she knew she made them uncomfortable, and because she was smarter than they were and so could not understand or could not believe the levels they lived on. She was to have a nervous breakdown before earning her PhD. in philosophy at the University of California, where she met and married a physicist and discovered within herself an untrammelled passion: she made love with her husband on the couch, the carpet, in the bathtub, and on the washing machine. By that time much had happened to her and she never thought of Louise. Barbara would finally stop growing and begin moving with grace and confidence. In college she would have two lovers and then several more during the six years she spent in Boston before marrying a middleaged editor who had two sons in their early teens, who drank too much, who was tenderly, boyishly grateful for her love, and whose wife had been killed while rock-climbing in New Hampshire with her lover. She would not think of Louise either, except in an earlier time, when lovers were still new to her and she was ecstatically surprised each time one of them loved her and, sometimes at night, lying in a man's arms, she would tell how in high school no one dated her, she had been thin and plain (she would still believe that: that she had been plain; it had never been true) and so had been forced into the week-end and night-time company of a neurotic smart girl and a shy fat girl. She would say this with self-pity exaggerated by scotch and her need to be more deeply loved by the man who held her.

She never eats, Barbara and Marjorie said of Louise. They ate lunch with her at school, watched her refusing potatoes, ravioli, fried fish. Sometimes she got through the cafeteria line with only a salad. That is how they would remember her: a girl whose hapless body was destined to be fat. No one saw the sandwiches she made and took to her room when she came home from school. No one saw the store of Milky Ways, Butterfingers, Almond Joys, and Hersheys far back on her closet shelf, behind the stuffed animals of her childhood. She was not a hypocrite. When she was out of the house she truly believed she was dieting; she forgot about the candy, as a man speaking into his office dictaphone may forget the lewd photographs hidden in an old shoe in his closet. At other times, away from the home, she thought of the waiting candy with near lust. One

GODINE PRESS

night driving home from a movie, Marjorie said: 'You're lucky you don't smoke; it's *incredible* what I go through to hide it from my parents.' Louise turned to her a smile which was elusive and mysterious; she yearned to be home in bed, eating chocolate in the dark. She did not need to smoke; she already had a vice that was insular and destructive.

She brought it with her to college. She thought she would leave it behind. A move from one place to another, a new room without the haunted closet shelf, would do for her what she could not do for herself. She packed her large dresses and went. For two weeks she was busy with registration, with shyness, with classes; then she began to feel at home. Her room was no longer like a motel. Its walls had stopped watching her, she felt they were her friends, and she gave them her secret. Away from her mother, she did not have to be as elaborate; she kept the candy in her drawer now.

The school was in Massachusetts, a girls' school. When she chose it, when she and her father and mother talked about it in the evenings, everyone so carefully avoided the word boys that sometimes the conversations seemed to be about nothing but boys. There are no boys there, the neuter words said; you will not have to contend with that. In her father's eyes were pity and encouragement; in her mother's was disappointment, and her voice was crisp. They spoke of courses, of small classes where Louise would get more attention. She imagined herself in those small classes; she saw herself as a teacher would see her, as the other girls would; she would get no attention.

The girls at the school were from wealthy families, but most of them wore the uniform of another class: blue jeans and work shirts, and many wore overalls. Louise bought some overalls, washed them until the dark blue faded, and wore them to classes. In the cafeteria she ate as she had in high school, not to lose weight nor even to sustain her lie, but because eating lightly in public had become as habitual as good manners. Everyone had to take gym, and in the locker room with the other girls, and wearing shorts on the volley-ball and badminton courts, she hated her body. She liked her body most when she was unaware of it: in bed at night, as sleep gently took her out of her day, out of herself. And she liked parts of her body. She liked her brown eyes and sometimes looked at them in the mirror: they were not shallow eyes, she thought; they were indeed windows of a tender soul, a good heart. She liked her lips and nose, and her chin, finely shaped between her wide and sagging cheeks. Most of all she liked her long pale blonde hair, she liked washing and drying it and lying naked on her bed, smelling of shampoo, and feeling the soft hair at her neck and shoulders and back.

Her friend at college was Carrie, who was thin and wore thick glasses and often at night she cried in Louise's room. She did not know why she was crying. She was crying, she said, because she was unhappy. She could say no more. Louise said she was unhappy too, and Carrie moved in with her. One night Carrie talked for hours, sadly and bitterly, about her parents and what they did to each other. When she finished she hugged Louise and they went to bed. Then in the dark Carrie spoke across the room: 'Louise? I just wanted to tell you. One night last week I woke up and smelled chocolate. You were eating chocolate, in your bed. I wish you'd eat it in front of me, Louise, whenever you feel like it.'

Stiffened in her bed, Louise could think of nothing to say. In the silence she was afraid Carrie would think she was asleep and would tell her again in the morning or tomorrow night. Finally she said Okay. Then after a moment she told Carrie if she ever wanted any she could feel free to help herself; the candy was in the top drawer. Then she said thank you.

They were roommates for four years and in the summers they exchanged letters. Each fall they greeted with embraces, laughter, tears, and moved into their old room, which had been stripped and cleansed of them for the summer. Neither girl enjoyed summer. Carrie did not like being at home because her parents did not love each other. Louise lived in a small city in Louisiana. She did not like summer because she had lost touch with Barbara and Marjorie; they saw each other, but it was not the same. She liked being with her father but with no one else. The flicker of disappointment in her mother's eyes at the airport was a vanguard of the army of relatives and acquaintances who awaited her: they would see her on the streets, in stores, at the country club, in her home, and in theirs; in the first moments of greeting, their eyes would tell her she was still fat Louise, who had been fat as long as they could remember, who had gone to college and returned as fat as ever. Then their eyes dismissed her, and she longed for school and Carrie, and she wrote letters to her friend. But that saddened her too. It wasn't simply that Carrie was her only friend, and when they finished college they might never see each other again. It was that her existence in the world was so divided; it had begun when she was a child creeping to the kitchen; now that division was much sharper, and her friendship with Carrie seemed disproportionate and perilous. The world she was destined to live in had nothing to do with the intimate nights in their room at school.

In the summer before their senior year, Carrie fell in love. She wrote to Louise about him, but she did not write much, and this hurt Louise more than if Carrie had shown the joy her writing tried to conceal. That fall they returned to their room; they were still close and warm, Carrie still needed Louise's ears and heart at night as she spoke of her parents and her recurring malaise whose source the two friends never discovered. But on most week-ends Carrie left, and caught a bus to Boston where her boy friend studied music. During the week she often spoke hesitantly of sex; she was not sure if she liked it. But Louise, eating candy and listening, did not know whether Carrie was telling the truth or whether, as in her letters of the past summer, Carrie was keeping from her those delights she may never experience.

Then one Sunday night when Carrie had just returned from Boston and was unpacking her overnight bag, she looked at Louise and said: 'I was thinking about you. On the bus coming home tonight.' Looking at Carrie's concerned, determined face, Louise prepared herself for humiliation. 'I was thinking about when we graduate. What you're going to do. What's to become of you. I want you to be loved the way I love you. Louise, if I help you, *really* help you, will you go on a diet?'

Louise entered a period of her life she would remember always, the way some people remember having endured poverty. Her diet did not begin the next day. Carrie told her to eat on Monday as though it were the last day of her life. So for the first time since grammar school Louise went into a school cafeteria and ate everything she wanted. At breakfast and lunch and dinner she glanced around the table to see if the other girls noticed the food on her tray. They did not. She felt there was a lesson in this, but it lay beyond her grasp. That night in their room she ate the four remaining candy bars. During the day Carrie rented a small refrigerator, bought an electric skillet, an electric broiler, and bathroom scales.

On Tuesday morning Louise stood on the scales, and Carrie wrote in her notebook: *October 14: 184 lbs.* Then she made Louise a cup of black coffee and scrambled one egg and sat with her while she ate. When Carrie went to the dining room for breakfast, Louise walked about the campus for thirty minutes. That was part of the plan. The campus was pretty, on its lawns grew at least one of every tree native to New England, and in the warm morning sun Louise felt a new hope. At noon they met in their room, and Carrie broiled her a piece of hamburger and served it with lettuce. Then while Carrie ate in the dining room Louise walked again. She was weak with hunger and she felt queasy. During her afternoon classes she was nervous and tense, and she chewed her pencil and tapped her heels on the floor and tightened her calves. When she returned to her room late that afternoon, she was so glad to see Carrie that she embraced her; she had felt she could not bear another minute of hunger, but now with Carrie she knew she could make it at least through tonight. Then she would sleep and face tomorrow when it came. Carrie broiled her a steak and served it with lettuce. Louise studied while Carrie ate dinner, then they went for a walk.

That was her ritual and her diet for the rest of the year, Carrie alternating fish and chicken breasts with the steaks for dinner, and every day was nearly as bad as the first. In the evenings she was irritable. In all her life she had never been afflicted by ill temper and she looked upon it now as a demon which, along with hunger, was taking possession of her soul. Often she spoke sharply to Carrie. One night during their after-dinner walk Carrie talked sadly of night, of how darkness made her more aware of herself, and at night she did not know why she was in college, why she studied, why she was walking the earth with other people. They were standing on a wooden foot bridge, looking down at a dark pond. Carrie kept talking; perhaps soon she would cry. Suddenly Louise said; 'I'm sick of lettuce. I never want to see a piece of lettuce for the rest of my life. I hate it. We shouldn't even buy it, it's immoral.'

Carrie was quiet. Louise glanced at her, and the pain and irritation in Carrie's face soothed her. Then she was ashamed. Before she could say she was sorry, Carrie turned to her and said gently: 'I know. I know how terrible it is.'

Carrie did all the shopping, telling Louise she knew how hard it was to go into a supermarket when you were hungry. And Louise was always hungry. She drank diet soft drinks and started smoking Carrie's cigarettes, learned to enjoy inhaling, thought of cancer and emphysema but they were as far away as those boys her mother had talked about when she was nine. By Thanksgiving she was smoking over a pack a day and her weight in Carrie's notebook was one hundred and sixty-two pounds. Carrie was afraid if Louise went home at Thanksgiving she would lapse from the diet, so Louise spent the vacation with Carrie, in Philadelphia. Carrie wrote her family about the diet, and told Louise that she had. On the plane to Philadelphia, Louise said: 'I feel like a bedwetter. When I was a little girl I had a friend who used to come spend the night and Mother would put a rubber sheet on the bed and we all pretended there wasn't a rubber sheet and that she hadn't wet the bed. Even me, and I slept with her.' At Thanksgiving dinner she lowered her eyes as Carrie's father put two slices of white meat on her plate and passed it to her over the bowls of steaming food.

When she went home at Christmas she weighed a hundred and fifty-five pounds; at the airport her mother marvelled. Her father laughed and hugged her and said: 'But now there's less of you to love.' He was troubled by her smoking but only mentioned it once; he told her she was beautiful and, as always, his eyes bathed her with love. During the long vacation her mother cooked for her as Carrie had, and Louise returned to school weighing a hundred and forty-six pounds.

Flying north on the plane she warmly recalled the surprised and congratulatory eyes of her relatives and acquaintances. She had not seen Barbara or Marjorie. She thought of returning home in May, weighing the hundred and fifteen pounds which Carrie had in October set as their goal. Looking toward the stoic days ahead, she felt strong. She thought of those hungry days of fall and early winter (and now: she was hungry now: with almost a frown, almost a brusque shake of the head, she refused peanuts from the stewardess): those first weeks of the diet when she was the pawn of an irascibility which still, conditioned to her ritual as she was, could at any moment take command of her. She thought of the nights of trying to sleep while her stomach growled. She thought of her addiction to cigarettes. She thought of the people at school: not one teacher, not one girl, had spoken to her about her loss of weight, not even about her absence from meals. And without warning her spirit collapsed. She did not feel strong, she did not feel she was committed to and within reach of achieving a valuable goal. She felt that somehow she had lost more than pounds of fat; that some time during her dieting she had lost herself too. She tried to remember what it had felt like to be Louise before she had started living on meat and fish, as an unhappy adult may look sadly in the memory of childhood for lost virtues and hopes. She looked down at the earth far below, and it seemed to her that her soul, like her body aboard the plane, was in some rootless flight. She neither knew its destination nor where it had departed from; it was on some passage she could not even define.

During the next few weeks she lost weight more slowly and once for eight days Carrie's daily recording stayed at a hundred and thirty-six. Louise woke in the morning thinking of one hundred and thirty-six and then she stood on the scales and they echoed her. She became obsessed with that number, and there wasn't a day when she didn't say it aloud, and through the days and nights the number stayed in her mind, and if a teacher had spoken those digits in a classroom she would have opened her mouth to speak. What if that's me, she said to Carrie. I mean what if a hundred and thirty-six is my real weight and I just can't lose anymore. Walking hand-in-hand with her despair was a longing for this to be true, and that longing angered her and wearied her, and every day she was gloomy. On the ninth day she weighed a hundred and thirty-five and a half pounds. She was not relieved; she thought bitterly of the months ahead, the shedding of the last twenty and a half pounds.

On Easter Sunday, which she spent at Carrie's, she weighed one hundred and twenty pounds, and she ate one slice of glazed pineapple with her ham and lettuce. She did not enjoy it: she felt she was being friendly with a recalcitrant enemy who had once tried to destroy her. Carrie's parents were laudative. She liked them and she wished they would touch sometimes, and look at each other when they spoke. She guessed they would divorce when Carrie left home, and she vowed that her own marriage would be one of affection and tenderness. She could think about that now: marriage. At school she had read in a Boston paper that this summer the cicadas would come out of their seventeen year hibernation on Cape Cod, for a month they would mate and then die, leaving their young to burrow into the ground where they would stay for seventeen years. That's me, she had said to Carrie. Only my hibernation lasted twenty-one years.

Often her mother asked in letters and on the phone about the diet, but Louise answered vaguely. When she flew home in late May she weighed a hundred and thirteen pounds, and at the airport her mother cried and hugged her and said again and again: You're so *beaut*iful. Her father blushed and bought her a martini. For days her relatives and acquaintances congratulated her, and the applause in their eyes lasted the entire summer, and she loved their eyes, and swam in the country club pool, the first time she had done this since she was a child.

She lived at home and ate the way her mother did and every morning she weighed. Her mother liked to take her shopping and buy her dresses and they put her old ones in the Goodwill box at the shopping center; Louise thought of them existing on the body of a poor woman whose cheap meals kept her fat. Louise's mother had a photographer come to the house, and Louise posed on the couch and standing beneath a live oak and sitting in a wicker lawn chair next to an azalea bush. The new clothes and the photographer made her feel she was going to another country or becoming a citizen of a new one. In the fall she took a job of no consequence, to give her something to do.

Also in the fall a young lawyer joined her father's firm, he came one night to dinner, and they started seeing each other. He was the first man outside her family to kiss her since the barbecue when she was sixteen. Louise celebrated Thanksgiving not with rice dressing and candied sweet potatoes and mince meat and pumpkin pies, but by giving Richard her virginity which she realized, at the very last moment of its existence, she had embarked on giving him over thirteen months ago, on that Tuesday in October when Carrie had made her a cup of black coffee and scrambled one egg. She wrote this to Carrie, who replied happily by return mail. She also, through glance and smile and innuendo, tried to tell her mother too. But finally she controlled that impulse, because Richard felt guilty about making love with the daughter of his partner and friend. In the spring they married. The wedding was a large one, in the Episcopal church, and Carrie flew from Boston to be maid of honor. Her parents had recently separated and she was living with the musician and was still victim of her unpredictable malaise. It overcame her on the night before the wedding, so Louise was up with her until past three and woke next morning from a sleep so heavy that she did not want to leave it.

Richard was a lean, tall, energetic man with the metabolism of a pencil sharpener. Louise fed him everything he wanted. He liked Italian food and she got recipes from her mother and watched him eating spaghetti with the sauce she had only tasted, and ravioli and lasagna, while she ate antipasto with her chianti. He made a lot of money and borrowed more and they bought a house whose lawn sloped down to the shore of a lake; they had a wharf and a boathouse, and Richard bought a boat and they took friends waterskiing. Richard bought her a car and they spent his vacations in Mexico, Canada, the Bahamas, and in the fifth year of their marriage they went to Europe and, according to their plan, she conceived a child in Paris. On the plane back, as she looked out the window and beyond the sparkling sea and saw her country, she felt that it was waiting for her, as her home by the lake was, and her parents, and her good friends who rode in the boat and waterskied; she thought of the accumulated warmth and pelf of her marriage, and how by slimming her body she had bought into the pleasures of the nation. She felt cunning, and she smiled to herself, and took Richard's hand.

But these moments of triumph were sparse. On most days she went about her routine of leisure with a sense of certainty about herself that came merely from not thinking. But there were times, with her friends, or with Richard, or alone in the house, when she was suddenly assaulted by the feeling that she had taken the wrong train and arrived at a place where no one knew her, and where she ought not to be. Often, in bed with Richard, she talked of being fat: 'I was the one who started the friendship with Carrie, I chose her, I started the conversations. When I understood that she was my friend I understood something else: I had chosen her for the same reason I'd chosen Barbara and Marjorie. They were all thin. I was always thinking about what people saw when they looked at me and I didn't want them to see two fat girls. When I was alone I didn't mind being fat but then I'd have to leave the house again and then I didn't want to look like me. But at home I didn't mind except when I was getting dressed to go out of the house and when Mother looked at me. But I stopped looking at her when she looked at me. And in college I felt good with Carrie; there weren't any boys and I didn't have any other friends and so when I wasn't with Carrie I thought about her and I tried to ignore the other people around me, I tried to make them not exist. A lot of the time I could do that. It was strange, and I felt like a spy.'

If Richard was bored by her repetition he pretended not to be.

But she knew the story meant very little to him. She could have been telling him of a childhood illness, or wearing braces, or a broken heart at sixteen. He could not see her as she was when she was fat. She felt as though she were trying to tell a foreign lover about her life in the United States, and if only she could command the language he would know and love all of her and she would feel complete. Some of the acquaintances of her childhood were her friends now, and even they did not seem to remember her when she was fat.

Now her body was growing again, and when she put on a maternity dress for the first time she shivered with fear. Richard did not smoke and he asked her, in a voice just short of demand, to stop during her pregnancy. She did. She ate carrots and celery instead of smoking, and at cocktail parties she tried to eat nothing, but after her first drink she ate nuts and cheese and crackers and dips. Always at these parties Richard had talked with his friends and she had rarely spoken to him until they drove home. But now when he noticed her at the hors d'oeuvres table he crossed the room and, smiling, led her back to his group. His smile and his hand on her arm told her he was doing his clumsy, husbandly best to help her through a time of female mystery.

She was gaining weight but she told herself it was only the baby, and would leave with its birth. But at other times she knew quite clearly that she was losing the discipline she had fought so hard to gain during her last year with Carrie. She was hungry now as she had been in college, and she ate between meals and after dinner and tried to eat only carrots and celery, but she grew to hate them, and her desire for sweets was as vicious as it had been long ago. At home she ate bread and jam and when she shopped for groceries she bought a candy bar and ate it driving home and put the wrapper in her purse and then in the garbage can under the sink. Her cheeks had filled out, there was loose flesh under her chin, her arms and legs were plump, and her mother was concerned. So was Richard. One night when she brought pie and milk to the living room where they were watching television, he said: 'You already had a piece. At dinner.'

She did not look at him.

'You're gaining weight. It's not all water, either. It's fat. It'll be summertime. You'll want to get into your bathing suit.'

The pie was cherry. She looked at it as her fork cut through it; she speared the piece and rubbed it in the red juice on the plate before lifting it to her mouth.

'You never used to eat pie,' he said. 'I just think you ought to watch it a bit. It's going to be tough on you this summer.'

In her seventh month, with a delight reminiscent of climbing the stairs to Richard's apartment before they were married, she returned to her world of secret gratification. She began hiding candy in her underwear drawer. She ate it during the day and at night while Richard slept, and at breakfast she was distracted, waiting for him to leave.

She gave birth to a son, brought him home, and nursed both him and her appetites. During this time of celibacy she enjoyed her body through her son's mouth; while he suckled she stroked his small head and back. She was hiding candy but she did not conceal her other indulgences: she was smoking again but still she ate between meals, and at dinner she ate what Richard did, and coldly he watched her, he grew petulant, and when the date marking the end of their celibacy came they let it pass. Often in the afternoons her mother visited and scolded her and Louise sat looking at the baby and said nothing until finally, to end it, she promised to diet. When her mother and father came for dinners, her father kissed her and held the baby and her mother said nothing about Louise's body, and her voice was tense. Returning from work in the evenings Richard looked at a soiled plate and glass on the table beside her chair as if detecting traces of infidelity, and at every dinner they fought.

'Look at you,' he said. 'Lasagna, for God's sake. When are you going to start? It's not simply that you haven't lost any weight. You're gaining. I can see it. I can feel it when you get in bed. Pretty soon you'll weigh more than I do and I'll be sleeping on a trampoline.'

'You never touch me anymore.'

'I don't want to touch you. Why should I? Have you *looked* at yourself?'

'You're cruel,' she said. 'I never knew how cruel you were.'

She ate, watching him. He did not look at her. Glaring at his plate, he worked with fork and knife like a hurried man at a lunch counter.

'I bet you didn't either,' she said.

That night when he was asleep she took a Milky Way to the bathroom. For a while she stood eating in the dark, then she turned on the light. Chewing, she looked at herself in the mirror; she looked at her eyes and hair. Then she stood on the scales and looking at the numbers between her feet, one hundred and sixty-two, she remembered when she had weighed a hundred and thirty-six pounds for eight days. Her memory of those eight days was fond and amusing, as though she were recalling an Easter egg hunt when she was six. She stepped off the scales and pushed them under the lavatory and did not stand on them again.

It was summer and she bought loose dresses and when Richard took friends out on the boat she did not wear a bathing suit or shorts; her friends gave her mischievous glances, and Richard did not look at her. She stopped riding on the boat. She told them she wanted to stay with the baby, and she sat inside holding him until she heard the boat leave the wharf. Then she took him to the front lawn and walked with him in the shade of the trees and talked to him about the blue jays and mockingbirds and cardinals she saw on their branches. Sometimes she stopped and watched the boat out on the lake and the friend skiing behind it.

Every day Richard quarrelled, and because his rage went no further than her weight and shape, she felt excluded from it, and she remained calm within layers of flesh and spirit, and watched his frustration, his impotence. He truly believed they were arguing about her weight. She knew better: she knew that beneath the argument lay the question of who Richard was. She thought of him smiling at the wheel of his boat, and long ago courting his slender girl, the daughter of his partner and friend. She thought of Carrie telling her of smelling chocolate in the dark and, after that, watching her eat it night after night. She smiled at Richard, teasing his anger.

He is angry now. He stands in the center of the living room, raging at her, and he wakes the baby. Beneath Richard's voice she hears the soft crying, feels it in her heart, and quietly she rises from her chair and goes upstairs to the child's room and takes him from the crib. She brings him to the living room and sits holding him in her lap, pressing him gently against the folds of fat at her waist. Now Richard is pleading with her. Louise thinks tenderly of Carrie broiling meat and fish in their room, and walking with her in the evenings. She wonders if Carrie still has the malaise. Perhaps she will come for a visit. In Louise's arms now the boy sleeps.

'I'll help you,' Richard says. 'I'll eat the same things you eat.'

But his face does not approach the compassion and determination and love she had seen in Carrie's during what she now recognizes as the worst year of her life. She can remember nothing about that year except hunger, and the meals in her room. She is hungry now. When she puts the boy to bed she will get a candy bar from her room. She will eat it here, in front of Richard. This room will be hers soon. She considers the possibilities: all these rooms and the lawn where she can do whatever she wishes. She knows he will leave soon. It has been in his eyes all summer. She stands, using one hand to pull herself out of the chair. She carries the boy to his crib, feels him against her large breasts, feels that his sleeping body touches her soul. With a surge of vindication and relief she holds him. Then she kisses his forehead and places him in the crib. She goes to the bedroom and in the dark takes a bar of candy from her drawer. Slowly she descends the stairs. She knows Richard is waiting but she feels his departure so happily that, when she enters the living room, unwrapping the candy, she is surprised to see him standing there.

"ARMED FOR WAR": NOTES ON THE ANTITHETICAL CRITICISM OF HAROLD BLOOM

by ALVIN ROSENFELD

from THE SOUTHERN REVIEW

nominated by Robert Boyers and Cynthia Ozick

> *A good critic . . . is armed for war. And criticism is a war, against a work of art —either the critic defeats the work or the work defeats the critic.*
>
> *–Jacob Glatstein*

IT IS A DUTY OF CRITICS, as Harold Bloom has recently defined it, to make a good poet's work harder for him to perform, for it is only in the overcoming of genuine difficulties that strong poetry emerges. A corollary of this view—never stated as such but clearly implicit in Bloom's writings—is that a critic should do his work in such a way as to make a *reader's* work also more difficult for him to perform, and for much the same reasons, namely, to achieve interpretations strenuous enough to be adequate to the age. "Strength" is a central term in Bloom's critical vocabulary, just as it is the goal of all of his intellectual labors. The designation "reader" must, in this case, apply to the professional reader—fellow critics, among whom Bloom values, and increasingly seems to write almost exclusively for— those relatively few "deep readers" of poetry who, in various independent ways, are attempting to formulate a theory of litera- ture that might serve as the basis for a new practical criticism. Certainly that is Harold Bloom's aim, yet those who have been encountering him in his latest and most difficult phase more often than not have been finding him perplexing and extravagant in his views, with the result that Bloom has emerged as not only the most powerful but also the most provocative and controversial critic of the day. More and more, in fact, the argument over his theories is set forth in personal terms: is Harold Bloom truly "brilliant" or just "mad"; "outrageous" by temperament or willfully "offensive" to the rest of the profession; "serious" or merely "putting us all on"?

Bloom's reply to such questions—and they are increasingly *ad hominem* in nature, increasingly polemical—is perhaps the most outrageous thing of all: *he writes another book*. The Anxiety of Influence (1973), the small volume that first presented the author's formulations of an antithetical criticism, was followed two years later by the companion volume, *A Map of Misreading* (1975), an effort at developing a new practical criticism based on a revisionist theory of poetic creation. If the first volume provoked a good deal of dismay in academic circles and generated a controversy in criticism rather rare in recent times, the second one heightened perplexity and exacer- bated the dispute. For in *A Map of Misreading* Bloom not only extended his earlier view that "the meaning of a poem can only be another poem" but pronounced against the very existence of the poem itself: "there are *no* texts, but only relationships *between* texts." In an attempt to discover and clarify the intricate nature of these relationships, Bloom developed, in *The Anxiety of Influence*, a set of six "revisionary ratios" that might aid the critic in traversing "the hidden roads that go from poem to poem." In the companion volume, these ratios were not only tested in a series of close readings of individual poets but drawn together into a "map of misprision," where they combined with coordinating sets of psychic defenses, poetic images, and rhetorical tropes to form the most elaborate apparatus for literary interpretation given us since the early work of Northrop Frye. Bloom's affinities with Frye have often been noted, but inasmuch as his evolving subject is now clearly in the realm of psychopoetics, or the philosophy of composition, he seems closer at this point to Kenneth Burke, our most gifted and perhaps most advanced rhetorician to date. Finally, though, Bloom seems destined to find a direction for his work independent of both Frye and Burke, a direction quite possibly that will move him to approximate or even partake of the most formidable system of textual commentary yet devised—Bible commentary, or, as Bloom would understand it, interpretation as a struggle for priority with Text Itself.[1] This prospect was hinted at in *A Map of Misreading* when the author turned to Lurianic Kabbalism as "the ultimate model for Western revisionism from the Renaissance to the present" and stated his intentions for further study along just these lines. With *Kabbalah and Criticism* (1975) and *Poetry and Repression* (1976) he has sought to make good on these promises.

Bloom has set himself a three-fold task in *Kabbalah and Criticism:* one, to offer an exposition of the rich but complex system of Kabbalistic thinking; two, to relate this thinking, and especially that branch of it formulated by Isaac Luria, to a theory of reading poetry; and three, to explain and defend the adoption of a Kabbalistic model for literary interpretation and to show its value for the practice of an antithetical criticism.

Antithetical criticism is a means of understanding poetry from within the long tradition of poetic history, which is to say, it is a nonreductionist attempt at appreciating poetic lineage. Poems, as Harold Bloom would have us see them, descend from and are "about" other poems before they arise from and are about the poet's reactions to life; as such, they share a "family relationship" not unlike human relationships. To grasp the essential character of poems, therefore, it becomes necessary to perceive a poetic text in terms of its formative precursors—those antecedent and influential texts that help to shape and misshape the literature that follows them. Creation is always a function of influence, and the "anxiety of influence" suffered by later poets in relationship to their forebears is the hidden but motive force behind all poetry. Bloom sees this anxiety of

[1] Bloom's devotion to the Hebrew Bible has often been expressed in his writings. For instance, in *A Map of Misreading*, he identifies himself "as a teacher of literature who prefers the morality of the Hebrew Bible to that of Homer, indeed who prefers the Bible aesthetically to Homer. . . ." If present signs hold, one expects to see more, not less, emphasis on biblical thinking and exegesis in his work.

influence as especially acute in the Post-Enlightenment period, where to write poetry at all means to wrestle for living space with the mightiest of the dead—principally Milton and Wordsworth in the British line, Emerson and Whitman in the American line—who among them not only defined but largely occupied the central ground of poetic tradition. Those who come after suffer the limitations of an inevitable belatedness, which they try to throw off in complex but identifiable ways. It becomes the goal of criticism to perceive and explain these moves to resist or offset a crippling influence, to expound poetry's life struggle with its own grand but limiting past. Antithetical criticism, dedicated to observing and clarifying the procedures of influence as it forms and malforms poets, is Harold Bloom's important theoretical contribution to such a practical criticism.

Bloom, an uncommonly learned and prolific scholar, has worked ambitiously in these four books to formulate and refine his ideas, yet it must be stressed that his theory is still very much a theory-in-progress, one beset by its own searchings and anxieties. The thinkers who have contributed most to it are Vico, Nietzsche, and Freud. But while these continue to exert their influence, it is apparent that Bloom has been attempting of late to assimilate a more ancient system of thought, namely Gnosticism[2]—more specifically, Jewish Kabbalism. Why align criticism with the Kabbalah? Because, in Bloom's view, Kabbalah, while generally valued as a form of mysticism, is most interesting as the embodiment of "a theory of writing" and, as such, "offers both a model for the processes of poetic influence, and maps for the problematic ways of interpretation." Accordingly, the author sets out in *Kabbalah and Criticism* to investigate the Kabbalistic system in terms of its rehetoric, to see it even as a *theory* of rhetoric, a mode of speculation whose ultimate importance lies less in the doctrines it announces than in the stance it takes against "not only a closed Book but a vast system of closed commentary." More than anything else, it was the ability of the Kabbalists to accept such a formidable system of canonical tests and, at the same time, to find the means for an independent spiritual assertion that moves Bloom to admiration in this book.

[2] There are a number of indications that Gnosticism is experiencing a resurgence in recent years. In addition to the prominent place it has won for itself in Bloom's work, one notices it as well in the recent publications of George Steiner (*After Babel* contains a lengthy chapter entitled "Language and Gnosis") and Saul Bellow (the "spiritual" plane of *Humboldt's Gift* is

Basing himself on the life work of Gershom Scholem,[3] as any student of this subject must, Bloom offers brief but reliable and wholly readable accounts of the evolution of Kabbalah from the *Sefer Yezirah* ("Book of Creation") and the *Sefer ha-Bahir* ("Book of Brightness") to the masterpiece of Jewish esoteric thinking, the *Sefer ha-Zohar* ("Book of Splendor"). Along the way he registers lucid and personally-felt appreciations of Moses Cordovero (1522–1570)—"the best example of a systematic thinker ever to appear among the Kabbalists"—and his pupil, Isaac Luria (1534–1572)— "the archetype of all Revisionists." The burden of exposition in this part of the book is carried with remarkable ease, and the resulting essay will stand for many as a most convenient and clarifying brief introduction to Kabbalah. Bloom works his way knowingly through powerful but recondite texts to offer an explanation of the ten *Sefirot*, the mystical names or emanations of God, in terms of poetic images and rhetorical tropes. To Bloom, the *Sefirot* are, in fact, very much like poems, and since to him poems are essentially commentaries on or readings of earlier poems, he advocates an appreciation of Kabbalism as among "the first Modernisms." The characteristic impulse in Modernism, as Bloom understands it, is revisionism, in this case "a reaction to the double priority and authority of both text and interpretation, Bible and the normative Judaism of rabbinic tradition." The importance of Kabbalah and its interest for literary interpretation, therefore, are to be found in the answers it managed to give to an abiding question, one that all new creativity of whatever kind must struggle with:

The Kabbalists of medieval Spain, and their Palestinian successors after the expulsion from Spain, confronted a peculiar psychological

---

an odd blend of Gnosticism and Anthroposophy). Ihab Hassan has made a groping and not very successful attempt to understand some contemporary aspects of Gnosticism in "The New Gnosticism: Speculations on an Aspect of the Post-modern Mind" (collected in his *Paracriticisms*). The best introductory work to the subject remains Hans Jonas's *Gnostic Religion* (2nd rev. ed.; Gloucester, Mass., 1963).

[3] Bloom's fine tribute to Scholem deserves to be quoted at some length:

Scholem's massive achievement can be judged as being unique in modern humanistic scholarship, for he has made himself indispensable to all rational students of his subject. . . . More than any other modern scholar, working on a comparable scale, he has been wholly adequate to his great subject. He has the same relation to the texts he has edited and written commentaries upon, that a later poet like John Milton had to the earlier poets he absorbed and, in some ways, transcended. Scholem is a Miltonic figure in modern scholarship, and deserves to be honored as such.

problem, one that demanded a revisionist solution. How does one accommodate a fresh and vital new religious impulse, in a precarious and even catastrophic time of troubles, when one inherits a religious tradition already so rich and coherent that it allows very little room for fresh revelations or even speculations?

Accepting the challenge of this dilemma—and in terms of poetic tradition every new poet must face something similar to it—the Kabbalists "developed implicitly a *psychology of belatedness*, and with it an explicit, rhetorical series of techniques for opening Scripture and even received commentary to their historical sufferings, and to their own, new theosophical insights." The genius of this development, and consequently the hero of *Kabbalah and Criticism*, is Isaac Luria, whose revisionary theory of creation as a *regressive* process is adopted by Bloom as "the classic paradigm upon which Western revisionism in all areas was to model itself ever since."

Just what was the system that Luria worked out? In brief, it stated that the world came into being as the result of a divine contraction—in Hebrew, *zimzum*, or God's withdrawing into Himself. What fell off or remained after this event was world—in Kabbalistic terms, an unredeemed fragment or vessel of divinity. Luria and his followers thereafter introduced an involved ethical system to coordinate with this startling version of genesis-as-catastrophe, but since Bloom's subject is origins and not ethics, he chooses to concentrate attention solely on the processes of creation. Nevertheless, he does adapt the ethical language of Lurianic Kabbalah to his concerns with writing and the problems of original genius and introduces two more basic terms to the discussion—*shevirat ha-kelim* and *tikkun*, the breaking apart and mending, or restitution, of the vessels. Taken together with *zimzum*, these comprise, in Bloom's summation and translation of Luria, a triple rhythm of "limitation, substitution, and representation," the model of Bloom's own dialectic of revisionism and, as he sees it, "the governing dialectic of Post-Enlightenment poetry."

The claim will startle, both for its boldness of assertion and its extravagant esotericism. Most poets and readers of poetry, after all, will never have heard of Isaac Luria; how then can Harold Bloom possibly expect them to give assent to Luria's sudden centrality? Bloom is willing to answer that question, but only in terms of his own working formulations of poetic influence. Digesting these from several separate passages, this is what results:

> The center of my theory is that there are crucial patterns of interplay between literal and figurative meanings in post-Miltonic poems, and these patterns, though very varied, are to a surprising degree quite definite and even over-determined. What determines them is the anxiety of influence. . . . I do not say that these patterns produce meaning, because I do not believe that meaning is produced *in* and *by* poems, but only *between* poems. . . . A modern poem begins with a *clinamen* that depends upon the renunciation of an earlier poem. . . . The creation through contraction of an internalized precursor text, which is the Kabbalistic mode, is precisely the dialectical mode of belated or Post-Enlightenment poetry. . . . The hidden roads that go from poem to poem are: limitation, substitution, representation; or the dialectic of revisionism.

To chart these hidden roads as they move through English poetry—from the great Romantics; through the major Victorians; to the American giants Emerson and Whitman; and finally to their modernist inheritors, Yeats and Stevens—Bloom has given us *Poetry and Repression*, a mapmaker's guide to poetic revisionism. The subject of this book is once more the psychopoetics of literary origins, although this time Bloom depends somewhat less on the Kabbalistic model of creation than he does on some of the theories of Nietzsche and Freud. His method is that of antithetical criticism, although by now this has become far more than a procedural means of literary investigation and amounts to a hermeneutical passion; indeed, Bloom has moved from an initial position that asserted the usefulness of an antithetical *approach* to the study of poetry to a point where he now views poetry in the Post-Enlightenment period as possessing an essentially anithetical *character.* One major consequence of this shift is that, more and more, the distinctions between poet and reader have begun to dissolve. As he stated it in *Kabbalah and Criticism,* the "ephebe's [or later poet's] misreading of the precursor is the paradigm for your misreading of the ephebe," a formula that renders all poetry a kind of errant criticism and all criticism, errant poetry. In his own words, which upon reflection are not in fact as mystifying as they may first appear, "reading is mis-writing and writing is mis-reading." The most notable element in *Poetry and Repression,* however, and the one that is certain to trouble most readers of the book, is its strongly deterministic stance as illustrated in such assertions as these:

> In studying poetry . . . we are studying a kind of labor that has its own latent principles, principles that can be uncovered and then taught systematically. . . . [The patterns of any poem] are as definite as those of any dance, and as varied as there are various dances. But poets do not invent the dances they dance, and we *can tell* the dancer from the dance. . . . I am afraid that there does tend to be one fairly definite dance pattern in Post-Enlightenment poetry, which can be altered by strong substitution, but still it does remain the same dance.

Attendant upon this view, Bloom sets out, in a series of intricate readings, "to uncover the pattern of revisionism" in key poems by ten different authors. His aim in each case is to "trace the network of ratios, tropes, defenses, and images" in the poems and, in such a manner, to answer the question that he finds at the center of all new poetic creativity: "*What is being freshly repressed?* What has been forgotten, on purpose, in the depths, so as to make possible this sudden elevation to the heights?" Such questions arise inevitably because "a poem's true subject is its repression of the precursor poem." What necessitates this repression? The fact that "poetry lives always under the shadow of poetry," so that in order to come into being at all, a new poem must find the means to translate its own belatedness into an earliness, must necessarily contend with and attempt to neutralize or escape the overriding power of priority. The history of poetry, in this view of it, is "an endless, defensive civil war," in which new poets engage the strongest of their precursors in a contest for and against canonization, "the final or transumptive form of literary revisionism."

Since Bloom understands poems themselves as "acts of reading" —instances not so much of fresh writing but of *re*writing —he turns his major attention to what he perceives to be the essential intertextual relationships that comprise poetry. Thus, in interpreting the well-known lyric "London," Bloom focuses on Blake and Ezekiel, the biblical text identified as the crucial antecedent for Blake's revisionary or anthithetical poem. In the cases of Wordsworth, Shelley, and Keats, the dialectical pairings are with Milton, in the case of Tennyson, with Keats; of Browning, with Shelley; of Yeats, with Browning, Blake, and Pater, etc. Bloom's emphases throughout are on the way poems originate and behave, or rather misbehave, for he has posited misprision as a basic principle of poetic existence and likes to concentrate particularly on the necessarily *wayward* behavior patterns of poems vis-a-vis their precursors. The results of his interpretive mappings are time and again startling, especially as he contends with works so central to the tradition that not only they but by now some of their readings have become "received" as basic. It is certain that there will be arguments with Bloom's analyses of such poems as "London" and "Tintern Abbey," "Prometheus Unbound" and "Song of Myself," for following his persistently revisionist impulse, Bloom has pitted himself, strength for strength, against all previous commentators on these works—including the earlier Bloom! The largest point of issue will come, however, not so much over particular differences in opinion between Bloom and other critics but over the method chosen to study poems in *Poetry and Repression*.

For it is clear that Bloom has turned away from the admirable insistence to avoid all reductionism in criticism, first voiced in *The Anxiety of Influence*, to a critical practice that now demands reduction—in this case to his network of "ratios, tropes, defenses, and images," as well as to certain fixed areas in which he finds poetic language invariably centering itself: "presence and absence, partness and wholeness, fullness and emptiness, height and depth, insideness and outsideness, earliness and lateness." These, he concludes, "are the inevitable categories of our makings and becomings," and although individual poets can give them a various emphasis, none can escape them. The dance pattern may alter, but it does remain the same dance.

The new gains for Bloom's practice as a critic must be carefully weighed against the losses, for while his critical cartography does unquestionably allow him some exceptionally challenging insights, it also tends to break down into the formulaic repetitions of a new jargon and, hence, to become monotonous; worse yet, it threatens to make the poetry itself appear severely limited and monotonous. Bloom would contend, of course, that it is not his interpretive method that restricts poetry but the consequences of poetry's own belatedness. This assertion will not easily be accepted by most readers, who will rightly resist the tendency to flatten poems into predetermined schemes, however ingeniously conceived. More than anything else, it is this reductionist, or algebraic, character of Bloom's critical method that must be questioned.

What accounts for it? Is reductionism an unavoidable consequence of Bloom's critical revisionism? At the time of *The Anxiety of Influence*, it seemed not to be, but, with the publication of *Poetry and Repression*, a book that completes a tetralogy of the author's studies in antithetical criticism, we are confronted by such an unexpected and sorrowful acknowledgement as this: "All reading is translation, and all attempts to communicate a reading seem to court reduction, perhaps inevitably." If that is so, then why reduce to the Kabbalistic paradigm and not some other?

Bloom reached this dilemma, it seems, when he turned to a hermeneutical principle that projects the reader as a commanding, even controlling, figure in the life of poetry—the critic suddenly elevated to a level that acknowledges him as equal in importance to and virtually one with the creator. That is a Gnostic turn— Gnosticism being in this case a defense against the blinding force of textual antecedence and a challenge to its authority. In the history of literature, there is only one Text with that kind of overpowering force, just as there is only a single Creator grand enough in conception to be responsible for it. Gnosticism, whose *stance* Bloom values as the central model for literary interpretation, was a thrust against this primacy, an exercise of the will-to-power over the Prime Precursor Himself. In its Jewish expression, the Kabbalah, this strain of revisionary defiance was greatly feared by the rabbis, who correctly understood its antinomian impulses. For to the Gnostic, knowledge is always knowledge of origins, ultimately *a rival claim* upon origins, which in human terms inevitably means an attempt to transform man into God. The means to this magical and forbidden end? A radical or revisionary hermeneutics, interpretation conceived as an effort to reach some equivalence with Original Text through substitution or displacement.

Now what, it can legitimately be asked, does all of this Jewish esotericism have to do with English and American poetry? In Bloom's case, just about everything. What, after all, is the ambition of "strength" in his work if not to reach an equality of power and place with textual priority? In his own words, "according to the strong reading, it and the text are *one*." A Talmudist could never say that, but a Kabbalist (at least in Bloom's conception of him) could and does say *only* that. The issue, once more, is one of stance—the Talmudist arguing for the maintenance of a proper piety, the preservation of some human distance from not only a canonized Text but a canonized Commentary; while the Kabbalist must argue—in revisionary, antithetical, and finally anti-textual terms—that the Text is no more than the mirror of his own making, his own *mis*-making, as Bloom likes to call it, his Necessary Error. Reduced to the secular plane, here is how Jacob Glatstein, the modernist Yiddish poet, formulated one side of this ongoing contest between reader and text: "The poet writes not only his poem, but in fact also his own criticism. The critic only transcribes the poet's criticism of himself, rewrites it and expands it. The poet puts the words in the critic's mouth, and tells him: 'This is what you will say.'" One can hardly imagine a situation more intolerable than this for a critic of Harold Bloom's disposition and drive. To accept the attitude of *secondariness* implicit in these words is tantamount to accepting servility, which may be all right for the pious but clearly is all wrong to one who maintains, with Bloom, that "a theory *of* poetry must belong *to* poetry, must *be* poetry, before it can be of any use in interpreting poems."

Now Bloom knows that criticism, however imaginative or "inspired," is *not* poetry, and that if it aspires to the condition of poetry, it is bound to find itself locked in a futile and unequal conflict which *it* can never win. If poets are not as self-begotten as they would have us and themselves believe—and no one has argued more forcefully and persuasively against the idealization of poetic origins than Harold Bloom—critics are even less independent and self-originating. It is in the nature of things that the critic depends upon and follows a primary text—for most critics, a normal enough state of affairs and the cause for no special anxiety. Yet just as there resides a *critic* within the soul of every powerful *poet*—a proleptic or forward-vaulting spirit that wants to dictate to others the interpretations of its own makings—so there resides a *poet* within the soul of certain powerful *critics*—a restless, contentious sprite that looks to traduce poetry and make of it a mere illustrative metaphor for theory or interpretation. Bloom is such a critic, one who comes to his work armed for war, for he understands that reading is "always a defensive process," even a form of "defensive warfare," a counter-thrust against an antecedent hegemony of mind that condemns the reader to the melancholy position of one-who-comes-after. In visionary or intellectual terms, that is tantamount to being expelled from paradise. No wonder, then, that Bloom has aligned himself with the Kabbalah, a paramount part of the elaborate Jewish defense system against expulsion and exile.

In adopting Kabbalah as a metaphor for the act of reading— reading here understood as an attempt to reclaim centrality by *undoing* the priority, autonomy, and singularity of text—however, Bloom has courted not only hyperbole but reduction. While he has revealed much of the heretofore unknown dynamics of the inter- textual, he has overleapt the bounds of the critically plausible by denying the legitimacy or even the existence of individual texts. On the strictly literal, even grammatical, level, he would surely acknowledge that there are both poems *and* relationships between poems. On this same level, he would have to grant as well the obvious and more sober distinctions between poetry and criticism, an acknowledgement that must see reading for what it is—an act that necessarily, even if reluctantly, follows upon the act of writing. Bloom has convincingly argued that the writer is a kind of reader, that there is no creative work that is not also interpretive, but that is not the same as proving that a critical reading of a poem, however "strong," and the text are *one*. To argue that point is to make a claim for solipsism—a claim not only for survival but for the solitary and exclusive right to survive. Poets, as Bloom has by now amply dem- onstrated, *may* be solipsists of this order, at least at their most "anxious," but there is no reason why critics *must* be, unless, of course, the poets within them become anxious for a fuller and freer release than they normally enjoy.

Actually, if Bloom is able to adjust his new hermeneutics a bit— modify his sense of the reader's ability to affect or determine mean- ing in poetry—he can retain the major emphases of antithetical criticism and perhaps escape the cul-de-sac of reductionism into which he has recently been led. Moreover, he can continue to do this from within the sphere of Jewish thinking—and from his earliest adaptations of Buber to his more recent expropriations of Luria and Freud his work is recognizably Jewish in its origins—a thinking which, in the Post-Biblical period, he correctly recognizes to be predominantly interpretive and commentative.

Biblical hermeneutics, in its most normative Jewish expression, maintains a continual dependency of text upon commentary, commentary upon text. To be sure, the world and all that flows from it rests upon the centrality of Torah, but far from being a closed text, the Torah remains open to study and commentary, without which it simply cannot exist intelligibly or be transmitted through the generations. "No interpretation of the Bible of the various traditional kinds," as Simon Rawidowicz has written, "means no expansion, no continuation of the *people* of the Bible." Consequently, "*interpretatio* is Israel's *creatio continua. . . . Interpret or perish* is the voice Israel hears incessantly since Sinai." According to at least one line of rabbinic thought, God Himself, the eternal Creator, is also an "eternal learner," whose passion it is to study the teachings of His interpreters. In a fine revision of Leviticus 19:2 that must delight any critical heart, Rawidowicz offers us this imperative:"Ye shall be *interpretatores* for I am an *interpretator*,"[4] Interpretation in this view of it is clearly more than an adjunct to text but provides the necessary language for its setting and transmission, its ongoing life.

Nevertheless, while interpretation is invested with an immense authority—to the point where it at times even takes for itself some of the power of the primary source that is its occasion—it can never fully wrest priority of place from the text but must coexist with it in a mutually reinforcing continuum:

> What did God give to Moses and Moses bring to Israel? A "text" for *interpretatio*; not a finished, independent, self-sufficient text, but one which is open and has to remain open to *interpretatio*; more than that, one which demands *interpretatio*, obliges Israel to go on interpreting, thus discovering in the process of learning the Torah the duty of *interpretatio*; also of *interpretatio* as a secret of the account Israel was able to give of itself in history.

Rawidowicz, himself a considerable master of interpretation, even if a generally unknown one, has described the dynamics of this interdependency in a way that both illuminates and confirms much of the thrust of Harold Bloom's theory of antithetical criticism while at the same time providing a necessary balance or corrective to it:

> *Interpretatio* lives by crisis in various degrees. . . . [It] can be characterized by a particular attitude of the *interpretator* who struggles

---

[4] All quotations from Rawidowicz are taken from his essay "On Interpretation," collected in N. Glatzer, ed., *Studies in Jewish Thought* (Philadelphia, 1975).

between preserving and rejecting some forms or content of the world at his interpretive "mercy," by a tension between continuation and rebellion, tradition and innovation. It derives its strength both from a deep attachment to the "text" and from an "alienation" from it, a certain distance, a gap which has to be bridged. *Interpretatio* is the "way out" when man is compelled to "take it" or "break it."

Within the Post-Enlightenment period, Harold Bloom would say, this "crisis" has heightened to the point where "breaking it" has become the familiar first option to succession, the "way out" of the tradition being a radical one for most aspiring poets. There is much in the four books considered here to bear him out. These writings also contain evidence of a hermeneutical crisis, however, the critic himself subjecting the canonized works of poetic tradition to a radical "breaking." There is a certain amount of good in that, for a closed thing is a dead thing, but the heavy critical determinism that marks the readings in *Poetry and Repression* seems calculated not so much to revive or "open" poetry as to reduce it, and hence to deprive it of much of its natural primacy. When that happens, when the interpretive stance takes precedence over the text at its mercy, the loss is near total for both.

What is needed now is some greater distance between poem and reader. That need not diminish the authority invested in criticism, which will remain considerable, but it may help to bring back into equilibrium the vitalizing tension that must exist for reading itself to exist—the tension between continuation and rebellion, tradition and innovation, preservation and loss. Bloom has shown us the awesome power of *shevirat ha-kelim*—"the breaking of the vessels." If he can now adjust his critical stance in a way that will allow for restitution, a new power may be his. The most humanizing move at this point would have to be *tikkun*—in critical terms, the restoration of those conditions of possiblity that permit the poem to be in the difficulty of what it is to be: a poem among poems, even a poem among commentaries, but also "a thing final in itself and, therefore, good."

POOR GOD

by CAROLYN CASSADY

from THE BEAT DIARY (Unspeakable Visions of the Individual)

nominated by Unspeakable Visions of The Individual

WHAT IS THERE TO DO? There must be something to *do*. I have heard the sentence, that clanging final sentence, clapping from the mouth of that old man who *dared* to presume to judge Neal. What does *he* know? And Neal standing there so quiet and polite and defenseless, while that apoplectic bigot screams "I don't *care* if there's no evidence, I DON'T LIKE HIS ATTITUDE!" Just because Neal wouldn't admit he smoked pot. I sit, I pace, I stand, I look up into the hills from whence has come so much help before . . . no good.

So I do what I always do and write to Jack and Allen . . . the only family I can share this with. As expected, they reply with distress, sympathy and encouragement. In addition here is a letter from Gregory Corso, totally unexpected . . . an act of Grace that not only corrects my negative impressions of him but provides a comforting anecdote to my anger and despair. Especially the last page:

> . . . This is hard to say yet I feel I have the earthly journey that is miles and miles of vision and sorrow and awakening to say: Neal's walk in life has always been pyloned by roses; and if a great old sick rose blocks his walk, he'd certainly not sidestep. That's what is so true and lovely in the man. When you see him please tell him for me that I well know that all things render themselves; I never knew this before, because when I used to come upon that obstructive rose I'd sidestep, yet would I continue on, venture on, but stand there and complain; well, I learned enough this last year in Europe to dispense with the complaints; how absurd I realized to complain that which is life. I hope this makes sense. I want it to, because I am very unhappy about what has happened to Neal. I'm almost apt to say, Poor God and not Poor Neal. my love, Gregory

Ironically, Neal begins officially serving his "time" on Independence Day, 1958, three months after his arrest. The sentence is five years to life on two counts, and the degrading three months doesn't count. I naively suppose he will be locked up for at least five more years, so Neal must explain to me that sentences don't mean what they say. Five years means two and life means around seven, though there are always possible variables. I don't understand again. It seems some sort of code or game they play, and it infuriates me. Why not say it like it is? Why have to study the rules, must you get a score-card? Where does one get an education for this sort of experience in life? I am ranting a lot, as I have for three months, and there is a good deal more to come, especially when I have to consider their plan for survival of the prisoner's family while the breadwinner is safely being sustained by the taxpayers. Dear Gregory, I will learn the futility of complaining "that which is life," but I bitterly resent the senselessness.

At first, Neal is sent to a medical facility at Vacaville, where prisoners undergo psychological testing supposedly to determine the most appropriate means and circumstances for their "correction." As far as we ever discover, this purpose is a carefully guarded secret, or a myth perpetrated, like so many others, to soothe the conscience of society. Perhaps, to be charitable, it is an attempt to soften the initial blow and shock of the real punishment to come.

At any rate, it is a fairly humane institution, and Neal lives in relative decency. His letters show him to be less bitter than when I'd seen him in the San Francisco City Jail, and there is a revival of his sense of humor, understandably sarcastic in tone. He has been at Vacaville a week, and I've received only one letter when he arrived. I assume he is kept busy adjusting to his new environment, his skull bristling with electrodes while he ponders a multiple-choice. I am wrong.

Dear Carolyn: unbelevable (no eraser) Unbelievable as it may seem, I've written you half a doz. letters since being here. Oh, I know you've received only one, the second I wrote (the first was rejected for writing above lines) besides this, the sixth. So here's the abridged story of my 3rd, 4th and 5th:

Wed. last, after devouring your 6-page beauty, proving more than mere Karma-spouse devotion, began preparing what I considered an equally uplifting .missive manifesting mutual matehood. By writing every spare moment that day & the next, I managed to get it mailed Thur. night, but, because trying to cover everything at once, I had conserved space by crowding lines on back of unruled page (just as I had on the letter you received, right?). It was rejected.

Expecting to be "pampered", like a fool, I proposed to sgt. in charge that it be allowed to pass "just this once", and, of course, I'd not write tiny again. After consulting with Capt, the hour I cooled my soon-to-be-subservient heels in the horseshoe pit, he recalled me to tell me the letter seemed full of "double-talk" . . . secret answers to your secret questions, and thus couldn't be sent; so ended letter #3.

All day Friday, with natural resentment tempered only by what I thought was the humor of it all, I composed an awkward, biting satire on "double-talk" and tried mailing this farce to you. But no go. Instead my supposed wit proved a bad mistake in judgement when Sat AM I was called in and chewed on for openly insulting the Capt. So this letter, the 4th and the funniest, I thought, was the most sternly rejected, as well as being, quite probably, put in my central file to show I disrespect authority.

Anyway, Sat. nite I mailed another, the 5th attempt to get thru a "message to Garcia"; this new one was a most sorry affair, reflecting much of my deep disgust over the whole sad hassel in which I'd stupidly involved myself. So despairingly blah was it that, altho already 5 days late answering you, I quickly regretted having written at all . . . but, hurray, my prayers working via a bum memory, it was returned this morning for forgetting to put my number, etc. on flap of envelope.

Well, now that I've wasted nearly a page by explaining somewhat my delay in writing . . . (tho have been scribbling so furiously all week I have writer's cramp) I'll begin anew this long-retarded reply to your #1.

As I read this detailed description, disbelief grows into awe. Here he is reviewing all the things that had been rejected by the censors, yet they allowed the retelling to pass. I can only suppose they bought his avowed contrition. Perhaps he is learning the game, albeit the hard way, but I abandon the hope of ever being able to outguess the probable behavior of those in control.

He now pushed his "unworried pencil . . . still minus eraser.." to the new answer telling me not to try and do any more toward his release and explaining the idiocies of the penal system and his speculations on his fate. "you see, all first-time 5-to-lifers, no matter the charge, go before the 3-man prison board in 18 months and THEN get their time set, & this is usually 2½ in, 2½ out on parole. Despite this more or less standard policy, God's Grace crowning our humble efforts, I'm still sure of being home to start our personal 'Easter of New Beginnings' at least by the exact date in 1960"

As evidenced in his prison letters, Neal had always been fascinated with the writing of Proust. He used to delight in reading aloud to Jack, marvelling at the non-stop sentences and the intricate dissection of thoughts. Not only does he play with these methods in his letters, but sometimes he'll write an entire page of alliteration. Doubtless these exercises are his only creative outlet, and although I enjoy them, I am aware that the therapy involved for him in searching for the right word is more important than the sentiments wrung from his labors. The *mot juste* in this case is not its meaning but its initial letter.

He is ever conscious of the censors and indulges in frequent gushes of conscience and remorse for their benefit . . . this his only avenue of conning in such a profitless environment. I do not begrudge him these rare moments.

For my part, the only joy I know during these two years is to find that small crumpled envelope in the mail box. One thanks I give the system is the absence of descriptive return address. My chief concern, of course, is for the children (now aged 10, 9 & 7) who do not know their father is in prison. They are usually in school when the mail arrives, and if not, I'm really the only one interested in it.

As the reader will appreciate, I think, I wait until I can settle down alone with coffee and cigarette to concentrate on these elaborate epistles, pencil-written on 5"×7" ruled paper in as small a hand as he can get by with.

From the beginning Neal shows an increasing absorption in religion. I certainly pray for a higher power to intervene, and that Neal may accept this test as an enforced monastic interlude. It has happened to others; Starr Daily, for one, whom Neal idolizes and had once sought out for advice. So much depends on attitude, and Neal knows it; his Cayce obsession had convinced him. When first arrested, he had managed a remarkable acceptance and eagerly and reverently told me of the "miracles" that had taken place that time, including his release. When he was re-arrested, his faith did not suffice to surmount the injustice. His bitterness was so intense it blinded him to not only the remembrance of the recent testimonials but to common sense as well. In both cases the higher law was aptly demonstrated, maddeningly clear to him, and his failure to overcome only increased his self-condemnation.

His sudden reversion to Catholicism saddens me at first. It seems nothing more than rote and dogma, surface declarations accomplishing nothing toward a basic change within. So the disappointment is the more acute when we learn Hugh Lynn Cayce has been refused the right to correspond with Neal; he had been a close friend and valued counsellor for many years. (Not too surprising, then, both Luanne and Jackie, two secret lovers, are granted this permission as well as that of visiting.)

By the time Neal is settled in Vacaville, he has made considerable progress already toward his religious routine:

. . . Amid other actions, disregarding my damning letter skit, to aid this happy Sunday happening & amongst other reasons for attempting even minimal valid repayment to Him, such as the invalid one of injury to callow pride by shallow shame suffered in ever-increasing recognition of weak sloth reinforcing strong lust, I've begun seriously composing prayers.

Most appropriate here, did not modesty (false, of course) & space (limited, yet unreal, you know) forbid quoting, would be the one to Apostle St. Paul that is based on his Epistle for the Easter Mass from Cor.5:7-8; I would quote this ex-Saul hoping to soon reenact his splendid rebirth . . . should I be called "Kneel"? No room for quote; you read it with Johnny.

To accompany my regular evening and morning prayers, I've made up several others, to St. Michael esp. who, remember, while not the Way, is Lord of the Way. I'm most proud . . . oops, that nemesis word again . . . of one of these that calls on (thru Holy Ghost, of course, who controls, nay, *is* all positive prayer power) every one of the 262 Popes, Peter to Pius XII, to help hasten my growth as well as all mankind. The better to emulate these leaders, I am memorizing their names & add a new one each day to the prayer, i.e., today's Pope . . . the 21st in order (I began July 1st) is St. Cornelius, who reigned from 251-263. Next week will get back to your wonderful 1st letter, the first paragraph of which is all I've managed to answer so far . . .

When I try to be subtle about my concern for his fervor, which I fear is bordering on fanaticism, he sees through me, as usual, and, not sidestepping, as usual, faces me with my own fears:

Dear Dynamo & Sweet Scrivner of Pretty Pages 99&100% pure Carolyn: As it allows of no tergiversation to concede that much worth in a picture depends on where the artist chooses to sit . . . or stand, as you usually do . . . so, too, a felon must admit that whatever value is gained by confinement rests largely on (a seeming paradox) his physical position.

While, of course, accentuating the all-important mental attitude, most attention, despite every effort contrariwise, is still naturally centered, being over ½ animal (you know . . . 4 glands to 3, or less, because one of those upper trio, the pineal, is partially fossilized by lime salts at puberty in practically everyone) on the restricted bodily activity which, tho in itself a small thing, when experienced without break over an extended length of time, considerably exaggerates the already tightly repressed emotional reaction until, if uncheckable by rational means, rubbed-raw nerves explode into a "stir-craziness".

Hence, such expressions among the "con-wise" as, "do your own time", meaning stay clear of another's tension; "keep your mind off the streets", meaning women, etc. Happily, thanks to you and God, as well as this State's enlightened penal system, there's little chance I could become seriously subject to unhingement thru any of these material fixations. No, if anything unbalanced me . . . further, that is . . . it would have the reverse type cause, i.e., inordinate dwelling on immaterial objects.

Actually, were there possible such an one nowadays, I *am* a "religious nut" and pray to become more so . . . and will! . . . for aren't we to be moderate in all things *except* love of God? (By its very definition and 1st principles there can't be any conscious moderation, i.e., holding back, in religion.) In fact, besides being poor slang & an incorrect term, there is no such person as a "religious nut", but only "nutty religion" (& not even'that) which is really what I meant to say, or warn myself especially against all along. But enuf line-consuming verbosity; back to realities of relationship . . .

. . . One last bit on the religion "kick" (& indeed it is this, whether in or out; it's really the only "kick" left, true?) I read that Postulant in Cisterian monastary spends 90 days at least as such; this corresponds to my 3 months in SF jail; 2 years as novice, equalling my term inside pen; 3 years under "simple" vows, my period of outside parole. So, just as they take over 5 years in all before being finally accepted, I'll be completely discharged & accepted back into society only after a similar passage of time. Interesting, what?

Here he is instructing me that he has lost none of his knowledge of metaphysics in spite of his new passion, but it would not be wise to reassure me too directly and thus enlighten his censors by the same means.

Neal is in Vacaville for three months. Although his keepers are obviously mad, the institution in general is not as deliberately degrading to the inmates as are the other prisons he passes through. There are psychological games to play, which Neal loves (as can be guessed from his letters) as well as more balanced and rewarding physical regimes.

I look out cell window and watch trains meeting and passing a half mile away and within few 100 yards there daily comes creeping a local freight over Sacramento Northern branch line. Ho hum, let 'um work; I'm on vacation.

Took gym test today. Ran 250 yards back & forth in 53 seconds, chinups 15, sit-ups 37 . . . all in "very good" category. Took 900-question quiz on "attitude & comprehension", then spelling, I.Q., mech.apt., scholastic, math, vocab. voc.skills, etc. Now all tests over & am in 2 week "Group Behavior Adjustment" class. Our ball team (tell Johnny I'm a Giant, too, just like on his cap) won 2 of last 3 & now in second place in league. Each Sat. go to confession to receive on Sun. the Holy·Euchurist from fine German priest here. Gained 10 lbs! Feeling increasingly purged of all old desires, especially of flesh.

If the good doctors read his repeated insistence that he is through forever of any former associates or habits, they can well believe they have a sure-fire system of reform. In spite of the accusations that Vacaville is a "country club", I do so wish he may stay there . . . or why isn't that sort of imprisonment sufficient punishment? A chance for increased self-respect to find a foothold in a crack of the confining wall.

Neal hopes to be sent to Soledad, where he says "the kissing facilities are better", but instead he draws San Quentin. I suppose the policy is consistent with that of the Armed Forces whereby given choices for stations, the only ones you may be sure you won't get are the ones you request.

Dearest Dear Carolyn, Wonder Wife: Even as they were striking my leg irons, that had, along with two sidearm-carrying officers, locked door, barred windows & snow-white pajamas (minus the half-expected bright red or yellow bulls-eye on the back) most adequately subdued any wild urge to disembark during the short bus ride from Vacaville, I began experiencing the generation of a not inconsiderable self-pity, soon to become, while the procedure progressed, almost overpowering by virtue of those repeated shocks every new dismal view bordering sheer disbelief administered in separate but accumulative blow to my so-sorry-for-myself-sharpened conception as, now buffeted from both within and without into a bewildering numbness, I at last encountered, when first stumbling across the "Big Yard", as the "cons" call it . . . in that characteristic state it seems to engender, a paradoxical one of hazelike concentration, the main source of what gloomy eminations my all-too-sympathetic mood had rendered it recipient; that psychical wall each convict's despair-ridden tension made to exist inside the, high and wide though they be, far weaker stone walls of this infamous old . . . 1859 is chisled atop the facade of one still-used building . . . prison, at which, accompanying 23 more, I finally arrived last week.

After a troubled sleep, in sagging bunk beneath one of a thug who'd escaped 8 times, much disturbed by an anxiety dream concerning some just-right blonde, fatty-cheeked both above and below (presumably you, since I personally know no other) & myself at a drive-in movie . . . remember the one in Kansas we attended so long ago? . . . the following day brought undoubtedly with the aid of a strong, yet abstractly felt, of course, sorrow, occasioned by news of the Holy Father's demise . . . Along this line, the next day another shared sadness, but in a far lighter vein of thought than the Pope's death, served for further perception into my always too weak realization of excessive self-centerdness, the demise, real enuf, tho figuratively and collectively, of the Milwaukee Braves in the World Series.

Much more, however, responsibility for lifting me from that blue funk of depression this place must naturally impress on "fish" (new convicts) can be attributed to an increasing awareness over this last week of the balancing factor it equally imposes: compassion. Truly, I've never seen, nor is there elsewhere in this noble country concentrated, surely not even in Sing Sing, such an assorted assemblage of absolutely pitiful misfits as are the 5,042 felons . . . latest count, which Radio KROW announced on 6 PM news as largest number here since 1942 . . . in whose routine I am daily . . . & nightly, ugh . . . immured until at least Easter of 1960.

Neal's first "job" in this grim new home is sweeping the floor of the textile mill.

. . . which reminds me how I've been using prayer lately, or how this exbeatster beats a beat bastille: Rule: blank mind-desire proportionately to each bodily nullification. Example: Hearing. To overcome eardrum-bursting racket made by the cotton textile mill's 4-million-dollars worth of 1745 R.P.M. 68x72″ hi-speed looms, whose constantly collecting flug is my weary job to sweep all day from beside & beneath, I, thus noisely assured safeguard from eavesdropping, deadening surfaced thought to equate the deafness, incessantly shout into that accompanying roar every prayer known & since . . . saying them hurriedly it takes just one hour to complete their entirety. Each minute, after the first 60, finds me repeating the very one said on that very moment last hour. Don't demurmer, it at least eliminates clock-watching.

Near the end of his first year, on our wedding anniversary, he tries to give me an idea of his living conditions, if living it is.

My dear wife, sweet April fool, laden doubly with toil because I did soil and foil the precious bloom of your tender love—bestowed in all its fresh entirety that glorious and (judge) Golden [We were married April 1, 1948 by Judge Joseph Golden, subsequently impeached to Neal's delight. He thought he overcharged us.] moment 11 years and

11 hours ago when we blew your practically last sawbuck to officially cinch that truly meant-to-be union which each day I, despite causing its previous & current adversity, sincerely thank Divine Providence for even permitting, as I mull it during those 16 of every 24 hours locked behind these 13 tan (to me) [Neal was color-blind.] colored bars fronting my 4½ x 7½ x 9½ foot cell:

To get some better idea of what lying so encaged is like, you might put car mattress in the bathtub, thereby making it softer, and if not as long, at least much cleaner than is my bug-ridden bunk; then bring in your 200 lb. friend, Edna, or the more neagatively aggressive, Pam. Lock the door, &, after dragging 11 rowdy kids into our bedroom to parallel the 1,100 noisy ones housed in this particular cell block; of course, in the bathroom, you must remove the toilet seat, towel racks, cabinet . . . anything other than a small mirror & 4½" shelf . . . remain almost motionless so as not to inadvertently irritate armed-robber-Edna, ponder past mistakes, present agonies & future defeats in the light of whatever insights your thus-disturbed condition allows . . .

About now I'm wondering if there are no censors at "Q". Perhaps they believe Neal sincere in an outburst like the following, but, yes, they are still with us, their objections tuned to a different wavelength than those at Vacaville:

. . . April 2 got a heartrending Easter card from John & Jamie . . . what no Cathy? . . . Tell John how pleased I was he got right number of humps (sand containers) on top of engine. Don't tell Jamie how tragically ironic I found it that she (guided by what mysterious hand beneath the surfactual ignorance?) spelled "Hey, Hey" as "hay, Hay" to innocently twist deeper in firmer-fix the sharp memory-knife cutting my remorse anew by her unwittingly giving such appropriate name to the vile weed used in that selfish habit of vice putting me here where everything once possessed, from job to joy, has gone irrevocably up the felon flu in a black smoke the more Hellishly felt for burning, conversely from Hay, so steel and concretely real . . . seared by the heat of which my reaction momentarily fanned resentment from still smoldering ember to blazing open flame in a self-piteous whale of a wail to my Godfather, which was so filled with frail whine, the censor wisely rejected & returned it with the curt command, "Write a *letter*". So, submerged under this further funk of having wounded pride pricked, the bubble of Literary smugness

burst as well, for the comment implied nonacceptance more for style
than complaint, since slip giving reason for letter's return had no
other mark whatsoever on it, not even a check in the space where it
should logically be. . .

In the early years, Neal had enjoyed letter-writing and was encouraged to consider style and technique by Jack and Allen. [It was
their urging that started him on *The First Third*.] Letters to them are
energized with a thrust of action, directed inward or outward and
often frustrated but nonetheless moving toward some progression.
It seemed to me his prison letters illustrated his own stymied
condition. With his intense and tortured efforts to create disciplined
phrases and choose exact words, I visualized his total Mind, lacking
means of expansion or broader forms of expression, trapped within
the intricate convolutions of his physical brain . . . turned, twisted,
folded back upon itself . . . like his driving . . . ever wary of the
cops, opening up on dangerous curves and risking a few dexterous
maneuvers to outwit and baffle them.

He was very much of this earth as well as in it; he grasped and
manipulated and developed incredibly perfected skills in the use of
his physical instrument, pitted mainly against himself rather than
other people even in sports. But he must master the requisite
imposed by any particular activity or object . . . whether railroad
cars, tire-recapping equipment or automobile driving. He was
equally intrigued with the manipulation of people.

Within, his intense energy raged the battle between exhuberant
Life and love and the destructive deamon: hostility toward women,
stupid authority and, most notably, himself. Before he died, this
Devil appeared in the form Neal had created, and "I talk to him all
the time," he told me.

The seeds of his later "raps" can be found in his letters. When he
was no longer capable of writing, except for a few times when in
some local jail, he was compelled to express his Aquarian insights in
talk, his agile intellect now struggling with the emotional whip of self-
hatred and the physical disintegration of drug-induced destruction.

Complex though the maze of thoughts is in his prison letters, the
ideas can, with effort, be followed. When he could only manage
verbalizing, the labyrinth becomes tangled, and increasingly are
there gaps and dead-end passages.

I pleaded with him to go to Mexico in 1968, knowing there were so many traffic warrants out against him, that if he were caught I feared he'd be returned to San Quentin for good. Gavin Arthur, who had been his teacher there, was furious with me. "Why did you do that?" he fumed. "Neal was at his very best in prison; it's the only place he could stay healthy and use that magnificent mind."

A lot could be said about that point of view.

A PUDDLE

by LARRY EIGNER

from THE WORLD AND ITS STREETS, PLACES (Black Sparrow)

nominated by Michael Lally

a puddle

 wind in the day and night

  all it takes
        a single branch
    to shower down
          and a few twigs

            reflections
              dissolve

       one center
     to rough edges

    walls

        and to see the sky
          as unreal

        the gnarl
          in the freshened water

WHAT LIGHT THERE IS

by MEKEEL McBRIDE

from THE AGNI REVIEW

nominated by THE AGNI REVIEW

Now the distance between us is a field.
What light there is I gather and plant.

Above me clouds build themselves into storm
into dark animals that splinter the sky with desire.

Where are you in this field? Beyond it,
taking apart the calendar box by white box.

Where am I? Here, walking in the dark,
waiting to see what will break earth first.

Now the air is thinner than it once was.
What wind there is touches me

the way an old man touches with surprise
the memory of himself as a child

and it is this wind, a little thinner
from travel, that days later will touch you.

MAKING A NAME
FOR MYSELF

by JOYCE E. PESEROFF

from THE HARDNESS SCALE (Alice James Books)

nominated by DeWitt Henry

It took long enough to get used to
& of course the jokes would piss me
off. Just yesterday a letter from Famous Writer's
Beauty Salon addressed J. Peteroff,
some crazy castrating bitch
the mailman assumes lives here.

When I was young & fat I guessed
each couple pondered & made up the family
name. Such a democrat,
I selected Silvergold, a rich sounding,
solid name. Why didn't my parents
pick Silvergold? So I pondered change & a fat bridal.

My grandfather was tailor to the Czar.
His sons, producing nothing but girls
& homosexuals, leave us alone
with his name. When he got off the boat,
his good wide pants wrapped double & up
to his sunken chest, he cut the "sky,"
meaning "Jew," from his name
and walked proud with a solid Russian label
in a land where Russian meant "Jew."

Grandfather, you were out of step
but your name is comfortable as an old shoe
except when I make appointments at Monsieur's salon
or a restaurant sometimes I'll give my husband's.
White, I used to say, W. C. Williams

EVEN AFTER A MACHINE IS DISMANTLED, IT CONTINUES TO OPERATE, WITH OR WITHOUT PURPOSE

fiction by Ascher/Straus Collective

from CHOUTEAU REVIEW

nominated by Stephen Dixon and Hugh Fox

THE AUTHOR CAN'T HELP feeling cornered in the summer home or cottage in the woods. The absurd wealth of nature that surrounds it is boring and repetitive, each leaf and pebble exactly the same and infinitely different from the others. To go on living here, one day after another, every '440 minutes settling on every other 1440 minutes, over a vast, perhaps rotten bed of hours, seconds and centuries, must seem something like this.

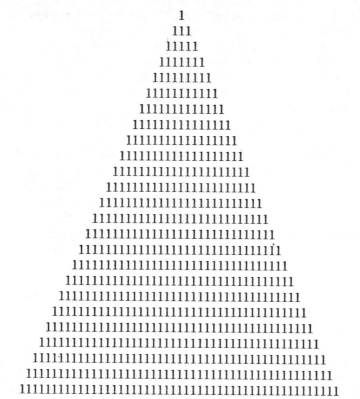

Still, something, perhaps the author, seems to prevent Elizabeth from leaving.

2.

One day Elizabeth borrows Walter's binoculars, which she finds in the living room, in a leather case. The sun is streaming through the bamboo shades and two dozen yellow rods of light slip off the smooth grain onto the slick cover of *Scientific American* and through the glass-topped coffee table. By accident she's facing the windows and doesn't see a vast yellow-red blot that would have to be focused down to a wall with paintings. She looks down through the windows into the underbrush and low trees. The "underbrush and low trees" become intersecting half curves: leaves, vines, branches, all steamrollered into a close-textured wall. Some dimension of depth or illusion of depth is removed. An illusion of lack of depth takes its place: distances disappear or flatten before and behind. Elizabeth, or the author, has this feeling: the binoculars sum everything up, perhaps a million years of tiny noises, deaths, aridity and fertile growth are packed tight and preserved like some sort of condensed food in dry ice or tubes of frozen jelly . . .

Elizabeth may imagine that she's discovered another scale of things in the black, glassed-over tubes. As if she can project glass bridges into the distance, toward any desired point. The binoculars make her feel alone with space. Nearer to things and yet further from a sense of reality. The valley is sucked into the tubes and compressed into these discs that contain a million yards of space. The underbrush flattens into stiff arcs or fans, the air silvery along their edges. Fan presses on fan presses on fan on fan on fan on fan on fan forward back and sidewise.

The middle distance of dark green hills is even more compact and thick-textured. Not one speck of light shows through the hills.

Beyond the hills the compactness of things gives way entirely. Some broad space intervenes. And in that space the condensing force of distance loses its hold. As if the hand that gripped things has opened up. Blue distances, level silver-grey stretches of water are released. Her being follows this material line of development and experiences a disturbing sense of freeing and opening . . . The view is like the one she had seen without the binoculars from the upper terrace, the lower terrace, the windows, the road, the lower terrace, the windows, the upper terrace, the road, etc., etc.

She wonders if she's free, why she's here, is this what her vacation was meant to be, is the real vacation beginning now, in the binoculars, is it all lies and fancy talk arising out of boredom, is William right for slipping himself like an extra suitcase into all the real and metaphysical baggage of these people who are returning to New York in two or three weeks, is there any freedom beyond the metaphoric one of an ideal and unlivable condition . . . These questions are packed into the steamrollered leaves, fans, trees, mountains, open spaces like glass in straw.

Or she may not think or wonder anything, she's long past the point of examining the nature of her condition or of all these steaming heaps of haphazard and rounded geometry, it's only we who seem to require an explanation, or at least a puzzle that can be solved in our leisure hours, like a crossword of infinite dimensions . . .

Elizabeth descends to the lower terrace with the binoculars. The view is very much the same. Let's say: she continues to feel lost in an ambiguous condition—slipping into open space along the doubtful shuttle of a metaphor. Bird cries: raspy and broken or threadlike and musical: materialize swiftly and become visible in her lenses. The audible or musical becomes the visible or spatial, so that it becomes possible to feel or imagine one is gazing at musical notes turned to yellow glass threads, red globes, blue spirals, etc.

Despite the fact that she's half-dissolved in an ambiguous and open condition on the hot flat of the terrace, she may wonder why she takes pleasure or interest in watching what may be nothing but a banal or hothouse reproduction of the fertile nature of our dreams: the unexpected and exaggerated forms of life, for example, that appear like drops of paint against a curiously flattened landscape. She isn't a bird-watcher by nature, Walter's *Temple's Field Guide,* his conservation magazines and so on leave her cold. All these charts, graphs, crossing files of words like Energy (Thousand Electron Volts) and Time (Minutes) or Depth (Feet) or Volume (Cubic Meters), strike her as a technical escape-route from reality. Automotive magazines come to mind, or manuals of electric equipment.

Or she may not be thinking about Walter and his magazines at all. She may be wondering what happens to birds when they die. Do they drop straight out of the air; rot in the grass; red, blue and yellow turning brown, black, grey; eaten by beetles, ants, flies, worms, larvae, bacteria, viruses; begin to resemble lumps of dung, then earth, then ash.

The screen door bangs on the upper terrace, breaking off her thoughts quite sharply.

A few seconds pass, the sound of shoes on the lawn, William appears on the lower terrace from the direction of the stairs, the lawn, the apple tree. His face is set and closed, as it has been on and off since they've rejoined. He has something to say but seems to be waiting for her to say it. She isn't willing to smooth the way: if he wants to "open up" it will be up to him.

The red-grey surface of the terrace becomes immeasurable.

"Walter took a look at my eyes. It may be nothing but a cold, but he isn't sure," he says.

It's true, each of his eyes looks something like a cherry pit. On the other hand, it isn't the first time he's complained or hidden behind his eyes. Perhaps if he said what was in his heart everything would return to normal, they would embrace. Elizabeth might even be willing to return or consider returning home.

She relents and smooths the way. Does he want to say anything? she asks. Is anything bothering him, aside from his eyes?

Oh, no, he protests. Of course not, no. He just wanted to see, well, how she was getting along.

"Well, I think I'll see what's on the radio."

His tone has a familiar ring: vacationer's false heartiness or something in that vein. The air remains tense with possiblities that seem bound to remain unexplored, bit by bit it slackens off and he fades away.

Ellen appears on the upper terrace, calls and waves gaily. Someone is with her. Both of them are wearing dungarees. Ellen invites Elizabeth to come up out of the heat and sit with them under the tree, where she's put out a few chairs. They'll have some whiskey sours and shoot the breeze.

Elizabeth is glad of the opportunity to escape from herself, mounts the steps and joins the others under the tree. She finds a chair and a whiskey sour waiting for her in the grass.

This apparent thoughtfulness surprises her. All solicitousness has begun to arouse her suspicions.

They talk about this and that—the new power station on the river, for example, where red-and-blue towers are just visible with the naked eye. Through Walter's binoculars one can almost spy on the operations of the plant, which, it's rumored in the community and in the conservation magazines, have something to do with atomic energy, count the number of bricks in the odd, dome-topped structure . . . Elizabeth says that she *has* counted the number of bricks and the number, supposing the back to be equal to the front, is 104,121. Everyone laughs over that, and Ellen's friend, who has driven down from her year-round home in the hills, objects that the number must be *much* greater than that, really, around a million.

Sooner or later they drop the subject of the power plant and the

question as to whether the touch of the human added to the valley by
the power plant and red-and-blue towers is ugly or beautiful and
Ellen raises the question of monogamous relationships. She knows
it's old hat, she says, but it seems to her the problem isn't a moral one
but one of boredom and stagnation.

Boredom and dependency, the friend modifies.

Monogamous relationships are the result of fear, insecurity, etc.
She sometimes worries about that. More recently than before.

"That you're dependent on Walter or that . . .?"

Both. More that Walter depends on her. But after a while, you lose
your freedom, boredom saps your energy and desire . . .

Sexually, marriage, or monogamy, is a stupid convention, a real
prison . . . Both love and desire melt away with the years and what's
left is pure mechanism, lies, false sentiment . . .

Or pornography. Eroticism with no emotional overtones or
undertones. She's not ashamed to admit that the sexual games one
plays in married life are infinitely let's say *dirtier* than anything
between lover and lover. Every new relationship is like the founding
of a new society. Everything is mysterious and invigorating. While
in marriage eroticism has to be whipped up through the most bizarre
fantasies . . .

Not that one can't continue to get a certain emotional satisfaction . . .

The only solution, *obviously,* is for both partners to come to an
intelligent understanding. Whereby one can satisfy one's erotic
needs, let off steam, without all the bourgeois deception, stifled
auto-eroticism, pornography, yet maintain one's relationship on an
emotional plane . . .

Yes. Doesn't Elizabeth agree that it's possible, and desirable, to
conduct two relationships at once? After all it's pure bull that sexuality has anything to do with sentiment. Nothing could draw more
attention to man's biological nature. What's more, an excursion or
vacation is sometimes essential to breathe in new life . . .

Elizabeth doesn't answer, but neither Ellen nor her friend seems
to care. The friend, in fact, begins to relate an anecdote of revitaliz-
ing infidelity.

Elizabeth's attention is absorbed by Ellen's dungarees, which are
faded, particularly at the knees, where there's no blue at all; and a
seam is open at the thigh, an inch of white skin showing softly

through. She strikes Elizabeth as self-indulgent and false. She begins to wonder if the conversation is purely theoretical. Ellen's face
and hair form a yellow aura against the hot masses of foliage and the
hairy mound of the middle distance.

3.

A few days later Walter, Elizabeth, William and Ellen go climbing. The climb is hot and exhausting, something like climbing a rope
of thorny vines that hangs from a naked and blazing sky. Bit-by-bit
they pass out of the familiar zone of black and silvered-over lakes
ringed round with green woodland speckled with green. Green light
gives way to brown shadow, paths of salmon-red clay that are like
bridlepaths sprinkled with tanner's bark. The forest is dotted with
luminous flakes of yellow, and brown-green with decaying vegetable
matter that resembles rotten sponges and steel wool soap pads.

Elizabeth feels more and more walled off by exhaustion and
wonders if all this labor and heat is worth reaching some local tourist
attraction, called "The Tip," "The Top," or, senselessly, "Le Temps,"
or "Le Tapis Vert," or "Tant Pis," which offers nothing but still
another view of the valley.

It seems to her that all along the way Walter takes the opportunity
to drop back, pass a remark—that such and such a rock is gneiss, or
shale, or pegmatite—lend her a hand in the dry stream beds, or else
fall behind altogether in order to watch her from behind.

She wonders about his peculiar behavior, which seems to be cut
from the same cloth as Ellen's solicitous chair and whiskey sour in
the shade, and finds it irritating.

Perhaps, she speculates, Walter has noticed her indifference or
coldness towards William and thinks he smells an opportunity. He
can see or thinks he can see that she's bored. Her detachment,
keeping to herself, borrowing his binoculars, mooning on the terrace, sitting in one place for 1 hour, 4 hours, 14 hours, 31 days, 300
years.

The yellow-brown speckles and decayed vegetable matter give
way to sunbaked rockfaces and stunted pines.

They reach a level space that may be the top. The trees, scrub
pines and some other broad-leafed variety are even more low and

twisted, the thin soil and bare, broken rockfaces are densely cross-hatched with blueberry runners. Blue-purple dots and pointed leaves. The footing is smooth and easy, but the bald rock is extremely hot. The four of them crawl around for a quarter of an hour, eating blueberries, pretending to find the tart and undeveloped little berries delicious. Elizabeth holds a dozen or so in her palm. Some are a delicate mauve, others are a deep violet. She loses interest, walks a few yards and parts the branches of the tough and spiny shrubbery. For an instant she feels as if she's passed through a wall into blue and empty space. The familiar valley spread out as something of a surprise, more vast and also more trivial than before. She sees dark green slopes a thousand inches or a hundred miles wide, swollen rivers of trees whose flow in time is fixed in countless spatial curves, a lifetime or a million lifetimes, all those mysterious, apparently inanimate existences one didn't have time to explore . . . In the central distance she discovers or postulates low-lying farmland, with its hard, shaved and sunbaked patches of red-brown. Here and there something sparkles like a coin.

She has Walter's binoculars with her and looks through them, perhaps wondering how many scraps of the human have, over the centuries, been hammered into this landscape like new nails. The sparkling coins, for example, may be aluminum silos or the silver fillings of murder victims who've been left to rot in the forest, but even with the binoculars she can't be certain. Instead four tremendous birds make wide pinwheels in the lenses, cut into and out of the mild silver of nothingness. The tubes pressed to her eyes block out everything else and she can't help feeling herself to be nothing but a mirror of the glittering emptiness of the atmosphere, the fertile desolation of the valley, three or four pinwheels of unreasonable fear . . .

The others lose interest in blueberrying. They gather around Elizabeth and speculate as to kind and purpose of the birds. Almost without question they're vultures, Walter asserts. And the way they're circling can only indicate one thing, a dead animal, and not a small one either.

They soon lose interest in that also. Perhaps all the hard work of climbing has nullified every semblance of freedom from cares or civilized-and-rational contemplation of nature and an unidentifiable craving is provoked. Or, Walter and Ellen have had a definite purpose in mind all along and only appear to make a spontaneous decision to walk a little further on. Elizabeth elects to stay where she is and look at the boring view for the next week or month or millisecond. William takes a hint and goes off to sulk. Everyone disappears. Elizabeth sits on the hot rock, her blouse is plastered to her back, she unbuttons two buttons at the top. A strong breeze blows out of the woods, propelling a moist and thermal shadow out of her body, over the valley. She feels cooler and weaker, though not quite ready to be picked apart by the birds of prey that are hidden behind some vast hump of rock and trees . . .

In five minutes Walter comes slipping back. He asks, "ah, you don't intend to come up where *we* are, do you, you're staying here?"

That's right, Elizabeth answers. Or it *was* right. Now of course he's succeeded in arousing her curiosity.

Ellen's taking a sunbath, he explains, and she doesn't want any strangers, or even William, to . . . He stops, looks hot and sly. Well, if she promises not to tell William, or to tell Ellen that he told, because he was just supposed to make sure no tourists were coming up the trail . . .

Elizabeth promises, out of indifference more than anything else.

Past those bushes, he says, there's another, even broader outcropping. One can lie down there very comfortably in the sun. Like a loaf of bread in a brick oven. Or like a brick red lizard. A girl who had hiked up here alone, and who was quite sure no one else was there, might very well choose the spot to sunbathe. Ellen is going to pretend she's the girl. She doesn't know he's been there the whole time, blueberrying, or contemplating suicide, and he's seen her go by. Right now she's taking off her blouse and her bra and she's lying down on the warm rock. He'll wait a few minutes, then sneak back through the shrubs and spy on her, maybe shoot some film. Then he'll have to decide what to do next. She may want to even out her tan and remove the rest of her clothes. Then he might sneak up and steal her things while she's sleeping, wait to see how she reacts when she wakes up, sees they're gone. Or else he'll just reveal himself and toy with his prisoner, whose naked back will be pressed up against a wall of open space. Or crawl forward and Ellen will pretend not to see him or pretend to be pretending she doesn't see him, turn over on her stomach, hoping he'll be satisfied and go away or enjoying this opportunity to have her rounded body examined from every angle . . .

Elizabeth doesn't feel much of anything. Or she doesn't know what she feels. Walter's motives are also a mystery.

Why did he tell her? she asks.

Walter seems puzzled. "Just like that," he says. Or, "because you asked, how should I know!" Or he may smile and say, "it doesn't have to be *one* girl, you know . . ." It's even possible that the two girls have chosen this arid spot because of its isolation, they want to be alone, to lie side-by-side in the blazing sun. She looks at him uncomprehendingly, he hesitates, shrugs, warns her again about William and slips off into the shrubbery.

4.

That night or the next night William is outside, possibly making a fire in the grate. Ellen is taking a bath.

Elizabeth is daydreaming behind a magazine in the living room.

Or it's just possible that her interest is actually absorbed in the Sunday supplement of a local newspaper, there's a two-page spread on a bizarre and grisly murder . . . No doubt there's some tale of murder or inexplicable brutality or sly exploitation every week, always in the same style: "Marie-Claire Janicek, a blonde, blue-eyed bundle of mini-skirted vitality, had high aspirations when she set out one day in her bright orange convertible . . ." The article goes on to recount how this Marie-Claire, with her somewhat incongruous last name, sets out one evening to audition as a singer in a nightclub or cabaret in a nearby city . . . The place isn't much to speak of, it's pretty seedy in fact, there are strippers, possibly topless dancers or something like that, but it may seem to her to be a step in the right direction, you never can tell who might drop in and notice her, stranger things have happened, and if she lands the job her husband will be thrilled . . . The reporter seems to make an effort to arouse one's sympathy or to gloss the ugly tale with a vaguely liberal social message: it seems, he or she points out, that Marie-Claire Janicek spent her girlhood in a small agricultural town, dreaming of the larger world. And so, when, after having put on her favorite purple minidress and tried her best to make herself into an object of love and seduction for all who heard-and-saw, or at least for the stocky owner of the Zanzibar Lounge, or the Eighth Wonder Cabaret, or the Malibu Club, she fails to get the job, she can't be more depressed. "Her booking agent and one of his employees walked the disheartened Marie-Claire to her car in the parking lot of the lounge. They watched her drive away and her agent noticed it was 10:35 p.m. Neither man was to know until much later that Marie-Claire pulled her yellow convertible into a gas station a few blocks from the lounge, on Bates Avenue, near the old Wheat Exchange, once considered to be a storage depot for underworld merchandise. It seems the car's tail light needed fixing." Elizabeth or the author can't help feeling that the reporter leaves various psychological avenues unexplored in relation to this crucial point. The most obvious being the trivial, even absurd reason offered for Marie-Claire Janicek's stopping into the station, thus delaying the moment when she would return, empty of possiblities, to her mediocre suburban street, her home, her husband: to all the static elements of a life that's already begun to slide into boredom and death . . .

"By all odds," the obtuse reporter continues, "Marie-Claire should have arrived at the Janicek home before midnight. As the hours passed and his wife failed to return, Sam Janicek wondered if he should report her missing to the police. He paced the floor and finally fell into a fitful doze shortly before 7 a.m. Tuesday."

At 8 o'clock, a retired hotel clerk named Arbogast is walking his dog, he allows it to pull him into a lot or field next to a rectangular structure of unadorned stucco or concrete that seems to house a printing plant. Among the weeds, soda caps and pulltags, flattened beer cartons, tablelegs, broken glass, bits of blue-ruled copybook notepaper covered with curls of scrawl like this: "In 1776 the colonists decided to live their own lives, threw off the yolk of the rulers and exploiters from across the sea . . .": he's amazed to see a naked blonde girl lying beside a turquoise-colored bulldozer about 10 feet from the edge of a paved parking lot.

"It was apparent to the first detective at the scene that the girl had been beaten, stabbed and strangled. She had been slashed numerous times across the throat. A single stroke had severed the larynx and the jugular vein. There was a circle of stab wounds in her chest. One knife wound had penetrated the heart. Several front teeth were missing; a deep gash stretched across the top of the girl's head.

A Coroner's Deputy said the young woman could have died as the result of any one of the numerous and massive wounds. Later examination was to reveal that she had bled to death.

"Police said the killer apparently had used two types of

weapons—a blunt instrument and a sharp one. Neither was found at the scene.

"The killer had stripped off his victim's clothing except for a silver shoe and the right leg of a beige-colored pair of panty hose. A dinner-type diamond ring on the third finger of the victim's left hand discounted robbery as a motive.

"Because of the small amount of blood found at the scene, investigators surmised that the killer had washed the body after death. Bloodstains on the pavement of the parking lot indicated that the body had been dragged from a car to the spot where it was found beside the bulldozer.

"The office of the Coroner reported that first examinations of the body indicated that the girl had been killed between 11 p.m. and 3 a.m.

"In the absence of any pinpointing clues to the identity of the dead girl or the killer, investigators swarmed out from the scene of the murder, questioning dozens of persons in the area."

Hundreds of detectives nose around, hoping some scrap of information will prove more real or unreal than the crossing highways, the littered fields, the small unadorned factories of stucco or concrete, the mediocre suburbs, the lounges or cabarets with their stocky owners who give two lines of grudging and useless information . . . "I wouldn't have known unless you told me that this girl was named Janicek. She used the name Cora Samuels. All these girls think it sounds better to have a name like that . . . She left about 10:30. She was wearing a purple dress. She sang five numbers or so, I wasn't impressed, you could see she was disappointed, and she left. That's all." "Nothing else?" "Yeah. She had nice legs, but a lousy voice."

"Initially, detectives had no luck in their attempts to trace Marie-Claire's movements after leaving the parking lot of the Zanzibar. Then, thanks to the conspicuous color of her convertible, they got an unexpected break. A woman reported to them that she had seen the red car with a blonde in a purple dress at the wheel, on Monday night at a service station on Bates Avenue.

"What particularly interested the investigators was the fact that the gas station was only two blocks from the Malibu and three blocks from the vacant field or lot where Marie-Claire's body was found.

"Police interrogated the owner of the station, Arthur Hitchcock, and his employees. They learned that the night before a new employee, H. Ronald Anthony, had been on duty. Anthony, lanky with a flat-top hairdo, had closed the station at midnight, on schedule, and on Tuesday had reported for work as usual."

The next morning, Anthony is brought in for arraignment. His wrists are handcuffed to the belt of his blue coveralls, he answers the questions that are put to him calmly and in a firm voice.

"At the hearing the assistant manager of the station reported that Anthony had worked the 2 p.m.-to-midnight shift. On Tuesday, the assistant manager had noticed one unusual thing. The clock in the gas station had stopped at 2:30. Then, on the following day, he had discovered that a tool—a punch—was missing from the station. He described it as about a foot long, ¾ of an inch square at the top and tapering down to about ¼ of an inch.

"And, he also testified, the station owner had called his attention to dark reddish smudges, apparently dried blood. They were on the wall near the clock, on the back of a company truck and on a tire. This macabre testimony," the reporter goes on, apparently feeling duty-bound after all this time to disassociate himself or herself from the ugliness and brutality in which he or she's imprisoned his or her readers, "was expounded on by a criminologist attached to the sheriff's office and who is qualified as an expert in the field of human blood.

"At the service station, he testified, he had detected spots of dried blood near the clock, in a rear washroom and on either side of the door frame, on a broom handle and on a hoist used to lift cars. He also had found wet blood in a drain, and he estimated that large amounts—at least a pint—had been poured down the drain.

"In the tongue well of the black boots that Anthony had been wearing, the expert witness told the court, there also had been blood. More, he disclosed that the plastic window which had been torn off Miss Janicek's car bore bootprints—and he linked the prints to Anthony's boots.

"The implication was that Marie-Claire was murdered in the garage, perhaps in the rest room, and then was later dumped into the vacant field."

It may seem to Elizabeth that the article is never going to end, the reporter and the readers of the supplement can't get enough of the technical details of this more-or-less conventionally senseless crime, with its melodramatic roots in Marie-Claire's aspirations, her depression, her poor childhood, the psychotic background of the murderer, which is also developed at great length . . . It comes as no surprise that he lives alone with his mother in an old frame house, that 8 or 12 years ago, when he was a marine stationed in Korea or something like that, he slit the throat of or strangled a barmaid after 12 seconds of making out . . . The evidence was flimsy, his mother pleaded with the court, he was given a relatively short sentence and so on . . . Everything fits into place: even chance plays its fore-ordained role and Marie-Claire's aspirations and disappointment, in the guise of a tail light that may or may not be on the blink, drives her into the isolated garage at the moment when the psychotic marine is alone in the station . . . Nothing is omitted, as if everyone had rehearsed his role for 1000 years.

All that's left is for the murderer to offer an explanation in his own words, no matter how irrational. Then everything will fall perfectly into place, the reporter will have done his or her job of piecing together a machine of psychological and circumstantial necessity that works to our satisfaction, and which comes to a definite end. The ex-Marine is therefore questioned, perhaps in court, and he responds satisfactorily:

"When she first drove her orange sports car into the station, I saw her pretty legs. The impulse to have relations with her was very strong. I hadn't touched a woman since that girl in Korea. This girl in the car was a lovely, warm person, I could see that right away. I could see the possiblity of romance. I looked into her eyes and saw the woman I had always waited for.

"I grabbed her by the arm and she sorta let out a gasp. 'Don't say anything,' I told her, 'or I'll kill you.' I kept her in the garage, but she tried awful hard to get out. I remember one time, after I'd taken off her clothes and beaten her and choked her pretty bad, she still tried to crawl out. I was surprised. So I had to find ways to keep her quiet so I could wait on customers. After I strangled her again it still looked to me like she was alive. She had a smile on her lips and seemed to be trying to tell me something. She had a secret. I suddenly realized the truth about myself and this truth was the only thing—that she wanted me to kill her."

Does anything else happen, or is it possible that this ugly story is the end of the road, Elizabeth fades into the murdered Marie-Claire Janicek, or perhaps the story is really American, it's been adapted for a European audience and the girl's name is Marian Crane or Marie Samuels . . . Walter may come in, drop into a chair, pick up a copy of something like *The German Journal of Conservation* or *The Modern Surgeon's Newsletter*. Minutes pass, the two of them sit there reading, there ought to be a fan that winds times into circles and distributes them throughout 100 years or 1,000,000 miles of space.

Walter looks up from his magazine and says sympathetically or analytically:

"You're bored, aren't you?"

"Is that the way it seems to you?"

He doesn't answer, and may even return to his magazine. He's reading an article about a river in South America. It seems that if a dam is constructed according to plans developed by local politicans and foreign industrial interests, the valley will be flooded like a bathtub, thousands will be homeless, in fact it will take no more than days or weeks for an entire sub-civilization to be lost forever, as if it had existed 2000 years ago . . . After a few minutes he renews his efforts.

"Have you ever thought how fascinating it would be if we could all change places?"

Elizabeth says uncomprehendingly that she doesn't understand. "Do you mean the four or us, or everyone?"

"Everyone, the four of us, it doesn't matter. It would be like one of those comedies, say *Twelfth Night, or What You Will*, where a pretty girl has a twin brother, she's in love with her lord, the Duke of Naples, but the Duke is in love with a certain lady, he disguises the girl as a boy and sends her to the lady's palace, to worm her way into her confidence somehow and find out who she loves or something like that . . . The lady falls in love with her . . . Meanwhile the twin brother gets mixed up in it somehow . . . If William and I could change places, it would be just the same, like a play . . ."

"What makes you think William will go for it?"

"No problem there, really."

"And me? Did it occur to you there might be a problem there, that you might not be the answer to my prayers?"

He laughs, says that he's surprised she fell for it, he was just pulling her leg . . . It's just that he's sometimes thought that nothing is more melancholy than literature in the face of life; unless it's life in the face of literature . . . Time is so short, one is never allowed to explore life's real depths . . . The only way out is for invention to be able, *actually*, to pass over into reality and reality into invention . . . To wish or invent a circumstance, to fantasize and have it become actual . . . And conversely to actually pass into the printed page . . . He has certain fantasies for example he wishes would materialize and there are certain books he wishes he could pass into . . .

And would others be aware that they were being, let's say, actualized or absorbed into these fantasies . . .?

That's something he hasn't worked out. But offhand he thinks some intermediate state of awareness with loss-of-will would be best . . . Everyone subject absolutely to the will and imagination of everyone else, while absolutely retaining his personality . . .

Elizabeth may allow Walter to return to his magazine, she thinks of everything Walter and Ellen have told her about themselves and about each other, all their queer little theories and anecdotes, and may become frightened. She doesn't like Ellen. She goes to the window and is surprised to find that it's already growing dark, not only in the forest, but from one end of the universe to the other.

ᕐ ᕐ ᕐ

STEPPING BACK

fiction by KATHLEEN COLLINS

from STORY QUARTERLY

nominated by M.D. Elevitch

I'M NOT TRYING to flatter myself, but I was the first colored woman he ever seriously considered loving. I know I was. The first one who had the kind of savoir-faire he believed in so devoutly. The first one with class, style, poetry, taste, elegance, repartee and haute cuisine. Because, you know, a colored woman with class is still an exceptional creature; and a colored woman with class, style, poetry, taste, elegance, repartee *and* haute cuisine is an almost non-existent species. Then breeding possibilities are slight.

I myself have never known another one like me, not one with my subtle understanding of art, music, drama, food, people, places, ambience, climate, dress, timing, correctness . . . whatever. As if all forms of cultural underdevelopment had somehow passed me by. As if I took my racial heritage (so to speak) and molded it to my spirit . . . then I emerged out of my cocoon like some new breed of butterfly.

I don't mean to go on like this but when people say to me "You don't know yourself to be colored! Don't you ever remember that you're black?" it makes me pause. I turn to my journal and devote pages to reminding myself that I am a colored lady. I try and bring myself up short. But again and again I am astonished at how uncolored I really am.

So I know it astonished him even more. At first he kept setting little traps for me. He would rattle on about Baudelaire and expect me to sit blankly by, bobbing my head. He would lay out his best china and silverware and watch while I set the table for a formal dinner. He took me to chic little intellectual gatherings and watched for signs of slovenliness . . . overindulgence in laughter, incorrect pronunciation, insensitivity in a delicate and nuanced situation . . . Always in the end he was baffled and enchanted by the effortlessness of my style, its unselfconscious elegance and flow, fitting so neatly into his mid-Victorian life, fitting so undemandingly into his careful cultivation of an elegant colored life.

There had been white women, of course, But that was too obvious. A too vulgar form of compensation. He did not like subjecting his cultivation to such overly sympathetic, such ingratiating discernment. The pain could destroy him, the humiliation crush a spirit already amputated by this reincarnation as a Negro. (Is it possible to imagine any greater amputation, any greater karmic debt than reincarnation as a Negro? And to make matters worse, a Negro with aristocratic tendencies, left over, of course . . . there is always some residue carried over from life to life.) But white women were out.

Instead he cultivated a kind of boyish asexuality, charming to men and women alike. At our first meeting he charmed me, too. Adolescently debonair with his clear lightly colored skin and his soft eyes. We lunched on the terrace of the Museum of Modern Art, allowing each other to perceive our distinctive tastes in books, films, music, theatre . . . whatever. We smiled frequently at each other, as if there were sufficient grounds for a truce.

The following week he invited me to his home for dinner. I imagined a simple country place with rustic charm, perhaps a few stuffed moose over the fireplace.

Nothing could have prepared me for the splendor in which he lived. That he should pass his hours amongst ancient treasures, Grecian busts, Italian neo-classical paintings, velvet mid-Victorian couches, shimmering gold candelabra—almost undid me. A hair's-breadth of a colored impulse escaped. I said, "Ain't this a blip!" but caught the words as they tumbled forth and coated them with charm. He appreciated the nuance and was delighted.

I made him *Coquilles St. Jacques* for dinner with a bottle of *Pouilly-Fuisse* (1970) and crepes filled with fresh strawberries for desert. A Botticelli painting flickered elegantly in the candlelight.

After dinner we took a stroll through the gardens and down to the river. The moon was full. His black crinkly hair glistened. He seemed more debonair, more boyish than ever. We kissed. No unpleasant tongue-kiss, either . . . no over moist search-and-seizure salivating the upper reaches of my throat. He focused on my lips, parted them softly, held it for a moment, then let go. Only to begin again this soft effortless contact. We stood a long while under the trellis. Where yellow roses bloom in Spring. Giving soft kisses.

It was delightful. Entrancing. Until my breasts began to tingle. I tried to imagine passing with him into the deep Heathcliffian gloom of his bedroom. I tried to imagine being lifted onto the splendid four-poster bed and undressed. My breasts stung. I longed to feel his fingers pull at them. Instead I caught myself stepping back. Retreating. In the face of our delicacy, our . . . how could I occupy the splendid four-poster bed? Tastefully enough. How could I pass beneath the candelabra and undress? Tastefully enough. And make love? Tastefully enough? No colored woman could. No colored woman could. No colored woman could.

BATHROOM WALLS

by MAURA STANTON

from PLOUGHSHARES

nominated by PLOUGHSHARES and *Raymond Carver*

A woman sobs on the toilet.
Hearing her through the wall,
I imagine the pink lace
unraveled from her nightgown
as she strokes her knees.
Upstairs there's a pop.
I suppose a retired barber
spread lather on a balloon
to test his swollen hands;
now he'll hang himself.
No, perhaps two teenagers
shyly undressing for love
with their backs to the mirror
each blew a final bubble.
Somewhere I hear glass breaking.
Of course it's the barber's
bifocals shattered in the sink
as he ties rope to a pipe.
Or is it the teenage girl
who smashed her mirror,
tossing her head in passion,
so that glass fragments fall
over her breasts in facets,
dazzling her lover's eyes
one moment before she bleeds?
You see, I think a man sleeps
downstairs in the bathtub;
when he hears my footsteps,

he thinks I'm someone,
like his grandmother, who darns
socks in her bathroom all night
because the light's brightest.
In his dream I stitch water.
In my dream drops accumulate
until his head goes under.

A COMFORT SPELL

by MAXINE SILVERMAN

from SUNBURY

nominated by Michael Lally

I
My father's teeth gap slightly.
Easy to spit seeds,
a natural grace.

II
"Pa," I write, "I'm low."
"Better soon," he swears. "Soon. Soon.
You're talkin to one who knows."

Lord, it's nearly time. October.
He'll pick some leaves off our sugar maples,
pressed, send them to New York.
Flat dry leaves,
and rusty rich.
Pa stays in Missouri,
bets the underdog each tv game,
and the home team, there or away.
"Lord," he whistles through his teeth,
"that boy's a runnin fool. Mercy me."

He names himself:
Patrick O'Silverman,
one of the fightinest!

Melancholy crowds him spring and fall,
regular
seasonal despair,
his brain shocked, his smile fraught with prayer.

I offer what remains of my childhood.
I offer up this comfort spell.

Whoever you are, run in nearly morning
to the center of the park.
There, rooted in the season,
maples send out flame.
Gather you to the river the furious leaf.
Mercy
Mercy Buck Up
Mercy Me
Mercy
Mercy Buck Up
Mercy Me

"Pa," I call, "what's new?"
"Nothin much. We're gettin on."

"Pa" I sing, "your leaves came today."
"Oh Maggie," he cries, "just want
to share the fall."

EMBARKMENT

by HUGH SEIDMAN

from PEQUOD

nominated by Jonathan Galassi

Is this yet to be the freight of Claude Lorraine

The gold of Sheba for a king's ennui
before his thousand wives and concubines
across the archaic night sea

Is this yet to be the anachronous Greek cartoon
calipered to the columns' groove

Are these sunbursts yet to be the blind
scapels that would sign
below the breasts of the fleshed sky
to fit the heart into the body to survive

Oh surely I do not like to care or to not care
that the passage of the soul
takes on some second-rate nubile queen

Altho I do not seem to turn the blade
from the prose of these rapes and revulsions

Perhaps it is how steel must remember the vein
or how sleep must unwind the bandages of the Pharaohs
who refuse to die
unclaimed as the shadows on their stones

But is this yet to be the reply
to the body drugged under the dawn as if alive
as the clouds ride slowly thru the rooms

Is this yet to be the verdict under the ductile beams

That a slave must be chained into the ribs
to beat like the heart of the figurehead
whose nipples spread the waves of that sea

That a rower must sweat under the sun's day in the hold
so that she can sail in the dream
on the dream of that sea

WHORES

fiction by JAMES CRUMLEY

from THE CALIFORNIA QUARTERLY

nominated by Raymond Carver and Joyce Carol Oates

I

ON LONG SUMMER AFTERNOONS when our idle time lay as heavily upon our minds and lives as the torpid South Texas air, often my friend and colleague, Lacy Harris, and I would happen to glance across our narrow office into each other's eyes. Usually we simply stared at each other, like two strangers who have wandered into an empty room at a party, ashamed of solitude among mirth, then we turned back to the disorderly stacks of freshman themes, heaped uncorrected upon our desks. Occasionally, though, the stares held;

one would shrug, the other suggest a beer, and in silence we would rise and go out, seeking a dark and calm beer joint.

Sometimes French's, a place south of town, where a cool highyellow bartender, Raoul, let us bask in the breeze of his chatter, as ceaseless and pleasant as the damp draft roaring from the old fashioned water-cooled window fan. Sometimes the Tropicana to joust with an obtuse pinball machine called the Merry Widow, while off-shift roughnecks slept drunk at the various tables scattered among the fake tropical greenery. Easy afternoons, more pleasant and possible than hiding in the air conditioned cage of our office, where the silences had no meaning. Dusty air, dark bars. Outside, the sun, white hot upon the caliche or shell parking lots, reminding us how pleasant the idle afternoon. Dim bars, cold beers, our mutual silence for company. Harmless.

Or so they'd seem until I'd catch Lacy's hooded blue eyes slipping toward the heated doorway. His wife, Marsha, was already prowling the town like a lost tourist, looking for him in the bars. Almost always she found us. One moment the doorway would be empty, the next a slim shade stood quietly just inside, perhaps a glint of afternoon sunlight off her long blond hair. Somehow I always saw her first. When I said "Lacy," he never moved, so I would walk to Marsha, welcome her with the frightened ebullience of a guilty drunk. She seldom spoke; when she did, in a hushed murmur, too quiet for words. She moved around me to Lacy's side, slipped her hand into the sweaty bend of his elbow, led him away. At the doorway, framed in heated light, his face would turn back to me, an apologetically arched eyebrow raised.

On those rare occasions when she didn't find us, we drank until midnight, but without frenzy or drunkenness, as if the evening were merely the shank of the afternoon. Then I drove Lacy home, let him out in the bright yellow glare of his porch light. As he sauntered up the front walk, his hands cocked in his pockets, his head tilted gently back, his tall frame seemed relaxed, easy. A tuneless whistle, like the repeated fragment of a birdsong, warbled around his head as he approached that yellow light. At the steps he'd stop, wave once as if to signal his safe arrival, then go inside the screened porch. Sometimes, glancing over my shoulder as I drove away, I'd see him sitting on the flowered pillows of the porch swing, head down, hands clasped before him, waiting.

On the mornings after, he never spoke of the evenings before, no hangover jokes shared, never hinted of those moments before sleep alone with Marsha in their marriage bed. And on the odd chance that I saw Marsha later, no matter how carefully I searched that lovely, composed face, no matter how hard I peered beneath her careful makeup, I caught no glimpse of anger. Unlike most of my married friends, the Harris' kept their marriage closed from view, as if secrecy were a vow. Aside from her sudden intrusions into our afternoons, his too casual saunter toward the bug light, as casual as a man mounting a gallows, and a single generality he let slip one night—"Never marry a woman you love"—I knew nothing about their marriage.

On rare and infrequent summer afternoons, when the immense boredom that rules my life stroked me like a cat and the heavy stir of desire rose like a sleepy beast within me, when our eyes met, I would say *Mexico*, as if it were a charmed word, and Lacy would grin instead of greeting me with a wry smile, a boy's grin, and I could see his boy's face, damp and red after a basketball game, expectant. On those afternoons, we'd fill a thermos with gin and tonics, climb into my restored 1949 Cadillac, and head for the border, bordertown whorehouses, the afternoon promenade of Nuevo Laredo whores coming to work at the Rumba Casino or the Miramir or the Malibu, the Diamond Azul or Papagayo's.

Perhaps it was the gin, or the memory of his single trip to Nuevo Laredo after a state basketball tournament, whatever, he maintained that grin, as he did his silences, all the way across the dry brush country of South Texas, my old Caddy as smooth as a barge. Or perhaps it was the thought of Marsha driving from bar to bar, circling Knight until full dark, then going home without him. He never went intending to partake of the pleasures, just for the parade.

Sometimes it seemed the saddest part, sometimes the most pathetic, sometimes the most exciting: the dreadful normalcy of the giggling girls. Dressed in jeans and men's shirts knotted above their brown dimpled bellies, they carried their working clothes, ruffled froth or slimy satin, draped over their young and tender shoulders. Although they chattered in Spanish, they had the voices of Texas highschool girls, the concerns of highschool girls. Dreadfully normal, god love them, untouched by their work, innocent until dark.

Occasionally, because I knew the girls more intimately than Lacy —unlike him, I'd never married either the loved or unloved—I could convince one or two to sit with us a moment before they changed clothes. But not too often. They seemed shy, unprotected out of their whoredresses, like virgins caught naked. If the mood seemed right, the shyness touching instead of posed, I'd have one then, slaking my studied boredom on an afternoon whore as the sun slanted into the empty room. Afterwards, Lacy often said, "I'll have to try that again. Someday." I always answered, as if wives were the antithesis of whores, "You've no need. You've a lovely wife at home." To which he replied, "Yes, that's true. But someday, some summer afternoon, I'll join you . . ." His soft East Texas accent would quaver like a mournful bird call, and a longing so immense that even I felt it would move over him. Even then I knew he'd want more than money could buy.

Most whores in Nuevo Laredo are carefully cloistered in a section of the city called, appropriately, Boys Town, a shabby place with raucous bars spaced among the sidewalk cribs, but the better-class whores worked in the clubs we frequented, outside of Boys Town. By *better-class* I don't mean more practiced, for Mexican whores don't German. I mean more expensive, less sullied by the hard life. More often than not, they're just good old working girls, pleasant and unhurried in bed, not greedy, and sometimes willing to have fun, to talk seriously. Many were sold into the business as young girls, many are married, making the most of a bad life. And then there are the rare ones, girls a man can fall in love with, though I never did, never will. Whores help me avoid the complexities of love, for which I am justly grateful. But even I have been tempted by the rare ones. Tempted.

One afternoon in Papagayo's in the blessed stillness after the parade—the waterfall silent, the jukebox dead—Lacy and I sipped our Tecate's. A moist heat had beaten the old air conditioners. Behind the bar one bartender sliced limes so slowly that he seemed hardly to move; the other slept at the end of the bar, his head propped on his upright arm. Lacy's whistle seemed to hover about us like a swarm of gnats. All of us composed, it seemed, for a tropical still life, or the opening act of a Tennessee Williams play. Absolute stasis. And when Elena came in, moving so slowly that she seemed not even to stir the hot air with her passing, she seemed to hold that moment with her lush body. As I turned my head, like some ancient sleepy turtle, she too turned hers toward me. A slack indifferent beauty, eyes always on the verge of sleep, the sort of soft full body over which frenzy would never leap. Otiosity sublime. Surely for a man to come in her would be to come already asleep.

I clicked my Tecate can lightly on the tile bar as she eased past us. The sleeping bartender, knowing my habits, looked up. I nodded, he asked her if she would join us for a drink. Halting like a tanker coming into dock, she nodded too, her eyes closing as she lowered her head. A life of indolence is really a search, I thought, a quest for that perfect place to place one's head, to sleep, to dream . . . but behind me, Lacy whispered, "This one, Walter." So I let her go. Walter Savage, perfect languor. Habits can be restrained; passions should not.

After the preliminaries, an overpriced weak brandy, an unbargained price—local airmen had ruined the tradition—Lacy left with his prize ship, walking away as casually as he wandered into the force of that yellow porch light, hands pocketed, loafers shuffling, head back, his aimless whistle. But as he held the door for Elena with one hand, the other cradled itself against her ample waist. I meant to warn him, but in the languorous moment all I could think was, "You've a lovely wife at home," and that seemed silly, the effort too much.

They were gone quite a time, longer than his money had purchased, so I knew it had to be an amazing passion, impotence, or death. Afternoon slipped into evening, the waterfall began flushing. Two students from the college came timidly in, then left when they recognized me. The girls returned in bright plumage. I took the gaudiest one, ruffled her as best I could, but when I came back, Lacy hadn't returned. The bartender cast me a slimy smile. I drank.

When Lacy finally came back, Papagayo's hummed with all the efficiency of a well-tuned engine, and I would have stayed to watch the dance, but Lacy said, "Let's go."

"Why?" Though I could guess.

Hesitating, unable to meet my eyes, he shook himself as if with anger, a flush troubling his pale face. Then he answered, "I don't want to see her working."

Not just impotence, but love, I thought, wanting to laugh.

More silent than usual on the trip back, he drank beer after beer, staring at the gray asphalt unwinding before us. Outside of Falfurrias, I ventured, "Impotent?" To which he answered, with hesitation, "Yes."

"It happens," I said, "Guilt before the deed. With whores and wives and random pieces . . ."

"Don't," he said, almost pleading.

"Hey, it doesn't matter."

"Yes," he whispered, "I know."

When I dropped him at his house, he said goodnight, then walked into that yellow haze quickly, as if he had unfinished business.

During the twenty years or so I've been beating love with border-town whoring, I've had it happen to me—drink or boredom or simple grief—and I knew most of the techniques with which whores handled the problem. Those who took simple pride in their work, those honest tradeswomen of the flesh, usually gave the customer his best chance, along with motherly comfort and no advice except to relax. Then they would try to laugh it off. Others, working just for the money and those few natively cruel, would pointedly ignore or even scoff at the flaccid gringo member. Or, as happened to me once, they would act terribly frightened, whimpering as if caged with a snake or a scorpion instead of a useless man, occasionally peeking out of the corners of their sly brown eyes to see if you'd left yet. Whatever the act was meant to do, it did. Perhaps because of my youth, when it happened to me, it kept me away from the whores for months, nearly caused me the grief of marriage with a rather chubby woman who taught Shakespeare very badly.

But Elena did none of those things. She was after all only a child, in spite of that woman's body, so she just started talking aimlessly, in her child's voice, winding her black hair with her fingers. What she did was, of course, more cruel: she talked to him, told him about her life. The dusty adobe on the Sonoran desert, the clutch of too many children, both alive and dead, the vast empty spaces of desert and poverty. When their time was up, he asked if he might pay for more, to which she shrugged, lifted a shoulder, cocked an eye at his member. And she answered, *why not*, she covered her breasts with a dingy sheet and smiled at him. God knows what she had in mind. When I told her, months later, of his death, she also shrugged at me, slipping into her dress.

Although Lacy and I were both in our thirties and both knew that, except for a miracle, we were going to ease out the rest of our academic careers at South Texas State trying to make them as painless as possible, I accepted my failure more gracefully than he. I'd been born in Knight, still lived in a converted garage behind my parents' house, and I taught because it was a respectable way to waste one's life. Unlike my mother's attachment to morphine and my father's to the American Conservative Party, teaching is respectable. The salary may be insulting, the intellectual rewards negligible, but when I tried doing nothing at all, the boredom drove me to drink. So I teach, my U.T. PhD a ticket to a peaceful life.

But Lacy, like so many bright, energetic young men, once had a future. Articles published in proper journals, one short story in a prestigious quarterly, an eastern degree, that sort of thing. And he came to South Texas State for the money, just for the money. When he came, he thought that, like a boulder tumbling down a hillside, he had only lodged for a moment, a winter's rest perhaps, and when spring came with heavy rains, he would be on his way once again. By the time he realized that no more showers were going to fall, he had been captured by the stillness, the heavy subtropical heat, the endless unchanging days of sun and dust. He hadn't accepted his defeat, but it didn't matter. By the time of this last summer, he had stopped writing letters of inquiry, had ditched his current Blake article, replacing somehow his fiery vision with Elena.

II

They say the second acts of all boring plays take place at parties, where truth looms out of the drunkenness with all the relentless force of a tidal wave. But in Knight the parties were dull, deadly dull, and whatever shouted insults rose above the crowd like clenched fists, whatever wives were hotly fondled by whomever in dark closets or under the fluorescent glare of kitchen lights, were beside the point. The truth lay in the burnished dullness, not in the desperate cries of hands clutching at strangely familiar bodies. The last party at the Harris' seemed no different, perhaps was no different, despite the death of our chairman.

Even Lacy had risen from his torpor long enough to become a bore. Each time he found me near enough to Marsha for her to overhear him, he would remind me loudly of our golf game the next day, suggesting earlier and earlier tee-offs. But he had El Papagayo's in mind, not golf. We had been back three or four times in less than a month, more often than was my habit, and his love remained unconsummated. He had passed through acceptance to sorrow to rage, and on quiet midnights in my apartment I had begun to think of Lacy and Marsha abed, he cursing his errant virility, she pliant upon their bed. His untoward passion had begun also to disturb the tranquillity of my life, and when he reminded me about our golf game the fifth or sixth time, I answered querulously, "I don't think I'll play tomorrow, I think I'll go to Mexico and get fucked." Then I left him, his stricken face like a painted balloon above the crowd.

It was then I noticed our chairman, a pleasant old gentlemanly widower who asked no more of life than I did, leaving the party. He wore a tweed jacket, as if fall in South Texas were autumn in Ithaca, that smelled lightly of pipe smoke, paper, and burning leaves. We chatted a moment, the usual graceful nothing, then bid each other good night. He suffered a coronary thrombosis just off the porch and crawled under the oleander bush at the corner of the Harris' house; slipped away to die, I like to think, without disturbing anyone. The party continued, somewhat relieved by his absence, until those wee dumb hours of the morning. Shortly before noon the next day, Marsha found him as she worked in the flower beds. On his side, his head cradled upon his clenched hands, he knees lifted toward his chest, the rictus of a smile delicate across his stubbled face, the faint stink of decomposition already ripe among the dusty oleander leaves. She brushed bits of grass and dirt from his face as she knelt beside him; she began crying and did not stop.

In an ideal, orderly world, on this day Lacy would have performed his necessary act, a final act of passion before we went home to his mad wife, but the world is neither ideal nor orderly, as the life we forge from the chaos must be. Elena, who was I can attest a very dull girl despite her interesting beauty, decided that day to become interested in Lacy's failure. She no longer babbled about her past but promised to cure his problem, if not with her antics, then surely with a *curanderas potion*. Of course, neither worked, and Lacy's life was complicated for the next month with an infernal dose of diarrhea. Even now, even in my grief, I know he deserved no better.

When he returned that night, we both noticed the absence of the porch light. He took it as a favorable omen, I thought it an oversight. Even as I unlocked my apartment door—unlike most folk in Knight, I lock my door; I have a small fortune in medieval tapestries and Chinese porcelain, two original Orozoco's—the telephone's shrill cry shattered the night. Lacy.

After the bodies had been disposed of, our chairman's beside his wife, Marsha into a Galveston hospital, instead of driving Lacy back to Knight, I made him stop with me in Houston, not so much to cheer him up as to hold him away from the scene of disaster for a few days. We stayed at the Warwick, drank at the nicest private clubs, where my father's money and name bought us privacy. Finally, on our third night, as we were sipping scotch at the Coronado Club, our nerves uneasy in their sheaths from seventy-two hours of waking and sleeping drunk, Lacy began to talk, to fill in the gaps, as if by breaking his silence, he could restore his shattered life.

His mother, as she often said, had made only one mistake in her life, she'd fallen in love with a Texas man and followed him out of Georgia and into exile in East Texas. In exile her native gentility grew aggressive, proud. No girls in Tyler met her standards, none quite good enough for Lacy, so except for one wild trip after a basketball tournament his senior year, a single fling to the border, Lacy knew nothing of girls. Where he found the courage to remove his clothes before a strange dark woman in a dank cubicle behind the 1-2-3 Club, and how he overcame his disgust long enough to place his anointed body upon hers, I'll never know. What guilt he suffered, those days he carried himself carefully around Tyler as if a sudden knock would unman him, he never said. I like to think of that first time, Lacy's body lean and as glossily hard as a basketball court, yet tender, vulnerable with innocence, a tee-shirt as white as his buttocks, flapping as he humped, his wool athletic socks crumpled about his ankles, his soul focused on the dark, puffy belly of a middleaged whore with an old-fashioned appendix scar like a gully up the center of her stomach.

In college, his career as young-man-about-campus kept him so busy that girls were just another necessary accessory, like his diamond-chip KA pin, his scuffed bucks and chinos with a belt in the back, and it wasn't until he began graduate school at Duke, where all the other teaching assistants seemed to have thin, reposed women at their elbows, that he discovered the absence of women in his life. Then too he looked over a freshman composition class and mistook that dark quietness in Marsha Long's wide eyes for intelligence, mistook her silence for repose.

The brief courtship could only be described as whirlwind, the wind of his stifled passion whirling around her pliant young body. Surprised that she wasn't virgin, he forgave her nonetheless, then confessed his single transgression in Mexico. Marsha nodded wisely, just as she did when he suggested marriage, expecting her to hold out for magnolia blossoms and fourteen bridesmaids. But she didn't.

They were married by a crossroads justice of the peace on the way to South Carolina to tell her parents.

They lived on the old family plantation on the Black River in a columned house right off a postcard, and as he drove up the circular way, Lacy thought how pleased his mother would be. But inside the house he found an old woman, perfumed and painted like a crinolined doll, who called him by any name but his own and confused Marsha with her long dead sister. In Marsha's father's regal face he saw her beauty, larded with bourbon fat. Everywhere he turned, each fact—black, white, or whitetrash—every face on the place had the same long straight nose, the broad mouth, the wide dark eyes. Only the blacks still carried enough viable intelligence in their genes to maintain some semblance of order. Marsha cried ten solid hours their first night, only shaking her head when he inquired as to why. By dawn he expected a black mammy to waddle in from the wings and comfort the both of them, but none came. At break-fast, Marsha had redrawn her face, and stare as he might through his own haggard eyes, he could see neither hint nor sign of whatever endless grief lay beneath her silence.

They left later that morning, since nobody seemed to mind. Mr. Long ran wildly out of the house, spilling whiskey, and Lacy, fearing now for both sanity and life, just drove on. But he heard the shouted, "Congratulations, son." He looked at this mad child, now his wife, seeing her now, dumb, painted, pliant. Perverse marriage vows followed; he made her silence his, vowed to love her.

"They were so old, old enough to be her grandparents, they didn't have her until they were in their forties. God knows what her childhood must have been like, locked on a movie set with those mad people, and every face she saw for ten miles in any direction, every club-foot, hump-back, cross-eyed genetic disaster, was her face. She thought she was ugly. You know that, ugly. In all the years we were married I saw her without make-up just twice. Once, when she had the flu so badly that she couldn't even crawl to the mirror. I found her like that, on her goddamned hands and knees, mewling and crying and holding back the vomit with clenched teeth. When I tried to carry her back to bed, she fought me like a madwo . . . fought like a wildcat, hiding her face from me as if she'd die if I saw her . . . Listen, I shouldn't be here, I should be back in that room, room, shit, cage with her. She needs me, she needed me and I wasn't there . . . And all those niggers in that house, so goddamned servile, so smug butter wouldn't melt in their assholes. Listen, drive me back to Galveston, will you? This isn't helping."

I led him out of the club, holding his elbow as if he were an elderly uncle. And it had helped. In the car he slept, quiet, not mumbling or twisting or springing awake. Slept really for the first time in days. I checked us out of the Warwick, drove us back to Knight on benzedrine—bordertown whorehouses are filled with more vices than those of the flesh. When I woke him in front of his house, dawn flushed the unclouded sky as birds chittered in the mimosa trees of his yard. He mumbled a simple thanks, grabbed his grip, and went into this empty house, his toneless whistle faint among birdsong. I thought he'd be all right.

III

He seemed all right for the next few months, more silent perhaps, uninterested in afternoons at French's or jousting with the Merry Widow, but accepting his life on its own terms. I hadn't the heart to suggest a trip to Nuevo Laredo, and Lacy didn't invite me to accompany him on the frequent weekends he spent in Galveston. So we began to see less of each other. He had his grief, I had a spurt of ambition and energy that threatened to destroy my wasted life. I handled it, as usual, by spending a great deal of my father's ill-gotten money. Christmas in Puerto Vallerta. An antique Edwardian sofa. Two Ung Cheng saucers in *famille rose* that made my father take notice of me and suggest that I was worse than worthless, expensively worthless. I even gave a party, a Sunday morning champagne breakfast, fresh strawberries, caviar, an excellent brie, and although Lacy didn't come, those good folk who did, didn't make church services that morning, not even that night. For reasons beyond me, I made the mistake of resuming my affair with my chubby Shakespearian, an affair it took me until spring to resign.

Spring in South Texas lacks the verdant burst of those parts of the world that experience winter, lacks even the blatant flowering of the desert, but it has its moments. A gentle mist of yellow falls upon the thorned *huisache;* tiny blossoms, smaller than the hooked thorns of the cat-claws, appear briefly; and the ripe flowers of the pricklypear, like bloody wounds, begin to emerge. And the bluebonnets, sown by a grim and greedy highway department, fill the flat roadside ditches.

On a Sunday when he hadn't gone to visit Marsha, I took Lacy out into the brush country north and east of Alice to show him the small clues of our slight season. But it only works for those who take pride in the narrowness of their vision, who stubbornly resist boredom, whatever the cost. By one o'clock we were drunk in the poolhall in Conception, by three, drinking margaritas at Dutch's across the border in Reynosa, at seven, stumbling into the waterfall hush of Papagayo's in Nuevo Laredo, giggling like schoolboys.

Lacy, standing straight, asked loudly for Elena, but she wasn't working that night, so he collapsed into his chair, morose and silent for the first time that day. I, ever-present nurse and shade, bought him the two most expensive girls in the place, sent him with them to find Elena's room. *Dos mujeres de la noche.* Where love had failed, some grand perversion might work.

And of course it did. When we met at the dry fountain in the courtyard afterwards, Lacy had a bottle of Carta Blanca in each hand, a whore under each arm, his shirt open to the waist, and a wild grin smack on his face.
"Hey, you old son-of-a-bitch, you set this whole fuckin' thing up, didn't you?"

I smiled in return, trying to look sly, but failing. My eyes wouldn't focus. "I'm responsible," I said. "How was it?"

"Ohhh, shit, wonderful," he said, stumbling sideways, his two ladies holding him up with a patient grace that my father's money hadn't purchased. "Listen," he said to them, "I want you to meet my best friend in the whole damned world, he's a good old boy." He lifted his arm from the right one's red satin shoulders, gathered me into his fierce grasp. "Stood by me, held me up, laid me down, introduced me to the woman I love . . ."

"We've met," I said, putting my arm around the abandoned whore. Her skin, warm and sweaty from the bed, smelled like all those things that men seek from whores: almonds and limes, dusty nights, cheap gin, anonymous love. I buried my face in her neck, had a moment's vision in which I bought both girls and fled south across the desert toward some other pleasantly idle life, a Yucatan beach, a mountain village, Egypt. But even as it came, it passed like a night wind. Lacy began to shout and shuffle our circle around.

"Ohhhh, what a great fucking night." The girls slipped out of the circle, whores again, leaving the two of us. Lacy hugged me until my breath faltered, repeating, as if it were a litany, "Ol' buddy, Ol' buddy, little ol' buddy."

It had been years since I'd been frightened by a man's embrace, or ashamed, or I must add in all honesty, aroused, but Lacy held me with such a fierce love, so much drunken power and love, that I clutched him, hugged him back, and for a few seconds we whirled, stumbling about the dark courtyard. Then—perhaps he thought it a disgusting revelation, perhaps he responded, I'll never know—he flung me from him as if I were a sack of dirty laundry. My knees hit the fountain wall, my head the fountain.

IV

The next morning I woke in the back seat of my car, not a great deal worse for the night. A bit stiff and sore, but no more. Because I am terribly responsible about the way I exhaust my life, I cleaned up, made a thermos of bloody mary's and went to my office. Lacy was already there.

"Listen," he said as I sat down, "I'm sorry."

"Hey, it doesn't matter."

"I know, I know."

He smiled once, nearly grinned, then raised his hand and left the office, walking with a bounce and energy that I'd never seen, striding as he must have onto the hardwood courts of his youth. I never saw him again. Elena says he was drunk, but I doubt it. She thinks he was drunk because of the wad of bills he offered her to flee across the border with him, because of the wonderful grin on his face.

"Did he make it?" I asked.

She shrugged again, not knowing what I meant until I showed her. Then her whore's face brightened, like a cheerleader's welcoming home a winner. "*Bueno*," she said, "*Muy bueno.*"

I tried to excuse her, telling myself that the craft of whoredom is lying; I tried to excuse myself, blaming my grief. But it didn't work. I paid her for another time, and as she slipped out of her yellow dress, she shrugged once again, as if to say *who knows about these gringo men.* Inside her, I slapped her dull face until she cried, until I came.

I don't go back to Nuevo Laredo anymore: I satisfy my needs up or down the border. Of late my needs are fewer. I visit Marsha occasionally. We sit in her room, I talk, she nods over the doll they've given her. Her parents would rather have her back than pay for her keep, so I pay; that is, my father pays. Even in her gray hospital robe, without a trace of makeup left on her face, she is still lovely, so lovely I know why men speak of the face of an angel. She neither ages nor speaks; she rocks, she nods, she clutches her painted doll. I believe she's happy. When I told her about Lacy, just about the accident, not the cause, she smiled, as if she knew he were happy too. I didn't tell her that it took a cutting torch to remove his body from the car.

As they say, the living must live. I don't know. From my parents' house I can hear them living: my mother's television tuned to an afternoon soap opera, the volume all the way up to penetrate her morphine haze: in the kitchen my father is shouting at a congressman over the telephone. I don't know.

I'll marry my chubby Shakespearean, or somebody so much like her that the slight differences won't matter. I'll still go bordertown whoring, and it will never occur to her to complain. And we'll avoid children like the plague.

TWO STRANGE STORIES

fiction by ROBERT WALSER

from THE LOWLANDS REVIEW

nominated by THE LOWLANDS REVIEW

T̶HE MAN WITH THE PUMPKIN HEAD. Once there was a man and on his shoulders he had, instead of a head, a hollow pumpkin. This was no great help to him. Yet he still wanted to be Number One. That's the sort of person he was. —For a tongue he had an oakleaf hanging from his mouth, and his teeth were cut out with a knife. Instead of eyes he had just two round holes. Back of the holes two candle stumps flickered. Those were his eyes. They didn't help him see far. And yet he said his eyes were better than anyone's, the braggart. —On his pumpkin head he wore a tall hat; he used to take it off when anyone spoke to him, he was so polite. Once this man went for a walk. But the wind blew so hard that his eyes went out. He

wanted to light them up again, but he had no matches. He started to
cry with his candle ends, because he couldn't find his way home. So
now he sat there, held his pumpkin head between his hands, and
wanted to die. But dying didn't come to him so easily. First there had
to come a June bug, which ate the oakleaf from his mouth; there had
to come a bird, which pecked a hole in his pumpkin skull; there had
to come a child, who took away the two candle stumps. Then he
could die. The bug is still eating the leaf, the bird is pecking still, and
the child is playing with the candle stumps.

THE MAID.   A rich lady had a maid and this maid had to look after
her child. The child was as delicate as a moonbeam, pure as freshly
fallen snow, and as lovable as the sun. The maid loved the child as
much as she loved the moon, the sun, almost as much as her own
dear God himself. But one day the child got lost, nobody knew how,
and so the maid went looking for it, looked for it everywhere in the
world, in all the cities and countries, even Persia. Over there in
Persia the maid came one night to a broad dark tower, it stood by a
broad dark river. But high up in the tower a red light was burning,
and the faithful maid asked this light: Can you tell me where my
child is? It got lost and for ten years I have been looking for it. —
Then go on looking for another ten years, said the light, and it went
out. So the maid looked for the child another ten years, in all the
parts and on all the bypaths of the earth, even in France. In France
there is a great and splendid city, called Paris, and to this city she
came. One evening she stood by the entrance to a beautiful garden,
wept, because she could not find the child, and took out her red
handkerchief to wipe her eyes. Then suddenly the garden opened
and her child came out. She saw it and died of joy. Why did she die?
Did that do her any good? Yet she was old now and could not endure
so much any more. The child is now a grand and beautiful lady. If you
should ever meet her, give her my best regards.

translated by Christopher Middleton

🔥 🔥 🔥

MOTHERS

fiction by LYDIA DAVIS

from THE THIRTEENTH WOMAN (Living Hand Press)

nominated by Jonathan Galassi

EVERYONE HAS A MOTHER SOMEWHERE. There is a mother at
dinner with us. She is a small woman with eyeglass lenses so thick
that they seem black when she turns her head away. Then, the
mother of the hostess telephones as we are eating. This causes the
hostess to be away from the table longer than one would expect. This
mother may possibly be in New York. The mother of a guest is
mentioned in conversation: this mother is in Oregon, a state few of
us know anything about, though it has happened before that a
relative lived there. A choreographer is referred to afterwards, in
the car. He is spending the night in town, on his way, in fact, to see
his mother, again in another state.

Mothers, when they are guests at dinner, eat well, like children, but seem absent. It is often the case that they cannot follow what we are doing or saying. It is often the case, also, that they enter the conversation only when it turns on our youth; or they accommodate where accommodation is not wanted; smile and are misunderstood. And yet mothers are always seen, always talked to, even if only on holidays. They have suffered for our sakes, and always in a place where we could not see them.

🔥 🔥 🔥

DOING GOOD

by JOHN BALABAN

from THE HUDSON REVIEW

nominated by THE HUDSON REVIEW, Teo Savory, Grace Schulman, and Louise Simons

PERHAPS THE CRUELEST THING the North Vietnamese did to Americans, which we will hold against them even more bitterly than our defeat, is their failure, after their victory, to bathe South Vietnam in blood. We needed a bloodbath, for even though we had lost the war, we could say that we had tried to save our half of the country from barbarous slaughter. Now it is harder to excuse the horrible things which we did in Vietnam.

If we sanctioned evil acts because they seemed to serve a greater good, perhaps we ought to forget them. The war is over. We could forget them if only we weren't so capable of performing them again, for even at the close of the war, with still another President making the decisions, we confused doing good with our own vague self-interest and the result once again was further suffering for others and increased moral confusion for ourselves. When defeat was clear, we baby-lifted hundreds of infants to save them from communist barbarism. Children who were left temporarily in orphanages were packed off to the United States. Brothers and sisters were separated and sent to unaware families thousands of miles apart. We never asked ourselves how these Asian, Eurasian and black Asian children would fare as adolescents and adults. We needed them immediately, like extras in a movie. Two scenes from our last venture at doing good in Vietnam are memorable: President Ford cradling an infant at the door of an Air Force plane (which had flown into Vietnam with arms and had flown out with babies) and an Air Force medic "giving an orphan its first drink in the U.S." (by squirting a hypodermic of Coca-Cola into its open mouth). We jammed the telephone lines with our requests for these children; when the adults came, we didn't like it.

Vietnam confused us. Most of us meant well. I am still sorting out my own involvement which began one warm afternoon in the spring of 1967 when I returned to my apartment from Widener library and encountered circumstances which more or less urged me to go: Plodding along with bookbag weighted with Middle Scots and Old English texts—the focus of my attention during my first year of graduate study at Harvard—with eyes itchy in the sunlight and shoulders stooped from reading too much, I came across a large crowd outside of Lowell House. They were students mostly and they were waiting to speak to Secretary of Defense Robert McNamara, who was talking to a small group of undergraduates while in Cambridge as a guest of the new Kennedy Institute. At that time, you remember, the Johnson Administration still got away with saying very little about the war. On this occasion, McNamara had been petitioned to speak to the academic community, which in Boston, with its several hundred colleges and junior colleges, is quite large. To make his position easier, some of his fellow guests at the Institute offered to share a platform with him. He refused. When I got to Lowell House perhaps five hundred persons were milling about. An SDS fellow was haranguing the crowd with a bull horn, but generally it was pleasant and amiable. Far down Mt. Auburn Street a bedsheet with an unintelligible protest was hung from a third-story window.

The tune and some of the words of "Mack the Knife" floated towards the crowd.

When McNamara did emerge, it was from a side exit into a narrow street to which the crowd rushed and, perhaps unintentionally, blocked his car. The Secret Service looked menaced and started pushing people out of the way. I stood behind an ABC camera team where it seemed safe and looked at the Secretary as he sat in his car. After a few minutes he got out and got up on the roof of his car, buckling the roof with a crackle which he ignored. The crowd hushed. He said, "I'll give you four minutes, then I must leave." He began, "When I was a student in California, I was as radical as you." The crowd groaned. "But there was one difference . . . I was more polite." The crowd booed. Someone yelled, "Fuck you!" Another yelled, "Murderer!" The cameras whirred. The sound man winked triumphantly at the camera man. McNamara was helped down by an agent and was driven off. Harvard apologized publicly.

And so I can thank Harvard and McNamara for my going to Vietnam, for both in their contrary ways had aroused in me an interest in *veritas*. During the following week, filled with decision, I wrote a poem about my going which was printed in the *American Scholar*, renewed an application that I had made more than a year earlier with the International Voluntary Services, and, even more to the point, I began dickering with my Pennsylvania draft board about trading in my student deferment for a conscientious objector rating on terms that would allow me to work in Vietnam as a civilian and without supervision.

My draft board, a group of old men who seemed frightened that I might make a speech, hearing that I was dropping my student deferment to perform good works in Vietnam, made me a conscientious objector in a four-minute hearing taken up mostly by my stating my name, by my swearing on the Bible, and by my answering "yes" when asked if I really intended to go to Vietnam. My hearing was so short that I thought they had turned me down out of hand. I had constructed answers regarding the sanctity of all life above the bird level (I still fished, and hunted grouse), and I was ready to reply that the Supreme Being was a kind of gas permeating the universe with goodliness and creation, but they did not ask one question.

In July, 1967, I arrived in Vietnam. In a few months, I was to teach at the University of Can Tho in the Mekong Delta as a volunteer with the International Voluntary Services, a kind of peace corps hired by the U.S. Agency of International Development to teach English, hand out seeds, and to relocate refugees. On the ride into Saigon from Tan Son Nhut airport, my white suit, which clothed slim confidence, was grimed with crankcase oil from the floor bed of the truck that ferried sixty of us new volunteers to a suffocating dormitory on the outskirts of town where idle small arms fire riddled one's sleep from dusk to dawn. My comrades were very keen on helping Vietnamese and seemed to suffer from none of the ambiguities that were aroused in me at the sight of all those ammo dumps and fighter-bombers at the airport; my comrades were missionaries and they found *virtus*, if not *veritas* in wretched food, stopped toilets, and sleepless nights. After some weeks of delay in Saigon, during which I tried to learn Vietnamese (my first words were "no" and "boiled water, please"), I flew to the center of the Delta where I taught descriptive linguistics. Soon I had my doubts that I was doing anybody any good, except by helping to keep a few Vietnamese draft dodgers in class and off the battlefields. And there was the worry that I was taking a job away from a Vietnamese instructor and putting him on the battlefield. And who could I help by deceiving these young people into believing that Americans could be as nice as I? Didn't I owe it to them to come to class drunk, loud, and lecherous? I only worried about these things for a few months. In February, the 1968 Tet Offensive began and the University and my house beside it were bombed by Americans and South Vietnamese.

This gave me a chance to do some *immediate* good which, of course, is the best kind because it comes without hesitation, is perfectly human to perform, and is immediately rewarding both to the receiver and to the giver. At the beginning of the Offensive, while there was fighting in the streets, and planes and Cobra helicopters were strafing overhead, I volunteered with three other young Americans to work in the general hospital. In the central courtyard of the hospital, whole families, shredded up and bleeding, lay moaning in the dirt or on reed mats under the broiling sun. My next door neighbor, raving himself, attended his delirious wife whose head was filled with slivers of shrapnel from a mortar that strayed into our dooryard as she peeked out during a lull. A teenage girl, still in the light cotton pajamas that Vietnamese wear around the house, had thrown her body over her old father because he was cold, because he was dying. A little boy thrashed about and would not be consoled by some adults because his ear drums were blown out and he could only hear pain. There were hundreds of such people. There were no doctors. In the U.S. I had talked about the war; marched against the war; I had lived in Vietnam eight months, and up until that moment I knew nothing about the war.

As the four of us stepped by the bodies and into the corridor leading to the surgery room, we met six or so heavily-armed American officers. They were military doctors, and with the fighting close by and the Vietnamese staff having already left, they were leaving too. They agreed to stay and operate if we would agree to serve as nurses and guards. So for a week, I gave blood (one unit), carried bodies, living and dead, learned how to clean and dress wounds, charged myself with closing the eyes of the dead (discharging myself from this duty when a number of stiffened eyelids refused to shut), and guarded the operating room as bullets made a sieve of the water tower near which I sat with a Red Cross band on my arm and a submachine gun in my hands. Without a guard, the surgeons wouldn't operate. If the surgeons didn't operate, many would die. Without medical stores, Vietcong soldiers would die too. To my shame and growing confusion (I had wanted to help *save* lives but I wanted the Vietcong to win) I was proposing to try to kill any that might get over the eight-foot stucco wall that surrounded the compound. Fortunately for me, none tried. Nonetheless, my sacrifice was marred. And the next day, while smuggling a sandwich to a Vietnamese friend who was holed up in a garage because he wasn't uniformed and might well have been shot in the mayhem on the streets, I got hit by a fingernail of shrapnel from a U.S. cluster bomb. After a few months of teaching and few days of doing good, all I wanted was to go home. If I could do anyone any good, it would be in the United States and not in Vietnam where do-gooder politics were mere pretension.

That spring I quit the International Voluntary Services and got a job as a field representative for the Committee of Responsibility to Save War-Injured Children. COR was a small organization among the hundreds of foreign voluntary agencies comprised of teams of Americans, French, English, Swiss, Germans, Japanese, Iranians, Spanish, Filipinos, Koreans, and some do-gooders from the UNESCO. There were Quakers, Baptists, Seventh-Day Adventists, Mennonites, Brethren, and all kind of Catholics, all doing good in some direct way by building hospitals and clinics, training nurses and doctors, doing specialized surgeries on brains, bones, eyes, and skins, making prosthetic limbs, and giving away blankets, food, vitamins, maternity kits, surgical equipment, clothing, vaccines, and medicines. Among this army of do-gooders there were legions of vampires who thrived on the war in separate, personal, and peculiar ways. G.I.'s betrayed their sense of this with their instant distrust of anyone who came to Vietnam of his own choosing. (Partly because of their suspicion and resentment, I avoided G.I.'s. I did not trust them either. Early on I had met a Navy medic who proudly showed me "V.C. ears" in a mason jar of formaldehyde. And, often, as I was hitch-hiking a ride or freeloading in a mess hall, I would talk to soldiers whose conversation centered on their urethral drips, and often they wanted, understandably enough, my assurance that killing Vietnamese was O.K. Twice, I called home to my parents to relay a message to the parents of a soldier I had just met, but generally I avoided soldiers because, very simply, it made my survival all the harder when I thought of the victimizer as victim too). Anyway, I also learned to suspect do-gooders, remembering the young American Medical Association volunteers who had come to experiment at surgeries they wouldn't dare perform on an American; the U.S. AID boozer escaping a rotten marriage; the French priest who finagled a law, in this country of Buddhists, that would give relief supplies only to Catholics; the sad, homely Englishwoman who hung around orphanages to cradle dying children, victims like herself; the Quaker who had come to adopt orphans for American families but who spent himself righteously tongue-lashing sullen bureaucrats until they froze him out of the country; the young IVS volunteer whose holiest mission was to become a Vietnamese; and his spiritual twin, the young volunteer, a shy twit among Americans, who became a powerful whore-master among slum-bound Vietnamese; the professional New York woman reporter of human interest stories who shed compassion on Vietnamese and acid and barbs on other journalists, a woman who, brilliant, bitter, raw-nerved and awkward, used Vietnam to explain her life; the Baptist missionary who preached relentless anti-Communism to his captive, refugee fiefdom near Danang; the radicals and doves who spent their obligatory week in Saigon so they could summon the cameras when they arrived back home; and remembering myself, the anonymous hero, the sensitive witness, morality's spy among the Nazis, the saver of lives, and in other self-congratulating guises.

For a period of six months I began each day by carrying a couple of raw eggs to Nhi Dong Children's Hospital for a 12-year old boy who had so many open wounds that he was dying of protein loss. Then I would go to the Ministry of Interior to sit all day, usually, in clerks' offices until one official found time to decide on the children's passport papers, papers that I had brought to his desk from another's desk, papers that I would carry to other desks. This was called "walking the papers." I was exhausted at the end of a day of doing good; my rage smouldered at the bureaucrats' distance from the war and at the Americans (this kind of work made one feel *above* nationality) who had maimed those innocent victims or had left them sick and homeless. At first the work had a very right feeling: children, like the boy with multiple wounds, had their lives saved. But generally I was worn out. How much good did it do? (This is the question that will ruin a do-gooder, if he asks it of himself). I ran around for six months comforting children and their families, placating hospital personnel about the beds we were taking up with our cases, ingratiating myself with boozy bureaucrats, hamstering my way through the Ministries, and making myself ridiculous by trying to browbeat the U.S. Embassy into pressuring the Saigon government into speeding up the evacuation process. At the end of six months, I put thirteen children on an airplane for hospital care in the U.S., and then headed out to the provinces to take on more cases. Thirteen, out of how many thousands?

Still, as I saw it, the Committee of Responsibility had a moral edge on the other groups because it provided some Vietnamese children with extensive medical care in the U.S. while remaining politically clear of the Saigon government. The idea was that if even a handful of war-injured children were to appear in a dozen or so American cities, then the American people would be so undeniably confronted, shocked and outraged that they would stop the war. The proposition held a basic, simple belief in the wellsprings of human goodness. My disappointment was inevitable.

Even if our proposition held, it wasn't as easy as bringing a child to the U.S., inviting the press to the airport, patching the kid up and then sending him home, as agreed, to his family (don't think we didn't anguish over sending the kids home to the war; our sense of good just wasn't sufficient for kidnapping). The only children that we were permitted to evacuate were the most severe cases for whom no one could even dare pretend that help could be gotten in Vietnam.

They required long term treatment, perhaps a dozen or so more surgeries and physical rehabilitation. They stayed a long time. Funny things happened to a few of them. The little ones started to forget their language after their Vietnamese convoyeuses returned home after three months. And while we all knew that once learned, a language could never really be forgotten and could easily be re-learned, especially by a child, still it was unsettling. Some of the teenagers tried to become Americans. They strutted before adults and competed nastily with other children, learned loud manners and ordered their nurses about. Some of them got greedy, for they were flooded with gifts by the good-willed who chanced to meet them. In Boston, when a kindly woman met a boy who had lost three limbs in a mining incident, she took off an $18,000 necklace and wanted to give it to him. In Vietnam I had to keep asking myself, "Now, is it better for a child here to die or be maimed for life or to risk his being screwed up by well-intentioned people back home?"

In May, 1969, as well as traveling to the provinces seeking evacuations, I was also returning children to their families. At the end of May two boys returned, Huynh Duc, 15 years old, and Ho Bau, 11. Duc was around the fiftieth child that COR had treated. There were, of course, thousands of civilians wounded every year, despite Robert McNamara's 1967 estimate of some one hundred and twenty (which was based on the number of compensations *paid* at that time by the Department of Defense). Duc had suffered an open fracture of his right forearm from gunshot wounds which also required below-the-knee amputation of both his legs at the Danang General Hospital where we found him in 1968. Through the recommendation of Dr. Phung Tuan Hanh, a general surgeon at the hospital, Duc was sent to Hawaii for treatment at Kauikeolani Children's Hospital and the Shriner's Hospital for Crippled Children. Ho Bau also had been evacuated from the Danang Hospital on Dr. Hanh's recommendation, for Hanh would sometimes initiate on behalf of a family the detailed evacuation papers—which involved thirty-five copies for some forms and trips to four Ministries and the U.S. Embassy. With a broad smile he would say, "It's legal and it's right. These are all my children," gesturing to the ward where the patients were crowded two and three to a bed. "These are all my relatives." Just the same I knew we were kidnapping a few, but just the same—and this was the one measure that saved me from total bewilderment in this business of doing good—they would have died. Bau would have died. In

June, 1968, about the time of the My Lai massacre, he was burned
by napalm dropped from a plane in a Free Strike Zone near his house
while he was playing with some other kids. He suffered third degree
burns over 25% of his body, right arm, left and right legs. In the U.S.
we had gotten him treatment in Boston at Massachusetts General
Hospital and the Shriner's Hospital for Crippled Children. While in
the U.S. Bau received a few letters from his mother (his father was
dead). Miss Bui Thi Khuy, the 22-year old woman who served as his
companion, translated them as best she could:

Duc, Duc, Feb. 5, 1969

Dear Son,

   Bau, we received many letters from you. But we couldn't send you
a letter. Bau, I know that you are alone in the different people and
country. I remember every day and night very very much. Each time
I call your name in my heart, I feel sadness and I don't know whom I
will talk to. The War separated us. The war took my good son away.
Because the situation of the War, so I must carry on. The first and last
letter I send to you. I don't know what I tell you. I always pray God
protects and gives you the good health. After you will return and live
together with us. On that time the peace will come to my heart. Now I
don't know when you come back. Today I write a letter let you know
that we are well. Please write to me when you receive this letter. Miss
Khuy, we are thankful and send you the best regards. Please our
family send the best regards and thankful to Bau's foster parents for
us. We will never forget them for their kindness to our son. Miss
Khuy, please help my son write a letter for us.

                              Bau's Mother
                              NGUYEN THI XUMG
                              DUC DUC Tinh Quang Nam
                              South Vietnam.

Now three months later, with Miss Khuy, who had returned to
Vietnam and who would soon take another group of children back to
the U.S., I met the boys when they got off the plane in Saigon. Bau,
except for his slightly scarred face, looked like a normal eleven-
year-old who had just taken a long plane ride; tired, a little spaced
out; wide-eyed at being in Vietnam. He was very happy to see Miss
Khuy. Duc, his hair thickly oiled, wearing a long-sleeved white shirt
and a tie with a bright stickpin, arrived with two mammoth suit-

cases, a Pan Am bag, and a crated pedal sewing machine. He would not speak Vietnamese, he hoped our house had a T.V., and said that he only intended to stay three months, for he would be returning to live in Hawaii. As proof that his return was already in the works, he produced a card showing his honorary membership in the Coast Guard Club of Hawaii.

At our house, for the next few days Duc complained that his stumps were sore from the chafing of his artificial limbs and that he couldn't eat Vietnamese food. When he started to hang in his room and play with his radios and watches, I began taking him out to lunch at working class restaurants in Saigon. Once some people snickered at his dressing like a middle-aged bureaucrat. Finally he gradually sold off most of his junk. And when gradually he found that Vietnam looked "a lot like Kailua," I decided it was time to get him home. Duc and Bau—who had meanwhile introduced Batman to the neighborhood kids—both lived in Duc Duc (Virtuous Teaching), a small village in the contested mountainous region of Quang Nam province.

Miss Khuy, Bau, Duc and I flew, with all their luggage, to Danang. At the hospital Dr. Hanh examined them with pleasure and had Duc walk about on his new legs. Duc walked proudly and without a waver. From Danang we had to take a U.S. Army Blackcat Huey helicopter for the road to Hoi An had been cut. Huey helicopters fly with their doors open and hold about six passengers besides the pilot, co-pilot, and gunner, who sits behind a big machine gun on a pivot post. Over the ocean the gunner opened up at the water. I couldn't see anything; maybe he was shooting at a whale. The noise was deafening. I suspected that he was firing to see the scare on Miss Khuy's face. From Hoi An we took another helicopter that was resupplying Marine field units patroling near Duc Duc. We flew for about thirty minutes over cratered fields, defoliated mountain forests and shining river loops. When we got to the village and hovered about a sea of brown thatch houses swelled by homes of new refugees, I wondered how we would find the boys' homes, for in a Vietnamese village there are no street names or addresses, and we had just a few hours before the supply helicopter would return; if we missed it we would have to spend the night, either in the village, which would not be safe for me, or in the Marine camp, which got mortared nearly every night and which would have been pretty rough on Miss Khuy.

Bau said he lived under a big pine tree. With all the luggage bouncing around on the rutted roads, we drove around in a jeep until we spotted, sure enough a large pine tree. Bau's mother was at market. His old grandmother was there and she hugged him and seemed bewildered as the rest of us as we waited for his mother to return. A crowd of neighbors gathered. I asked Bau where the place was where he had been wounded; he pointed to an area about seventy-five yards from where we were standing. That was the Free Strike Zone. Anyone could be shot there at any time.

While Miss Khuy was talking to the grandmother and Duc was chafing to get to *his* home, Bau's mother came walking up the road. When a neighbor rushed out to tell her we were there, she threw her hands to her face and ran the thirty yards to the house, pushed through the crowd, and hugged her son. She wept and called his name. Bau looked at me, and then under the sheer weight of his mother's love, he was overwhelmed and began to cry too. Everybody was crying. Miss Khuy, who was crying (Miss Khuy, who, a week later in Saigon, was to be crushed to death by a two-ton military truck out of the control of its drunken driver), looked at me and I was crying. Bau's minutes of burning, his pain and endurance, his mother's love and the enormous distance that had separated them overwhelmed us all. After a few minutes, Miss Khuy spoke to Mrs. Xung and told her how to contact us if they needed help. Khuy gave Bau a hug and his mother some stamped, addressed envelopes.

Duc's father, Huynh Cat, who made rice paper for his living, was at their home near the market (It was in the market that Duc had been cut down with other villagers when a G.I. went crazy and opened up on the crowd.) However, Duc's mother had just gone to Danang in response to our telegram to meet us at the hospital. Seeing his father waiting for us outside their house, Duc jumped down from the back of the jeep and strode to Mr. Cat, whose smile grew wider as he saw his son grown older, looking more like his father, and walking to him.

Back in Saigon, I congratulated myself on how well it had gone. Few complications. So, we had messed with their lives . . . we had done no harm. We had done some good. As I drew my work to a close and prepared a testimony on civilian casualties for the Senate Sub-committee on Refugees, Escapees, and Civilian Casualties, I liked to consider cases like Duc and Bau. (Forgetting, as best I could, the 9-year old girl who had her nose shot off and for whom we made, in

New York, a veritable red garden hose of a replacement which closed up as soon as she returned to Vietnam.)

Some weeks before the collapse of the Saigon troops, as I was having breakfast and reading *The New York Times* just before walking up to the Penn State campus where I teach composition and poetry to students who were in junior high school when I was in Vietnam, I read on the fifth or sixth page that the village of Duc Duc had been caught in a crossfire and burned. I wondered what happened to Bau and Duc, especially Duc who can't run. At best, I could say, if they had escaped, that I had returned them home so they could become homeless. I had always known that it could happen. As I see it, there was nothing else I could have done. One must act, even if his acts fail, or, if they seem to succeed, are contaminated by other men. It is hopeless to look for personal reward in good works. This isn't a rationalization to protect oneself from disappointment. It means merely that as soon as one tries to profit personally from a good act, it is poisoned. There are no personal rewards in good works unless one is stupid (which only means "blind to consequence") in which case one's good works are more or less evil.

There is no one to talk to about this for like many who have returned from Vietnam, I have returned a foreigner, one whose experiences and emotions are honed on the edge of memories from a place Americans seldom think of or would like to forget. For some reason which I do not understand American pleas for my help make me angry. Hitchhikers and United Fund collectors annoy me. Just the other day I was flying back to New York on a crowded flight when a young woman with two small boys asked me and the woman next to me if we would change seats with her and her 8-year old son so they could be next to her other, 7-year old son. "If you don't want to, just say so," she smiled when she noted my hesitation. She was seated across the aisle, one row up; her son was at her right; the son in question was across the aisle from her, in front of me, on her left. She wanted to sit right behind him. Handbags and passengers were pushing through the aisle. I had just sat down and had gotten my luggage stowed and I did not feel like moving. I said that if she didn't mind, I would stay where I was. She said "O.K." and then, in tears, suddenly lit into me: "People today are so unfeeling, so selfish," she said. "If you had children, you would understand!" Puzzled, I looked at her. If she had reached out her arm, she could have touched her son. I thought of the children who had littered the village battle-fields to be picked up, perhaps, by U.S. helicopters, children who perhaps died on route or in field hospitals, whose parents would never know what had happened to them. I thought of the children I had evacuated, children separated from their families by years and by 10,000 miles. This American woman's distress seemed selfish and absurd, but, on her terms, reasonable. She was suffering a tragedy of a kind that I can no longer recognize. I should have been delighted that she had such a limited sense of personal tragedy, but personal tragedies are pretty easily felt, aren't they? And, more importantly, do they open up Americans to the pain of others? That we had waged war in Vietnam for ten years is evidence in response. Sorry, madam, I am an adept measurer of pain and yours doesn't count for much. I thought of explaining, but I didn't feel like it. Instead, I stiffly told her, "I understand."

TURTLE

fiction by JOHN PILCROW

from DECEMBER

nominated by DECEMBER *and Harry Smith*

HE LAID OUT THE DAY'S NEWS and put down the turtle, bottom side up. It rocked like a half a melon. With a honed jackknife he cut out the neck. Lying on the want ads the neck contracted, trying to pull in a head that wasn't there. Leeches waved excitedly on the meat and on his wet hands. He razored through the tough cables of tendon to pull out four waving legs and the tail. These he skinned with pliers and put in a pan of brine. He viewed the task completed, anatomy in disarray across the counter, tissues and organs still throbbing with the effort to escape. He dumped the entrails into the shell, opened the screen door and tossed it all out for the cats. In the dark the torn-off claws still slowly clutched and unclutched, the heart still beat. He barbecued the flesh and ate it with a quart of malt liquor. Then he went out looking for a woman.

THE CROW IS MISCHIEF

by LAURA JENSEN

from OPEN PLACES

nominated by Tess Gallagher and Grace Schulman

The crow is mischief.
He is the shadow of the sun
as the owl is shadow of the moon—
wisdom and mischief, evening and dawn.
He wakes you when you sleep near the water
in a white bed.
I saw the crow, a lone shadow
high in an evergreen. This is his call
of discovery—a piece of black bread.
I pounded something with a stone.
Sometimes I think it was my heart.
Sometimes I think it was a stranger's heart,
someone now I will never know.

MY MOTHER'S LIST OF NAMES

by BILL KNOTT

from SELECTED AND COLLECTED POEMS (Sun Press)

nominated by Sun Press

My mother's list of names today I take it in my hand
And I read the places she underlined William and Ann
The others are my brothers and sisters I know
I'm going to see them when I'm fully grown

Yes they're waiting for me to join em and I will
Just over the top of that next big hill
Lies a green valley where their shouts of joy are fellowing
Save all but one can be seen there next a kin

And a link is missing from their ringarosey dance
Think of the names she wrote down not just by chance
When she learned that a baby inside her was growing small
She placed that list inside the family Bible

Then I was born and she died soon after
And I grew up sinful of questions I could not ask her
I did'not know that she had left me the answer
Pressed between the holy pages with the happy laughter
Of John, Rudolph, Frank, Arthur, Paul,
Pauline, Martha, Ann, Doris, Susan, you all,

I did not even know you were alive
Till I read the Bible today for the first time in my life
And I found this list of names that might have been my own
You other me's on the bright side of my moon

Mother and Daddy too have joined you in play
And I am coming to complete the circle of your day
I was a lonely child I never understood that you
Were waiting for me to find the truth and know

And I'll make this one promise you want me to:
I'm goin to continue my Bible study
Till I'm back inside the Body
With you

THE TEARING OF THE SKIN

by Yvonne

from WILLMORE CITY

nominated by Naomi Lazard

All white
the boards, the shutters,
a long shrill schoolteacher throat
is Aunt Ida's house
shouting up and down
the dirt brown neck of Brunswick Avenue:
"I pledge allegiance"
straight up to the stark electric hair

of sudden rain.
Sudden white
is Aunt Ida's house
like the silk lining of dreams—
we women of color learn to hide
porcelain flame,
mandala pearl,
but not our flag of surrender riding

riding the night like a tattered star
into the grey drowned hair
of a silent morning.

We women of color learn to brush away
water of a harpsichord
like lint from a husband's suit.
But Aunt Ida slipped
out of the scream she could not pull

(and it would not rot)
into her smooth strong bone
of a house, her good dry lace
hugging the front porch windows.
And after dark, her twenty-five pale
window shades seem to uncurl
(as if champagne) whatever sleeps.
And each ruffled organdy curtain

like an antebellum skirt
is light diverting cream
to bring in the cat. And why not?
"If you work for less,
you won't get more."
Each room is a sedative,
a cup of camomile tea.

Each room is a key.
Some are like vellum, and some
are prim as soap. Each room
is a view. Far within
her old incurability calls "not pretty, not
pretty" like an unrequited love.
And Aunt Ida replies "not at home,
not at home" and begins her work.

Her work is to bury (if not
heal) the beggar in herself,
to rebuild the altar, the foreplay,
the white corset melting as wax.
Pale as a fingernail,
her carpets open their thighs,
the shorn and the shepherd alike
gathered in her wool.

And who will condemn?
The hungry? The one who is eaten?
Each is tight-lipped
about their wisdom.
(because the paws of marriage
are permitted to sweat)
Each chair and spoon and sheet
is an act of aggression.

And why not? The icebox purrs.
Her first anniversary plates,
aspirin white,
are heavy as skulls.
Because the famine is always with us.
The sink and the cupboard are wise.
The stove is puritan white
with hot blue paws.

Because every whatnot
is costing less than disaster.
Less than opium, self-pity, the first white
song of the apple.
This first white sugar
of a house. White bread. White shoulder.
Her brazen back
to the world.

Now it is written
"Women have no wilderness in them"
but "provident instead, content
in the tight hot cell".
Aunt Ida's house—a harvest so perverse,
so bereft of fruit and tradition!
Washing the right hand of starvation
with the elegant claw of her left.

ƙ *ƙ* *ƙ*

THE ESSENTIAL ELLISON

excerpts from an interview with RALPH ELLISON

by STEVEN CANNON, ISHMAEL REED and QUINCY TROUPE

from Y'BIRD

nominated by Y'BIRD *and Harry Smith*

editor's note: The following interview took place in Ralph Ellison's apartment in New York in 1977. In his introduction to the interview, Steve Cannon remarks: "The interview, including the riffs, the tangents and digressions, came alive in what Albert Murray (*Stompin' the Blues*) likes to call that 'uphere, downhome' sort of fashion. Collard greens and hamhocks. And tensions (which were essentially on the surface) vanished under that onslaught of verbiage, verbal contests, and that rich interchange of ideas, information and everyday experiences—four Southern writers, for all it's worth, having a ball, discussing the ways of 'Western Culture.' "

QT: I notice that in the interview that you did with Steve quite a while back, you commented on the writers of the Forties and Fifties. Now I would like for you to talk about some of the specific differences in regard to vision and influence that you see between the writers of the Forties and Fifties and those who emerged during the Sixties and Seventies. Would you address yourself to the novelists first, and then to the poets?

RE: Well, I don't care to talk about specific works because so much has been published and so many writers have appeared that I wouldn't pretend to know what all of them are doing. that's no longer possible. Now, let's go back a bit. One could say that during the Forties we were still being influenced by the attitudes and values of the Twenties and Thirties, and by perspectives introduced to our specific community of writers by Stalinists and the Trotskyist Left. There was also the influence of the WPA, which provided a number of us with our first opportunity for becoming writers. It also provided others who were already working at the craft with an opportunity to earn a living. And there was also present a current of intellectual influence derived from existentialism. I became aware of Kierkegaard and Unamuno a good while before existentialism became a literary "movement." I picked it up through the writings of André Malraux, who was depicting existential concepts long before Sartre and Camus made them fashionable. I became interested after reading *Man's Hope,* in which Unamuno appears as a character. In 1937, I was present at a party where Malraux was raising funds for the Spanish Loyalists, and shortly afterwards, Richard Wright and I were reading and discussing Unamuno's *The Tragic Sense of Life.* Such ideas were new to me and very exciting in that they made me aware of existential elements in the spirituals and the blues. At the time, I was trying to make connections between my own background and the world of ideas, connections that I hadn't been taught in college but which I felt to exist. As a musician, I had no problem in seeing connections between European and Afro-American music, so why not between my segregated condition and the world of ideas? So, I was groping. Marx and Freud were the dominant intellectual forces during that period, and I had become aware of Freud even before finishing high school. Marx, I encountered at Tuskegee—but how did you put the two together? I didn't know, so I read, I talked, I asked questions and I listened. Such ideas concerned me as I turned from music to literature.

Now for the main ideological and intellectual forces operating within the small group in which I found myself: There was the psychological in the form of Freudianism, the political in the form of Marxism, and in Malraux's fiction and criticism, which questioned the assertions of both, there were the concepts of existentialism. With these there was the living presence of Langston Hughes, Claude McKay, Countee Cullen, Sterling Brown and Alain Locke. Now I don't mean that these figures were "influences" in any simple-minded way, but that their examples were part of the glamour of Harlem and thus important to your sense of opportunity. And, although you had a vague but different set of tunes tinkling in your head and sought other solutions and perhaps a more complex form in which to work, you respected them and their achievements. You respected them even after you discovered that some of them like, say, McKay, were inarticulate when it came to discussing technique. In fact, Wright was far more articulate in that area than either Hughes or McKay.

But, there was another factor which I found most important. The writers I've just mentioned related to Harlem and to the waning influence of the Negro Renaissance, but there was a wider world of culture to be found in New York, and I made my closest contacts with it on the Writers Project. There you were thrown in contact not only with black and white writers of your own age grouping, but with a number who had already achieved broad reputations. McKay was one of these, but most were white. Then there was the old League of American Writers whose programs made it possible for me to meet important writers who had nothing to do with the WPA. My friendship with Wright gave me entree to a number of such people, and they came to form, for me at least, a scattered but most meaningful intellectual community. Within it, the craft of fiction was passionately discussed. The philosophical and political implications of artistic styles were given endless attention. Myth, ritual and revolution got slammed around. On the project, I hung out with a few fellows of my own general age and the same subjects were discussed. Incidentally, most of them were Jewish, but this was before we realized what Hitler was really up to, so little time was spent discussing race or religion. Instead, we discussed craft, form, and ideas relating more immediately to writing. And even in Harlem, there was no such concentration upon what is now termed the "Black experience" as one encounters it today, not even between Wright and myself. I was concerned, but I felt it to be something one worked out for oneself. I was *living* that experience, so what I wanted was to be able to make my own intellectual sense of it. Nor was there any question in my own mind about who I was or where I came from. It's in my face, it's in the neighborhoods where I grew up, it's in the Afro-Methodist Episcopal Church into which I was baptized, it was in the ex-slaves I knew as a child. I'm out of slaves on both sides of my family. That was history, and I couldn't undo it; my question was how did one bridge the gap intellectually (or at least *imaginatively*), between what one felt about Negro life, between what one felt about our people, and what was said about us—that is, the sterotyped identity imposed upon us by society. Yes, and what was there being written in areas lying beyond the confines of our own neighborhoods that could be used in the task of adequately defining our humanity? How did one get American Negro life, that great, bursting, expressive capacity for life, into writing? Where did one discover ideas and techniques with which one could free one's mind and achieve something of one's possibilities? . . .

IR: It's said that you were influenced by Richard Wright and Chester Himes. Were they influenced by you?

RE: [Laughter] I tried my damnedest to influence Chester Himes, but I got nowhere with him. After all, Chester preceded me as a writer, you know. He goes way back. Chester and I used to argue over technique and ideas, but I don't know to what extent I influenced him; but, certainly Wright influenced me, although it was not in the simplistic way that certain pseudocritics would insist. I've recorded in writing that I sought out Wright the day after he arrived in New York. I was still a musician, and it was at his suggestion that I wrote my first review and attempted my first short story. Obviously, he influenced me to begin writing. What gets overlooked is the fact that I was a rather well-read young trumpeter from Oklahoma who had studied music for most of my life, including four years of harmony in junior high and high school. I had tried composing marches and popular song and had arranged spirituals, and I had majored in music theory and trumpet at Tuskegee. My point is that I had been concerned with art and its creation long before I met Wright. I was also a bookworm who became interested in Wright because I had discovered Eliot, Pound and Edwin Arlington Robinson at Tuskegee. It's interesting that no one says that I was influenced by Langston Hughes, whose work was taught in my grade school and whom I knew longer than I did Wright. I don't think that Wright appreciated the background that I brought to his discussion of creative writing because frequently he seemed to assume that I was totally ignorant of the works under discussion. But, I didn't argue with him. He possessed the certainty that came from having an organized body of ideas, and he could write—so having confidence in my own ability to think, I listened to him and kept my disagreements to myself. . . .

IR: I'm just saying that in essays and interviews you always mention Hemingway as an influence.

RE: Well, he was.

IR: But, you don't mention Wright. I may be wrong—

RE: You're wrong as hell [laughter].

IR: All right.

IR: Damn right, you're wrong as hell.

IR: OK.

RE: People are still arguing over what I've said or haven't said about Wright as though I have no right to disagree with him. But, they forget that I wrote some of the most appreciative criticism of him that's ever been published. Wright and I were friends, but I quit showing him any of my fiction in 1940 after I was unable to get his reaction to a novelette. Finally, I pressed him for an opinion and he became very emotional about it and said, "Well, this is *my* stuff." You might say that with that he influenced me *not* to be influenced by his style of writing.

SC: Was this when he was living over in Brooklyn?

RE: No, he was living on 140th Street, across from City College; I was living on Hamilton Terrace. Chester Himes mentioned the incident during a television interview . . .

SC: With John A. Williams?

RE: No, with Nikki Giovanni . . . I find the assumption that no Negro can do anything unless another *Negro* has done so before him rather simple-minded, and as far as I'm concerned, it's an inverted form of racism. An artist can't do a damn thing about his relatives, but he can sure as hell choose his artistic ancestors. I had read Mark Twain and Hemingway, among others, long before I even heard of Wright.

IR: I wanted to mention that because I read about the incident in a book on the WPA which just came out. There's a new thing going around called "super fiction," which is a term invented by Jerome Klinkowitz and others. They claim that the modern writer is influenced by more than writing. When I read your work and when I read Wright's work, I do see influences of the movies. Would you say there are popular influences in your work and Wright's?

RE: Oh, sure, I use anything from movies to comic strips.

IR: Radio?

RE: Anything; radio, sermons, practical jokes. In fact, anything that suggests ideas for handling narrative; even jazz riffs. I've never been squeamish about using whatever there is to use.

IR: It's not a new thing then, like they're saying?

RE: Far from it. Mark Twain drew on the minstrel show. Fitzgerald and Faulkner did time in Hollywood. Henry James was a fan of P.T. Barnum's museum and Dos Passos adapted devices from the newsreel.

SC: Chester Himes said he saw the first draft of *Invisible Man*, did he?

RE: He might have seen parts of it, but I doubt if I showed him the whole thing. I rewrote so continuously that one draft blended into the other. But, Chester and I were friends. My wife and I knew him and his first wife, Jean, rather well, but I didn't show my manuscript around; the 1940 incident with Wright had made me leery. I was close to Wright, but I quit showing him my fiction because I had no desire to offend him. I accepted the fact that our sensibilities were different, as were our feelings for style. But, I held no antagonism toward him. Questions of style and influence aside, we still had a broad basis for a relationship. I admired and respected him, and we remained friendly. During the Fifties whenever I was in Paris, I visited him, and whenever he returned to New York, he got in touch with me.

IR: I call you a Hoodooist.

RE: Do you know who he is? That's the master. You see, he's looking at you from both the front and back of his head [points to a sculpture of Eshu, the trickster god].

IR: No, you said in *The Invisible Man* that New Orleans was the home of mystery, that's the reason I called you a Hoodooist.

SC: You mentioned over the years (you were addressing yourself to the National Academy), do you find that Kenneth Burke was only one of the few critics that you could learn anything from who was around at the time? Or were there other people? The second part of the question is who do you see, as far as criticism is concerned, who's qualified on the scene right now, for the type of stuff that you're doing?

RE: Critics?

SC: Yeah. The first part of the question was—do you feel you learned a lot from Kenneth Burke in terms of dealing with the type of writing that you were doing at that time? In other words, going back to *Invisible Man*, in terms of vocabulary, in terms of speaking—of kinds of things that were going on in the novel. Second part of question: Who do you see as good interpretive critics who're around nowadays?

RE: What I learned from Burke was not so much the technique of fiction but the nature of literature and the way ideas and language operate in literary form. I first became interested in Burke after hearing him read his essay, "The Rhetoric of Hitler's Battle." It was a critique of *Mein Kampf*, and the time was 1937. I was absolutely delighted because in the essay, he made a meaningful fusion of Marx and Freud, and I had been asking myself how the insights of the two could be put together. On that occasion, Burke was hooted at by some of the left-wing intellectuals, but not too many years later, the discovery of the gas ovens revealed that Burke knew what he was doing. I was just starting out as a writer, and as I went on struggling to understand his criticism, I began to learn something of the nature of literature, society, social class, and psychology as they related to literary form. I began to grasp how language operates, both in literature and as an agency of oral communication. In college and on my own, I had studied a little psychology, a little sociology, you know, dribs and drabs, but Burke provided a *Gestalt* through which I could apply intellectual insights back into my own materials and into my own life.

Critics are all over the place, and there's always been something that I could learn from a few of them. Sometimes, you get a man who is very good with comparative literature, so you go to him. Joe Frank, for instance, who's over at Princeton, is a very good Dostoyevsky man, but, in order to be a good Dostoyevsky man, he has to know a hell of a lot about literature generally. John McCormick, who teaches at Rutgers, is very good on American literature, in the comparative context. And R.W.B. Lewis, the expert on Edith Wharton, is very good on American literature generally. But, I don't go to any of these people expecting the whole thing. I learn what I can and use what I'm prepared to use. During the late 1940s when I was walking around with holes in my shoes, I was spending twenty-five dollars a volume for Malraux's *The Psychology of Art*. Why? Because trying to grasp his blending of art history, philosophy, and politics was more important that having dry feet. So that's the way it continues to go: anywhere I find a critic who has an idea or concept that seems useful, I grab it. Eclecticism is the word. Like a jazz musician who creates his own style out of the styles around him, I play it by ear.

QT: I wanted to ask you another question. You said here in this interview with Steve, Quote:

> What is missing today is a corps of artists and intellectuals who evaluate Negro American experience from the inside, and out of a broad knowledge of how people of other cultures live, deal with experience and give significance to that experience. We do too little of this. Rather, we depend on outsiders, mainly sociologists, to interpret our lives for us.

I'd like to ask if you still think that is true?
RE: No—or at least it isn't as true as it once was. Perhaps I shouldn't have made the statement at that time since Steve and the others were making such an attempt. Still, such groups are still quite small while the sociologists with their "benign neglect" and "affirmative discrimination," their "pathology of the Black family" and their "psychological castration of the Black male," so forth and so on, are legion.

SC: We want to get out of that world anyway.
RE: Well, you're still badly needed. Returning to your question, I'll say something which is apt to outrage certain people—present company not included. During the Sixties, I observed the attention paid the intellectual pronouncement of an intellectually, not too sophisticated ex-pimp who had sprung to prominence. Now I don't mean to imply that pimps can't be intellectuals or intellectuals pimps, or that they can't become politically responsible and even become capable of heroic action. Obviously, this man had undergone a profound transformation and had learned how to exploit the media for his own purposes. I myself took him seriously as a political activist, or at least as a political force, but not as an intellectual. As an

exhorter, yes. As a rabble rouser who had transformed Afro-American barbershop and poolhall rhetoric into a force for scaring the hell out of white folks over television, yes. But, as an intellectual leader capable of making insightful analyses of American culture and politics, no! So, given his effectiveness among so many of us, I concluded that many of us hadn't overcome our Afro-American vulnerability to easy formulations and slick slogans. Just give the most banal statement a rhyme and a rhythm, put a little strut into it, and we'll grab it like a catfish gulping down a piece of dough-bait. Toss us a slick, emotional phrase and we victimize ourselves, even go up against Sherman tanks with shotguns.

QT: I think that's very good, because I had a question to ask you along that line. It's about the glorification of people who have been in prison. They come out, and all of a sudden, you know . . .
RE: Sure, they're treated as though serving time has endowed them with a mysterious, god-granted knowledge. And, especially if they say that they've been to the depths of hell and have been reborn into a new vision. Well, I've known a few guys who spent time in prison and none of them underwent any such mystical transforma-tion. Nevertheless, for Americans—and especially Christians—the confession of sin and the assertion of rebirth and redemption has tremendous appeal. This is especially true of our own people, who understandably are hungry for heroes and redeemers. I used to collect the handbills distributed by fly-by-night faith-healers in Harlem, and most of them stated that after being up to their eyeballs in crime, they'd had the scales struck from their eyes while in prison, and this had prepared them to lead their people. During the Sixties, this myth of the redeemed criminal had a tremendous influence on our young people, when criminals guilty of every crime from con games, to rape, to murder exploited it by declaring themselves political activists and Black leaders. As a result, many sincere, dedicated leaders of an older generation were swept aside. I'm speaking now of courageous individuals who made sacrifices in order to master the disciplines of leadership and who created a continuity between themselves and earlier leaders of our struggle. The kids treated such people as if they were Uncle Toms, and I found it outrageous. Because not only did it distort the concrete historical differences between one period of struggle and another, it made heroes out of thugs and self-servers out of dedicated leaders. Worse,

it gave many kids the notion that there was no point in developing their minds; that all they had to do was to strike a militant stance, assert their unity with the group and stress their "Blackness." If you didn't accept their slogans, you were dismissed as a "Neegro" Uncle Tom. Years ago, DuBois stress a leadership based upon an elite of the intellect. During the Sixties, it appeared that for many Afro-Americans all that was required for such a role was a history of criminality (the sleazier the better), a capacity for irresponsible rhetoric, and the passionate assertion of the mystique of "Blackness." At least, that's how it appeared to me.

QT: There are some great writers who suffered tremendously at the hands of a certain clique of people out in Chicago. For example, my favorite poet, Robert Hayden.
IR: He is a bit high-strung, though; I like his work very much, and I like him as a person.
QT: But, I think that he suffered . . .
IR: Well, everybody suffered . . .
QT: But, they stomped on him, I thought because of the fact that he is a great poet.
RE: He's a fine poet.
QT: And he did his homework.
IR: I was thinking of *Kaleidoscope,* in which Hayden seemed to make condescending remarks about other Afro-American poets.

QT: I thought that too, and I told him to his face that it wasn't the job of an editor to make those kinds of remarks in terms of biography. I think he should have said this man is from so-and-so, and this man has been published and so forth. He didn't have to say that this man didn't rewrite and things like that. That was ridiculous. Why should he say something like that: Why even include it?

IR: . . . Around the country we have this feminist movement, which always reminds me that the Amazons came out of Dahomey, and we have a situation which people murmur about but don't bring out in the open. And, I think, I'm all for the oppressed getting their share of everything—whatever they want—but when today's oppressed become tomorrow's jailers and start picking up habits of people they're trying to get rid of—which always happens, we have a situation where homo-erotics, both in the closet and out of the closet, are commenting on the behavior of hetero-erotics [laughter]. We have people going around talking about conflict between Third World men and Third World women when the birth rate is soaring, so somebody must be getting along you know. And I'm saying it's possible that some of these homo-erotics are using their literacy power to create some kind of conflict between hetero-erotics to get defections. [Laughter.] I know it's a pretty delicate question, but the people have a lot of influence. They're writing novels that have overtones of lesbianism, which is okay and all that. I could name you some novels and poetry in which you don't know the gender of the person who's getting laid. And these people get currency, they get into newspapers, they have influence—what do you think about that?

RE: I would answer that by saying that when old Black Moses starts blowing *his* top the whole country goes nuts [Laughter]. Seriously, though, I'd add that the abstract Black Man is so deeply associated in the American mind with the concept of freedom and the denial of freedom that when we roil up the American conscience and consciousness, all other repressed groups get out and start doing their thing—and in public. And just as some of the Blacks are using the opportunity of freely expressing themselves to put the damper on other Afro-Americans, other hitherto quiescent, repressed groups are attempting to repress people *they* don't like.

IR: Yes, and some of these people are high yellows.
RE: With black declared beautiful the lighter the skin the blacker the rhetoric.
IR: At least it looks that way.
SC: They talk the loudest.
RE: They give me more hell that the whites did down in Alabama.

QT: I want to ask a couple of different questions. I see that you have a wonderful art collection. Wonderful . . .
RE: Thank you.
QT: I love African art, and as many times as I've been over there, I still find it beautiful. But, in this regard, I want to get back to the question of influences. I know there's obviously the influence of music on your work, but what about the influence of certain artists like Romare Bearden? What about the technique of collage and

such? And beyond that, what other American artists, painters, and sculptors are you interested in today?

RE: First, I should tell you that although I've been collecting African art for a long time, I am not a Pan-Africanist. I love the art for itself. Nor am I anti-Africa. [Laughter.] No, as far as writing goes, I've not been influenced by Bearden, although I met him during what I believe was his first period. He was doing the heroic, mural type of painting which was developed by such artists as Diego Rivera. Later, I was to have many talks with him, and over the years, I always found him stimulating and conscious of where he was going. As a serious artist in his own field, Bearden still affirms and strengthens me in my own work.

SC: You've written a piece on him, too.

RE: Yes, it was the catalogue copy for one of his shows.

QT: Yes, I've got the catalogue.

RE: Getting back to your question concerning the influence of one artist upon another, I'd say that it frequently takes other forms than that of copying or trying to do what another artist or writer does in his precise manner. That is mere imitation. But, sometimes, by working in his chosen form, a fellow artist can affirm one's own efforts and give you the courage to struggle with the problems of your medium. So, in that light, you might say that Bearden influenced me. Just by knowing him at a time when we were both working hard and without much recognition, I found strength for my own efforts. He had faith in the importance of artistic creation, and I learned something about the nature of painting from listening to his discussions of his craft. Look around, and you'll see that I own a number of his works. So, as I see it, it's not the imitation of an artist's work, or even his endorsement of your talent, that's of basic importance, but his assertion of artistic ideals and the example of his drive to achieve excellence. But, then I've found a similar affirmation in the examples of football players, jazz musicians—who for me are the most important—tap dancers, and even a few bootleggers [Laughter]. Such people attract me with a certain elegance and flair for style, as have certain preachers and teachers. I never attended anything but segregated schools, from first grade through graduation, and yet certain fine teachers inspired me to do the best I had in me. Being angry over segregation, it took me a while to realize that despite a handful of indifferent teachers, I also had a few that were excellent, people who still inspire me.

QT: Did you know Melvin Tolson?
RE: Yes, I knew Tolson.
QT: Could you give us something about him?
RE: I knew Tolson first when I was in high school and he was teaching in Texas at Wiley College. He was the coach of the Wiley debating team, and I became aware of him when they came to Oklahoma City to debate the team from Langston University. This serves to highlight one of the crazy aspects of segregation in the United States: Tolson's team wasn't allowed to debate the teams of white colleges in Oklahoma, but the English team from Oxford University used to come out to Oklahoma on tour and were known to be defeated by the debaters of Tolson's segregated college. This gave us a tremendous sense of affirmation. Ishmael Reed here has taken a few potshots at the art of rhetoric, but, man, rhetorical skill is a vital part of Afro-American cultural heritage. Tolson was a skilled rhetorician, as was true of Frederick Douglass and many other 19th century leaders.

I got to know Tolson personally during the Forties, when he was in New York for an extended period. We had many long discussions and one of the subjects we fought over was my admiration for the work of Pound and Eliot. At the time, being dedicated to earlier poetic styles, Tolson saw nothing in Eliot, who had inspired my half-conscious attempts to write poetry at Tuskegee. But, later, in '53, when I was given a reception at the old Paul Laurence Dunbar Library in Oklahoma City, Tolson gave a talk in which he castigated the teachers for not encouraging our kids to go into creative writing. After pointing to me as an example of what could happen, he shocked hell out of me by complaining that segregation was preventing [mimicking Tolson's voice] "our young Black boys and girls from becoming acquainted with the works of Tee Sssssssss Elllllliot and Ezzzzzzzra Pound!" (He was very precise in his diction.) This was so different from his position back in New York that it both shocked and pleased me. But then, Tolson was a very complex man. I don't quite understand the combination of forces that led to his later poetry, but, perhaps our arguments had something to do with it—but for god's sake don't interpret this as meaning that I "influenced" him! He was very knowledgeable, and I know that he was shaped in his earlier life by those eddying currents of New England education which were brought into Negro schools with Emancipation—

SC: Oh, you're talking about the "Mississippi school marm"; they came down when the abolitionists came down.
RE: Right! They introduced the Freedmen to the New England educational tradition. I myself had a few teachers who were just old enough to have been taught in such schools; people who knew Greek, Hebrew and Latin. There weren't a lot of them, but they were dedicated products of New England classical education.
SC: That was almost a black-face minstrel show in reverse, huh?
RE: Perhaps. It appeared impractical, but knowledge is colorless, and I wish that *I* knew those languages.

IR: Trollope's mother set up schools for Blacks around Nashville and wanted to make it the Athens of the South. [Laughter]
SC: That's what I mean.
IR: They all ran away. [Laughter]
QT: I'd like to ask you who, if any, of the younger poets do you know?
IR: Did you mention names?
QT: Yes, I've got some names . . .
IR: Good, I've got some names too.
QT: OK. But, I mean poets that you might admire, or if you know anything about their work. I've got some names.
RE: You'd better give them to me because I don't know many of them.
SC: I've got some novelists, but you know them.

QT: OK, here are the poets: Jayne Cortez, Calvin Hernton, Al Young, Kay Curtis Lyle, Eloise Lofton, Stanley Crouch, Lorenzo Thomas, Sonya Sanchez, Don L. Lee, Baraka, Nikki Giovanni—
RE: When did Baraka become *young?* I know Stanley Crouch as a correspondent; he's a very intelligent guy, but I don't know him as a poet.
QT: We went to school together, he and I.
RE: Is that right?
QT: Jayne Cortez and myself.
SC: He's writing jazz criticism for the *Village Voice* now.

RE: I know that he can write prose, but I don't know his poetry. As with Hernton, I've only read a few of the poems by people you've mentioned, so I wouldn't be able to judge their work. I don't think very much of what Miss Giovanni does, but that doesn't mean anything; it's a matter of taste.

IR: And Don L. Lee?

RE: Once, I met Lee on a plane, leaving Buffalo, I think, and flew beside him to Chicago. He sent me some of his work. He was very amiable, but his ideological emphasis got in the way of my really getting to his poetry. Maybe it's a case of generation gap.

QT: My last question: Can you tell us the difference in terms of form and structure and language and character between your works in progress and *Invisible Man?*

SC: Quincy, I had a question in mind before you get to that. I was looking at *Invisible Man* while thinking about a few things that happened in 19th Century American literature, and the whole narrative sequence of events updated to the turn of the century. It reads very much like a slave narrative, doesn't it? Would you say you've borrowed the techniques?

RE: No, that's coincidental. And, frankly, I think too much has been made of the slave narrative as an influence on contemporary writing. Experience tends to mold itself into certain repetitive patterns, and one of the reasons we exchange experiences is in order to discover the repetitions and coincidences which amount to a common group experience. We tell ourselves our individual stories so as to become aware of our *general* story. I wouldn't have had to read a single slave narrative in order to create the narrative pattern of *Invisible Man*. It emerges from experience and from my own sense of literary form, out of my sense of experience as shaped by history and my familiarity with literature. However, one's sense of group experience comes first because one communicates with the reader in terms of what he identifies as a viable description of experience. You project your vision of what *can* happen in terms of what he accepts as the way things *have happened* in the past, his sense of "the way things are." Historically, we were trying to escape from slavery in a scene consisting of geographical space. First, to the North and then to the West, going to the Nation (meaning the Indian Nation and later the Oklahoma Territory), just as Huckleberry Finn decided to do, and as Bessie Smith states in one of her blues. Of course, some of us escaped south and joined the Seminoles and fought with them against the U.S. Geography forms the scene in which we and our forefathers acted and continue to act out the drama of Afro-American freedom. This movement from region to region involved all of the motives, political, sociological, and personal, that come to focus in the struggle. So, the movement from the South to the North became a basic pattern for my novel. The pattern of movement and the obstacles encountered are so basic to Afro-American experience (and to my own, since my mother took me North briefly during the Twenties, and I came North again in '36), that I had no need of slave narratives to grasp either its significance or its potential for organizing a fictional narrative. I would have used the same device if I had been writing an autobiography.

Then, there is the imagery and the incidents of conflict. These come from all kinds of sources. From literature, from the spirituals and the blues, from other novels and from poetry, as well as from my observations of socio-psychological conflicts and processes. It comes from mythology, fool's errands, children's games, sermons, the dozens, and the Bible. All this is not to put down the slave narrative, but, to say that it did not influence my novel as a conscious functional form. And, don't forget, the main source of any novel is other *novels*; these constitute the culture of the form, and my loyalty to our group does nothing to change that; it's a cultural, literary reality.

SC: Well, I happened to notice a parallel, that's all, such as your putting Douglass's picture on the wall and the whole bit.
RE: Oh!—But, that's *allusion*, that's riffing. When you put a detail in its proper place in an action, it gathers up associations and meanings and starts speaking to the reader's sense of significance. Just as it spoke to *you* as you struggled to give order to your material. Placed in the right context, and at the optimum stage of an action, it vibrates and becomes symbolically eloquent. That's poetry, I mean, in the larger sense of the term. That's how we use the little marks on the page to communicate and evoke a symbolic reality. It's symbolic action. In *Mr. Sammler's Planet*, Saul Bellow has a Black pickpocket make the symbolic gesture of drawing his pecker out on the main character. The thing sets up all kinds of reverberation in the narrative. It becomes damn nigh metaphysical. It certainly caused a lot of comment, but if I had written the scene, I would have tried to make it even more eloquent by having the pickpocket snatch it out and hit

the hero over the head with it. I would have further physicalized the metaphysic—soma to psyche! [Laughter] It reminds me of the story of the proud Negro who goes to the doctor to be examined for the clap—which he doesn't have, and knows it—simply because he wants an "expert" to admire what he believes to be an unusually fine member. "Hell, doc," he says, "I knew wasn't nothing *wrong* with it. I just wanted you to see what a fine one I have." Forgive me, Steve, for getting away from your question.

SC: Well, maybe what I meant by it was simply that the movement, the whole sweep through Georgia on the Greyhound bus suggested the slave narratives. The other question is, why since you hear the sounds we do, the sounds of technology, particularly the sounds of trains, why do you think they're absent from novels nowadays?

RE: Because the trains no longer have those whistles on them. [Laughter]

IR: What about Baldwin's *Tell Me How Long the Train's Been Gone?* That could be like a mournful train wail.

SC: OK. I remember what's his name—you knew a guy by the name of Bledsoe, didn't you? I was told last night that you did.

QT: Jules Bledsoe. He was an opera singer.

RE: I knew about him, but I never met him. My character is imaginary.

SC: I meant functionally . . .

IR: There was also a guy in the Civil War named Bledsoe . . .

RE: There are a number of Bledsoes, but I used the name for its sound and the associations it evoked. I did the same with Trueblood. I associate the names with the characters and their actions. I was trying to pun with them. Bledsoe "bled" his people.

SC: We were going to bring up a question about Rinehart . . .

IR: I want to ask you about novelists—Toni Morrison, Gayl Jones, John McClusky, Charles Johnson . . .

RE: Toni Morrison's work I know.

IR: You know her work?

RE: Yes, she's a good novelist.

IR: And Gayl Jones, you know her work?

RE: No. I have a book of hers that came during the summer, but I haven't read it.

IR: It's an excellent book, not like a lot of the feminist tracts and that sort of thing. Ah, (William Gardner Smith)?

RE: Smith's first book, *The Last of the Conquerors*, I liked; I didn't like the next one, I forget the title. He's dead, isn't he?

IR: Yeah, he died last year. And, Charles Johnson?

RE: I've never read him. I know the work of a writer named Boles, he has a certain skill.

SC: Robert Boles, an excellent novelist.

IR: —

QT: Would you like to comment on Bill Demby and Al Murray? Did you look at Murray's first novel, the one he published I mean. I don't know how many he's got at the house.

QT: *Train Whistle Guitar?*

RE: Sure, I think it's a fine book. The, ah, Demby, which title?

QT: *Beetle Creek.*

RE: It's a good book.

IR: What do you think of Joseph Okpaku, a Nigerian, representing Afro-American writers—

RE: What's his name?

IR: Joseph Okpaku, Third World Press. He received $250,000 from the Ford Foundation to begin a publishing company here. What do you think of the propriety of a Nigerian testifying before an American Senate committee concerning the plight of Afro-American writers? [Laughter]

RE: [Laughs] Well, ah, very seriously, I would ask how much does he know about it? If he knows about it——

QT: He's trained as an engineer. [Laughter]

RE: Come on now, there are writers who were trained in other disciplines. MacLeish was a lawyer and my discipline was music.

QT: No, I was just saying that in jest, but I don't think he knows that much about it after talking with him. . . .

RE: Well, strange things happen. I don't know how this could have come about. I just hope that he does well with it. Have you any idea why he was appointed, how he succeeded in . . .

IR: It just seems to be a general trend. Many timid Afro-American intellectuals, really, murmur about it. It seems to be something that the liberal establishment began when Afro-Americans stopped talking to them for a while. They brought over Africans to teach Afro-American literature.

RE: Now I see what you mean. Well, haven't the Blacks been telling the white liberals that we are all Africans? So, after taking a lot of criticisms from angry people with their hands out the whites say, "Hell, so we'll go and get us some *real* Africans." It's an ironic development. I've had nasty things said about me because I say that I'm not an "African"—which is a geographical abstraction anyway. I don't even know what tribes my great great great great great grand-addies came from, so I'm certainly in no position to identify myself as an African. Q.T.'s been to Africa, I haven't. I wouldn't be able to tell you anything about it except what I've read in books. And I certainly wouldn't be able to set up a press for Africans except as a technician—if I *knew* the techniques of running a publishing house. But often we help to confuse white people, and sometimes this can be used to our disadvantage.

QT: Let me ask you, what do you think about the writing of Garcia Marquez, Pynchon, and, say, Chinua Achebe?
RE: Well, I don't know Achebe's work too well. I've read a couple of his books which I liked. However, Achebe raised the question of what, precisely, is an "African" writer? He strikes me as a Western writer—just as certain writers from former French colonies, such as Cesaire, Senghor, and Ouologuem who are French writer-intellectuals, no matter what they tell you about negritude. I think that Amos Tutuola, who wrote *The Palm-wine Drunkard*, is far more "African" than any of the others. Marquez? As far as I'm concerned, his *One Hundred Years of Solitude* is the work of a great novelist.

SC: Pynchon?
RE: Pynchon gets away from me. I find his work too diffused for my own sense of things, which doesn't mean that I'm right about him. Anyway, he doesn't need my OK. He's doing all right, despite my lack of interest in his work.

SC: Would you like to comment on what Quincy was asking before, as to why you got away from the "I" form, the first person narrative, why you changed technique for your new book?
RE: There's no mystery about it, you change technique according

to the demands of your material. In *Invisible Man*, I used the first person just to see what I could do with it, and by way of arguing across the centuries with Henry James, who considered the first person as contributing to formal looseness. I'm now struggling to wind up my current novel by using various points-of-view because the material seems to call for it.

SC: Is it a big book?

RE: Well, it has a lot of pages, but whether it's going to be a big book in impact is something else. It's a crazy book, and I won't pretend to understand what it's about. I do think there are some funny passages in it.

QT: Could you say when you think you might finish it?

RE: No, I've done that too many times and been wrong.

CARLTON FISK IS MY IDEAL

by BERNADETTE MAYER

from BASEBALL I GAVE YOU ALL THE BEST YEARS OF MY LIFE
(North Atlantic Books)

nominated by David Wilk

He wears a beautiful necklace
next to the beautiful skin of his neck
unlike the Worthington butcher,
Bradford T. Fisk (butchers always
have a crush on me), who cannot even order veal
except in whole legs of it.
Oh the legs of a catcher!
Catchers squat in a posture
that is of course inward denying orgasm
but Carlton Fisk, I could
model a whole attitude to spring
on him. And he is a leaper!
Like Walt Frazier or, better,
like the only white leaper,
I forget his name, in the ABA's
All-star game half-time slam-dunk contest
this year. I think about Carlton Fisk
in his modest home in New Hampshire
all the time, I love the sound of his name
denying orgasm. Carlton & I
look out the window at spring's first
northeaster. He carries a big hero
across the porch of his home to me.
(He has no year-round Xmas tree

like Clifford Ray who handles the ball
like a banana). We eat & watch the storm
batter the buds balking on the trees
& cover the green of the grass
that my sister thinks is new grass.
It's last year's grass still!
And still there is no spring training
as I write this, March 16, 1976,
the year of the blizzard that sealed our love
up in a great mound of orgasmic earth.
The pitcher's mound is the lightning mound.
Pudge will see fastballs in the wind,
his mescaline arm extends to the field.
He wears his necklace.
He catches the ball in his teeth!
Balls fall with a neat thunk
in the upholstery of the leather glove he puts on
to caress me, as told to, in the off-season.
All of a sudden he leaps from the couch,
a real ball has come thru the window
& is heading for the penguins on his sweater,
one of whom has lost his balloon
which is floating up into the sky!

UNTITLED

by LORIS ESSARY

from CLOWN WAR

nominated by Richard Kostelanetz

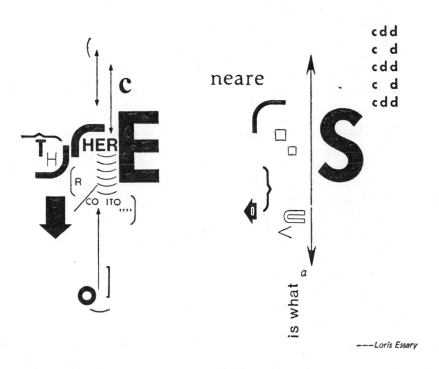

—Loris Essary

MY MOTHER'S NOVEL

by MARGE PIERCY

from PAINTED BRIDE QUARTERLY

nominated by Barbara Damrosch and Louise Simons

Married academic woman ten
years younger holding that microphone
like a bazooka, forgive
me that I do some number of things
that you fantasize but frame
impossible. Understand:
I am my mother's daughter,
a small woman of large longings.

Energy hurled through her
confined and fierce as in a wind
tunnel. Born to a mean
harried poverty crosshatched
by spidery fears and fitfully
lit by the explosions
of politics, she married her way
at length into the solid workingclass:
a box of house, a car she could
not drive, a TV set kept turned
to the blare of football,
terrifying power tools, used wall
to wall carpeting protected
by scatter rugs.

Out of backyard posies
permitted to fringe
the proud hanky lawn
her imagination hummed
and made honey,
occasionally exploding
in mad queen swarms.

I am her only novel.
The plot is melodramatic,
hot lovers leap out of
thickets, it makes you cry
a lot, in between the revolutionary
heroics and making good
home-cooked soup.
Understand: I am my mother's
novel daughter: I
have my duty to perform.

THE MAN FROM MARS

fiction by MARGARET ATWOOD

from ONTARIO REVIEW

nominated by ONTARIO REVIEW, *Paula Deitz, Maxine Kumin, and Anne Tyler*

A LONG TIME AGO CHRISTINE was walking through the park. She was still wearing her tennis dress; she hadn't had time to shower and change, and her hair was held back with an elastic band. Her chunky reddish face, exposed with no softening fringe, looked like a Russian peasant's, but without the elastic band the hair got in her eyes. The afternoon was too hot for April; the indoor courts had been steaming, her skin felt poached.

The sun had brought the old men out from wherever they spent the winter: she had read a story recently about one who lived for three years in a manhole. They sat weedishly on the benches or lay on the grass with their heads on squares of used newspaper. As she

passed, their wrinkled toadstool faces drifted towards her, drawn by
the movement of her body, then floated away again, uninterested.

The squirrels were out too, foraging; two or three of them moved
towards her in darts and pauses, eyes fixed on her expectantly,
mouths with the ratlike receding chins open to show the yellowed
front teeth. Christine walked faster, she had nothing to give them.
People shouldn't feed them, she thought, it makes them anxious and
they get mangy.

Halfway across the park she stopped to take off her cardigan. As
she bent over to pick up her tennis racquet again someone touched
her on her freshly-bared arm. Christine seldom screamed; she
straightened up suddenly, gripping the handle of her racquet. It was
not one of the old men, however: it was a dark-haired boy of twelve
or so.

"Excuse me," he said, "I search for Economics Building. It is
there?" He motioned towards the west.

Christine looked at him more closely. She had been mistaken: he
was not young, just short. He came a little above her shoulder, but
then, she was above the average height; "statuesque," her mother
called it when she was straining. He was also what was referred to in
their family as "a person from another culture": oriental without a
doubt, though perhaps not Chinese. Christine judged he must be a
foreign student and gave him her official welcoming smile. In high
school she had been President of the United Nations Club; that year
her school had been picked to represent the Egyptian delegation at
the Mock Assembly. It had been an unpopular assignment—nobody
wanted to be the Arabs—but she had seen it through. She had made
rather a good speech about the Palestinian refugees.   •

"Yes," she said, "that's it over there. The one with the flat roof.
See it?"

The man had been smiling nervously at her the whole time. He
was wearing glasses with transparent plastic rims, through which his
eyes bulged up at her as though through a goldfish bowl. He had not
followed where she was pointing. Instead he thrust towards her a
small pad of green paper and a ballpoint pen.

"You make map," he said.

Christine set down her tennis racquet and drew a careful map.
"We are here," she said, pronouncing distinctly. "You go this way.
The building is here." She indicated the route with a dotted line and
an X. The man leaned close to her, watching the progress of the map

attentively; he smelled of cooked cauliflower and an unfamiliar brand of hair grease. When she had finished Christine handed the paper and pen back to him with a terminal smile.

"Wait," the man said. He tore the piece of paper with the map off the pad, folded it carefully and put it in his jacket pocket; the jacket sleeves came down over his wrists and had threads at the edges. He began to write something; she noticed with a slight feeling of revulsion that his nails and the ends of his fingertips were so badly bitten they seemed almost deformed. Several of his fingers were blue from the leaky ballpoint.

"Here is my name," he said, holding the pad out to her.

Christine read an odd assemblage of G's, Y's and N's, neatly printed in block letters. "Thank you," she said.

"You now write *your* name," he said, extending the pen.

Christine hesitated. If this had been a person from her own culture she would have thought he was trying to pick her up. But then, people from her own culture never tried to pick her up: she was too big. The only one who had made the attempt was the Moroccan waiter at the beer parlour where they sometimes went after meetings, and he had been direct. He had just intercepted her on the way to the Ladies' Room and asked and she said no; that had been that. This man was not a waiter though but a student; she didn't want to offend him. In his culture, whatever it was, this exchange of names on pieces of paper was probably a formal politeness, like saying Thank You. She took the pen from him.

"That is a very pleasant name," he said. He folded the paper and placed it in his jacket pocket with the map.

Christine felt she had done her duty. "Well, goodbye," she said "it was nice to have met you." She bent for her tennis racquet but he had already stooped and retrieved it and was holding it with both hands in front of him, like a captured banner.

"I carry this for you."

"Oh no, please. Don't bother, I am in a hurry," she said, articulating clearly. Deprived of her tennis racquet she felt weaponless. He started to saunter along the path; he was not nervous at all now, he seemed completely at ease.

"Vous parlez français?" he asked conversationally.

"Oui, un petit peu," she said. "Not very well." How am I going to get my racquet away from him without being rude, she was wondering.

"Mais vous avez un bel accent." His eyes goggled at her through the glasses: was he being flirtatious? She was well aware that her accent was wretched.

"Look," she said, for the first time letting her impatience show, "I really have to go. Give me my racquet please."

He quickened his pace but gave no sign of returning the racquet. "Where you are going?"

"Home," she said. "My house."

"I go with you now," he said hopefully.

"*No,*" she said: she would have to be firm with him. She made a lunge and got a grip on her racquet; after a brief tug of war it came free.

"Goodbye," she said, turning away from his puzzled face and setting off at what she hoped was a discouraging jog-trot. It was like walking away from a growling dog, you shouldn't let on you were frightened. Why should she be frightened anyway? He was only half her size and she had the tennis racquet, there was nothing he could do to her.

Although she did not look back she could tell he was still following. Let there be a streetcar, she thought, and there was one, but it was far down the line, stuck behind a red light. He appeared at her side, breathing audibly, a moment after she reached the stop. She gazed ahead, rigid.

"You are my friend," he said tentatively.

Christine relented: he hadn't been trying to pick her up after all, he was a stranger, he just wanted to meet some of the local people; in his place she would have wanted the same thing.

"Yes," she said, doling him out a smile.

"That is good," he said. "My country is very far."

Christine couldn't think of an apt reply. "That's interesting," she said. "Très interessant." The streetcar was coming at last; she opened her purse and got out a ticket.

"I go with you now," he said. His hand clamped on her arm above the elbow.

"You . . . stay . . . *here,*" Christine said, resisting the impulse to shout but pausing between each word as though for a deaf person. She detached his hand—his hold was quite feeble and could not compete with her tennis biceps—and leapt off the curb and up the streetcar steps, hearing with relief the doors grind shut behind her. Inside the car and a block away she permitted herself a glance out a side window. He was standing where she had left him; he seemed to be writing something on his little pad of paper.

When she reached home she had only time for a snack, and even then she was almost late for the Debating Society. The topic was, "Resolved: That War Is Obsolete." Her team took the affirmative, and won.

Christine came out of her last examination feeling depressed. It was not the exam that depressed her but the fact that it was the last one: it meant the end of the school year. She dropped into the coffee shop as usual, then went home early because there didn't seem to be anything else to do.

"Is that you, dear?" her mother called from the livingroom. She must have heard the front door close. Christine went in and flopped on the sofa, disturbing the neat pattern of the cushions.

"How was your exam, dear?" her mother asked.

"Fine," said Christine flatly. It had been fine, she had passed. She was not a brilliant student, she knew that, but she was conscientious. Her professors always wrote things like "A serious attempt" and "Well thought out but perhaps lacking in *élan*" on her term papers; they gave her B's, the occasional B+. She was taking Political Science and Economics, and hoped for a job with the Government after she graduated; with her father's connections she had a good chance.

"That's nice."

Christine felt, resentfully, that her mother had only a hazy idea of what an exam was. She was arranging gladioli in a vase; she had rubber gloves on to protect her hands as she always did when engaged in what she called "housework." As far as Christine could tell her housework consisted of arranging flowers in vases: daffodils and tulips and hyacinths through gladioli, iris and roses, all the way to asters and mums. Sometimes she cooked, elegantly and with chafing-dishes, but she thought of it as a hobby. The girl did everything else. Christine thought it faintly sinful to have a girl. The only ones available now were either foreign or pregnant; their expressions usually suggested they were being taken advantage of somehow. But her mother asked what they would do otherwise, they'd either have to go into a Home or stay in their own countries, and Christine had to agree this was probably true. It was hard anyway to argue with her mother, she was so delicate, so preserved-looking, a harsh breath would scratch the finish.

"An interesting young man phoned today," her mother said. She had finished the gladioli and was taking off her rubber gloves. "He asked to speak with you and when I said you weren't in we had quite a little chat. You didn't tell me about him, dear." She put on the glasses which she wore on a decorative chain around her neck, a signal that she was in her modern, intelligent mood rather than her old-fashioned whimsical one.

"Did he leave his name?" Christine asked. She knew a lot of young men but they didn't often call her, they conducted their business with her in the coffee shop or after meetings.

"He's a person from another culture. He said he would call back later."

Christine had to think a moment. She was vaguely acquainted with several people from other cultures, Britain mostly; they belonged to the Debating Society.

"He's studying Philosophy in Montreal," her mother prompted. "He sounded French."

Christine began to remember the man in the park. "I don't think he's French, exactly," she said.

Her mother had taken off her glasses again and was poking absentmindedly at a bent gladiolus. "Well, he sounded French." She meditated, flowery sceptre in hand. "I think it would be nice if you had him to tea."

Christine's mother did her best. She had two other daughters, both of whom took after her. They were beautiful, one was well married already and the other would clearly have no trouble. Her friends consoled her about Christine by saying, "She's not fat, she's just big-boned, it's the father's side," and "Christine is so healthy." Her other daughters had never gotten involved in activities when they were at school, but since Christine could not possibly ever be beautiful even if she took off weight, it was just as well she was so athletic and political, it was a good thing she had interests. Christine's mother tried to encourage her interests whenever possible. Christine could tell when she was making an extra effort, there was a reproachful edge to her voice.

She knew her mother expected enthusiasm but she could not supply it. "I don't know, I'll have to see," she said dubiously.

"You look tired, darling" said her mother. "Perhaps you'd like a glass of milk."

Christine was in the bathtub when the phone rang. She was not prone to fantasy but when she was in the bathtub she often pretended she was a dolphin, a game left over from one of the girls who used to bathe her when she was small. Her mother was being bell-voiced and gracious in the hall; then there was a tap at the door.

"It's that nice young French student, Christine," her mother said.

"Tell him I'm in the bathtub," Christine said, louder than necessary. "He isn't French."

She could hear her mother frowning. "That wouldn't be very polite, Christine. I don't think he'd understand."

"Oh all right," Christine said. She heaved herself out of the bathtub, swathed her pink bulk in a towel and splattered to the phone.

"Hello," she said gruffly. At a distance he was not pathetic, he was a nuisance. She could not imagine how he had tracked her down: most likely he went through the phone book, calling all the numbers with her last name until he hit on the right one.

"It is your friend."

"I know," she said. "How are you?"

"I am very fine." There was a long pause, during which Christine had a vicious urge to say, "Well, goodbye then," and hang up; but she was aware of her mother poised figurine-like in her bedroom doorway. Then he said, "I hope you also are very fine."

"Yes," said Christine. She wasn't going to participate.

"I come to tea," he said.

This took Christine by surprise. "You do?"

"Your pleasant mother ask me. I come Thursday, four o'clock."

"Oh," Christine said, ungraciously.

"See you then," he said, with conscious pride of one who has mastered a difficult idiom.

Christine set down the phone and went along the hall. Her mother was in her study, sitting innocently at her writing desk.

"Did you ask him to tea on Thursday?"

"Not exactly, dear," her mother said. "I did mention he might come round to tea *some*time, though."

"Well, he's coming Thursday. Four o'clock."

"What's wrong with that?" her mother said serenely. "I think it's a very nice gesture for us to make. I do think you might try to be a little more co-operative." She was pleased with herself.

"Since you invited him," said Christine, "you can bloody well stick around and help me entertain him. I don't want to be left making nice gestures all by myself."

"Christine *dear*," her mother said, above being shocked. "You ought to put on your dressing gown, you'll catch a chill."

After sulking for an hour Christine tried to think of the tea as a cross between an examination and an executive meeting: not enjoyable, certainly, but to be got through as tactfully as possible. And it *was* a nice gesture. When the cakes her mother had ordered arrived from *The Patisserie* on Thursday morning she began to feel slightly festive; she even resolved to put on a dress, a good one, instead of a skirt and blouse. After all, she had nothing against him, except the memory of the way he had grabbed her tennis racquet and then her arm. She suppressed a quick impossible vision of herself pursued around the livingroom, fending him off with thrown sofa cushions and vases of gladioli; nevertheless she told the girl they would have tea in the garden. It would be a treat for him, and there was more space outdoors.

She had suspected her mother would dodge the tea, would contrive to be going out just as he was arriving: that way she could size him up and then leave them alone together. She had done things like that to Christine before; her mother carefully mislaid her gloves and located them with a faked murmur of joy when the doorbell rang. Christine relished for weeks afterwards the image of her mother's dropped jaw and flawless recovery when he was introduced: he wasn't quite the foreign potentate her optimistic, veil-fragile mind had concocted.

He was prepared for celebration. He had slicked on so much hair cream that his head seemed to be covered with a tight black patent-leather cap, and he had cut the threads off his jacket sleeves. His orange tie was overpoweringly splendid. Christine noticed however as he shook her mother's suddenly-braced white glove that the ballpoint ink on his fingers was indelible. His face had broken out, possibly in anticipation of the delights in store for him; he had a tiny camera slung over his shoulder and was smoking an exotic-smelling cigarette.

Christine led him through the cool flowery softly-padded livingroom and out by the French doors into the garden. "You sit here," she said. "I will have the girl bring tea."

This girl was from the West Indies: Christines's parents had been enraptured with her when they were down at Christmas and had brought her back with them. Since that time she had become pregnant, but Christine's mother had not dismissed her. She said she was slightly disappointed but what could you expect, and she didn't see any real difference between a girl who was pregnant before you hired her and one who got that way afterward. She prided herself on her tolerance; also there was a scarcity of girls. Strangely enough, the girl became progressively less easy to get along with. Either she did not share Christine's mother's view of her own generosity, or she felt she had gotten away with something and was therefore free to indulge in contempt. At first Christine had tried to treat her as an equal. "Don't call me 'Miss Christine,'" she had said with an imitation of light, comradely laughter. "What you want me to call you then?" the girl had said, scowling. They had begun to have brief, surly arguments in the kitchen, which Christine decided were like the arguments between one servant and another: her mother's attitude towards each of them was similar, they were not altogether satisfactory but they would have to do.

The cakes, glossy with icing, were set out on a plate and the teapot was standing ready; on the counter the electric kettle boiled. Christine headed for it, but the girl, till then sitting with her elbows on the kitchen table and watching her expressionlessly, made a dash and intercepted her. Christine waited until she had poured the water into the pot. Then, "I'll carry it out, Elvira," she said. She had just decided she didn't want the girl to see her visitor's orange tie; already, she knew, her position in the girl's eyes had suffered because no-one had yet attempted to get *her* pregnant.

"What you think they pay me for, Miss Christine?" the girl said insolently. She swung toward the garden with the tray; Christine trailed her, feeling lumpish and awkward. The girl was at least as big as she was but she was big in a different way.

"Thank you, Elvira," Christine said when the tray was in place. The girl departed without a word, casting a disdainful backward glance at the frayed jacket sleeves, the stained fingers. Christine was now determined to be especially kind to him.

"You are very rich," he said.

"No," Christine protested, shaking her head; "we're not." She had never thought of her family as rich, it was one of her father's sayings that nobody made any money with the Government.

"Yes," he repeated, "You are very rich." He sat back in his lawn chair, gazing about him as though dazed.

Christine set his cup of tea in front of him. She wasn't in the habit of paying much attention to the house or the garden; they were nothing special, far from being the largest on the street; other people took care of them. But now she looked where he was looking, seeing it all as though from a different height: the long expanses, the border flowers blazing in the early-summer sunlight, the flagged patio and walks, the high walls and the silence.

He came back to her face, sighing a little. "My English is not good," he said, "but I improve."

"You do," Christine said, nodding encouragement.

He took sips of his tea, quickly and tenderly as though afraid of injuring the cup. "I like to stay here."

Christine passed him the cakes. He took only one, making a slight face as he ate it; but he had several more cups of tea while she finished the cakes. She managed to find out from him that he had come over on a Church fellowship—she could not decode the denomination—and was studying Philosophy or Theology, or possibly both. She was feeling well-disposed towards him: he had behaved himself, he had caused her no inconvenience.

The teapot was at last empty. He sat up straight in his chair, as though alerted by a soundless gong. "You look this way, please," he said. Christine saw that he had placed his miniature camera on the stone sundial her mother had shipped back from England two years before: he wanted to take her picture. She was flattered, and settled herself to pose, smiling evenly.

He took off his glasses and laid them beside his plate. For a moment she saw his myopic, unprotected eyes turned towards her, with something tremulous and confiding in them she wanted to close herself off from knowing about. Then he went over and did something to the camera, his back to her. The next instant he was crouched beside her, his arm around her waist as far as it could reach, his other hand covering her own hands which she had folded in her lap, his cheek jammed up against hers. She was too startled to move. The camera clicked.

He stood up at once and replaced his glasses, which glittered now with a sad triumph. "Thank you, Miss," he said to her. "I go now." He slung the camera back over his shoulder, keeping his hand on it as though to hold the lid on and prevent escape. "I send to my family; they will like."

He was out the gate and gone before Christine had recovered; then she laughed. She had been afraid he would attack her, she could admit it now, and he had; but not in the usual way. He had raped, *rapeo, rapere, rapui, to seize and carry off*, not herself but her celluloid image, and incidently that of the silver tea service, which glinted mockingly at her as the girl bore it away, carrying it regally, the insignia, the official jewels.

Christine spent the summer as she had for the past three years: she was the sailing instructress at an expensive all-girls camp near Algonquin Park. She had been a camper there, everything was familiar to her; she sailed almost better then she played tennis.

The second week she got a letter from him, postmarked Montreal and forwarded from her home address. It was printed in block letters on a piece of the green paper, two or three sentences. It began, "I hope you are well," then described the weather in monosyllables and ended, "I am fine." It was signed "Your friend." Each week she got another of these letters, more or less identical. In one of them a colour print was enclosed: himself, slightly crosseyed and grinning hilariously, even more spindly than she remembered him against her billowing draperies, flowers exploding around them like firecrackers, one of his hands an equivocal blur in her lap, the other out of sight; on her own face, astonishment and outrage, as though he was sticking her in the behind with his hidden thumb.

She answered the first letter, but after that the seniors were in training for the races. At the end of the summer, packing to go home, she threw all the letters away.

When she had been back for several weeks she received another of the green letters. This time there was a return address printed at the top which Christine noted with foreboding was in her own city. Every day she waited for the phone to ring; she was so certain his first attempt at contact would be a disembodied voice that when he came upon her abruptly in mid-campus she was unprepared.

"How are you?"

His smile was the same, but everything else about him had deteriorated. He was, if possible, thinner; his jacket sleeves had sprouted a lush new crop of threads, as though to conceal hands now so badly bitten they appeared to have been gnawed by rodents. His hair fell over his eyes, uncut, ungreased; his eyes in the hollowed face, a delicate triangle of skin stretched on bone, jumped behind his glasses like hooked fish. He had the end of a cigarette in the corner of his mouth and as they walked he lit a new one from it.

"I'm fine," Christine said. She was thinking, I'm not going to get involved again, enough is enough, I've done my bit for internationalism. "How are you?"

"I live here now," he said. "Maybe I study Economics."

"That's nice." He didn't sound as though he was enrolled anywhere.

"I come to see you."

Christine didn't know whether he meant he had left Montreal in order to be near her or just wanted to visit her at her house as he had done in the spring; either way she refused to be implicated. They were outside the Political Science building. "I have a class here," she said. "Goodbye." She was being callous, she realized that, but a quick chop was more merciful in the long run, that was what her beautiful sisters used to say.

Afterwards she decided it had been stupid of her to let him find out where her class was. Though a timetable was posted in each of the colleges: all he had to do was look her up and record her every probable movement in block letters on his green notepad. After that day he never left her alone.

Initially he waited outside the lecture rooms for her to come out. She said Hello to him curtly at first and kept on going, but this didn't work; he followed her at a distance, smiling his changeless smile. Then she stopped speaking altogether and pretended to ignore him, but it made no difference, he followed her anyway. The fact that she was in some way afraid of him—or was it just embarrassment?—seemed only to encourage him. Her friends started to notice, asking her who he was and why he was tagging along behind her; she could hardly answer because she hardly knew.

As the weekdays passed and he showed no signs of letting up, she began to jog-trot between classes, finally to run. He was tireless, and had an amazing wind for one who smoked so heavily: he would speed along behind her, keeping the distance between them the same, as though he was a pull-toy attached to her by a string. She was aware of the ridiculous spectacle they must make, galloping across campus, something out of a cartoon short, a lumbering elephant stampeded

by a smiling, emaciated mouse, both of them locked in the classic
pattern of comic pursuit and flight; but she found that to race made
her less nervous than to walk sedately, the skin on the back of her
neck crawling with the feel of his eyes on it. At least she could use
her muscles. She worked out routines, escapes: she would dash in
the front door of the Ladies' Room in the coffee shop and out the back
door, and he would lose the trail, until he discovered the other
entrance. She would try to shake him by detours through baffling
archways and corridors, but he seemed as familiar with the architec-
tural mazes as she was herself. As a last refuge she could head for the
women's dormitory and watch from safety as he was skidded to a halt
by the receptionist's austere voice: men were not allowed past the
entrance.

Lunch became difficult. She would be sitting, usually with other
members of the Debating Society, just digging nicely into a
sandwich, when he would appear suddenly as though he'd come up
through an unseen manhole. She then had the choice of barging out
through the crowded cafeteria, sandwich half-eaten, or finishing her
lunch with him standing behind her chair, everyone at the table
acutely aware of him, the conversation stilting and dwindling. Her
friends learned to spot him from a distance; they posted lookouts.
"Here he comes," they would whisper, helping her collect her
belongings for the sprint they knew would follow.

Several times she got tired of running and turned to confront him.
"What do you want?" she would ask, glowering belligerently down
at him, almost clenching her fists; she felt like shaking him, hitting
him.

"I wish to talk with you."

"Well, here I am," she would say. "What do you want to talk
about?"

But he would say nothing; he would stand in front of her, shifting
his feet, smiling perhaps apologetically (though she could never
pinpoint the exact tone of that smile, chewed lips stretched apart
over the nicotine-yellowed teeth, rising at the corners, flesh held
stiffly in place for an invisible photographer), his eyes jerking from
one part of her face to another as though he saw her in fragments.

Annoying and tedious though it was, his pursuit of her had an odd
result: mysterious in itself, it rendered her equally mysterious.
No-one had ever found Christine mysterious before. To her parents
she was a beefy heavyweight, a plodder, lacking in flair, ordinary as

bread. To her sisters she was the plain one, treated with an indulgence they did not give to each other: they did not fear her as a rival. To her male friends she was the one who could be relied on. She was helpful and a hard worker, always good for a game of tennis with the athletes among them. They invited her along to drink beer with them so they could get into the cleaner, more desirable Ladies and Escorts side of the beer parlour, taking it for granted she would buy her share of the rounds. In moments of stress they confided to her their problems with women. There was nothing devious about her and nothing interesting.

Christine had always agreed with these estimates of herself. In childhood she had identified with the False Bride or the ugly sister; whenever a story had begun, "Once there was a maiden as beautiful as she was good," she had known it wasn't her. That was just how it was, but it wasn't so bad. Her parents never expected her to be a brilliant social success and weren't overly disappointed when she wasn't. She was spared the manoeuvering and anxiety she witnessed among others her age, and she even had a kind of special position among men: she was an exception, she fitted none of the categories they commonly used when talking about girls, she wasn't a cock-teaser, a cold fish, an easy lay or a snarky bitch; she was an honorary person. She had grown to share their contempt for most women.

Now however there was something about her that could not be explained. A man was chasing her, a peculiar sort of man, granted, but still a man, and he was without doubt attracted to her, he couldn't leave her alone. Other men examined her more closely than they ever had, appraising her, trying to find out what it was those twitching bespectacled eyes saw in her. They started to ask her out, though they returned from these excursions with their curiosity unsatisfied, the secret of her charm still intact. Her opaque dumpling face, her solid bear-shaped body became for them parts of a riddle no-one could solve. Christine knew this and began to use it. In the bathtub she no longer imagined she was a dolphin; instead she imagined she was an elusive water-nixie, or sometimes, in moments of audacity, Marilyn Monroe. The daily chase was becoming a habit; she even looked forward to it. In addition to its other benefits she was losing weight.

All those weeks he had never phoned her or turned up at the house. He must have decided however that his tactics were not having the desired result, or perhaps he sensed she was becoming bored. The phone began to ring in the early morning or late at night when he could be sure she would be there. Sometimes he would simply breathe (she could recognize, or thought she could, the quality of his breathing), in which case she would hang up. Occasionally he would say again that he wanted to talk to her, but even when she gave him lots of time nothing else would follow. Then he extended his range: she would see him on her streetcar, smiling at her silently from a seat never closer than three away; she could feel him tracking her down her own street, though when she would break her resolve to pay no attention and would glance back he would be invisible or in the act of hiding behind a tree or hedge.

Among crowds of people and in daylight she had not really been afraid of him; she was stronger than he was and he had made no recent attempt to touch her. But the days were growing shorter and colder, it was almost November, often she was arriving home in twilight or a darkness broken only by the feeble orange streetlamps. She brooded over the possibility of razors, knives, guns; by acquiring a weapon he could quickly turn the odds against her. She avoided wearing scarves, remembering the newspaper stories about girls who had been strangled by them. Putting on her nylons in the morning gave her a funny feeling. Her body seemed to have diminished, to have become smaller than his.

Was he deranged, was he a sex maniac? He seemed so harmless, yet it was that kind who often went berserk in the end. She pictured those ragged fingers at her throat, tearing at her clothes, though she could not think of herself as screaming. Parked cars, the shrubberies near her house, the driveways on either side of it, changed as she passed them from unnoticed background to sinisterly-shadowed foreground, every detail distinct and harsh: they were places a man might crouch, leap out from. Yet every time she saw him in the clear light of morning or afternoon (for he still continued his old methods of pursuit), his aging jacket and jittery eyes convinced her that it was she herself who was the tormentor, the persecuter. She was in some sense responsible; from the folds and crevices of the body she had treated for so long as a reliable machine was emanating, against her will, some potent invisible odour, like a dog's in heat or a female moth's, that made him unable to stop following her.

Her mother, who had been too preoccupied with the unavoidable fall entertaining to pay much attention to the number of phone calls Christine was getting or to the hired girl's complaints of a man who hung up without speaking, announced that she was flying down to New York for the weekend; her father decided to go too. Christine panicked: she saw herself in the bathtub with her throat slit, the blood drooling out of her neck and running in a little spiral down the drain (for by this time she believed he could walk through walls, could be everywhere at once). The girl would do nothing to help; she might even stand in the bathroom door with her arms folded, watching. Christine arranged to spend the weekend at her married sister's.

When she arrived back Sunday evening she found the girl close to hysterics. She said that on Saturday she had gone to pull the curtains across the French doors at dusk and had found a strangely contorted face, a man's face, pressed against the glass, staring in at her from the garden. She claimed she had fainted and had almost had her baby a month too early right there on the livingroom carpet. Then she had called the police. He was gone by the time they got there but she had recognized him from the afternoon of the tea; she had informed them he was a friend of Christine's.

They called Monday evening to investigate, two of them; they were very polite, they knew who Christine's father was. Her father greeted them heartily; her mother hovered in the background, fidgeting with her porcelain hands, letting them see how frail and worried she was. She didn't like having them in the livingroom but they were necessary.

Christine had to admit he'd been following her around. She was relieved he'd been discovered, relieved also that she hadn't been the one to tell, though if he'd been a citizen of the country she would have called the police a long time ago. She insisted he was not dangerous, he had never hurt her.

"That kind don't hurt you," one of the policemen said. "They just kill you. You're lucky you aren't dead."

"Nut cases," the other one said.

Her mother volunteered that the thing about people from another culture was that you could never tell whether they were insane or not because their ways were so different. The policeman agreed with her, deferential but also condescending, as though she was a royal halfwit who had to be humoured.

"You know where he lives?" the first policeman asked. Christine had long ago torn up the letter with his address on it; she shook her head.

"We'll have to pick him up tomorrow then," he said. "Think you can keep him talking outside your class if he's waiting for you?"

After questioning her they held a murmured conversation with her father in the front hall. The girl, clearing away the coffee cups, said if they didn't lock him up she was leaving, she wasn't going to be scared half out of her skin like that again.

Next day when Christine came out of her Modern History lecture he was there, right on schedule. He seemed puzzled when she did not begin to run. She approached him, her heart thumping with treachery and the prospect of freedom. Her body was back to its usual size; she felt herself a giantess, self-controlled, invulnerable.

"How are you?" she asked, smiling brightly.

He looked at her with distrust.

"How have you been?" she ventured again. His own perennial smile faded; he took a step back from her.

"This the one?" said the policeman, popping out from behind a notice board like a Keystone Cop and laying a competent hand on the worn jacket shoulder. The other policeman lounged in the background; force would not be required.

"Don't *do* anything to him," she pleaded as they took him away. They nodded and grinned, respectful, scornful. He seemed to know perfectly well who they were and what they wanted.

The first policeman phoned that evening to make his report. Her father talked with him, jovial and managing. She herself was now out of the picture; she had been protected, her function was over.

"What did they *do* to him?" she asked anxiously as he came back into the livingroom. She was not sure what went on in police stations.

"They didn't do anything to him," he said, amused by her concern. "They could have booked him for Watching and Besetting, they wanted to know if I'd like to proffer charges. But it's not worth a court case: he's got a visa that says he's only allowed in the country as long as he studies in Montreal, so I told them to just ship him up there. If he turns up here again they'll deport him. They went around to his rooming house, his rent's two weeks overdue; the landlady said she was on the point of kicking him out. He seems happy enough to be getting his back rent paid and a free train ticket to Montreal." He paused. "They couldn't get anything out of him though."

"*Out* of him?" Christine asked.

"They tried to find out why he was doing it; following you, I mean." Her father's eyes swept her as though it was a riddle to him also. "They said when they asked him about that he just clammed up. Pretended he didn't understand English. He understood well enough, but he wasn't answering."

Christine thought this was the end, but somehow between his arrest and the departure of the train he managed to elude his escort long enough for one more phone call.

"I see you again," he said. He didn't wait for her to hang up.

Now that he was no longer an embarrassing present reality he could be talked about, he could become an amusing story. In fact he was the only amusing story Christine had to tell, and telling it preserved both for herself and for others the aura of her strange allure. Her friends and the men who continued to ask her out speculated about his motives. One suggested he had wanted to marry her so he could remain in the country; another said that oriental men were fond of well-built women: "It's your Rubens quality."

Christine thought about him a lot. She had not been attracted to him, rather the reverse, but as an idea only he was a romantic figure, the one man who had found her irresistible; though she often wondered, inspecting her unchanged pink face and hefty body in her full-length mirror, just what it was about her that had done it. She avoided whenever it was proposed the theory of his insanity: it was only that there was more than one way of being sane.

But a new acquaintance, hearing the story for the first time, had a different explanation. "So he got you too," he said, laughing. "That has to be the same guy who was hanging around our day camp a year ago this summer. He followed all the girls like that. A short guy, Japanese or something, glasses, smiling all the time."

"Maybe it was another one," Christine said.

"There couldn't be two of them, everything fits. This was a pretty weird guy."

"What . . . *kind* of girls did he follow?" Christine asked.

"Oh, just anyone who happened to be around. But if they paid any attention to him at first, if they were nice to him or anything, he was unshakeable. He was a bit of a pest, but harmless."

Christine ceased to tell her amusing story. She had been one among many, then. She went back to playing tennis, she had been neglecting her game.

A few months later the policeman who had been in charge of the case telephoned her again.

"Like you to know, Miss, that fellow you were having the trouble with was sent back to his own country. Deported."

"What for?" Christine asked. "Did he try to come back here?" Maybe she had been special after all, maybe he had dared everything for her.

"Nothing like it," the policeman said. "He was up to the same tricks in Montreal but he really picked the wrong woman this time—a Mother Superior of a convent. They don't stand for things like that in Quebec—had him out of here before he knew what happened. I guess he'll be better off in his own place."

"How old was she?" Christine asked, after a silence.

"Oh, around sixty, I guess."

"Thank you very much for letting me know," Christine said in her best official manner. "It's such a relief." She wondered if the policeman had called to make fun of her.

She was almost crying when she put down the phone. What *had* he wanted from her then? A Mother Superior. Did she really look sixty, did she look like a mother? What did convents mean? Comfort, charity? Refuge? Was it that something had happened to him, some intolerable strain just from being in this country; her tennis dress and exposed legs too much for him, flesh and money seemingly available everywhere but withheld from him wherever he turned, the nun the symbol of some final distortion, the robe and the veil reminiscent to his nearsighted eyes of the women of his homeland, the ones he was able to understand? But he was back in his own country, remote from her as another planet; she would never know.

He hadn't forgotten her though. In the spring she got a postcard with a foreign stamp and the familiar block-letter writing. On the front was a picture of a temple. He was fine, he hoped she was fine also, he was her friend. A month later another print of the picture he had taken in the garden arrived, in a sealed manila envelope otherwise empty.

*   *   *

Christine's aura of mystery soon faded; anyway, she herself no longer believed in it. Life became again what she had always expected. She graduated with mediocre grades and went into the

Department of Health and Welfare; she did a good job, and was seldom discriminated against for being a woman because nobody thought of her as one. She could afford a pleasant-sized apartment, though she did not put much energy into decorating it. She played less and less tennis; what had been muscle with a light coating of fat turned gradually to fat with a thin substratum of muscle. She began to get headaches.

As the years were used up and the war began to fill the newspapers and magazines, she realized which eastern country he had actually been from. She had known the name but it hadn't registered at the time, it was such a minor place; she could never keep them separate in her mind.

But though she tried, she couldn't remember the name of the city, and the postcard was long gone—had he been from the North or the South, was he near the battle zone or safely far from it? Obsessively she bought the magazines and poured over the available photographs, dead villagers, soldiers on the march, colour blowups of frightened or angry faces, spies being executed; she studied maps, she watched the late-night newscasts, the distant country and terrain becoming almost more familiar to her than her own. Once or twice she thought she could recognize him but it was no use, they all looked like him.

Finally she had to stop looking at the pictures. It bothered her too much, it was bad for her; she was beginning to have nightmares in which he was coming through the French doors of her mother's house in his shabby jacket, carrying a packsack and a rifle and a huge bouquet of richly-coloured flowers. He was smiling in the same way but with blood streaked over his face, partly blotting out the features. She gave her television set away and took to reading nineteenth century novels instead; Trollope and Galsworthy were her favourites. When, despite herself, she would think about him, she would tell herself that he had been crafty and agile-minded enough to survive, more or less, in her country, so surely he would be able to do it in his own, where he knew the language. She could not see him in the army, on either side; he wasn't the type, and to her knowledge he had not believed in any particular ideology. He would be something nondescript, something in the background, like herself; perhaps he had become an interpreter.

KEY LARGO

by BRUCE ANDREWS

from HILLS

nominated by Michael Lally and Harry Smith

a respectable avoidance

                          b.
                          c.

measuring

    back blue does incites
    will pasture slowly

        narrate daughter

        ideaed

            universe

        crystal

go biography

    slight making
    whicker
    whim

        pape
        coalesce

buoyance i *am* to do teeter mum naw harked gold wood
alm dire tenting
blue
            of lube
        stooge
                    senators

THE IRON TABLE

fiction by JANE BOWLES

from ANTAEUS

nominated by ANTAEUS

THEY SAT IN THE SUN, looking out over a big new boulevard. The waiter had dragged an old iron table around from the other side of the hotel and set it down on the cement near a half-empty flower bed. A string stretched between stakes separated the hotel grounds from the sidewalk. Few of the guests staying at the hotel sat in the sun. The town was not a tourist center, and not many Anglo-Saxons came. Most of the guests were Spanish.

"The whole civilization is going to pieces," he said.

Her voice was sorrowful. "I know it." Her answers to his ceaseless complaining about the West's contamination of Moslem culture had become increasingly unpredictable. Today, because she felt that he was in a very irritable mood and in need of an argument, she automatically agreed with him. "It's going to pieces so quickly, too," she said, and her tone was sepulchral.

He looked at her without any light in his blue eyes. "There are places where the culture has remained untouched," he announced as if for the first time. "If we went into the desert you wouldn't have to face all this. Wouldn't you love that?" He was punishing her for her swift agreement with him a moment earlier. He knew she had no desire to go to the desert, and that she believed it was not possible to continue trying to escape from the Industrial Revolution. Without realizing he was doing it he had provoked the argument he wanted.

"Why do you ask me if I wouldn't love to go into the desert, when you know as well as I do I wouldn't. We've talked about it over and over. Every few days we talk about it." Although the sun was beating down on her chest, making it feel on fire, deep inside she could still feel the cold current that seemed to run near her heart.

"Well," he said. "You change. Sometimes you say you *would* like to go."

It was true. She did change. Sometimes she would run to him with bright eyes. "Let's go," she would say. "Let's go into the desert." But she never did this if she was sober.

There was something wistful in his voice, and she had to remind herself that she wanted to feel cranky rather than heartbroken. In order to go on talking she said: "Sometimes I feel like going, but it's always when I've had something to drink. When I've had nothing to drink I'm afraid." She turned to face him, and he saw that she was beginning to have her hunted expression.

"Do you think I *ought* to go?" she asked him.

"Go where?"

"To the desert. To live in an oasis." She was pronouncing her words slowly. "Maybe that's what I should do, since I'm your wife."

"You must do what you really want to do," he said. He had been trying to teach her this for twelve years.

"What I really want. . . . Well, if you'd be happy in an oasis, maybe I'd really want to do that." She spoke hesitantly, and there was a note of doubt in her voice.

"What?" He shook his head as if he had run into a spiderweb. "What is it?"

"I meant that maybe if you were happy in an oasis I would be, too.

Wives get pleasure out of making their husbands happy. They really do, quite aside from its being moral."

He did not smile. He was in too bad a humor. "You'd go to an oasis because you wanted to escape from Western civilization."

"My friends and I don't feel there's any *way* of escaping it. It's not interesting to sit around talking about industrialization."

"What friends?" He liked her to feel isolated.

"Our friends." Most of them she had not seen in many years. She turned to him with a certain violence. "I think you come to these countries so you can complain. I'm tired of hearing the word *civilization*. It has no meaning. Or I've forgotten what it meant, anyway."

The moment when they might have felt tenderness had passed, and secretly they both rejoiced. Since he did not answer her, she went on. "I think it's uninteresting. To sit and watch costumes disappear, one by one. It's uninteresting even to mention it."

"They are not costumes," he said distinctly. "They're simply the clothes people wear."

She was as bitter as he about the changes, but she felt it would be indelicate for them both to reflect the same sorrow. It would happen some day, surely. A serious grief would silence their argument. They would share it and not be able to look into each other's eyes. But as long as she could she would hold off that moment.

CONTRIBUTORS NOTES

WALTER ABISH is the author of a book of poems *Duel Site* (Tibor de Nagy Editions, 1970) and three books of fiction from New Directions. He has published extensively in literary magazines.

BRUCE ANDREWS co-edits the critical magazine, L-A-N-G-U-A-G-E and directs the political program at Fordham University in New York.

VICENTE ALEIXANDRE lives in Spain and recently was awarded The Nobel Prize for Literature.

THE ASCHER/STRAUS COLLECTIVE is composed of Sheila Ascher and Dennis Straus, who write separately, but publish together as a "verbal collective." Their work has appeared in *The Paris Review*, *Chicago Review* and elsewhere.

MARGARET ATWOOD of Alliston, Ontario has published novels, several collections of poetry and a gathering of her short stories. She was awarded the Governor General's Award for Poetry in 1967.

JOHN BALABAN teaches English at Pennsylvania State University and won the 1974 Lamont Award of the Academy of American Poets.

WESLEY BROWN's novel, *Tragic Magic*, will soon be published by Random House. He lives in New York City.

MICHAEL DENNIS BROWNE is the author of the poetry collection *The Wife of Winter* and the long poem *Sun Exercises*. He teaches at The University of Minnesota.

ROBERT BURLINGAME teaches comparative literature and modern poetry at the University of Texas, El Paso. He is the author of 250 poems and has appeared in many literary magazines.

JANE BOWLES' collected works, *My Sister's Hand In Mine*, was published in Fall, 1977 by The Ecco Press.

CAROLYN CASSADY lives in Los Gatos, California and won a Fels Award for her first published piece, "Coming Down" which appeared in *The Beat Book* (Unspeakable Visions, 1974).

NAOMI CLARK's first collection of poems *Burglaries and Celebrations* (Oyez Pres, 1977) will soon be followed by a second which she is assembling. She teaches at San José State University.

KATHLEEN COLLINS teaches at City College in New York and has just completed a novel, *Long Before We Said Goodbye*. She is also the author of two plays.

JANE COOPER's first book *The Weather of Six Mornings* won the Lamont Poetry Award. Her second book is *Maps and Windows*.

JAMES CRUMLEY lives in Kennedy, Texas. His latest book is *The Wrong Case*.

RICHARD DAUENHAUER lives in Anchorage, Alaska and is the author of four books from small presses.

LYDIA DAVIS lives in rural New York State.

"H. BUSTOS DOMECQ" is the pen name for Jorge Luis Borges and Adolfo Bioy Casares.

NORMAN DUBIE's latest book is *The Illustrations* (Braziller).

ANDRE DUBUS's collection of fiction is *Adultery and Other Choices* (The Godine Press, 1977).

LARRY EIGNER has published over twenty books of verse, most recently *Stirring Together or Far Away* (1974), and *The World And Its Streets, Places* (Black Sparrow, 1977).

RALPH ELLISON is the author of *Invisible Man* and is at work on a novel. He lives in New York.

LORIS ESSARY is an editor of *Interstate*.

JAMES GALVIN was one of the Nation/Discovery, winners in 1977. He teaches at Murray State University.

JOHN GARDNER is the author of *Grendel, Wreckage of Agathon, Sunlight Dialogues, Nickel Mountain, October Light, The Life and Times of Chaucer* and books for children. *Moral Fiction* is just out from Basic Books and includes the selection in this volume.

LOUISE GLÜCK is the author of several poetry collections and is teaching creative writing at the University of Cincinnati.

LORRIE GOLDENSOHN's poetry and criticism have appeared in *Ploughshares, Shenandoah, American Book Review, Carlton Miscellany* and elsewhere. She teaches at Goddard College.

C.W. GUSEWELLE has had stories published in *The Antioch Review, Transatlantic Review* and elsewhere. He is foreign editor of *The Kansas City Star*.

YUKI HARTMAN's first book, *A One of Me* (Grasp Press) has been followed by "a dynamite work from Telephone Books, *Hot Footsteps*, both adding up to an incredible writer" says Maureen Owen, Telephone Books.

ROBERT HASS lives in Berkeley, California and publishes widely in the literary presses.

SEAMUS HEANEY lives in Ireland. His recent collection is *North* (Oxford University Press).

DON HENDRIE's first novel, *Boomkitchwatt*, was published by John Muir Press in 1973. He is writing another novel in San Miguel de Allende, Mexico.

ANNE HERBERT is assistant editor of *The CoEvolution Quarterly.*

CHRISTOPHER HOWELL's books include *The Crime of Luck* (Panache Books, 1977), *The Bear In The Mirror* (Raincrow Press, 1977) and *Why Shouldn't I* (L'Epervier Press, 1977). He lives in Burton, Washington.

GYULA ILLYÉS, the Hungarian poet, was born in 1902.

BILL KNOTT's latest book is *Selected and Collected Poems* (Sun Press, 1977).

LAURA JENSEN's poetry collection *Bad Boats* has just been published by The Ecco Press. She lives in Tacoma, Washington.

DAN MASTERSON's first volume of poems *On Earth As It Is* was published by The University of Illinois Press in 1978. He won the 1977 Borestone Poetry Award, The *Poetry Northwest* Bullis Prize and the CCLM Fels Award.

BERNADETTE MAYER co-edits *United Artists* with Lewis Warsh and is the author of seven books from Angel Hair Books, Kulchur Foundation, Big Sky Books, 0 To 9 Press and North Atlantic Books.

MEKEEL MCBRIDE lives in Cambridge, Massachusetts and is working on a book of poems, *No Ordinary World.*

DAVID MCCANN is doing research on Japanese and Korean poetry of the early period and he lives in Ithaca, .NY.

STEPHEN MINOT is the author of a novel, *Chill of Dusk* and a collection of short stories, *Crossings.* He is Adjunct Professor of writing at Trinity College, Hartford, Ct.

ANAÏS NIN was a Founding Editor of *The Pushcart Prize* series and is known for both her literary work and her encouragement of small presses and new authors. She died in 1977.

GEORGE PAYERLE's novel *The Afterpeople* was published in 1970 by The House of Anansi press.

JOYCE PESEROFF is co-editor of *Green House* magazine, and was a Fellow of The University of Michigan from 1973–1976.

MARY PETERSON teaches at The University of New Hampshire and has published fiction in *North American Review, Ploughshares, South Dakota Review* and elsewhere.

MARGE PIERCY is a poet and novelist and appears frequently in small press publications. She lives in Wellfleet, Massachusetts.

JOHN PILCROW is "a peripatetic, sometime Chicago writer," says Curt Johnson of December Press.

RUTHELLEN QUILLEN teaches writing at the University of Maryland and is the author of the novel *The Raisin Cake*.

ADRIENNE RICH's tenth and most recent collection of poetry is *The Dream of A Common Language: Poems 1974–77* (Norton, 1978). She is also author of *Of Women Born: Motherhood as Experience And Institution.* (Norton, 1976). Her poem "Power" appeared in the first *Pushcart Prize* volume, reprinted from *The Little Magazine.*

WILLIAM PITT ROOT has published five volumes of poetry and has appeared in twenty current anthologies and in many magazines. He has been awarded fellowships from the Rockefeller and Guggenheim Foundations, Stanford University and The National Endowment for The Arts.

ALVIN ROSENFELD is Associate Professor of English at Indiana University. He is writing a book on *The Literature of the Holocaust* to be published by Indiana University Press.

PINCHAS SADEH lives and writes in Israel.

LYNNE SHARON SCHWARTZ's stories appeared in *Ploughsares, The Smith*, and *Ontario Review* and elsewhere during 1977. She is at work on a novel and lives in New York.

CHARLES SCRUGGS teaches at The University of Arizona, Tucson.

HUGH SEIDMAN's poems have been collected in *Collecting Evidence* (Yale Series of Younger Poets, 1970) and *Blood Lord* (Doubleday, 1974). He lives in New York.

BETH TASHERY SHANNON is working on a collection of short experimental pieces and a novel, *Neluna*, about a woman knight errant. She lives in Lexingt :n, Kentucky.

MAXINE SILVERMAN is the author of *Survival Song* (Sunbury Press, 1976) and is completing a second collection of poems, *Knowing Luck Counts.*

LESLIE MARMON SILKO grew up on the Laguna Pueblo Reservation where she now lives with her husband and two children. *Ceremony* is her new novel.

WILLIAM SPRUNT's latest poetry collection is *A Sacrifice of Dogs* (St. Andrews Press, 1977).

MAURA STANTON's poetry collection *Snow On Snow* was published by Yale University Press in 1975. She is the author of a novel, *Molly Companion* (Bobbs Merrill).

RICARDO DA SILVEIRA LOBO STERNBERG was born in Brazil, lives in Cambridge and is a member of the Society of Fellows at Harvard.

ROMAN VISHNIAC's books of photographs include *Polish Jews* (Schocken) and *Roman Vishniac* (ICP Books).

ROBERT WALSER lived from 1878 to 1956 and has been described as one of the most important German language writers of this century. He wrote over a thousand short stories and eight novels.

NANCY WILLARD lives in Poughkeepsie, N.Y. and is the author of *Carpenter of the Sun* (Liveright, 1974).

ROBLEY WILSON, JR. is editor of *North American Review*, professor of English at the University of Northern Iowa and the author of two story collections published by Fiction International and The University of Illinois Press.

"THE WORKERS UNIVERSITY" teaches in Brussels, Belgium.

YVONNE publishes widely in the small presses and frequently appears in *MS* magazine. She lives in New York City.

MAX ZIMMER is a member of the English Department at the University of Utah, Salt Lake City.

🔥 🔥 🔥

OUTSTANDING WRITERS

(The editors also wish to mention the following important works published by small presses in 1977. Listing is alphabetical by author's last name. Asterisk indicates that work by this author may also be found in a previous *Pushcart Prize* edition, one asterisk for the first edition, two for the second.)

POETRY

Erase Words—Keith Abbott (Blue Wind)
Attempting to Convince . . .—Michael Benedikt (Ploughshares)
Healing—Wendell Berry (Antaeus)
Mother/Daughter Poem—Susan Biskeborn (Write Poems Women)
On Water—Randy Blasing (Persea)
Lines for Her Leaving—Richard Blessing (Ahsahta Press)
Viol—Ralph Burns (CutBank)
Hermie—David Budbill (Crow's Mark)
For Evil and Destruction—William Bronk (Handbook)
462-0614—Charles Bukowski (Northwest Review)*
From That Moment On—Cynthia Carr (Heresies)
Dialogue—Richard Cecil (Ploughshares)
On "The Therapeutist. . ." James Cervantes (CutBank)
White Squirrel—David Childers (Buffalo Books)
My House—Michael Cuddihy (Gallimaufry)
Cleared for Approach—Ann Darr (Dryad)
Daughters With Toad—Mark Defoe (Carolina Quarterly)
St. Elmos of Assateaque—G. Donahue (Nightwords)
Narratives of New Netherland—S. Farragher (Beloit Journal)
About Me, About You, About Us—Marlene Fine (Zone)
Eight Women—Wallace Fowlie (Archive)
Seeing—Malcolm Glass (Sewanee Review)
Rose of the West—Jaimy Gordon (Woodbine)

Blowing Feathers—Gunter Grass (Canto)
My Mother Walked Out—M. Hannon (Kaldron)
Unlikely Marriage—Annette Hayn (Rutherford Books)
A Simple Memoriam For My Father—James Hazard (Crossing Press)
Snow Angels—Anita Helle (Prescott Street Press)
Waiting For A Friend—Dick Higgins (Unpublished Editions)
Another Part of the Field—Michael Heffernan (Shenandoah)
The Liberation Films—William Heyen (Ontario Review)
For A Prison Poet—Michael Hogan (Joint Conference)*
Old Space Cadet Speaking—Anselm Hollo (Blue Wind)
Already The Leaves—Barbara Hughes (Invisible City)
Changes At Meridan—Richard Hugo (Graham House)**
"Captain, Circa 1972"—Lawson Fusao Inada (Gallimaufry)
Thinking of My Father . . .—Colette Inez (West Branch)
Stone Soup—C. Itzin (Massachusetts Review)
Our Mothers Were Sisters—Marilyn Johnson (Partisan Review)
The Abandoned Fairgrounds—Rodney Jones (Puddingstone)
April At the Ruins—Rolly Kent (Maguey Press)
The Briefing—David Kirby (Southern Poetry Review)
Plowing the North 40—Lillian Kloefkorn (Pentagram)
Georgia Island Turtles—Herbert Krohn (Chelsea)
Signs—Larry Levis (Ohio Review)
Wasps—Larry Levis (Ploughshares)
The Bridge of Change—John Logan (Paris Review)
For Sale: Girl Poet Cheap—Lynn Lonidier (Manroot)
Armadillo—S. Lyne (Virginia Quarterly)
The Perfect Horse—Jim Martin (Impact)
The Guidebook—Alice Mattison (Massachusetts Review)
Ripples—Jerome Mazzaro (Modern Poetry Studies)
Feast of the Epiphany—Mark McCloskey (Bellingham)
How It is—Judith McCombs (Modern Poetry Studies)
Mother Night—Carol McNeary (Ali Baba Press)
The Mouse—Sandra McPherson (Field)
The Must-Be-Admired Things—Gary Miranda (Poetry)
Binge—Paul Nelson (Iowa Review)
Starting With Roses—Allen Neff (Windless Orchard)
Four Parts—Carole Oles (Ploughshares)
That Year—Sharon Olds (Kayak)
Image—George Oppen (Montemora)

Write It Down-Allen Said—Peter Orlovsky (Unspeakable Visions)
Who Needs It—Maureen Owen (Crossing Press)
Cloud Forms—Michael Palmer (Black Sparrow)
Setting the Table—Linda Pastan (Field)
Life and Literature—Linda Pastan (Plum)
Alter Ego—Cesare Pavese (Canto)
Giacometti's Race—Robert Phillips (Modern Poetry Studies)
Ghazal/Insomnia—Stanley Plumly (Ohio Review)
The Tree—Stanley Plumly (Iowa Review)
The First Time—David Ray (Paris Review)*
The Silver Swan—Kenneth Rexroth (Red Hill)
Your Circle—N. Russell (Red Earth)
Language Lessions—P. K. Saha (bits press)
Harvest—Susan F. Schaeffer (Hampden-Sydney)
Song of the Self-Stimulator—Lloyd Schwartz (Green House)
Sad Dogs—Margaret Shafer (Confrontation)
Tight Like That—Harvey Shapiro (N.Y. Arts Journal)*
Zenobia Camprubi Jimenez—Greg Simon (Porch)
A Day In Which . . .—Dave Smith (Kansas Quarterly)
Sometime I Think I Will Ride . . .—Dave Smith (Northwest Review)
What's Money Good For—Joan Smith (Vagabond)
Tantrum of Bones—Margoret Smith (Boston U. Journal)
Eva Braun—W. D. Snodgrass (BOA Editions)
A Face—William Stafford (Partisan Review)
The Chiffonier—Diane Stevenson (Ailanthus)
Lines for Winter—Mark Strand (Field)*
Cascades—Pamela Stewart (Maguey Press)
Nearing Christmas—Tony Towle (Sun)
October—David Unger (Persea)
Consider Anything—Cornelia Veenendaal (Alice James)
from Harmatan—Paul Violi (Sun)
Black Leaves—Michael Waters (Croissant)
Sitting The Night . . .—Nancy Westerfield (Western Humanities)
Tamsen Donner—Ruth Whitman (Alice James)
Companions for the Dark Slate—Jonathan Williams (St. Andrews)
The Bells Are Ringing—Terence Winch (Z Press)
Cloud River—Charles Wright (Three Rivers)
Safari In Ulster—Y. Yevtushenko (Transatlantic)
Four About Death—David Young (Cleveland State)

NON-FICTION

Essays—Djuna Barnes (UnMuzzled Ox)

From the Notebooks of Louise Bogan—Louise Bogan (Antaeus)

Allen Ginsberg—James Breslin (Iowa Review)

Cotton-Mouth Whirlpool—Jim Brodey (432 Review)

Autumn's Bread—Douglas Bullis (Snowy Egret).

I Wonder What Mr. Santini Dreamed—Eleanor Clark (Georgia Review)

Interview with John Gardner—Joe Cuomo, Marie Ponsot (Shout In the Street)

Poetry Today—Andrew Glaze, Norman Rosten (The Smith)

On The Limits of Language—Denis Donoghue (Sewanee Review)

From "Towards a New Poetics"—Ekbert Faas (Black Sparrow)

"The Tempest," Or Repetition—Jan Knott (Mosaic)

The Prophet Is A Fool—Mary Kinzie (Salmagundi)

TV: The Minus Multiplier—Kenneth Lash (North American Review)

Escape Routes—Ursula Le Guin (Antaeus)

After Enjoying 6 or 7 Essays on Me—Robert Lowell (Salmagundi)

The Continuity of James Wright's Poems—William Matthews (Chicago Review)

Latin America Trip —Mark Mirsky (Confrontation)

A Second Occupation—Eugenio Montale (Pequod)*

"A Remembrance of Things Past"—Ira Sadoff (Carleton Miscellany)

The Real Cowboys and Indians—Thomas Sanchez (Capra)

Chief Seattle's Message—(Peace Press)

Document in Film and Literature—Roger Shattuck (Partisan Review)

Place in American Culture—Paul Shepard (North American Review)

Disappearance of the Word . . .—Ron Silliman (A Hundred Posters)

Dylan: A Documentary—William Van Wert (Antioch Review)

Generation—Christine Wade (Heresies)

There Ain't No Graceful Way—interview, Peter Warshall (Co-Evolution)

Turkey Drop—T. Williams (CoEvolution)

FICTION

Dead Slow—M. P. Battin (Quarterly West)
The Man Who Loved Dylan—Ann Beck (Ascent)
Getting It On—Anne Bernays (Ploughshares)
Invention of Architecture—Dennis Boyles (Dryad)
Queen Constance—Virgil Burnett (TriQuarterly)
A Gradually Dwindling Play—Marvin Cohen (Wormwood)*
The Hippopotamus—James Cortese (Epoch)
Down—H. E. Francis (Confrontation)*
Happy Deathday—Hugh Fox (Vagabond)
Four Prose Tone Poems—David Glines (Chicago Review)
Columbus Discovering America—Oscar Hijuelos (Persea)
Witchdoctor—Angela Jackson (Chicago Review)
Two Seaside Yarns—Steve Katz (Fiction Collective)
The Third Wheel—Tamara Kennelly (North American Review)
Caraway—W. P. Kinsetta (The Spirit That Moves Us)
A Rifle Is Not Funny—Fred Knipe (South Shore)
Slot Queen—David Kranes (Ascent)*
In the Bag—David Madden (Southern Review)
Excerpts from *Inlet*—Clarence Major (Black Scholar)*
Mad Dog—Bob Minick (Red Earth)
Common Pleas—Dallas Miller (Transatlantic)
Story Time—Peter Najarian (Berkeley Poets Co-op)
Sentimental Journey—Joyce Carol Oates (South Carolina Review)*
Staus—Mary A. M. Rishel (Hudson Review)
Negroes I Have Known—David Rosner (Ploughshares)
Belief: A Tale of Aran—Richard Selzer (Antaeus)
Exes—Issac B. Singer (Confrontation)
O'Mara Of No Fixed Abode—Gilbert Sorrentino (TriQuarterly)
People One Knows—John Updike (Transatlantic)
Natty Hallelujah—Heathcote Williams (Transatlantic)

OUTSTANDING SMALL PRESSES

(These presses made or received nominations for the 1978–79 edition of *The Pushcart Prize*. See the *International Directory of Little Magazines and Small Presses*, Dustbooks, Box 1056, Paradise, CA 95969, for subscription rates, manuscript requirements and a complete international listing of small presses.)

Abraxas Press, 2322 Rugby Rd., Madison, WI 53705
Acrobat Books, 409 N. Las Palmas, Los Angeles, CA 90004
Action Magazine, 710 Lowdi St., Syracuse, NY 13203
Agenda, 5 Cranbourne Court, Albert Bridge Rd., London SWII 4PE England
The Agni Review, Box 349, Cambridge, MA 02138
Ahsahta Press, English Dept., BSU, Boise, ID 83725
Akwesasne Notes, Mohawk Nation via Rooseveltown, NY 13683
Aldebaran Review, 2209 California St., Berkeley, CA 94703
Ailanthus Press, 200 W. 83rd St., New York, NY 10024
Aleph, 7319 Willow Ave., Takoma Park, MD 20012
Alcheringa/Ethnopoetics, 745 Commonwealth Ave., Boston, MA. 02215
Ali Baba Press, 746 N. Highland, #9, Atlanta, GA 30306
Alice James Books, 138 Mt. Auburn, Cambridge, MA 02138
Allegheny Mountain Press, 111 North 10th St., Olean, NY 14760
The Ally Press, 1764 Gilpin St., Denver, CO 80218
American Literature, College Sta., Box 667, Durham, NC 27708
American Poetry Review, 1616 Walnut St., Philadelphia, PA 19103
American Scholar, 1811 Q. St. NW, Washington DC 20009
Anemone Press, 550 Alta Vista Way, Laguna Beach, CA 92651
Angel Hair, Box 718, Lenox, MA 02140
Annex Press, 301 East Ann St., Ann Arbor MI
Antaeus, 1 West 30th St., New York, NY 10001

The Antioch Review, Box 148, Yellow Springs, OH 45387
Apalachee Quarterly, Box 20106, Tallahasee, FA 32304
Applezaba Press, 333 Orizaba, Long Beach, CA 90814
Aquila Magazine, Box 174-B, Petersburg, PA 16669
Arbitrary Closet Press, Box 54, Onondaga, MI 49264
The Archive, Box 4665, Duke Station, Durham, NC 27706
Ardis, 2901 Heatherway, Ann Arbor, MI 48104
Ark River Review, Box 14 WSU, Wichita, KS 67208
Art Direction Book Co., 19 West 44th St. New York, NY 10036
Artifact, 1050 Old Pecos Trail, Santa Fe, NM 87501
Ascent, English Dept., University of Illinois, Urbana, ILL 61801
The Asia Mail, Box 1044, Alexandria, VA 22313
Aspect, 12 Rogers Ave., Cambridge, MA 02140
Aspen Anthology, Box 3185, Aspen, CO 81611
Assembling Press, Box 1967, Brooklyn, NY 11202
Astro Black Books, Box 46, Sioux Falls, SD 57101
The Atlanta Poetry Collective, Box 7952, Atlanta, GA 30357
Auntie Bellum, Box 3473, Columbia, SC 29230
Aura Literary/Arts Review, University of Alabama, Box 348 NBSB,
    U. Sta., Birmingham, AL 35294
Autumn Press Inc., 7 Littell Rd., Brookline, MA 02146
Avery Color Studies, Box 95, Autrain, MI 49806

Bachy, 11317 Santa Monica Blvd., West Los Angeles, CA 90025
Back Row Press, Box 12845, St. Paul, MN 55112
Ball State University Forum, English Dept., BSU, Muncie, IN
    47306
Bardic Books, Box 992, Bryn Mawr, PA 19010
Barbeque Planet, 2513-B Ashwood, Nashville, TN 37212
Bare Wires, Box 9779, San Diego, CA 92109
The Bellingham Review, 2600 Hampton Place, Bellingham, WA
    98225
Beloit Poetry Journal, Box 2, Beloit, WI 53511
Berkeley Poet's Co-op, Box 459, Berkeley, CA 94701
Beyond Baroque Foundation, Box 806-N, Venice, CA 90291
Bezoar, Box 535, Gloucester, MA 01930
The Bielex Press, 4603 Shore Acres Rd., Madison, WI 53716
Big Deal, Box 830, Stuyvesant Sta., NY 10009
Big Moon, Box 4731, Modesto, CA 95352
Big Sky, Box 389, Bolinas, CA 94924

Biography Press, Rte. 1, Box 745, Arkansas Pass, TX 78336
Biohydrant Publications, RFD #3, St. Albans, VT 05478
Birthstone Magazine, 1319 6th Ave., San Francisco, CA 94122
Bits Press, English Dept., CWR University, Cleveland, OH 44106
Bittersweet, Lebanon High School, Lebanon, MO 65536
BKMK Press, 5725 Wyandotte, Kansas City, MO 64113
Black Forum, GPO Box 1090, Bronx, NY 10451
Black River Writers: West, Box 15853, Sacramento, CA 95813
The Black Scholar, Box 908, Sausalito, CA 94965
Black Sparrow Press, Box 3993, Santa Barbara, CA 93105
Black Warrior Review, Box 2936, University, AL 35486
Bleb, Box 322, Times Square Sta., New York, NY 10036
Bloodroot, 316 Harvard St., Grand Forks, ND 58201
Blue Cloud Quarterly, Blue Cloud Abbey, Marvin, SD 57251
Blue Moon Press, UA English Dept., Tucson, AZ 85721
Blue Mountain Press, 511 Campbell St., Kalamazoo, MI 49007
Blue Wind Press, 820 Miramar, Berkeley, CA 94707
BOA Editions, 92 Park Ave., Brockport, NY 14420
Bonsai Press/JaMa Press, Box 7211, Phoenix, AZ 85011
Border-Mountain Press, Box 1296, Benson, AZ 85602
Boston U. Journal, 775 Commonwealth Ave., Boston, MA 02215
Brilliant Corners, 1372 W. Estes #2n, Chicago, IL 60626
Buffalo Books, 15 Gladstone Dr., San Francisco, CA 94112
Burning Deck, 71 Elmgrove, Providence, RI 02906

California Quarterly, 100 Sproul Hall, Davis, CA 95616
Calliope Press, Wentworth Rd., Walpole, NH
Calyx, RT 2 Box 118, Corvallis, OR 97330
Canadian Fiction Magazine, Box 46422, Sta. G, Vancouver, B.C.
Canto, 11 Bartlett St., Andover, MA 01810
The Cape Rock, SEMO State Univ., Cape Giradeau, MO 63701
Capra Press, 631 State St., Santa Barbara, CA 93101
Carey House, Box 453, Concord, NH 03301
The Carleton Miscellany, Carleton College, Northfield, MN 55057
Carma Press, Box 12633, St. Paul, MN 55112
Carolina Quarterly, Box 1117, Chapel Hill, NC 27514
Carolina Wren Press, Box 209, Carrboro, NC 27510
Carpenter Press, Rte 4, Pomeroy, OH 45769
Caryatid Press, 7724 Cohn St., New Orleans, LA 70118

Cat Anna Press, Box 301, Dexter, MI 48130
The Cauldron Press, St. Louis, MO
Cedar Rock, 1121 Madeline, New Braunfels, TX 78130
Center, English Dept. USM, Hattiesburg, MISS 39401
Centerfold, 561 Piermont Rd., Demarest, NJ
Centergram, 401 N. Plank Rd., Newburgh, NY 12550
Centering, ATL EBH MSU, E. Lansing, MI 48824
Chandler & Sharp Publishers, 5643 Paradise Dr. #10, Corte Madera, CA 94925
Chariton Review, NE Missouri State U., Kirksville, MO 63501
Chelsea, Box 5880, Grand Central Sta., New York NY 10017
Cherry Valley Editions, Box 303, Cherry Valley, NY 13320
Chicago Review, University of Chicago, Chicago, IL 60637
Choomia, Box 4204, Tucson, AZ 85719
Chouteau Review, Box 10016, Kansas City, MO 64111
Chowder Review, 2858 Kingston Dr., Madison, WI 53713
Chthon Press, 39 Hawthorne Village, Concord, MA 07142
Cibola Press, 1295 Wilson St., Box 1495, Palo Alto, CA 94301
Cimarron Review, Oklahoma State U., Stillwater, OK 74074
Cine-Tracts, 4227 Esplanade Ave., Montreal, Quebec
Clahdamanelle Publishers, 235 E. 77th St., New York, NY 10021
Clown War, Box 1093, Brooklyn, NY 11202
Coe Review, Coe College, Cedar Rapids, IA 52402
Coastal Quarterly, Savannah, GA
Co-Evolution Quarterly, Box 428, Sausalito, CA 94965
Cocono, Suite 217, 564 Central Ave., Alameda, CA 94501
Columbia, 404 Dodge, Columbia U., New York NY 10067
The Commentator's Press, Box 61297, Sunnyvale, CA 94088
The Communication Press, Box 22541, Sunset Sta., San Francisco, CA 94122
Conditions, Box 56, Brooklyn, NY 11215
Confluence Press, Lewis-Clark Campus, Lewiston, ID 83501
La Confluencia, Box 409, Albuquerque, NM 87103
Confrontation, Long Island U. English Dept., Brooklyn, NY 11201
Confrontation/Change Review, 32 College St., Dayton, OH 45407
Copper Canyon Press, Box 271, Port Townsend, WA 98368
Cornell Review, 124 Roberts Place, Ithaca, NY 14850
Cornerstone Press, Box 28048, St. Louis, MO 63119
Corycian Press, Box 1524, Iowa City, IA 52240

Cosmic Circus, 521 33rd St., Oakland, CA 94609
Crawl Out Your Window, 704 Nob Ave., Del Mar, CA 92014
Creación, Apartado 111, Estacion 6-UCRR, Ponce, P.R. 00731
Critical Inquiry, University of Chicago Press, 5801 S. Ellis Ave., Chicago, IL 60637
Critical List Magazine, 32 Sullivan St., Toronto, Ontario
Croissant & Co., Rt. 1 Box 51, Athens, OH 45701
Cross Country, Box 21081, Woodhaven, NY 11421
Cross Currents, West Nyack, NY 10994
Crosscurrents, 516 Ave. K South, Saskatoon, Sask.
The Crossing Press, Trumansburg, NY 14886
Crow's Mark Press, Johnson, VT 05656
Curbstone, 321 Jackson St., Willimantic, CT 06226
Curveship Press, St. Andrews College, Laurinburg, NC 28352
Cut Bank, English Dept., University of Montana, Missoula, MT 59812
Cycle Press, 18 Warren Pl., Cobble Hill, Brooklyn, NY 11201

Dacotah Territory, Box 775, Moorhead, MN 56560
Dark Horse, 47 Stearns St., Cambridge, MA 02138
Dawn Valley Press, Box 58, New Wilmington, PA 16142
December Press, 4343 N. Clarendon, Chicago, IL 60613
Delirium/Libra Press, 611 S. Pennsylvania, Denver, CO 80209
Denver Quarterly, University of Denver, Denver, CO 80210
Desert First Works, Inc., 3870 N. Vine Ave., Tucson, AZ 85719
A Different Drummer, 18 Union St., Toms River, NJ 08753
Drivel Press, 354 Hoover Rd., Santa Cruz, CA 95065
Druid Books, Ephraim, WI 54211
Drunken Poet Press, 216 West Ridderow Ave., Maple Shade, NJ 08052
Dryad Press, Box 1656, Washington D.C. 20013

Earth Publishing Enterprises, Box 430273, S. Miami, FL 33143
East River Review, 128 E. 4th St., New York NY 10701
E & E Enterprise, Box 405, Howell, NY 07731
El Fuego de Aztlar, 3408 Dwinelle Hill, U.C., Berkeley, CA 94720
Emerald City Press, Box 1239, Berkeley, CA 94704
En Passant Poetry Quarterly, 1906 Brant Rd., Wilmington, DE 19810
Epoch, 251 G. Smith Hall, Cornell University, Ithaca, NY 14853

Epos, English Dept. T.S.U., Troy, AL 36081
Euterpe, 418 E. 83rd St. #5D, New York, NY 10028
Event, Douglas College, Box 2503, New Westminster, B.C., Canada

Fag Rag, Box 331, Kenmore Sta., Boston, MA 02215
Famous/Famous Last Words, 1732 Webster St. No 301, Oakland, CA 94612
Fantome Press, 720 North Park Ave., Warren, OH 44483
Fels & Firn Press, 1036 Colorado Ave., 'C', Palo Alto, CA 94303
Fiction, Dept. English, CCNY, New York, NY 10031
Fiction Collective, Dept. English, Brooklyn College, Brooklyn, NY 11210
Fiction International, St. Lawrence University, Canton, NY 13617
Fiction Magazine, 339 Newburg St., Boston, MA 02115
Fido Productions, 86 E. 3rd St., New York, NY 10003
Field, Rice Hall, Oberlin College, Oberlin, OH 44074
Fighter's Peace, Box 8111, University Sta., Grand Forks, ND 58202
Floating Island Publications, Box 516, Point Reyes Sta., CA 94956
Florida Sun-Gator Publishing Co., Box 365, Oveida, FL 32765
Four-Three-Two Review, % Schuchat, Box 1030, Stuyvesant St., New York, NY 10009
Four Quarters, La Salle College, Philadelphia, PA 19141
Four Zoas Press, Box 461, Ware, MA 01082
Free Life Editions, 41 Union Square West, New York, NY 10003
Front Street Trolley, 2125 Acklen Ave., Nashville, TN
Frozen Waffles, 321 N. Indiana, Bloomington, IN 47401

Gallimaufry, 807 N. Daniel St., Arlington, VA 22201
Gargoyle, 160 Boylston St. #3, Jamaica Plain, MA 02130
Gay Sunshine, Box 40397, San Francisco, CA 94140
Generation, Box 110, Princeton, NJ 08540
Genesis, Box 1194, Greenwich, CT 06830
The Georgia Review, University of Georgia, Athens, GA 30602
Georgia State University Press, Atlanta, GA 30303
Gerry de la Ree Scientifantasy, 7 Cedarwood Lane, Saddle River, NJ 07458
Ghost Dance Press, 526 Forest, E. Lansing, MI 48823
Giorno Poetry Systems, 222 Bowery, New York, NY 10012
Glass Bell Press, 5053 Commonwealth, Detroit, MI 48202

Glassworks, Box 163, Rosebank Sta., Staten Island, NY 10305
Gnormen Press, Box 106, Frankfort, KY 40601
David Godine, Publisher, 306 Dartmouth St., Boston, MA 02116
C. P. Graham Press, Box 5, Keswick, VA 22947
Graham House Review, Box 489, Englewood, NJ 07631
The Gramercy Review, Box 15362, Los Angeles, CA 90015
Granite, Box 1367, Southampton, NY 11968
Graywolf Press, Box 142, Port Towsend, WA 98368
Great Basin Press, Box 11162, Reno, NV 89510
Great Lakes Review, Northeastern Illinois U., Chicago, IL 60625
Great Society Press, 451 Heckman St. #308, Phillipsburg, NJ 08865
Green Horse Press, Box 1691, Santa Cruz, CA 95061
Green House, 53 Beacon St., Dedham, MA 02026
Green Hut Press, 24051 Rotunda Rd., Valencia Hills, CA 91355
Greenhouse Review, 126 Escalona Dr., Santa Cruz, CA 95060
Greensboro Review, UNC-G, Greensboro, NC 27412
Green's Magazine, Box 313, Detroit, MI 48231
Greenwich Meridian, 516 Ave. K South, Saskatoon, Saskatchewan
Grilled Flowers, U.A. Poetry Center, 1086 N. Highland Ave., Tucson, AZ 85719
Grist Press, 195 Lakeview Ave., Cambridge, MA 02138

The Hampden-Sydney Poetry Review, Box 126, Hampden-Sydney, VA 23943
Handbook, 184 W. N. Broadway, Columbus, OH 43214
Hanging Loose Press, 231 Wyckoff St., Brooklyn, NY 11217
Happiness Holding Tank, 1790 Grand River, Okemos, MI 48864
Hard Pressed, 2830 Third Ave., Sacramento, CA 95818
Harian Creative Press, 47 Hyde Blvd. Ballston Spa, CT 12020
Harold House Publishers, 2144 Harold St., Houston, TX 77098
Harvard Advocate, 21 South St., Cambridge, MA 02138
Hearthstone Press, 708 Inglewood Dr., Broderick, CA 95605
Heidelberg Graphics, Box 3404, Chico, CA 95927
Heirs Magazine, 657 Mission St., San Francisco, CA 94105
Heresies, Box 766, Canal St. Station, New York, NY 10013
High/Coo Press, 26-11 Hilltop Dr., W. Lafayette, IN 47906
Lawrence Hill and Co., 24 Burr Farms Rd., Westport, CT 06880
Hills, 1220 Folsom, San Francisco, CA 94104
Hit & Run Press, Box 1041, Fort Bragg, CA 95437
The Hollins Critic, Box 9538, Hollins College, VA 24020

Hollow Spring Review, Box 76, Berkshire, MA 01224

Homosexual Information Center, 6715 Hollywood Blvd., Los Angeles, CA. 90028

Hudson Review, 65 E. 55th St., New York, NY 10022

A Hundred Posters, Box 415, Kenmore Sta., Boston, MA 02215

Huron Review, 423 South Franklin Ave., Flint, MI 48503

Hyacinths & Biscuits, Box 392, Brea, CA 92621

Idaho Heritage, Box 9365, Boise, ID 38707

The Illustrated Orb, Box 111, Royal Oak, MI 48068

Images, English Dept., Wright State University, Dayton, OH 45431

In a Nutshell, Hibiscus Press, Box 22248, Sacramento CA 95822

International Poetry Review, Box 2046, Greensboro, NC 27402

Interstate, Box 7068, U.T. Station, Austin TX 78712

Intrepid Press, Box 1423, Buffalo, NY 14214

The Iowa Review, 321 EPB, University of Iowa, Iowa City, IA 52242

Ithaca House, 108 North Plain St., Ithaca, NY 14850

Iris Press, 27 Chestnut St., Binghamton, NY 13905

Iron Mountain Press, Box 28, Emory, VA 24327

Ironwood Press, Box 49023, Tuscon, AZ 85717

The Jacek Publishing Co., 38 Morris Lane, Milford, CT 06460

The Jackpine Press, 3381 Timberlake Lane, Winston-Salem, NC 27106

Jacksonville Poetry Quarterly, 5340 Weller Ave., Jacksonville, FL 32211

Jam To-day, Box 249, Northfield, VT 05663

Jalmar Press, 6501 Elvas Ave., Sacramento, CA 95819

Jeopardy, Western Washington University, Bellingham, WA 98225

Jim Brodey Books, 439 E. 12th St. #29, New York, NY

John Blair Publisher, 1406 Plaza Dr., Winston-Salem, NC 27103

Jungle Garden Press, 47 Oak Rd., Fairfax, CA 94930

Kaldron, Rainbow Resin Press, 441 N. 6th St., Grover City, CA 93433

Kanchenjunga Press, 22 Rio Vista Lane, Red Bluff, CA 96080

Kansas Quarterly, English Dept. Kansas State University, Manhattan, KS 66506

Karmic Revenge Laundry Shop Press, Box 14, Guttenberg, NJ 07903

Kayak, 325 Ocean View, Santa Cruz, CA 95062

Kelsey Street Press, 2824 Kelsey St., Berkeley, CA 94705

King Publications, Box 19332, Washington D.C. 20036

Konglomerati Press, 5719 29th Ave. South, Gulfport, FL 33707

Kontexts Publications, Eerste van der Helststr. 55, Amsterdam, Holland

Kroesen Books, 97 Kenmore St., New York, NY 10012

The Kulchur Foundation, 888 Park Ave., New York, NY 10021

Kurios Press, Box 946, Bryn Mawr, PA 19010

Kylix Press, 1485 Maywood, Ann Arbor, MI 48103˙

Là-bas, Box 509, Hollywood Sta., College Park, MD 20740

Lake Superior Review, Box 724, Ironwood, MI 49938

Lame Johnny Press, Box 66, Hermosa, SD 57744

Lamplighters Roadway Press, 500 Bohemia Highway, Freestone, CA 95472

Laughing Bear Press, Box 14, Woodinville, WA 98072

The Laurel Review, West Virginia Wesleyan College, Buckhannon, WV 26201

Lenape Publishing, 608 Whitby Dr., Wilmington, DE 19803

L'Epervier Press, 1219 E. Laurel, Fort Collins, CO

Linden Publishers, 27 W. 11th St., New York, NY 10011

Literary Messenger, Albany, CA

The Literary Review, Fairleigh Dickinson University, 285 Madison Ave., Madison, NJ 07940

Litmus, Inc., 574 3rd Ave., Salt Lake City, UT 84103

The Little Magazine, Box 207 Cathedral Sta., New York, NY 10025

Living Hand, Box 252, Millis Rd., Stanfordville, NY 12581

Lodestar Publishing, 3075 W. 7th St., Los Angeles, CA 90005

Longhouse, Bob Arnold, Green River, Brattleboro, VT 05301

Love Street Books, Box 58163, Louisville, KY 40258

Lowlands Review, 8204 Maple #1, New Orleans, LA 70118

Lucille, 5 Kern Ramble, Austin, TX 78722

Lucky Heart Books, Box 1064, Quincy IL 62301

Luna Bisonte Prods, 137 Leland Ave., Columbus, OH 43214

Lynx House Press, Box 800, Amherst, MA 01002

Madonna, 4730 Latona NE, Seattle, WA 98105

Mafdet Press, 1313 South Jefferson Ave., Springfield, MO 65807

Magazine, Pima College, 2202 W. Anklam Rd., Tucson, AZ 85709

Magic Circle Press, 10 Hyde Ridge, Weston, CT 06880
The Maguey Press, Box 3395, Tucson, AZ 85722
Malpelo, 1916 Court Ave., Newport Beach, CA 92663
Maneater, Box 2148 College Sta., Pullman, WA 99163
ManRoot, Box 982, South San Francisco, CA 94080
The Massachusetts Review, University of Mass., Amherst, MA
     01002
The Mediaworks, Box 4494, Boulder, CO 80306
Me Too, 400 E. 74th St., New York, NY 10021
Miam, Box 14083, San Francisco, CA 94114
The Midatlantic Review, Box 398, Baldwin Place, NY 10505
Midnight Sun, 223 E. 28th St., New York, NY
Midstream, 515 Park Ave., New York, NY 10022
Milk Quarterly/Yellow Press, 2394 Blue Island Ave., Chicago, IL
     60608
Mississippi Mud, 3125 S.E. Van Water, Portland, OR 97202
Mississippi Review, Box 37, Southern Sta., Hattiesburg, MS 39401
Mixed Voices, 163 West 17th St., New York, NY 10011
Modern Poetry Studies, 147 Capen Blvd., Buffalo, NY 14226
Modernismo Publications Ltd., 155 Ave. of the Americas, New York,
     NY 10013
Modus Operandi, Box 136, Brookeville, MD 20729
Momentum, 10508 W. Pico Blvd., Los Angeles, CA 90064
Montemora Foundation, Box 336 Cooper Sta., New York, NY 10003
Monument, 4508 Mexico Gravel Rd., Columbia, MO 65201
Mosaic, 208 Tier Bldg., University of Manitoba, Winnipeg, Canada
Mountain Summer, Tennessee Ave., Sewanee, TN 37375
Mountain Union Books, 107A Earwood St., Beckley, WV 25801
Moving Out, 4866 Third, Wayne State University, Detroit, MI
     45202
Mu Publications, Box 612, Dahlgren, VA, 22448
Mundus Artium, University of Texas at Dallas, Box 688, Richardson,
     TX 75080

Nada Press, 696 48th St. SE, Grand Rapids, MI 49508
Nebula Press, 970 Copeland St., North Bay, Ontario, Canada
New America, University of New Mexico, Albuquerque, NM 87131
New Atlantean Journal, 4280- 68th Ave. N., Pinellas Park, FL 33565
New Collage Magazine, 5700 North Trial, Sarasota, FL 33580
New Earth Books, 58 St. Marks Place, New York, NY 10003

The New Jersey Poetry Monthly, Box 824, Saddle Brook, NJ 07662

New Letters, University of Missouri, 5100 Rockhill Rd., Kansas City, MO 64110

New Orlando Publications, Box 296 Village Sta., New York, NY 10014

New Orleans Review, Loyola University, 6363 St. Charles Ave., New Orleans, LA 70118

New Renaissance, 9 Heath Rd., Arlington, MA 02174

New River Review, Radford College Sta., Radford, VA 24142

New Rivers Press, 90 Oxford Place, Staten Island, NY 10301

Newscribes, 1223 Newkirk Ave., Brooklyn, NY 11230

News Novel, 3639 University Ave., Riverside, CA 92509

New Voices, Box 308, Clintondale, NY 12515

New Wilderness Letter, 365 West End Ave., New York, NY 10024

New York Arts Journal, 560 Riverside Dr., New York, NY 10027

New York Literary Society, 417 W. 56th St., New York, NY 10019

Niagra Magazine, 195 Hicks St., Apt., 3-B, Brooklyn, NY 11201

Nightwords, 24 Jay St., Succasunna, NJ 07876

Nobodaddy Press, 100 College Hill Rd., Clinton, NY 13323

No Deadlines, 241 Bonita, Portola Valley, CA 94025

The North American Review, University of Northern Iowa, Cedar Falls, IA 50613

North Atlantic Books, 456 Hudson St., Oakland, CA 94618

Northeast/Juniper Books, 1310 Shorewood Dr., LaCrosse, WI 54601

The Northwest Matrix, 1628 E. 19th Ave., Eugene, OR 97403

Northwest Passage, 1017 E. Pike, Seattle, WA 98102

Northwest Review, University of Oregon, Eugene, OR 97403

Northwoods Journal, RD #1, Meadows of Dan, VA 24120

Nostoc, 101 Nehoiden Rd., Waban, MA 02168

Noumenon Press, Box 7068, U.T. Sta., Austin, TX 78712

NRG, 621 NW 23rd #304, Portland, OR 97210

Nummo News, The Collegian, University of Massachusetts, Amherst, MA 01003

Oberon Press, 555 Maple Lane, Ottawa, Ontario, Canada

Observations From the Treadmill, RFD #1, Union, ME 04862

The Ohio Journal, English Dept. OSU, 164 W. 17th Ave., Columbus, OH 43210

The Ohio Review, Ellis Hall, Ohio University, Athens, OH 45701

Ontario Review, 6000 Riverside Dr. E., Windsor, Ontario, Canada
Open Places, Box 2085, Stephens College, Columbia, MO 65201
The Original Art Report, Box 1641, Chicago, IL 60690
Origins, Box 5072 St. E, Hamilton, Ontario, Canada
Outerbridge, Staten Island Community College, 715 Ocean Terr., Staten Island, NY 10301
The Outland Press, Box 94, Lewisville, PA 19351
Out There Press, 6-D, 280 Lafayette, New York, NY 10012
Ox Head Press, 414 N. 6th St., Marshall, MN 56258
Oxymoron, Box 3423, Charlottesville, VA 22903
Oyez Press, Box 5134, Berkeley, CA 94705
Oyez Review, Roosevelt University, 430 S. Michigan Ave., Chicago, IL 60605
Oz Publications, Inc., 447 E. 15th Ave., Eugene, OR 97401

Packrat Press, House 3, Madrid, NM 87010
Padan Aram, 52 Dunster St., Cambridge, MA 02138
Padma Press, Box 56, Oatman, AZ 86433
Padre Productions, Box 1275, San Luis Obispo, CA 93406
Painted Bride Quarterly, 527 South St., Philadelphia, PA 19147
P.A.N., Annex 21 U.N.O. Box 688, Omaha, NE 68101
Panache, Box 77, Sunderland, MA 01375
The Paris Review, 541 E. 72nd St., New York, NY 10021
Parnassus, Poetry in Review, 205 W. 88th St., New York, NY 10024
Partisan Review, 1 Richardson St., Rutgers University, New Brunswick, NJ 08903
The Passage, 5 Market St., Portsmouth, NH 03801
The Pawn Review, 2806 Reagan #204, Dallas, TX 75219
Peace & Pieces Press, Box 99394, San Francisco, CA 94109
Peace Press, 3828 Willat Ave., Culver City, CA 90230
Pembroke Magazine, Box 756, Pembroke, NC 28372
Pentagram Press, Box 11609, Milwaukee, WI 53211
Pequod, Box 491, Forest Knolls, CA 94933
Periodical of Art In Nebraska, Box 688, Downtown Sta., Omaha, NE 68101
Perishable Press Ltd., Mt. Horeb, WI
Perivale Press, 13830 Erwin St., Van Nuys, CA 91401
Persea Books, Box 804, Madison Square Sta., New York, NY 10010
Petronium Press, EWA Tower 1813, 1255 Nuuanu Ave., Honolulu, HI 96817

Phantasm, Box 3404, Chico, CA 95927

Philologos, Box 2586, Tallahassee, FL 32304

Pig Iron Press, Box 237, Youngstown, OH 44501

Plexus, 2600 Dwight Way, Berkeley, CA 94708

Ploughshares, Box 529, Cambridge, MA 02139

Plum Magazine, Box 218, Reisterstown, MD 21136

Poem, Box 1247 West Sta., Huntsville, AL 35807

The Poem Company, Box 3294, Vancouver, B.C., Canada

Poésie U.S.A., Box 811, Melville, NY 11746

Poet Gallery Press, 224 West 29th St., New York, NY 10001

Poet Papers, Box 528, Topanga, CA 90290

Poetry, 1228 N. Dearborn Pkwy., Chicago, IL 60610

Poetry &, Box A 3298, Chicago, IL 60690

Poetry Flash, 1371-47th Ave., #2, San Francisco, CA 94122

Poetry Northwest, 4045 Brooklyn Ave., NE, University of Washington, Seattle WA 98105

Poets and Writers of New Jersey, 21 Lake Dr., Roosevelt, NJ 08555

Poets On:, Box 255, Chaplin, CT 06235

The Poet's Press, 386 Dean St., Brooklyn, NY 11217

Porch, 1422-37th Ave., Seattle, WA 98122

Portland Review, Box 751, Portland, OR 97207

Prairie Schooner, 201 Andrews, University of Nebraska, Lincoln, NE 68588

Prescott Street Press, 407 Postal Building, Portland, OR 97204

Present Tense, 165 E. 56th St., New York, NY 10022

Press Porcepic, 536 Gladstone Ave., Toronto, Ontario, Canada

Primavera, University of Chicago, 1212 E. 59th St., Chicago, IL 60637

Primer, 18 E. 40th St. #1, Indianapolis, IN 46205

Puckerbrush Press, 76 Main St., Orono, ME 04473

Puddingstone, Box 8800 University Sta., Knoxville, TN 37916

Quarry West, 88 College V, University of California, Santa Cruz, CA 95064

Quarterly Review of Literature, 26 Haslet Ave., Princeton, NJ 08540

Quarterly West, 312 Olpin Union, University of Utah, Salt Lake City, UT 84112

Quintessence Publications, 356 Bunker Hill Mine Rd., Armador City, CA 95601

Ragnarok Press, 1719-13th Ave. S., Birmingham, AL 35205

Rainbow Resin, 426 Pearl, Shell Beach CA 93449

Raincrow Press, 728 Orchard St., Toledo, OH 43609

Raindust Press, Box 1823, Independence, MO 64055

The Raintree Press, 4043 Morningside Dr., Bloomington, IN 47401

Raspberry Press, Rt. 6 Box 459, Bemidji, MN 56601

Rebis Press, 5806 Lawton Ave., Oakland, CA 94618

The Record Sun, 982 University Ave., Berkeley, CA 94710

Red Cedar Review, English Dept., Michigan State University, E. Lansing, MI 48824

Red Earth Press, Box 26641, Albuquerque, NM 87125

Red Fox Review, Mohegan C.C., Norwich, CT 06360

Red Hill Press, 6 San Gabriel Dr., Fairfax, CA 94930

Red Osier Press, 121 E. Gilman St. #6, Madison, WI 53703

Red Weather, Box 1104, Eau Claire, WI 54701

Reject, Box 9779, San Diego, CA

Remington Review, 505 Westfield Ave., Elizabeth NJ 07208

Revista Chicano-Riquena, Indiana University NW, 3400 Broadway, Gary, IN 46408

RFD, 4525 Lower Wolf Creek Rd., Wolf Creek, OR 97497

River Bottom Press, Box 252, Iola, WI 54945

River Sedge Press, Box 1547, Edinburg, TX 78539

River Styx, 7420 Cornell Ave., St. Louis, MO 63130

Rochester Routes, 50 Inglewood Dr., Rochester, NY 14619

Roof, 300 Bowery, New York, NY 10012

The Rose Bower Press, Rt. 3 Box 252, Farmville, VA 23943

The Rufus, Box 16, Pasadena, CA 91102

Rumba Train Press, 4497 Barrett St. S., Salem, OR 97302

St. Andrews Press, S.A. Presbyterian College, Laurinburg, NC 28352

St. Luke's Press, 1474 Harbert, Memphis, TN 38104

St. Mawr, Box 615, Middleburg, VT 05753

Salmagundi, Skidmore College, Saratoga Springs, NY 12866

The Salt Cedar, Rt. 3 Box 652, Fort Collins, CO 80521

Salt-Works Press, Box 649, Dennis, MA 02638

Sam Houston Literary Review, English Dept., Sam Houston State University, Huntsville, TX 77340

Samisdat, Box 231, Richford, VT 05476

Sand Dollar Press, 1205 Solano Ave., Albany, CA 94706

San Jose Studies, San Jose State University, San Jose, CA 95192
Scarecrow Books, 1050 Magnolia #2, Millbrae, CA 94030
Scopcraeft Press, 2816 Indiana Ave. #H, Stevens Point, WI 54481
Scree, Box 761, Fallon, NV 89406
The Scrimshaw Press, 6040, Claremont Ave., Oakland, CA 94618
Seamark Press, Box 2, Iowa City IA 82240
Second Coming Press, Box 31249, San Francisco, CA 94131
Segue Press, 300 Bowery, New York, NY 10012
Seven Stars, Realities Library, Box 33512, San Diego, CA 92103
The Seventies Press, Odin House, Madison, MN 56256
The Sewanee Review, Sewanee, TN 37375
Shankpainter, The Fine Arts Work Center, Provincetown, MA
Shantih, Box 125 Bay Ridge Sta., Brooklyn, NY 11220
Shelly's Kent Area Poets, 501 Franklin St., Kent, OH 44240
Shenandoah, Box 722, Lexington VA 24450
Shitashi, 1255 Nuuanu Ave., E. 1813, Honolulu, HI 96817
A Shout In the Street, English Dept. Queens College, Flushing, NY
    11367
S.H.Y., Hydra, Greece
Sibyl-Child, Box 1773, Hyattsville, MD 20788
Side Car Press, 5428 Tennis Ave., Philadelphia, PA 19120
Singing Wind Publications, Box 1426, Columbia, MO 65201
Sinister Wisdom, 3116 Country Club Dr., Charlotte, NC 28205
Skywriting/Blue Mountain Press, 511 Campbell St., Kalamazoo, MI
    49007
Slit Wrist, 333 E. 30th St.-14F, New York, NY 10016
Slough, 184 Q St. #2, Salt Lake City, UT 84103
The Slow Loris Press, 923 Highview St., Pittsburgh, PA 15206
Small Moon, 12 Cooney St., Somerville, MA 02143
The Smith, 5 Beekman St., New York, NY 10038
Snakeroots, Pratt Institute, Brooklyn, NY 11205
Snowy Egret, 205 S. Ninth St., Williamsburg, KY 40769
Soft Press, 1050 St. David St., Victoria, B.C., Canada
The Sole Proprietor, 2770 N.W. 32nd Ave, Miami, FL 33142
Solo Books, 1209 Drake Circle, San Luis Obispo, CA 93401
Some, 309 W. 104th St. (9-D), New York, NY 10025
Song, 808 Illinois Ave., Stevens Point, WI 54481
South Carolina Review, Clemson University, Clemson, SC 29631
Southern Exposure, Box 230, Chapel Hill, NC 27514

Southern Poetry Review, English Dept. UNCC., Charlotte, NC 28223

The Southern Review, Drawer D., Univ. Sta., Baton Rouge, LA 70893

South Shore, Box 95, AuTrain, MI 49806

Southwest Review, Southern Methodist University, Dallas, TX 75275

Sparrow, 103 Waldron St., West Lafayette, IN 47906

Spectrum Productions, 979 Casiano Rd., Los Angeles, CA 90049

The Spirit That Moves Us, Box 1585, Iowa City, IA 52240

Stardancer, Box 128, Athens, OH 45701

Statement Magazine, C.S.U. English Dept., Los Angeles, CA 90032

Stile, 1705 Giles, Austin, TX 78722

Stone Country, 20 Lorraine Rd., Madison NJ 07940

Stonehenge Press, Box 9779, San Diego, CA 92109

Stone Post Press, 5399½ Bryant, Oakland, CA 94618

Stony Hills, Box 715, Newburyport, MA 01950

Story Quarterly, 820 Ridge Rd., Highland Park, IL 60035

Strange Faeces Press, Box 301, Barton VT 05822

Street, Box 555, Port Jefferson, NY 11777

Studies in Poetry, English Dept. Texas Tech., Lubbock, TX 79409

Sun, 456 Riverside Dr., New York, NY 10027

Sun & Moon, 4330 Hartwick Rd. #418, College Park, MD 20740

Sun Publishing, Box 4383, Albuquerque, NM 87106

Sunbury, Box 274 Jerome Ave. Sta., Bronx, NY 10468

Sunrise Press, Box 742, Chandler, AZ 85224

Sunstone Press, Box 2321, 239 Johnson St., Santa Fe, NM 87501

Syracuse Guide, 500 S. Warren St., Syracuse, NY 13202

Syzygy/Cincinnati Women's Press, 3901 Hedgewood Dr., Cincinnati, OH 45229

Taurean Horn Press, 601 Leavenworth #45, San Francisco, CA 94109

Telephone Books, Box 672, Old Chelsea Sta., New York, NY 10011

Telepoem, 230 San Juan Ave., Venice, CA 90291

Third Eye Publications, 250 Mill St., Williamsville, NY 14221

13th Moon, Inc., Box 3, Inwood Sta., New York, NY 10034

Thistledown Press, 668 East Place, Saskatoon, Sask., Canada

Three Trees Press, Box 70 Sta. 'V', Toronto, Canada

The Thumbprint Press, 307 NW 14th Ave., Gainesville, FL 32601

This, 326 Connecticut St., San Francisco, CA 94107

Time Capsule, English Dept. Livingston College, New Brunswick, NJ 08903

Titanic Books, 1920 S. Street NW #506, Washington D.C. 20009

Tomboucton Books, Box 265, Bolinas, CA 94924

The Toothpaste Press, Box 546, West Branch, IA 52358

The Transatlantic Review, Box 3348, Grand Central Sta., New York, NY 10017

Transition, 537 NE Lincoln St., Hillsboro, OR 97123

Translation P.E.N., School of the Arts, Columbia, New York, NY 10027

TriQuarterly, University Hall 101, Northwestern U., Evanston, IL 60201

Truck Press, 1645 Portland Ave., St. Paul, MN 55104

Trunk Press, Hanover, MD 21750

Tuesday Nights, 2014 Locust St., Philadelphia, PA 19103

Tunbridge Press, Box 345, New York, NY 10021

Lana Turner, 825 West End Ave., 13-b, New York, NY 10025

Tuumba Press, 2639 Russell St., Berkeley, CA 94705

Two Hands News, 1125 Webster, Chicago, IL 60614

Unaka Range, Rt. 1 Box 58 A, Bryson City, NC 28713

Under The Sign of Pisces, 1858 Neil Ave. Mall, Columbus, OH 43210

The Unicorn, 4501 N. Charles St., Baltimore, MD 21210

Unity Press, 113 New St., Santa Cruz, CA 95060

Unmuzzled Ox, Box 840, Canal St. Sta., New York, NY 10013

Unpublished Editions, Barton, VT

Unrealist Press, Box 53, Prince, WV 25907

The Unspeakable Visions of the Individual, Box 439, California, PA 15419

U.S. 1 Poets' Cooperative, 21 Lake Dr., Roosevelt, NJ 08555

Uzzano, Box 169, Mount Carroll, Il 61053

Vagabond, Box 879, Ellensburg, WA 98926

Van Dyk Publications, 303 Wikiup Dr., Santa Rosa, CA 95401

Vanderbilt Poetry Review, 50 Inglewood Dr., Rochester, NY 14619

Vehicle, 238 Mott St., New York, NY 10012

Velvet Wings, 1228 Oxford St., Berkeley, CA 94709
Vesta Publications, Box 1641, Cornwall, Ontario, Canada
Virginia Quarterly Review, U. of VA, Charlottesville, VA 22903
Voyeur, 301 Hicks St., Brooklyn, NY 11201

Wares, 128 Founders College, York University, 4700 Keele St., Downsview, Ontario, Canada
Washington Review of the Arts, 404 10th St. S.E., Washington D.C. 20003
Washington Review, 404 10th St. SE, Washington, D.C. 20003
West Branch, English Dept. Bucknell University, Lewisburg, PA 17837
West Coast Poetry Review, 1335 Dartmouth Dr., Reno, NV 89509
The Western Humanities Review, Spencer Hall 330, U. UT., Salt Lake City, UT 84112
Western Poetry Quarterly, 3253 Q. San Amadeo, Laguna Hills, CA 92653
Westbee Review, 229 Cumberland St., Brooklyn, NY 11205
The Westigan Review, English Dept. Univ. of Utah, Salt Lake City, UT 84112
White Mule, 2710 E. 98th Ave., Tampa, FL 33612
Wild Places, Rd. 2 Box 305A, Red Hook, NY 12571
Willmore City, Box 1601, Carlsbad, CA 92008
Wind/Literary Journal, Rt.#1 Box 809K, Pikeville, KY 41501
The Windless Orchard, English Dept. Indiana University, Fort Wayne, IN 46805
Whimsy Press, 1822 Northview Dr., Arnold, MO 63010
Windmill, Box 78, Farmington, CT 06032
Wini Press, 704 De Mott Ave., Baldwin, NY 11510
Wire Press, 392 San Jose Ave., San Francisco, CA 94110
Wisconsin Trails, Box 5650, Madison, WI 53705
Womanspirit, Box 263, Wolf Creek, OR 97497
Woodbine Press, 65 Allen Ave., Riverside, RI 02915
The WorDoctor, Box 9761, North Hollywood, CA 91606
The Workingman's Press, 833 Bancroft Way, Berkeley, CA 94710
Work/Shop Press, Box 56052, Atlanta, GA 30343
The Wormwood Review, Box 8840, Stockton, CA 95204
Writ Magazine, 2 Sussex Ave., Toronto, Canada
Write Poems Women Workshop, 238 W. 22nd St., New York, NY 10011

Writers Resources, 48 Kinnaird St., Apt. 3, Cambridge, MA 02139
Wyro, Box 6302, Albany, CA 94706

Xanadu/Pleasure Dome Press, 2441 Riverside Dr., Wantagh, NY 11793
X-Press Press, 524 Henry St., Brooklyn, NY 11231

Y'Bird Magazine, 2140 Shattuck Ave., Berkeley, CA 94704
The Yale Review, 1902 A. Yale Sta., New Haven, CT 06520

Z Press, Poets Corner, Calais, VT 05648
Zahir Press, Box 715, Newburyport, MA 01950
Ziesing Brothers Publishing, 768 Main St., Willimantic, CT 06226
Ziggurat, 2546 S. KK., Milwaukee, WI 53207
Zone One, Box 194, Bay Station, Brooklyn, NY 11235
Zone Press, Box 194, Bay Station, Brooklyn, NY 11235
Zvezda, Box 9024, Berkeley, CA 94709

🔥 🔥 🔥

CALEDONIA, the type in which this book was set is one of those referred to by printers, as a "modern face". It was designed around 1939 by W.A. Dwiggins (1880–1956) and it has been called "the most popular all-purpose typeface in U.S. history".

It is an original design, but, as from the beginning, fresh and exciting designs have often evolved from variations on the old, done by competent and disciplined hands. Caledonia shows marks of the long admired Scotch roman type-letters cut by Alexander Wilson in Glasgow in the 19th century. It also shows a trace from the types that W. Bulmer & Company used, cut in London, around 1790 by William Martin.

That Dwiggins was aware of the particular needs of our time is soundly attested to the enduring good reception his "hard working, feet-on-the-ground" type has received from countless printers, authors and readers alike.

This book was designed and produced for the publisher, by RAY FREIMAN & COMPANY, Stamford, Connecticut.